NO PLACE FOR BEGINNERS

BATTLE OVER MALTA
JUNE 1940 – SEPTEMBER 1941

TONY O'TOOLE

No Place for Beginners
Battle over Malta:
June 1940 - September 1941
© Tony O'Toole 2013

ISBN 978-1-905414-18-5

First published in 2013 by
Dalrymple & Verdun Publishing
33 Adelaide Street, Stamford, PE9 2EN
United Kingdom
Tel: 0845 838 1940
mail@dvpublishing.co.uk
www.dvpublishing.co.uk

© Concept and design
Dalrymple & Verdun Publishing
and the late Stephen Thompson
Page layout by Russell Strong
Artwork © Steve Nichol
Editor Martin Derry

The right of Tony O'Toole to be identified as the author of this work has been asserted in accordance with sections 77 and 78 of the Copyright Designs and Patents Act, 1988.

Printed in England by
Buxton Press Limited
Palace Road, Buxton
Derbyshire, SK17 6AE

All rights reserved. No part of this publication may be reproduced or transmitted in any form or by any means, electronic or mechanical, including photocopy, recording, or any other information storage and retrieval system, without permission in writing from the publishers.

CONTENTS

Introduction & Acknowledgements 4

Chapter 1: Setting the Scene 6
   Why Malta was so important 7
   Defence denied:
      The Fleet is instructed to leave Malta 8
   Strike Base Malta 11
   Malta's Strike Forces 16
      Royal Air Force: strike, reconnaissance,
      special duties aircraft and units 16
      Fleet Air Arm: strike, reconnaissance,
      night-intruder aircraft and units 25
      Royal Navy: submarine and surface forces 27
   Other Malta-based units and their contribution 30
   In support of Malta: non Malta-based personnel 32
   'No Place For Beginners' 35

Chapter 2: Holding the fort 1940;
   Sea Gladiators and the first Hurricanes 40
   The road to war in the Mediterranean 41
   Tension Builds in the Mediterranean 42
   Italy declares war:
      The legend of 'Faith, Hope and Charity' is born . . . 45
   The first air raids 45
   Reinforcements arrive: Malta's first aerial victory 49
   The second ferry flight across France 51
   First kills and losses 53
   Operation *Hurry*: The first carrier delivery flight.
      More Hurricanes arrive 55
   Number 261 Squadron: A new unit emerges 60
   Picchiatelli: Ju 87s appear over Malta 63
   Italian raids continue: Reconnaissance receives a boost . 65
   New Arrivals: Sunderlands, Wellingtons and
      Clandestine Frenchmen 67
   November 1940 68
   Disaster at sea: Operation *White* 70
   1940 draws to an end 72
   The lull before the storm: Italian attacks continue . . . 73
   Build-up of German strength 75

Chapter 3: The Hurricane takes the strain 84
   1941: A new year commences and the Germans arrive . 85
   HMS *Illustrious* and the *Illustrious Blitz*: The build-up . 86
   The Fulmars of 806 Naval Air Squadron 89
   10th January 1941: *Stuka* attack on *Illustrious* 90
   Safety of a sort: the *Illustrious Blitz* 93

The *Blitz* begins in earnest 95
Malta's first Spitfire: *Illustrious* leaves 99
The surviving Sea Gladiators 104
After *Illustrious*: the onslaught continues 105
7/JG 26: The Muncheberg menace arrives 105
Raids continue: Fulmars depart 108
Operation *Winch*: Hurricane IIs finally arrive 115
Photo Reconnaissance Hurricanes 117
Hurricane IIs go into action 117
Anti-shipping Blenheims arrive: and so do further
   Hurricanes courtesy of Operation *Dunlop* 120
Operation *Tiger*: A vital convoy 121
Operation *Tiger* 123
'Maltese Griffons': A new Hurricane unit is formed . . . 127
German efforts wind down and the Italians take over:
   Operation *Splice* commences 128
Further Blenheims arrive: and French Marylands too . . 131
Italy assumes the offensive once more:
   A third Hurricane unit arrives 134
A new AOC arrives: Offensive operations mount 135
Hurricane IIs flood in (and out again!) 136
Operation *Substance*: another vital convoy 138
The Italian seaborne attack on Grand Harbour 139
Malta's summer offensive 140

Appendices
Regia Aeronautica units based in Sicily
   on 10th June 1940 164
Regia Aeronautica engaged on operations
   against Malta in late 1940 165
Regia Aeronautica engaged on operations
   against Malta early 1941 166
Regia Aeronautica engaged on operations
   against Malta May-June 1941 167
Regia Aeronautica unit composition 168
Regia Aeronautica unit designations 168
Regia Aeronautica Ranks: Officers & Senior NCOs . . . 168
Fliegerkorps X units based in Sicily in 1941 169
A general explanation of *Luftwaffe* units 170
Luftwaffe ranks 170
RAF and Fleet Air Arm rank abbreviations 171
Aircraft deliveries to Malta by aircraft carrier 1940-41 171
Aircraft specifications: RAF / Fleet Air Arm 172
   Regia Aeronautica / *Luftwaffe* 174

Bibliography 176

INTRODUCTION & ACKNOWLEDGEMENTS

Anybody who knows modern day Valletta will be shocked by this 1942 view of the top end of Kingsway, now known as Republic Street, which is the main high street of the Maltese capital. The ruins of the old Opera House are on the right and this building has never been rebuilt as a reminder of the devastation that the wartime bombing caused. Behind the rubble next to the parked cars, which are finished in the effective 'Malta Rubble' or 'Stone Wall' colour scheme worn by most vehicles on the island, is a row of kiosks which remain today as the only part of the old Opera House in existence.
via Carl Vincent

INTRODUCTION

The Air Battle of Malta has been the topic of countless books since the end of World War Two and has always been a subject of great interest to the author who has produced here a detailed narrative, primarily from the Allies perspective, of Malta's aerial defence (and offence) from June 1940 to September 1941.

This volume deals with the early years of the siege imposed upon Malta when small numbers of RAF Sea Gladiators and Hurricanes, occasionally accompanied by a handful of Fleet Air Arm Fulmars, blunted Axis aerial attacks against the islands at a time when an embryonic Malta-based strike force began to emerge that would develop to become the scourge of Axis supply convoys across the Mediterranean.

A later volume will cover the use of the Spitfire as well as night-fighter and intruder operations which employed Hurricanes, Fulmars, Beaufighters and Mosquitos on the Allied side and Fiat CR.42s, Bf 110Cs and Ju 88Cs with the Axis.

An additional aspect of the approach to this book is the fresh examination of the camouflage schemes worn by the combatant aircraft involved in this battle, particularly those employed by the British. Using evidence garnered from a number of sources, including interviews and correspondence with veterans and by reinterpretation of selected photographs, reappraisals of the colours worn by many of the aircraft are considered.

General notes:

1) Throughout this work Malta's capital city has been rendered as 'Valletta' as opposed to the more common English practice of 'Valetta'. The city was originally named after Grand Master Jean Parisot de Vallette and in deference to both him and the Maltese people it is that spelling which is retained here.

2) Unsurprisingly, general references are frequently made throughout this volume to 'British forces', 'Britain's forces' or similar. Such terms should be viewed by the reader as a shorthand reference to British, British Imperial and Crown Colony personnel as significant numbers of servicemen and woman from Britain's Empire as it then stood were employed in the Mediterranean and North African theatres.

ACKNOWLEDGEMENTS

I would like to extend my heartfelt gratitude to the host of contributors that have helped to make this project a reality. In this respect I would especially like to thank the following: Frederick Galea, Honorary President of Malta's National War Museum Association and Honorary Director of the Malta Aviation Museum Foundation who has provided many of the photographs in this book; Paul Lazell, whose father Bill was a keen photographer and who served with the Malta-based 7th AA Regiment RA; author and artist Steve Nichol, who patiently listened to my point of view whilst creating all of the artwork contained within this volume; Alverino 'Nino' Capatti; Eddy Creek; Brian Cull; Leonard Hesling; Roberto Lionello; Colin Pomeroy who put me in contact with many of Malta's veterans; Mark Anthony Vella; Neil Page and Peter Watson DSM.

Additionally, I would also like to thank Mr Dennis Hogg for kindly lending me the wartime diaries of his older brother, the late Sub Lieutenant Graham Angus Hogg DSO, RNVR (806 NAS, Fleet Air Arm), who became the top-scoring pilot to fly the Fairey Fulmar before he was sadly killed during a training flight.

It has also been my great privilege to interview and correspond with a number of Malta veterans, namely: Walter Gillman; Jack Paternoster; Colin White DSC; Ernest Humphreys; Malcolm Oxley; John Tipton, Jack Waterfield, Harold Revill, Malcolm Oxley, Ron Bramley, Douglas Newton and Anthony Stephens, all of whom provided anecdotes, information or photographs from their private collections. It was a pleasure to have made your acquaintance, gentlemen.

Further, I would also like to extend my gratitude to Dalrymple & Verdun Publishing for commissioning this book – particularly for the work accomplished by Russell Strong, Chris Salter, Doug Derry and, last but not least, a huge thank you to Martin Derry for all of his hard work in editing my script into something legible that makes sense.

Finally, and most importantly, I would like to thank and dedicate this book to my wife Alison and son Robert. Without their support, affection, encouragement and countless cups of tea this work might never have been completed – perhaps I might request more of the same for volume two please.

1 | SETTING THE SCENE

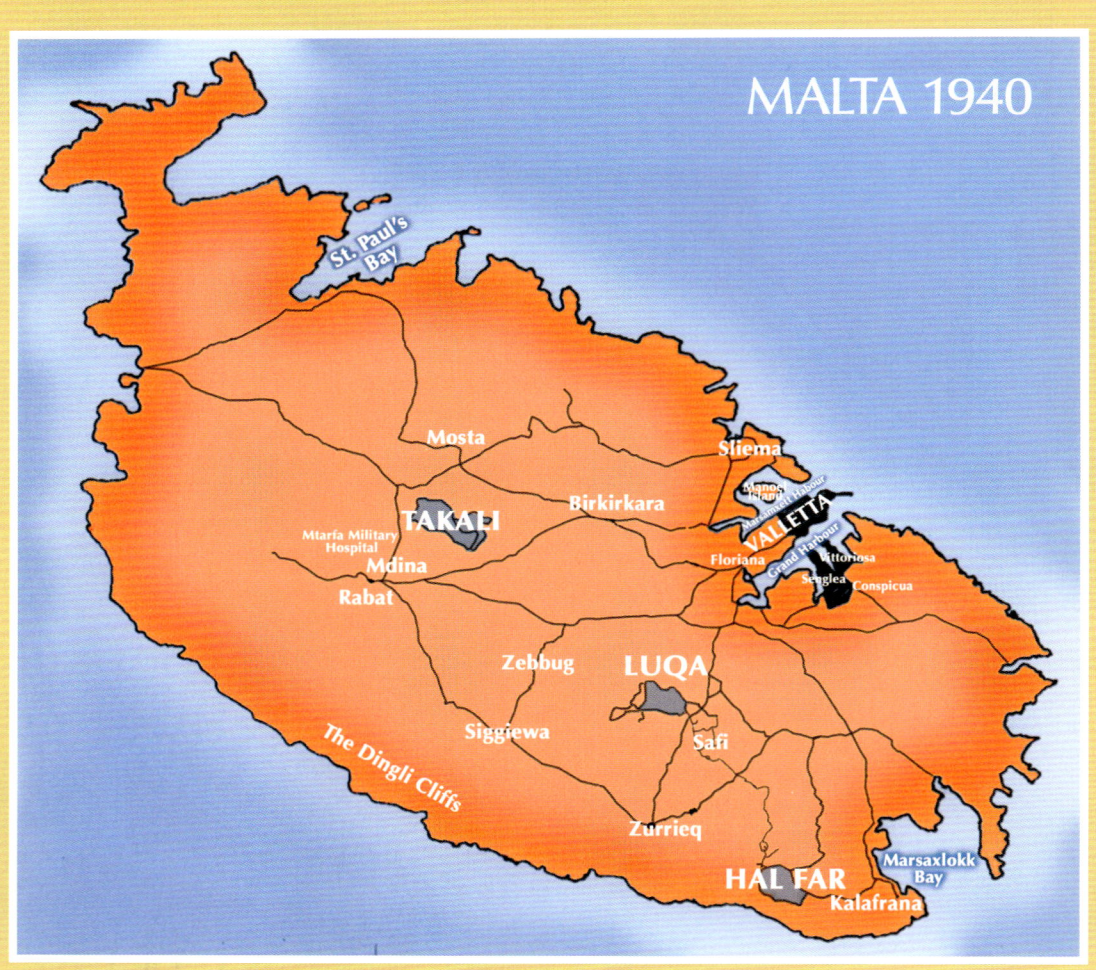

WHY MALTA WAS SO IMPORTANT

The three Maltese islands of Malta, Gozo and Comino, lying as they do just 60 miles south of Sicily, have always held an important, even dominant, strategic position. Crucially, they are situated virtually in the middle of the Mediterranean Sea, astride most of the region's major shipping routes.

Following Italy's entry into World War Two as a member of the Axis in support of Hitler's Germany on 10th June 1940, one of Britain's principal lines-of-supply, the Mediterranean Sea, at once came under the threat of sustained Italian air and naval attack. Assuming that the Italians were to be challenged by Britain and the Sea was not to become the '*Mare Nostrum*' (Our Sea) as decreed by Italy's dictator Mussolini (*Il Duce*: The Leader), then Malta would prove pivotal in prosecuting any war against the Italians.

It is perhaps relevant at this early stage to draw attention to the fact that some post-war comments have questioned whether Britain should have fought for the Mediterranean at all, that all convoys to and from the UK could have been routed around South Africa if the Mediterranean was to be blocked at the chokepoints of Gibraltar and Suez. In early June 1940, Britain's future efforts to maintain a fighting presence in the region was not, in the view of some, a foregone conclusion. In fact, a strong proposal was raised in late-May 1940, endorsed shortly thereafter by the Royal Navy's First Sea Lord and Chief of Naval Staff, Sir Dudley Pound, that consideration be given to abandoning the Mediterranean. For two months prior to this date, Mussolini had become ever more belligerent towards Britain and France and hostilities appeared increasingly likely, despite which, British and French politicians still hoped and believed that Italy would remain neutral for the foreseeable future. Pound however was deeply concerned that if a war with Italy was to transpire, then maintaining a fleet in the Mediterranean as well as the Far East, (in terms of strategy, Singapore was seen as Britain's greatest overseas priority) would stretch naval resources beyond their limit – resources which he felt should be directed primarily against the greatest of all threats to Britain's survival: Germany. Its surface fleet, raiders and U-boats menaced Britain's vital supply lines in the North Sea, English Channel, Atlantic Ocean and, to a lesser degree, the Indian Ocean. He also endorsed the view, held by many, that the Mediterranean Fleet's new base in Alexandria, (discussed later) was unsound for several reasons, not least that geographically and hence strategically it lay in entirely the wrong place, Egypt rather than the central Mediterranean.

In answer to Pound's doubts, a complex series of powerful political, economic and military arguments emerged in support of maintaining the Royal Navy's presence in the region which lie beyond the scope of this book, but it was Britain's new Prime Minister who formally rejected the views of Pound and his supporters regarding Mediterranean strategy. Winston Churchill had become both Britain's Prime Minister and Minister of Defence on 10th May 1940, and on 23rd June he rejected Pound's proposal to withdraw the Fleet from the Mediterranean. In early July, Churchill endorsed a memorandum stating that the Middle East, defined particularly as Egypt, Aden, Sudan, Iraq, Palestine and the oil wells of Persia, would be held and a fleet in the Eastern Mediterranean maintained. Egypt in particular offered the only front (other than the Horn of Africa) where British and Commonwealth soldiers were in contact with the enemy as, by this time, Allied ground forces had been expelled from Europe by the Germans. Ever alert to the possibility of offensive action, he thus anticipated great opportunities for British, Commonwealth and Empire forces to take the war to the Italians at the earliest occasion.

All other considerations to one side, Churchill's decision ensured that Malta would be returned to its familiar strategic role, as dictated by geography, despite the virtual abandonment of the island militarily speaking and its lack of modern defences by June 1940. In this war, Malta's survival would quickly prove to be the Allied key to success in the region.

Malta from the air looking approximately to the north-west and showing the islands of Malta in the foreground, Gozo furthest away, with diminutive Comino lying between. The nearest bay in the photo is Marsaxlokk Bay where Kalafrana seaplane base was situated, with Hal Far airfield close by on the left-hand corner of the island as viewed here. The capital city, Valletta, is situated on the peninsular seen to the centre-right of the image dividing Grand Harbour from Marsamxett Harbour, the latter being the location of Manoel Island where once the 10th Submarine Flotilla was based. (See also accompanying map). via Paul Lazell

DEFENCE DENIED:
THE FLEET IS INSTRUCTED TO LEAVE MALTA

As stated, the hub of any successful British strategy in the Mediterranean would be Malta. Captured from France by the British in 1800, it became a Crown Colony 15 years later and was developed by Britain to become a major facility for the Royal Navy. In conjunction with Malta, British Mediterranean naval strategy also relied on Gibraltar, 1,100 miles to the west, plus Egypt 900 miles to the east wherein lay the ports of Alexandria and Port Said, the latter guarding the entrance to the Suez Canal. Their geographic locations offered a considerable strategic advantage to the Royal Navy in time of conflict by enabling it to largely bar hostile vessels from entering the Sea, (a consideration for Italy which until 1940 imported 60% of its oil and coal via Suez and Gibraltar), although by themselves they could of course do nothing to prevent the existence of regional navies, particularly Italy's own navy – the *Regia Marina*. Additionally, and significantly by 1940, it could do nothing either to counter another more recent threat to any ship or army: the aeroplane.

As storm clouds began to gather over the Mediterranean, the existence of an apparently powerful, hostile and combat experienced Italian air force (*Regia Aeronautica*) located scarcely 60 miles north of Malta, would be both an obvious and immediate threat to any vessel berthed within the walls of Malta's Grand Harbour. Yet in June 1940, Malta lay virtually undefended from this and any other threat. Why?

Although Malta's central location made it *the* obvious choice for housing a fleet capable of striking at targets within the Mediterranean, the British government was pessimistic and declined to accept this despite the lessons of history. Rather, they doubted the island's ability to withstand an aerial attack. Thus in April 1937, the British Cabinet made the decision to move the Mediterranean Fleet's main base from Malta to the comparative safety of Alexandria, which had temporarily acted as the main naval base for the Royal Navy during the Italian-Abyssinian conflict in 1935-36, despite its very limited facilities. Their decision was heavily influenced by the great international fear of the day; airpower, and, most particularly, '…the bomber', proponents of which predicted, for its own sake, the dire consequences that would fall, without notice, upon Europe's cities, populations, ports, armies and navies alike. The presence of an entire Italian air force located in such close proximity to Malta, its dockyard and the Royal Navy was perceived as a grave threat.

Although a port, Alexandria was in 1937 a *naval* dockyard in name only and would have to be constructed from almost nothing at great expense; such was the fear of the bomber. In hindsight it would have been far cheaper to have greatly improved Malta's defences, particularly with regard to fighter aircraft. However, in 1938, in order to accomplish savings within the defence budget and doubtless to help offset some of the costs implicit with developing Alexandria, the funding for Malta's defences was much reduced, (as too were those for Gibraltar and Hong Kong). Hence Malta was denied the four squadrons of fighters which it was felt was the minimum required to provide an adequate air defence. Although the concept of providing the four fighter squadrons for Malta was to be reconsidered following the declaration of war on 3rd September 1939, it was not acted upon. Equally unfortunate in light of subsequent events, was that funding for the completion of bomb-proof tunnels in which to moor submarines was stopped and their construction, (commenced in the mid-1930s) was abandoned. As a result of this the Royal Navy could not be regarded as properly prepared for war in the Mediterranean unless it

Air power over Malta between the wars was for the most part provided by disembarked carrier aircraft which were shore based at Hal Far airfield. Possibly taken during the second half of 1930, three Fairey IIIF spotter-reconnaissance aircraft from 446 Flight, HMS *Courageous*, are seen over Malta, the leader of which, S1307 '40', features the later style fin and rudder by comparison to the other two. S1307's barely discernable chequered markings on the tailplane consist of red and white cheques; the diagonal stripe on the fuselage was light blue. S1307 was eventually sold for scrap in November 1937. via Martin Derry

was able to use Malta as a base for offence, which in turn was centred on Malta's ability to protect the ships from aerial attack. The latter would not be provided, and so the Mediterranean fleet departed for Alexandria. Even so, while Italy remained neutral, Malta reverted to being a fleet base from November 1939 until May 1940 as many of Alexandria's facilities remained incomplete and with a drydock that could not accommodate any vessel in excess of a mere 5,000 tons or so; a situation partially remedied by the transfer from Portsmouth of a floating dock capable of a 60,000 ton lift.

Yet, if a British strike force had been properly maintained and sustained on Malta it would have been ideally placed to threaten the vulnerable Italian supply routes crossing the Mediterranean, both in peacetime or in the event of war. However, when Italy declared war on 10th June 1940, Malta possessed no offensive capability with which to strike at either Italy itself or its principal colony, Libya, which maintained a garrison of approximately 200,000 troops and was reliant on Italy for virtually all of its food, fuel, tanks and munitions, most of which went by sea. Any sustained disruption to this somewhat vulnerable flow of supplies would have a significant effect on the Italian war effort in North Africa. If the supply chain could be broken or largely disrupted then it would inevitably weaken the Axis forces in the Western Desert which, from early 1941 onwards, included Germany's well-known Afrika Korps led by General (later Field-Marshal) Erwin Rommel.

An offensive capability was one thing, in June 1940 however there was little defensive capability either, with no fighter aircraft based in Malta at all. The Army's pre-war presence comprised just five infantry battalions serving with the Malta Brigade whose main responsibility was ground defence. As for anti-aircraft defences, these scarcely existed beyond 34 heavy AA guns, eight 40mm Bofors guns and 24 searchlights out of an originally approved pre-war establishment of 112 and 60 respectively; a later proposal increased the number of heavy AA guns to (a theoretical) 172. Just one radar set existed on the island, with a second due to arrive that month. It proved fortunate therefore when a cache of Royal Navy Gloster Sea Gladiator biplane fighters was found stored in crates at Malta's Kalafrana seaplane base. They were re-erected and manned by a scratch force of RAF pilots (whose presence there is discussed later), in order to provide Malta with some semblance of aerial defence. These biplanes were soon supplemented by a small number of Hawker Hurricane monoplane fighters which were retained whilst en-route to Egypt via Malta. Almost unbelievably a footnote to the Sea Gladiator story exists whereby, weeks later, Britain's Commander-in-Chief (C-in-C), Mediterranean Fleet, Admiral Sir Andrew Cunningham, received an indignant communication from a bureaucrat in the Admiralty stores division demanding to know why he, the C-in-C, had allowed Fleet Air Arm (FAA) spares to be handed to the RAF!

Above: Another common inter-war visitor to Malta was the Fairey Flycatcher, a small, nimble, single-seat carrier-borne fighter that entered service in 1924 and remained in the frontline for 11 years. This aircraft, N9945, had departed from Hal Far, was photographed over Dingly Cliffs and belonged to 406 Flight, HMS *Glorious*. Taken during 1930/31, N9945 wears the code '2' on a diagonal yellow fuselage band; its ultimate fate is unknown. via Martin Derry

Below: Saro London II, K9682 'C', a flying boat belonging to 202 Squadron, is finished in overall silver, and seen at Kalafrana seaplane base in 1938. This unit was Malta-based from 1929 until September 1939 and received its first Londons in 1937. They were retained until replaced by Consolidated Catalinas in April 1941, although by that time the Squadron was operating from Gibraltar, having been transferred there in September 1939 to patrol the Mediterranean's approaches. Delivered to the RAF in September 1937, K9682 went missing during a reconnaissance off Vichy-French Casablanca on 14th September 1940, although its crew was rescued and interned. via Martin Derry

As related, the majority of the Royal Navy's ships had departed Malta prior to the start of hostilities with Italy, the only vessels remaining comprised small auxiliaries and two gunboats. There was one exception however, as the World War One vintage monitor HMS *Terror* arrived in Malta from Alexandria on 4th April 1940 to help bolster the island's weak defences. The monitor was armed with a pair of recently refurbished 15in guns in a single turret that far outranged Malta's existing half-dozen or so 9.2in coastal defence guns, and fired shells weighing 1,920 lb each as opposed to the 380 lb shell of the smaller weapon. Of greater significance, as it transpired, was the fact that *Terror* mounted six 4in anti-aircraft guns that provided a considerable addition to the islands AA capability. In fact, on June 11th alone, the vessel fired over 210 rounds at Italian aircraft and continued to contribute in this way until further land-based AA artillery units arrived at Malta in September 1940.

As related in detail in the following chapter, the Royal Navy made a further early contribution to Malta's military capabilities by deploying 12 Fairey Swordfish biplane torpedo bombers to form 830 Naval Air Squadron (NAS) and thus become the island's first aerial strike force. The Swordfish were already old aircraft from the initial 1936 production batch that had been relegated to a training role due to their somewhat limited instrumentation, however, nothing better was then available and they were based at Hal Far airfield alongside the RAF operated Sea Gladiators. This small collection of biplanes formed the nucleus of a Malta-based strike force which would grow over the next three years and become key to strategic operations across the entire Mediterranean and Middle East.

STRIKE BASE MALTA

As the war developed, the extent of Malta's relevance to the Allies – always important – would vary in proportion to the ebb and flow of the frontline in North Africa. This was due to the fact that the Axis shipping lanes across the Mediterranean were often beyond the range of Allied strike aircraft based on African soil, their location being dependent upon where the front line in the desert happened to be at any given time. Frequently therefore, the only Allied aircraft capable of striking at enemy vessels were those based in Malta which operated in conjunction with Malta based warships when possible. This of course made Malta vital to the fortunes of the 8th Army, a force consisting of British and Commonwealth troops, which was fighting in North Africa in the defence of Egypt, Suez and the vital oil supplies from the Middle East. Thus it was imperative that the island should remain in Allied hands and that it should possess a strong strike force – a force which needed to be defended and kept operational at all costs.

Naturally, Malta's importance was not lost on the Axis either, both the Italians and Germans sought to cut off the island and grind it into submission. As with most islands, Malta has always been vulnerable to the tactics of blockade, especially so given that most of its foodstuffs had to be imported. From mid-1940 much of the Mediterranean coastline was under hostile Italian, German or Vichy-French control, making it hazardous for any Allied vessels, warship or merchantman, to reach or depart Malta as they had to run a gauntlet, or the threat at least, of almost continuous air and sea attacks, irrespective of whether they were heading east or west, throughout the Mediterranean. The situation was to worsen considerably with the later invasion and occupation by Axis forces of Greece, Crete and Yugoslavia.

During their attempts to neutralize Malta, as well as later whilst 'softening' it up in preparation for a planned invasion, codename Operation *Herkules*, (to be spearheaded by paratroopers of the Italian *Folgore* Airborne Division and the 7th German *Fallschirmjager* Division), the bombers of the Italian and German air forces pounded the tiny nation to such an extent that it became the most heavily bombed place on Earth! Indeed the total tonnage of bombs dropped on Malta each week during the more intense periods of attack, easily equalled the amount used to level Coventry during the blitz on Britain. In fact, during a period of six weeks in April and May 1942, more bombs were dropped on Malta (6,700 tons) than were dropped on Coventry (670 tons) or on London throughout the entire London Blitz. By comparison Dresden in Germany received 1,700 tons, while Britain received 18,000 tons throughout the war. In Malta 30,027 buildings were damaged or destroyed and Takali (present day Ta' Qali) became the most bombed Allied airfield in the world, receiving 296 tons of bombs during one 24 hour period alone on 20th and 21st March 1942. In fact, towards the end of 1942 the islands had been so devastated that *Luftwaffe* crews commonly complained of having no more targets left to hit! Yet the island of Gozo, which was the principle source of home grown food for the Maltese islands, was relatively unaffected by targeted bombing and was only lightly guarded by British troops who used the rural setting as a rest centre.

In order to try and break the siege and ensure that Malta received sufficient food and supplies for it to survive, let alone strike at Axis shipping, a series of supply convoys had to be run from either end of the Mediterranean despite frequent and often appalling losses. The supplies carried by those vessels which did succeed in running the gauntlet had, by necessity, to last for as long as possible, leaving the civilian and military inhabitants of Malta with no option but to survive on starvation rations eked out for months on end. As a measure of the severity of the shortages, even the anti-aircraft guns were at times rationed to using a single shell per air raid or sometimes none at all if a raid was 'small'!

Left: Within the Great Ditch or dry moat that protects the battlements of Valletta's St James bastion, lay the heart of the Maltese war effort – the Lascaris underground battle headquarters complex, its tunnel entrance is visible here, from where the air and sea battles which occurred over and around Malta were co-ordinated. The vertical lattice structure was a lift that once led to the Upper Barracca Gardens and allowed easy access to and from the main HQ building in the Auberge de Castille, from which a red flag was raised as a warning to evacuate any shipping then being unloaded in the harbour, as it meant that an air raid was imminent. via Paul Lazell

Below: The reason why Malta was so important to the Allied war effort. German *Panzer*'s of the *Afrika Korps* photographed being unloaded from a ship in Tripoli harbour, Libya. Excluding minute quantities of supplies delivered by air, all Axis supplies for North Africa had to travel by sea from Italy or Sicily, for which Malta proved to be a well situated thorn in the Axis side. Author's collection

Finally, during the summer of 1942, the island was just weeks away from being starved into submission completely. Their dilemma was only eased by the arrival of the celebrated Operation Pedestal convoy during August 1942 and, as most of the few surviving ships arrived during the Roman Catholic feast of 'Santa Maria', the devout peoples of Malta have referred to this convoy ever since as the 'Santa Maria Convoy'. Further convoys would arrive over time and reserves built up, but it was not until mid-1943 that the siege was finally lifted – for good.

With time modern fighters were made available for the defence of Malta, including improved versions of the Hurricane and, later, Supermarine's Spitfire. The majority of these had to be flown to Malta from the decks of aircraft carriers, others arrived in crates aboard merchant ships and some were also flown in from Egypt having been delivered via the Takoradi Route. The latter was a supply route created to deliver warplanes to Egypt as a supplement to the hazardous Mediterranean and lengthy Red Sea convoy routes. Takoradi is located in present-day Ghana on Africa's western coast, but in 1940 was known as the Gold Coast and it was where aircraft were off-loaded, re-assembled and flown in aerial convoys, led by navigational aircraft, to Nigeria and then across the heart of Africa to Khartoum in the Sudan and finally north into Egypt.

The effectiveness, or otherwise of Malta's fighter defences would have a profound effect not only on the fortunes of the islands themselves but also on the entire war in North Africa; their principal role therefore was to protect the airfields as well as docks, munitions and any vessels at sea within their operational radius of action. Should they fail, then the islands' strike forces in turn would be vulnerable to destruction at their respective bases, or rendered inoperative through lack of supplies, thus preventing them from attacking Axis shipping and, by extension, allowing greater quantities of troops and supplies to reach the Axis armies in North Africa.

The Swordfish torpedo bombers of 830 NAS could only operate safely under the cover of darkness, therefore the RAF began to deploy faster, more powerful strike aircraft which could operate from Malta in daylight as well as by night. The RAF's strike force was slowly expanded to include the Vickers Wellington, Bristol Blenheim, Bristol's Beaufort and Beaufighter and, from 1942, 23 Squadron's De Havilland Mosquito NF.IIs to conduct night intruder sorties. The Fleet Air Arm also sent further reinforcements to Malta which included Fairey Albacore torpedo bombers and Fairey Fulmars, the latter flying as fighters and also as night intruders over Sicily in 1941. Due to constant bombing, the number of Swordfish and Albacores had been reduced to a mere handful of serviceable airframes by the summer of 1942 although, unlike other strike forces, they were never withdrawn to safety which ultimately resulted in all the Fleet Air Arm units in Malta being combined into a composite unit known as the Royal Naval Air Squadron Malta.

Despite being heavily outnumbered most of the time, Malta's Sea Gladiators and Hurricanes were usually able to cope with their Italian opposition. However, following a catalogue of setbacks suffered by Italy's military (and naval) forces throughout their Mediterranean and Adriatic theatres of operations, Italy asked Germany for help which resulted in the latter's expeditionary *Afrikakorps* being deployed to North Africa from February 1941. In order to help protect the Korps supply lines, the *Luftwaffe* moved *Fliegerkorps* X, a highly experienced anti-shipping unit from Norway to Sicily during January 1941 equipped with Junkers Ju 88 and Heinkel He 111 bombers, Messerschmitt Bf 110 twin-engine fighters and long-range Junkers Ju 87R Stuka dive-bombers. Their main priorities were to eliminate Malta as a threat and to sink British warships.

Initially the German bombers were escorted by Italian fighters. However, a *Staffel* (loosely equivalent to a small RAF squadron) of *Luftwaffe* '*experten*' equipped with the excellent Messerschmitt Bf 109E-7 soon arrived to bolster the Italian fighters and, although they never possessed more than 14 E-7s, they totally outclassed the RAF's Hurricanes to leave Malta at the mercy of enemy bombers. Many British aircraft were destroyed on the ground and havoc ensued in the harbours, yet before the Germans could complete their task several *Fliegerkorps* X's units were despatched from Sicily to assist with operations in both North Africa and the Balkans in April 1941. Two months later the remainder left for Russia to participate in Operation *Barbarossa*.

The *Luftwaffe*'s withdrawal left the Italians solely responsible for attacks upon Malta and provided RAF Hurricane pilots with an opportunity to regain the upper hand which, as a further consequence, allowed the British to regain some freedom of operations against Axis shipping. Ominously for the Italians, their losses began to rise once again. In one incident, following a report from a Malta-based reconnaissance aircraft on 15th April 1941, a naval engagement ensued in

An aerial view of Malta's capital, Valletta, on the left-hand peninsular, with Grand Harbour out of view to the left and Marsamxett Harbour on the right encompassing Manoel Island. via Paul Lazell

the early hours of the following day. Aware that elements of a German armoured division would be embarking at Palermo, Sicily, for the Libyan port of Tripoli from perhaps the 8th of April, Admiral Cunningham deployed four of the RN's larger destroyers: *Jervis*, *Janus*, *Mohawk* and *Nubian* to Malta shortly afterwards under the command of Captain Mack. (The four vessels collectively formed Force K and were the first to use this designation in the Mediterranean, though not, as will be seen, the last.) A reconnaissance aircraft from Malta found the convoy at sea and the destroyers sailed in pursuit to successfully engage three Italian destroyers and five merchant vessels in a night action off the Tunisian port of Sfax, en route to Tripoli. All eight Italian vessels were sunk, as too was *Mohawk*. As a consequence of this action nearly 400 men, 300 vehicles and over 3,500 tons of stores was denied to

Royal Artillery Bofors anti-aircraft gun and crew in Grand Harbour. This hard-hitting weapon fired a 2 lb shell at a rate of c120 rounds per minute and possessed a maximum horizontal range of 10,000yds, and an absolute ceiling of 23,500ft. Such extreme ranges it must be stressed, were far more theoretical than practical, especially prior to the advent of radar-predicted gun-laying. Needless to say, the weapon's *practical* ceiling was considerably less, extending to approximately 5,000ft using open sights as shown here. Paul Lazell

A Vickers 3.7in anti-aircraft gun from 10 Battery, 7th Heavy Anti-Aircraft Regiment, Royal Artillery, sited at Zabbar and wearing the distinctive and effective 'Malta Rubble' camouflage scheme. A very advanced weapon when it first entered service in 1937, it remained in British service for 22 years. Trained by a predictor these hand-loaded weapons had a rate-of-fire of up to 10 rounds per minute. The 3.7 had a practical ceiling of between 23,000 and 32,000ft, dependent upon mark and other modifications, and fired a 28 lb shell at a maximum elevation of 80°. Malcolm D Oxley via Colin Pomeroy

Rommel. Although impressive, such a loss by itself represented little more than a dent in the armour of the Axis war machine, but the engagement served to prove, if proof was needed, the relevance of, and strategic potential provided by a functioning base on Malta, for both reconnaissance and offensive operations.

Eventually, mounting shipping losses began to cripple the Axis war effort in North Africa causing the *Luftwaffe* to return to Sicily in even greater numbers during November 1941, this time with the intention of breaking the islands once and for all in preparation for the planned invasion (Operation *Herkules*).

The fighter units of *Fliegerkorps* II were by this time equipped with the latest Bf 109F fighters that totally outclassed Malta's Hurricanes, many of which included the increasingly common Mark II variant featuring the more powerful Rolls-Royce Merlin XX engine. Of the sub-variants available, the Hurricane IIa retained the familiar battery of eight .303in machine guns, the Hurricane IIb increased this number to 12 such weapons, while the Hurricane IIc carried four powerful 20mm cannons. Despite their best efforts, the RAF's fighter pilots were so busy contending with the enemy's fighters that the German bombers were able to penetrate the defences in large numbers and cause devastation throughout Malta. Matters deteriorated to such a point whereby, excepting the FAA's torpedo bombers at Hal Far, the majority of Malta's strike aircraft, ships and submarines which had not already been too badly damaged, destroyed or sunk at their moorings were deployed to North Africa to ensure their continued survival.

Unsurprisingly, this led to a significant increase in the quantity of supplies reaching Axis forces in North Africa – despite the occasional success obtained by the naval biplanes based at Hal Far. Meanwhile, in Sicily large numbers of gliders, Junkers Ju 52/3m and Savoia Marchetti SM.82 transport aircraft began to congregate on its airfields, indicating that the airborne invasion of Malta was being prepared. In the event however, following the huge losses incurred by German paratroopers during the invasion of Crete, Hitler baulked, he became hesitant about carrying out a similar operation against Malta unless the defences could indeed be totally broken first.

In an all-out attempt to destroy Malta's defences prior to an invasion, Axis air raids became ever more intense resulting in the then current AOC, Air Commodore Hugh Pugh Lloyd, to make repeated requests to the Air Ministry in London for more fighters to be sent to Malta, which initially resulted in the despatch of further Hurricanes; yet it was Spitfires that were needed. Requests for the latter finally bore fruit in April 1942, when the first batch of Spitfire Vs arrived on the island having been conveyed within flying range aboard the carrier HMS *Eagle* to reinforce the surviving Hurricanes, and in so doing, became the first fighter version of the Spitfire to be permanently based overseas. Following much bitter fighting and further deliveries of Spitfires, the RAF finally regained control of the skies over Malta, quelling any threat of invasion and allowing the rejuvenated strike forces in Malta to continue their offensive against the Axis. Ultimately the see-saw battle for North Africa ended on 13th May 1943 when the remnants of the German-Italian Panzer Army in Africa surrendered in Tunisia. For them the epithet of Malta as the 'thorn in Rommel's side', rang true until the bitter end.

A Morris Quad belonging to a Royal Artillery Field Regiment and serialled H1163137, it bears the name Drake on its front bumper and is camouflaged with the distinctive 'Malta Rubble' camouflage scheme. The commander wears a distinctive Pith Helmet, indicating that his unit had only recently arrived in Malta as this form of headgear was standard tropical issue to troops leaving the UK. It was soon discarded in favour of a tin hat! Author's collection

Above: A Cruiser A13 Mk.IIA tank of the Malta Independent Tank Squadron, Royal Tank Regiment, patrols an exposed section of coast road in 1942. Three of this model, plus five Cruiser A9s, had arrived in Malta during January 1942 when X Squadron (originally A Squadron) of 6th RTR was redeployed from Egypt. Their numbers would have been higher, but five other Cruisers were lost en route when the convoy conveying them was heavily attacked. The newcomers were amalgamated with the existing Independent Troop to become the Malta Independent Tank Squadron, RTR. The 'Malta Rubble' or 'Stone Wall' camouflage scheme of Light Stone with a disruptive pattern on top replicates the many walls found on the island. Author's collection

Below: Only four Valentine tanks were sent to Malta where they arrived (from Egypt) during April/May 1943. Two were Mk.IIs equipped with a two-man turret, while the other pair were Mk.IIIs equipped with a larger three-man turret. Both variants were fitted with a 2-pounder gun. The Valentine seen here, named *ADONIS*, is a Mk.III equipped with the larger turret and lots of children! This is one of only two known photographs of a Malta-based Valentine and was taken in Palace Square, Valletta, on 2nd June 1943, during the King's birthday celebrations. The Valentines were stationed in defence of Malta's airfields and were frequently used to tow damaged aircraft clear of the runway. Author's collection

MALTA'S STRIKE FORCES

ROYAL AIR FORCE: STRIKE, RECONNAISSANCE, SPECIAL DUTIES AIRCRAFT AND UNITS

Due to space constraints an early decision was made to deal solely with the aerial defence of Malta and to exclude strike operations. However, it was quickly realised that mention of the strike units was very necessary in order to present a wider, more balanced account, as many actions, both defensive and offensive, often occurred simultaneously. Therefore, a number of strike operations have been included in order to help the reader gain a wider appreciation of Malta's struggle. Accordingly, a list of the principal types of strike aircraft employed (accompanied by a brief description of their role) while flying from Malta is included.

Vickers Wellington

The Wellington (nicknamed 'Wimpey' after Wellington J Wimpey of 'Popeye' fame) was the first of the RAF's offensive aircraft to be based in Malta although it was employed in three widely varying roles whilst based on the island; each role attracted its own more specific nickname.

'Bombington'

This was the name used in Malta and North Africa for the standard bomber version whether it be the Bristol Pegasus-powered, radial-engined Wellington Ic or the Rolls-Royce Merlin-powered inline-engined Wellington II. Although they sometimes operated against convoys at sea, their principal role was the night-time bombing of the ports in which merchant vessels were to be found in Sicily, Italy and North Africa – especially Tripoli and the Sicilian ports of Catania and Palermo.

The first Wellington unit to operate from Malta was the Malta Wellington Flight (MWF). This unit began arriving at Luqa from the UK during October 1940, for what its dozen crews were mistakenly led to believe was a 10 day detachment from their parent Bomber Command units of 38, 99 and 115 Squadrons. Amongst other duties performed, it was one of this unit's aircraft that was used to drop flares during the famous attack by FAA Swordfish against Italian battleships at Taranto, Italy, on the night of 11th/12th November 1940. Following the arrival of additional aircrew and aircraft from 37, 38 and 99 Squadrons, the MWF was redesignated to become 148 Squadron between 1st and 14th December 1940, which probably reflects the length of time taken for all of the units aircraft to arrive at Luqa. Wellingtons usually left the UK for Malta individually with two, three or four aircraft following at intervals. The first leg, covering the UK-Gibraltar section, risked encounters with Ju 88 fighters over the Bay of Biscay. Following a night spent in a fully-lit and unrationed

Left: **A Martin Maryland of either 431 Flight or 69 Squadron at Luqa airfield in one of the stone aircraft pens built mostly by soldiers.** Paul Lazell

Below: **Royal Navy destroyers entering Grand Harbour. The lead vessel is one of the RN's modern J, K or N Class destroyers equipped with three twin 4.7in gun mountings and, as designed at least, two sets of quintuple 21in torpedo tubes. It became common for British destroyers however to have one set of torpedoes removed and replaced with a single AA gun in an attempt to partially rectify their woeful lack of AA capability. Behind is an older destroyer, probably one of the interwar A-I classes.** Author's collection

Gibraltar, the final leg was a night flight and dawn landing in Malta. Gibraltar was unable to accommodate any more than four large aircraft in transit until 1942 as it was still a very small airfield, thus extending the amount of time taken to equip an entire squadron in Malta.

While the inhabitants of Malta endured the heavy blitz, Luqa-based 'Bombingtons' mounted retaliatory night raids against enemy bomber bases in Sicily in addition to their usual targets and, on the 12th January 1941, they managed to destroy 10 enemy bombers on the ground followed three nights later by 10 more. Unfortunately, the large Wellingtons with their black painted sides proved to be far too vulnerable on the ground themselves and before long Luqa airfield was littered with the burnt-out remains of 10 or more of them, each easily identified by their distinctive geodetic skeletons. What remained of 148 Squadron was withdrawn to Egypt in March 1941 and, from then on, only short-term detachments of Wellingtons could be maintained in Malta.

The next unit to arrive at Luqa with its 'Bombington' Ics was a detachment from 38 Squadron based in Egypt that arrived on 9th August 1941 and remained until 26th October. They were joined by 15 Wellington IIs detached from the UK-based 104 Squadron which began arriving from 18th October 1941 and both units combined to mount a large raid against Naples prior to 38 Squadron's departure. Number 104 Squadron's detachment remained in Malta until early January 1942, when it too departed for Egypt. Another 38 Squadron detachment visited Malta in 1942 from where, on one occasion, the unit bombed Palermo harbour twice in one night, sinking three ships. Detachments to Malta from various Wellington-equipped units continued including those from 104 and 40

Most of the British fighters that succeeded in reaching Malta arrived there courtesy of the RN's carrier decks, most particularly those of HMS *Argus*, *Eagle*, *Furious* and *Ark Royal*. However, the US Navy was also instrumental in supplying aircraft to Malta after President Roosevelt famously agreed to Winston Churchill's request to allow the carrier USS *Wasp* to deliver urgently needed Spitfires to Malta in April-May 1942. Having offloaded most of its own air group (other than Grumman Wildcats for self-defence), she embarked approximately 94 Spitfires at Glasgow and conveyed them to within flying distance of Malta during the course of two Mediterranean incursions. Although built along somewhat basic lines and of much lighter displacement than the contemporary HMS *Ark Royal*, physically *Wasp* was not much smaller and was able to accommodate 76 aircraft which, by 1942, was a much greater quantity than Britain's surviving carriers could accommodate. USS *Wasp* was sunk in the Pacific on 15th September 1942 by the Japanese submarine I-19. via Carl Vincent

Squadrons which arrived at Luqa during November 1942 in support of Operation *Torch*, the Anglo-American landings in North Africa; an operation which ultimately helped to ease Axis pressure on Malta.

Wellington Units Detached to Malta 1940-41

Unit	Period	Codes	Type
37 Sqn	November 1940 - November 1940	LF	Mk.Ic
38 Sqn	August 1941 - October 1941	-	Mk.Ic
40 Sqn	October 1941 - May 1942	BL	Mk.Ic
104 Sqn	October 1941 - January 1942	EP	Mk.II
148 Sqn	December 1940 - March 1941	-	Mk.Ic
221 Sqn (Special Flight) Malta	September 1941 - August 1942 (became 69 Sqn-C Flt)	-	Mk.VIII
Wellington Flight	November 1940 - December 1940	-	Mk.Ic

'Goofington'

These were Air-to-Surface-Vessel Mk II, (ASV) radar-equipped Wellington VIIIs which, bristling with 'stickleback' antenna, went out at night in search of Axis convoys. Often these and other reconnaissance assets used immensely valuable, top-secret, *Ultra* intelligence (derived from German *Enigma* transmissions) provided by a Malta-based Y Service detachment, via the code breakers based at Bletchley Park in the UK to indicate a rough search area. *Ultra*-derived intelligence however was never to be utilised without a 'cover' to protect the source and frequently the cover employed was a reconnaissance aircraft that had seemingly happened upon the enemy and discovered his position. Having been seen by the enemy and a sighting transmission sent, *Ultra*'s continued protection was preserved. Once found, the 'Goofington' would shadow a convoy whilst homing in an attack force of Swordfish, Albacores, 'Fishingtons' (q.v.) or warships. Once in a position to attack, the 'Goofington' dropped flares on the opposite side of the target vessels so as to leave them silhouetted while the strike force struck at them from out of the darkness.

The first three 'Goofingtons' arrived on detachment to Malta from 221 Squadron at Limavady in Northern

Top left: An unidentified torpedo-equipped Fairey Swordfish I coded 'M' of 830 NAS, Hal Far. Flying mainly by night they soon gained black undersides and, to increase endurance, a long-range fuel tank too; the latter, located in the observer's cockpit, reduced the crew from three to two. When ASV radar-equipped Swordfish arrived, the third crew member was required to operate it and he thus displaced the cockpit fuel tank. The latter was replaced by a Hurricane-type long-range tank carried on the fuselage torpedo crutches which limited ASV Swordfish to the carriage of under-wing stores only. Consequently they usually became lead aircraft with the CO as observer, and, using flares, illuminated the target for the torpedo carriers. Frederick Galea

Above left: An unidentified Fairey Albacore I, the other type of Malta-based naval torpedo-bomber, was operated by 828 NAS and later 821 NAS and supplemented the Swordfish of 830 NAS. Following severe losses, surviving elements from all of the biplane torpedo-bomber units were eventually amalgamated to form the Royal Naval Air Squadron Malta (RNAS-Malta). This aircraft, reportedly from 828 NAS, was in the process of having its codes changed to 'S5R' when this photograph was taken. Of interest is the black nocturnal camouflage combined with the Temperate Sea Scheme of Extra Dark Sea Grey and Dark Slate Grey on the aircraft's sides and upper surfaces. The rectangular object above the engine cowling is a Vokes tropical filter which interfered with the pilots forward vision; presumably the U-shaped torpedo sight mounted on a pole in front of the windscreen, though vital, didn't do much to improve the pilot's view either! W Forster via Colin Pomeroy

Above: Fleet Air Arm personnel dressed in a combination of naval bellbottoms, army battledress and gumboots loading a torpedo onto an Albacore of 821 NAS at Hal Far. In all probability this is either a staged photograph or the men were very confident that the torpedo shackles holding the 1,548 lb weapon would not fail, as even a strong back and right shoulder would scarcely prove sufficient to hold the 'fish' in place. Additionally they are all wearing their naval headgear – possibly the last thing one would wish to wear when working in the confined spaces witnessed here! It may also be noticed that the application of black paint has partially obscured a line of stencilling which now reads '...ing point'. The Albacore could carry a full load of 6 x 250 lb bombs beneath the lower wings or an underslung torpedo, but not both.
Author's collection

Ireland during September 1941, to become the 'Special Duties Flight' and soon had their front turrets removed and the aperture faired over in order to save weight and extend their endurance. However, when the remainder of 221 Squadron moved from the UK to the Middle East to operate in the torpedo-bomber role, the Special Duties Flight became C Flight of 69 Squadron, Malta's resident reconnaissance unit in which guise the 'Goofingtons' continued operating, as before, until the end of the siege.

'Fishington'

This name was applied to one of the rarer forms of Wellington. Following the conversion of a quantity of Mk.Ics belonging to No.38 Squadron to carry torpedoes or 'fish', the Squadron having commenced experiments with air-dropped torpedoes from January 1942, albeit while still employed in its more usual bombing role. Amongst other changes, the front turret was removed and the aperture was covered by a fairing with a lowered profile which enabled the pilot to obtain a better view whilst flying over the sea at low level. Additionally, the pilot was equipped with a Heath Robinson-looking torpedo sight mounted in front of the cockpit which featured wooden pegs nailed into place onto a length of wood that looked not unlike the head of a garden rake. This device helped the pilot to judge the speed of the target ship and provide the necessary 'aim-off' prior to dropping his 'fish'.

A pair of Mk XII or MkXII* 18in torpedoes were usually mounted, one-above-the-other, inside the bomb bay which had a V-shaped section cut out of the lower rear fuselage to house the air-tails of each torpedo that were designed to keep it stable in the air and which detached upon striking the water. Mark XII torpedoes each weighed 1,548 lb, were 16ft 3in long and carried a TNT explosive charge weighing 388 lb. Specially developed to be dropped by aircraft, Mk XII torpedoes had a range of 1500 yards at 40 knots and needed to be dropped at less that 150 knots, the Mk XII* was strengthened and improved, while the Mk XII** was further strengthened and improved to offer a range of 2,000 yards at 40 knots and a drop speed of 250 knots.

Operating mostly by night and with a greater range than Swordfish, Albacores or Beauforts, Wellingtons proved especially useful against the warships of the Italian navy. It was one of these Wellingtons which succeeded in hitting and damaging the Italian battleship *Littorio* with a torpedo during the night of 15/16th June 1942, whilst the vessel and its attendant warships were en-route to the port of Taranto following an abortive foray against a British convoy. The original 'Fishingtons' did not carry radar, but during 1942 and 1943 ASV-equipped Wellington VIIIs arrived in Malta with 221 Squadron and 458 (Australian) Squadron which were fitted for the torpedo-strike role and ultimately, it was some of these aircraft that helped to escort the Italian Battle Fleet to Malta when it surrendered to the Allies in September 1943, following Italy's capitulation.

Bristol Blenheim

The first RAF anti-shipping aircraft to be based in Malta was the Bristol Blenheim IV light bomber, the majority of which were deployed on rotational detachments employing units from No.2 Group, Bomber Command in the UK. The majority of No.2 Group's Blenheim squadrons had already been engaged in anti-shipping strikes over the North Sea against German convoys and were consequently well versed in this type of operation.

Most Blenheim units flew from the UK to Malta, via Gibraltar, in specially tropicalised aircraft fitted with long-range fuel tanks in the wing leading edges. The first unit to deploy was 139 Squadron from Horsham St Faith, Norfolk, on 11th June 1941. The last Blenheim detachment was a double deployment by 18 and 21 Squadrons which ended in February 1942 when their surviving Blenheims were destroyed on the ground by bombing.

In between these dates other Blenheim IV detachments were also sustained by 82, 105, 107, 110 and 113 (from Egypt as opposed to No.2 Group) Squadrons, with 21 and 107 Squadrons deploying more than once with each deployment usually consisting of between 12 to 18 aircraft. While operating from the UK, the casualty rate amongst the Blenheim crews had been very high and were in fact amongst the highest in the entire RAF, but for those operating from Malta, the casualty rate rose higher still. Although they proved quite successful against Axis convoys in the Mediterranean and at times sank individual vessels in excess of 10,000 tons or more, most Blenheim detachments were left with a mere handful of aircraft by the time their deployment ended and, in some instances, no Blenheims survived at all. Once relieved by the arrival of a following detachment, the outgoing Blenheim units were usually disbanded in situ as a result of the losses suffered and the survivors were either posted elsewhere in the Middle East or returned to the UK as a nucleus to form or reform a squadron from scratch.

Blenheim IV Units detached to Malta from No.2 Group, UK

Unit	Period	Codes
18 Squadron	October 1941 - January 1942	WV
21 Squadron	April - May 1941	
	December 1941 - March 1942	YH
82 Squadron	May 1941 - July 1941	UX
105 Squadron	July 1941 - October 1941	GB
107 Squadron	September 1941 - January 1942	OM
110 Squadron	July 1941 - July 1941	VE
139 Squadron	May 1941 - June 1941	XD
113 Squadron*	September 1941 - September 1941	-

* Not from No.2 Group. A single flight from 113 Squadron, equipped with the Blenheim IVf (fighter variant), was detached from Egypt to Malta between 23rd - 29th September 1941.

A Wellington VIII 'Goofington' of the Special Duties Flight which eventually became part of 69 Squadron. Seen at Luqa coded 'X' and fitted with ASV antenna, this is an early photograph as a later one exists that depicts it with the nose turret removed and faired over to reduce weight and help extend patrol times. via Author

Bristol Beaufighter

Other than a small detachment of radar-equipped Beaufighter If night fighters from Egypt-based 89 Squadron which worked alongside the Malta Night Fighter Unit (MNFU) and their nocturnal Hurricanes, the majority of Malta's Beaufighters were in fact Mk.Ic long-range fighter variants belonging to 248 and 272 Squadrons. These two units were detached from Coastal Command in the UK to the Middle East in order to provide long-range fighter support for convoys approaching Malta and subsequently became permanently based in the Mediterranean theatre. They were later joined by 227 Squadron which was formed from a detachment of 248 Squadron (although some sources quote 235 Squadron) at Luqa during August 1942. With time the Beaufighter Ic units developed techniques for flak suppression whilst escorting strike sorties by Blenheims and Beauforts and also conducted strikes in their own right against Axis convoys, airfields and any vehicles caught carrying supplies along the exposed North African coastal roads. They were also involved in a particularly successful series of operations flown against Sicilian airfields which resulted in substantial enemy losses.

Following local modifications made in Malta and North Africa, these Beaufighters became the first of their breed to be equipped with a rear-facing 'stinger', i.e. a single magazine-fed .303in Vickers K machine-gun (mg) on an improvised mount which, by cutting away the rear half of the observer's blister, provided it with a good field of fire. The modification proved to be so successful that it later became standard on the improved Beaufighter X, albeit using a .303in Browning mg mounted within a further modified blister.

Bristol Beaufort

In order to provide Malta with a daylight torpedo-bomber capability, detachments of Bristol Beaufort torpedo bombers were deployed to Luqa, mainly from units passing through the Middle East en route to the Far East, or from units already based in North Africa. As with the Blenheims and their crews, they would also suffer heavy losses but they proved to be very successful, especially against tankers and troopships. Most of Malta's Beauforts were detached from Nos.39, 69, 86 and 217 Squadrons, with surviving elements from each of these units being later amalgamated to form a strike force of approximately 20 Beauforts, based at Luqa, led by Wing Commander (W/C) Pat Gibbs.

According to 39 Squadron's records, this unit (which later absorbed elements of 86 and 217 Squadrons) was required to exchange their existing Pratt & Whitney Twin Wasp-powered Beaufort IIs, for Bristol Taurus-powered Beaufort Is while operating from Malta as the ground crews were apparently unfamiliar with the American

Left: A further Malta-based Wellington variant was the torpedo-equipped 'Fishington' (see text) which carried a pair of 'fish' one above the other in its bomb bay but which required the rear of the bomb doors and part of the adjacent fuselage to be cut away. Early Fishingtons were not fitted with ASV radar, though later ones were, and to provide better visibility for the pilot at low-level the nose turret was usually deleted to be replaced by a fairing that incorporated a lowered profile. A Heath Robinson-looking torpedo sight was also mounted just in front of the cockpit which had wooden pegs attached to help judge the speed of a ship and the deflection of the attack. via Author

Opposite: It wasn't always sunny in Malta and when it rained the island's airfields often became quagmires as seen in this image taken between October 1941 and January 1942 when Merlin-engined Wellington IIs of 104 Squadron were based on the island. As with other Wellington night bomber units based in Malta, their main targets were the Italian, Sicilian and North African ports used by Axis convoys. Author via Kev Darling

engine. This cannot have been a widespread problem however as several images exist depicting Beaufort IIs and similarly powered Martin Marylands and Martin Baltimores operating from Malta regularly, making the veracity of the Squadron's statement difficult to confirm; more likely perhaps was that this was a temporary problem encountered by that unit due to a shortage of trained personnel at the time.

Aerial Reconnaissance
Although not usually expected to conduct strikes against the Axis, Malta's reconnaissance aircraft were nevertheless a vital asset to the island's strike forces, not least for providing essential intelligence which they had discovered in their own right, but also for safeguarding *Ultra* decrypts by supplying a plausible alternative to the 'co-incidental' discovery of Axis forces.

Malta's aerial reconnaissance capability began modestly using a few Short Sunderland I flying boats detached to Kalafrana seaplane base on an ad hoc basis from Gibraltar, but was placed on a somewhat more certain footing by the arrival of Lockheed Hudson I, N7324, on 21st June 1940. Belonging to 233 Squadron and based at Leuchars, Fife, the Hudson and its crew were retained on the island to become Malta's sole land-based reconnaissance asset after having helped to lead the first delivery of Hurricanes to the island from the UK, via France, before that route was closed by the latter's capitulation. In August 1940, the Hudson was joined by Blackburn Skua II, L2911, that had acted as the navigational lead aircraft for the first carrier-borne delivery of Hurricanes to Malta, (Operation *Hurry*), and thereafter was employed for a time in the same role as the Hudson, particularly after the latter had been shot down by a Fulmar on 1st September 1940. An ex-Vichy French Latécoère 298B floatplane from Escadrille 2HT, coded HB2-5, also joined this growing but disparate collection of reconnaissance aircraft when its crew defected in July 1940 and flew it to Malta from Bizerte, Tunisia. However, following the arrival of 431 Flight from the UK in September 1940, equipped at first with just three Martin Marylands, Malta's aerial reconnaissance aircraft became a little more standardised and rather less ad hoc.

An undated image of Martin Maryland I, AR733, which was operated first by 431 Flight and later by 69 Squadron. A battle-scarred AR733 is seen at Luqa looking much the worse for wear. Taken shortly after its return and subsequent wheels-up landing, it had been flown back to Malta by the ever-capable W/C Warburton. Warburton was a famous photo-reconnaissance pilot who achieved ace status while flying Marylands which, usefully, were equipped with four wing-mounted, forward firing, machine-guns. While engaged upon his reconnaissance duties, Warburton ultimately claimed the destruction of seven enemy aircraft in air-to-air engagements (including a Macchi MC.200 and a Fiat G.50), one probable and six damaged with three more destroyed on the ground. For a time AR733 was Warburton's regular mount and, in order to obtain as much additional speed as possible, the machine was lacquered and polished and had its propellers 'tweaked' to add 15mph to its cruising-speed and supposedly as much as 32mph at full speed ! AR733 was written-off following a crash-landing at Luqa on 13th February 1942 having earlier been engaged by Bf109s. Paul Lazell

Upon arrival the Flight lacked ground crews, so, as a consequence, Malta's resident No.3 Anti-Aircraft Co-Operation Unit (AACU) was disbanded and its personnel assigned to the new Flight as was Skua L2911, while most of the AACU's Swordfish target-tugs had their floats replaced by wheels and were passed on to 830 NAS. Following a disastrous attempt to deliver Hurricanes to Malta from HMS *Ark Royal* on 17th November 1940, the Flight also acquired the surviving navigational lead Skua, L2882. Due to a pressing lack of Marylands at least two Blenheim IVs were also acquired and further Blenheims may also have been obtained, possibly taken over from the Overseas Air Delivery Unit (OADU) while en route to Egypt. By early November 1940, 431 Flight's strength was recorded as having been reduced to just two Maryland Is, plus the two Skuas, although both of the latter were returned to FAA control at Dekheila, Egypt, during December. At a later stage, and in order to carry out the more dangerous overland photographic reconnaissance (PR) missions, a few Hurricane Is and IIs were locally converted to carry cameras and although the exact number of conversions is difficult to ascertain, it probably only numbered three or four at most.

One of 431 Flight's original pilots was destined to become both a legend and an ace while flying from Malta, to become perhaps the most famous reconnaissance pilot of all time. His name was Adrian Warburton who, initially at least, experienced difficulty in mastering the sprightly American aircraft, as the Maryland could prove to be a handful for pilots new to the type and was prone to ground-looping if not handled carefully. It was though his CO, Flight Lieutenant (F/Lt) 'Titch' Whiteley, who conducted one of the best known reconnaissance flights of the war to date, when he flew Maryland AR705 over Taranto harbour to obtain the final set of photographs used to brief Swordfish crews aboard the carrier HMS *Illustrious* prior to their famous attack upon the Italian fleet on the night of 11th/12th November 1940. Indeed the images were so important that *Illustrious* had sent a Swordfish to sit on the tarmac at Luqa ready to pick up the camera film as soon as it was unloaded from the Maryland, whence it was flown to the carrier to be developed onboard. Whiteley also flew the sortie on the morning following the raid, returning with photographs of the extensive damage that the Swordfish had caused.

As further Marylands arrived in Malta, 431 Flight was redesignated to become 69 Squadron on 10th January 1941 with a 'paper' establishment of 12 such aircraft, although a miscellany of other camera-equipped types were also employed by the unit including a pair of Beaufighter PR.Ics. These Beaufighters were locally modified to carry cameras by 2 Photo Reconnaissance Unit (2 PRU) in North Africa and were painted overall 'Bosun Blue' with red and blue roundels. One of them, T4705 became a favourite mount of Warburton who had been steadily promoted during the course of his outstanding career and who would eventually rise to become the commanding officer of 69 Squadron from 11th August 1942 until March 1943. He was a man who would obtain photographs whatever the danger and often flew across heavily defended ports in broad daylight, at zero feet, in order to obtain the best images and intelligence possible, frequently by capturing the names on the sides of ships! Despite its increase in size, the Squadron's role remained the same as it had as 431 Flight: flying out in search of Axis convoys whilst maintaining surveillance of enemy ports and airfields.

On 19th January 1941, a new type of reconnaissance aircraft that offered a very different performance to that of a camera-equipped Hurricane arrived in Malta in the form of Spitfire I (PR Type D), P9551, which, having taken off from Britain, diverted to Malta during a long-range sortie to Turin in northern Italy. Permission was subsequently granted for its pilot, F/Lt Corbishley, to remain there temporarily in order to conduct a number of PR sorties from the island, although in fact he was to be shot down before he could return to the UK. Further PR Spitfires were to follow and Spitfire PR.IVs were duly received on detachment from both the UK and (later) from

Above: An unidentified Bristol Blenheim IV, 'GB-X', of 105 Squadron seen in its usual low-level element. The Blenheim IV was the first type of aircraft employed to conduct *daytime* anti-shipping strikes from Malta, all of which were provided, on detachment, from the RAF's No.2 Group in the UK. It is uncertain as to whether or not this particular image was obtained whilst the subject aircraft was operating from Malta. Blenheim losses in each of the operational theatres that they served in proved to be severe, but in operating from Malta their losses were murderous. Author's collection

Below: Unidentified Blenheim IV, 'VE-X', of 110 Squadron seen following a collision with a stone wall. During its month-long deployment to Malta, 110 Squadron lost seven out of seventeen aircraft (four falling on 9th July 1941, their first sortie), which included the CO, W/C Theo Hunt DFC, who was shot down by an Italian Fiat CR.42 on 18th July while attacking the Trapani power station in Sicily. Despite such losses however, the Squadron sank no less than eight Axis vessels.
via Carl Vincent

2 PRU in North Africa, and it was with these that the hazardous over land sorties, previously undertaken by PR Hurricanes, were flown. In due course the Maryland was replaced in the maritime reconnaissance role by its more powerful stable-mate, the Martin Baltimore from June 1942. As previously mentioned, 69 Squadron obtained 'Goofingtons' too and by the summer of 1942, 69 Squadron comprised of: A Flight, flying Baltimores; B Flight with PR Spitfires and C Flight with Wellingtons. Eventually B Flight became 683 Squadron, while C Flight was absorbed by the Wellington VIII equipped 458 (Australian) Squadron.

Special Duty Aircraft

In addition to the aircraft, units and roles already discussed, Malta also played host to aircraft that were engaged on special duties, of which a few examples might hopefully serve to illustrate their diversity.

One relates to eight Armstrong Whitworth Whitley V bombers provided by UK-based 51 and 78 Squadrons which flew directly across Europe to Malta. Late on 10th February 1941, six Whitleys took off from Malta carrying 35 British paratroopers who were to be dropped near to the Tragino Aqueduct on mainland Italy during Operation *Colossus*, while the remaining Whitleys carried bombs in order to create a diversion elsewhere in what was the first operational mission ever undertaken by Britain's embryo airborne forces. Unfortunately the operation proved to be unsuccessful as the aqueduct could not be destroyed, only damaged, due to a lack of explosives some of which were lost in the drop. Subsequently, all of the men were captured en route to the coast to rendezvous with a submarine. One Whitley was lost to anti-aircraft fire.

The ex-Vichy French Latécoère 298B floatplane referred to earlier was used, as were Swordfish from No. 830 NAS, to carry agents to North Africa, especially into Vichy-held territory where at least one Swordfish was lost when it overturned upon landing on a muddy field in the dark.

In addition, two German-built, ex-Norwegian operated, escapee Heinkel He 115 floatplanes were also used to undertake clandestine flights. The first arrived at Kalafrana in June 1941, without national markings but wearing RAF night bomber colours and with the British serial BV185 applied (ex-Norwegian F.58), as well as the code '115PP1'. Unfortunately it caught fire and crashed soon after taking off for North Africa on the night of 21st/22nd September 1941 while being flown by ex-Latécoère pilot, Flight Sergeant (F/Sgt) Georges Blaize, who along with his gunner, F/Sgt Gatien and FAA Observer Sub-Lieutenant (S/Lt) Drake were all killed. Identifiable parts of this aircraft have recently been recovered from the Mediterranean and are now on display in Malta, although some sources state that this aircraft was lost to bombing at Kalafrana. BV185 was replaced by BV187, the pilot of which was Lieutenant Haakon Offerdal, a Norwegian who flew this aircraft on a number of audacious special operations. On one occasion he allegedly landed inside the enemy-held harbour at Tripoli in broad daylight to pick up Allied agents in an aircraft which apparently wore full German markings. Unfortunately BV187 was strafed and sunk at its moorings at Kalafrana by German Bf 109Fs on 5th February 1942.

FLEET AIR ARM: STRIKE, RECONNAISSANCE, NIGHT-INTRUDER AIRCRAFT AND UNITS

Fairey Swordfish

Amongst the most potent of Malta's strike squadrons and the longest serving was 830 NAS. Equipped with an anachronistic, World War One-looking, biplane torpedo-bomber, the Fairey Swordfish proved to be a deadly efficient anti-shipping aircraft with which the Squadron was to account for a truly impressive total of Axis shipping sunk while flying from Malta. Based at Hal Far, it, unlike other units, was never withdrawn from Malta during the siege – despite the most trying of circumstances.

Fairey Albacore

The Albacore was a refinement of and an intended replacement for the Swordfish. Eleven Albacores (and one Swordfish) belonging to 828 NAS arrived in Malta on 18th November 1941, having been delivered to within flying

---

Opposite page:

The importance of the Bristol Aeroplane Company and its contribution to Britain's aero industries, particularly during World War Two, can scarcely be overstated, not simply because of the plethora of engines that the company designed and produced, but because of the aircraft it manufactured too. Three of the company's products; the Blenheim, Beaufort and Beaufighter, featured prominently in the epic of Malta although the type portrayed here, a Beaufort, remains perhaps the lesser known. The Beaufort depicted is a Bristol Taurus-powered Mk.I from the DD serial range and is coded 'O'. It is equipped with ASV radar, the antennas for which can be seen beneath the wings and nose, from which protrude two Vickers K mg barrels; their purpose was to provide suppressive fire against whatever target the aircraft was attacking. For offence, the Beaufort could carry a semi-recessed 18in torpedo or bombs as required. The aircraft's camouflage is most probably the Temperate Sea Scheme with Azure Blue undersides although some appear to have worn shades similar to Ocean Grey and Dark Green. via Carl Vincent

A familiar image of Bristol Beaufighter Ic T5038 'V' from 272 Squadron, a Malta-based unit engaged on anti-shipping and long-range fighter operations. It portrays several points of interest including the dorsal 'stinger', a .303 Vickers K mg fitted locally to provide rearward defence, an early non-dihedral tailplane with an area of pale yellow paint applied beneath the tailplane and rear fuselage. The latter was a local recognition feature in the Middle East to help distinguish Beaufighters from Axis Ju 88s. Although much worn and stained, colour images of this aircraft show that the desert scheme of Middle Stone, Dark Earth and Azure Blue has been locally altered for over-water operations by covering the Middle Stone areas using a greenish colour which is mostly likely Dark Slate Grey, although other Beaufighters also had the more appropriate Extra Dark Sea Grey applied instead and flight colours of red or blue were applied to the lower nose. Normally operated by a crew of two, a third occupant is seen behind the pilot. According to Mr A Pontet, who flew 17 sorties in T5038 '. .V-Vic was the longest serving Beaufighter on the Squadron with 480 flying hours and by mid-1943 it bore 14 swastikas on its nose and another by the observer's gun.' Records state T5038 was operated solely by this unit until struck off charge on 27th October 1944. Author's collection

distance by HMS *Ark Royal* during Operation *Callboy*; a second Swordfish was lost en route. The Squadron, though initially confined to bombing sorties only, was soon trained in the art of delivering torpedoes and operated in either role alongside the Swordfish of 830 NAS. The naval fliers continued to be extremely effective against Axis ports and convoys although operational losses, combined with others lost to the heavy bombing of 1942, reduced aircraft numbers to such a degree that both 830 and 828 NAS were ultimately combined to form the Royal Naval Air Squadron Malta.

Reinforcements arrived from North Africa during November 1942 in the form of 12 Albacores from 821 NAS which had previously operated in the pathfinder role over the Western Desert in support of RAF Wellington bombers. Upon arrival, this unit, its aircraft and personnel was absorbed into the Royal Naval Air Squadron Malta, and remained active until the end of the siege.

Blackburn Skua

Designed as a two-seat, carrier-borne fighter/dive-bomber, the Skua, by virtue of its ability to carry a navigator, made a suitable guide with which to lead groups of Hurricanes from carriers at sea to Malta. Two of them were retained in Malta for maritime reconnaissance duties until replaced by more suitable types. On 17th November 1940, during Operation *White*, a pair of Skuas each led a flight of six Hurricanes from HMS *Argus* bound for Malta although Skua L2987, flown by Petty Officer Stockwell, became hopelessly lost in bad weather and all six of its Hurricanes ran out of fuel over the sea and their pilots never seen again. L2987 just managed to reach Sicily however and crash-landed on the coast where both crewmembers were taken prisoner. The other Skua, L2882 flown by S/Lt Norwell, arrived over Malta with four of its six Hurricanes still in company, although all were found to have empty fuel tanks upon landing.

Fairey Fulmar

The first Fulmars to arrive in Malta were Mk.Is from 806 NAS after their parent carrier, HMS *Illustrious*, had been

Throughout the siege of Malta, transport aircraft, both civil (BOAC) and military (RAF) maintained a regular passenger service to Malta from the UK and Egypt. For a while BOAC used converted Whitley V bombers of which G-AGDY (seen here) was one. Originally allocated the military serial BD386, this Whitley was one of a batch of 157 such aircraft constructed and delivered between February and July 1942, with BD386 receiving its civil registration on 16th April 1942. Operated by BOAC, and having been used on the Malta service, G-AGDY came to grief in October 1942 when, having suffered an engine failure and a propeller that refused to feather, it was ditched off the Aberdeenshire coast – although its registration wasn't finally cancelled until April 1943. As may be seen, other than its civil registration and BOAC titles, this Whitley's upper colour scheme remained essentially that of Bomber Command (Dark Earth and Dark Green) albeit with silver undersides. Author's collection

damaged by Stuka dive-bombers in January 1941 and they remained for several months operating alongside RAF Hurricanes in the fighter role. The Squadron's inventory was increased when the island's surviving (RAF operated) Sea Gladiators reverted to naval ownership and flew alongside the Fulmars, albeit principally on Meteorological duties. When the Squadron left for Egypt, the surviving Sea Gladiators remained behind in Malta and returned to RAF charge, joining 185 Squadron.

The next Fulmars Is to arrive in Malta were from 800X Flight which had been responsible for leading Hurricanes to Malta during Operation *Splice* on 21st May 1941. Upon arrival they were to have continued on to the island of Crete in order to bolster its defences, but the German invasion of that island prevented this from taking place and so the unit remained in Malta to operate in a night intruder role instead. Operating mostly over Sicily, the Flight's Fulmars often carried small bombs under their wings while at least one was fitted with Hurricane long-range tanks beneath its wings and possibly used to drop supplies to a Sicilian agent. Originally 800X Flight had departed the UK equipped with brand-new Fulmar IIs, but they were commandeered by *Ark Royal*'s captain following an instruction from Admiral Sir James Somerville to swap the new aircraft with the worst of the *Ark*'s 'old crocks' despite fears that they would not reach Malta though ultimately all but one did in fact complete the journey. The errant Fulmar, which had originally failed to start, subsequently suffered engine failure en route to Malta and ditched, although the pilot and his crewman survived to fall into less-than-tender Vichy-French hands. The surviving aircraft were not expected to last long due to their poor mechanical condition and a complete lack of spares; however, their unexpected longevity may perhaps be explained by them finding a cache of Fulmar parts and by salvaging whatever they could from the wrecked airframes left behind by 806 NAS. Malta never boasted more than eight Fulmars at any one time and, although several Swordfish and Albacores were lost to bombing, it is not known whether any Fulmars were lost to this cause.

Hurricane

After Spitfires had begun to replace Hurricanes as fighters over Malta, permission was granted during August 1942 for Fleet Air Arm torpedo-bomber pilots from the composite Royal Naval Air Squadron Malta to operate four surplus ex-RAF Hurricane IIs in the fighter-bomber and night intruder roles over Sicily and the North African coastline. The idea was instigated by S/Lt Ernest Pratt who asked the then current AOC Malta, Air Vice-Marshal Sir Keith Park, if he could 'borrow' some stored RAF Hurricanes and fly offensive operations in them as there were insufficient Swordfish and Albacores available for the purpose. The 'meeting' between a lowly sub lieutenant and the AOC occurred early one morning whilst Pratt was jogging around the Hal Far perimeter track when he came across Sir Keith Park – a fellow New Zealander – who readily agreed.

Having received instruction from the fighter pilots of 185 Squadron, the naval fliers were allocated four machine-gun armed Hurricanes equipped to carry small bombs on converted Beaufighter bomb racks. Pratt and fellow pilots, Sub-Lieutenants Colin White and Reg Elliott, were later joined by Sub-Lieutenant Simpson, while their first Hurricanes were replaced by cannon-armed Mk.IIc variants that offered far greater firepower and proved particularly effective against the Axis railway system, one of their favoured targets. Later, the RAF banned Hurricane intruder sorties over Sicily and so the naval fliers switched their attention to the North African coast for which purpose their bomb racks were replaced by long-range tanks. Additionally, they were also used much closer to home in support of the RAF Air Sea Rescue Launches, by helping to locate survivors offshore and by protecting those vessels from aerial attack.

THE ROYAL NAVY: SUBMARINE AND SURFACE FORCES

Despite the Mediterranean Fleet's relocation to Alexandria, a few individual warships remained at Malta, often bolstered by the arrival of others for varying lengths of time. The duration and viability of their attachment was dictated not only by the prevailing circumstances of the besieged islands, but also by the availability of suitable destroyers and light cruisers, which, other than submarines, were the two predominant types of warship to operate from there in 1941/1942.

No capital ships operated from Malta during the siege, although Grand Harbour was to provide refuge for the aircraft carrier HMS *Illustrious* which limped into Malta following damage received from the all too capable hands of German dive-bombers. No battleship entered Malta's harbours between HMS *Warspite*'s brief visit in December 1940, and the arrival of the sister ships HMS *Nelson* and *Rodney* in July 1943.

Excluding therefore warships which conveyed essential supplies to the islands, the Royal Navy's Malta-based offensive campaign was conducted principally by small flotillas of destroyers, light cruisers and submarines.

Submarines

Although several types of submarine operated from Malta and elsewhere in the Mediterranean during World War Two, it is the exploits of Malta's 10th Submarine Flotilla that are most commonly recalled. Designated as such in September 1941, the Flotilla had an initial complement of seven submarines and went on to take an impressive toll of Axis shipping. The 10th Flotilla was shore-based at HMS

Talbot, the old quarantine hospital built by the Knights of St John on Manoel Island, but was known to the submariners as 'Man Hole Island' and lay within Marsamxett Harbour. Most of the submarines, or more simply the 'boats', were moored in Lazzaretto Creek and, when the bombing was at its worst, they were submerged during daylight hours with a skeleton crew on board.

The Flotilla's reputation lay not only with the professionalism of its crews however, but also to one class of small submarine in particular; the 'U' Class. Originally designed to act as submerged targets for anti-submarine training purposes, they were later used to train nascent submariners themselves. Initially just three of these diminutive craft were ordered, all of which were completed in 1938 with each measuring less than 200ft in length and displacing a mere 540 tons. As war approached their suitability for offensive purposes was realised, particularly for use in shallow waters or where the seas themselves were generally quite clear – or both, for which the 'U's dimensions could offer a marked advantage; thus the type was put into large-scale production with 46 further examples being built. The class did however suffer from many of the shortcomings inherent with most small submarines: limited range; low surface speed; and, except for the first three, an armament of just four bow torpedo tubes and a meagre total of just eight torpedoes. By comparison, the initial group of the much larger 'T' Class submarines deployed no less than 10 forward-firing torpedo tubes, illustrating further perhaps the remarkable accomplishments of both the 'U's and their crews and that their lack of size could often work in their favour as the Mediterranean could indeed prove to be both relatively shallow and clear.

Ultimately the 10th Flotilla claimed almost 400,000 tons of Axis shipping accounting for 75 ships sunk in the Mediterranean; more than any other British strike asset in the theatre. Its most famous submarine was HMS *Upholder*, commanded by Lieutenant Commander Wanklyn VC, which sank 21 ships for a total of 128,353 tons. Sadly *Upholder* was lost with all hands on 14th April 1942 during her twenty-fifth patrol, the last prior to their scheduled return home.

Submarines of the 10th Submarine Flotilla

Name*	Name*	Name*
Upholder	Utmost	ORP Sokol (Polish; *ex-Urchin*)
Umbra	Union	P.31 (later *Ullswater/Uproar*)
Unbeaten	Undaunted	P.32
Unbending	Usk	P.33
Unbroken	United	P.34 (later *Ultimatum*)
Unique	Unison	P.36
Upright	Unbeaten	P.38
Urge	Una	P.39
Ursula	Urge	

* Listed by the name used between 1940-42, renamed vessels in italics.

Axis losses to 10th Flotilla Submarines

Name	Tonnage	Comprising
Upholder	128,353 tons	2 destroyers, 3 submarines, 3 transports, 10 supply ships, 2 tankers, 1 trawler
Urge	74,669 tons	2 cruisers, 1 destroyer, 1 transport, 5 supply ships, 2 tankers
Utmost	43,993 tons	1 transport, 6 supply ships
Unbeaten	30,616 tons	2 submarines, 2 supply ships, 1 tanker, 1 collier, 2 schooners
Upright	23,408 tons	1 cruiser, 1 destroyer, 4 supply ships, 1 floating dock
Unique	20,408 tons	1 armed merchant cruiser, 1 transport, 2 supply ships
Una	15,355 tons	1 supply ship, 1 tanker, 1 schooner
Ursula	14,640 tons	2 supply ships
P.31	12,100 tons	1 cruiser, 1 supply ship
Sokol	7,642 tons	1 destroyer, 2 supply ships, 1 schooner
P.33	6,600 tons	1 supply ship
P.35	4,471 tons	1 supply ship, 1 salvage tug
P.38	4,170 tons	1 supply ship
Union	2,800 tons	1 supply ship
P.34	1,461 tons	1 submarine
TOTAL	**390,660 tons**	**75 Vessels**

Surface forces

Malta often hosted surface warships in order to form a naval strike force, the most famous of which were the vessels of Force K. Formed and disbanded as circumstances dictated, the first Force K was not involved with the Mediterranean theatre at all – it having been built around HMS *Renown* and *Ark Royal* during the opening months of the war for operations in the South Atlantic against German surface raiders. Mention has already been made of the first *Mediterranean*-based incarnation of Force K which had existed briefly in April 1941, following which the designation was soon resurrected and applied to the 5th Destroyer Flotilla. Led by Captain the Earl Mountbatten, aboard HMS *Kelly* and accompanied by HMS *Jackal*, *Kipling*, *Kashmir* and *Jersey*, Force K's existence expired once more shortly after the debacle of Crete, as did two of its destroyers, *Kelly* and *Kashmir*, which were sunk by dive-bombers on 23rd May 1941.

Force K's fourth reincarnation commenced upon its arrival in Malta on Trafalgar Day (21st October) 1941 and initially consisted of four ships: HMS *Aurora*, *Penelope*, *Lance* and *Lively*. The first pair were light cruisers mounting a primary armament of six 6in guns in three twin turrets – the term 'light' being a reference to the calibre of a cruiser's main armament, *not* their displacement. However, as it happened, *Aurora* and *Penelope* (and their two sisters) were in fact the smallest modern cruisers in the Navy, conferring upon them the twin benefits of quick acceleration and manoeuvrability; ideal attributes when leading destroyers into battle. *Lance* and *Lively* were 'L' Class destroyers mounting eight 4in guns in four twin mountings rather than the six 4.7s originally intended, plus eight 21in torpedo tubes in two quadruple mountings and it was these that constituted a fleet destroyer's main armament, despite the occasional cynic's view that they actually formed the 'main ornament'! They would however make good use of these weapons, six of which also equipped each cruiser.

Despite its small size Force K accomplished much and, during the early hours of 9th November 1941, achieved a considerable success. On this occasion the force attacked and sank all seven merchantmen in an Italian North African-bound convoy that represented a shipping loss of almost 40,000 tons in addition to an Italian destroyer which was also sunk. This was despite an enemy escort force consisting of two heavy cruisers and 10 destroyers! To add to the carnage *Upholder*, on patrol nearby, sank a second destroyer. The success was brought about as a direct result of deciphered intelligence, which in turn caused a Maryland to be sent to the appropriate area with the dual purpose of 'discovering' the convoy and to provide the necessary cover in order to protect the source. Hence the despatch from Malta of Force K and the convoy's interception. Similar circumstances prevailed later that month when Force K intercepted and sank two German supply vessels en route to Libya – one carried munitions, the other fuel for the *Luftwaffe*.

On 29th November, Force K was reinforced by Force B which consisted of the two *Leander* class light cruisers HMS *Ajax* and *Neptune*, and two destroyers, HMS *Kandahar* and *Jaguar*. On the afternoon of the 18th December 1941 several units of the combined force, commanded by Captain Rory O'Conor in *Neptune*, left Malta to intercept an important enemy convoy bound for Tripoli. The cruisers *Neptune*, *Aurora* and *Penelope*, supported by the destroyers *Kandahar*, *Lance* and *Lively* were accompanied by HMS *Havock*, (not *Havelock* as is sometimes stated) an older destroyer that had then been passing through Malta. While steaming south in single line ahead, 20 miles north of Tripoli, *Neptune*'s paravanes detonated a mine at 00:40. *Aurora*, the next in line immediately turned to starboard only to strike another mine, as too did *Penelope*. As *Neptune* sought to disentangle herself from the uncharted minefield by going astern, another mine was detonated which wrecked her steering gear and propellers and brought her to a standstill. *Aurora* managed to exit the minefield followed by *Penelope*, but by then dawn was approaching and, given their proximity to the enemy occupied coast and that *Aurora*'s damage had reduced her maximum speed to just 10 knots, the first priority was for both cruisers to close with Malta as quickly as possible before daybreak. At 01:00 *Neptune* struck a third mine. *Kandahar* and *Lively* entered the minefield in an attempt to rescue the cruiser's crew and secure a towline, however, *Kandahar* struck a mine too at 03:18 which killed 73 of her crew and left her severely damaged. Captain O'Conor flashed a warning from the bridge of *Neptune* for ships to keep away and at 04:03 she struck a fourth mine which caused the cruiser to roll over and sink rapidly, taking 764 officers and men with her; only one of her crew survived. Unfortunately the badly damaged *Kandahar* could not be saved either and 24 hours later the stricken destroyer was scuttled by a torpedo fired from *Jaguar*.

Despite their damage, both *Aurora* and *Penelope* reached Malta safely although, once again, Force K had effectively ceased to exist. While undergoing repairs in Malta the number of air raids intensified greatly thus putting the safety of the ships based there in doubt. Therefore, any vessels deemed fit enough to sail were despatched elsewhere but the damage to HMS *Penelope* was such that she had to remain in Grand Harbour where she received direct bomb hits fore and aft plus hundreds of shrapnel holes in the hull which earned her the epithet 'HMS *Pepperpot*'. Despite her damage *Penelope* survived the bombing and, on 9th April 1942, with wooden shoring protruding from her punctured, riddled hull the battered cruiser made a successful 'dash' to Gibraltar.

Several other vessels proved to be less fortunate than *Penelope* and were sunk at their moorings. These included: destroyers HMS *Maori* and HMS *Legion*, with three other destroyers damaged beyond repair in dry dock and either scuttled (HMS *Kingston* and HMS *Gallant*) or scrapped (HMS *Lance*); three minesweepers (excluding those sunk offshore by mines or enemy aircraft); two Submarines – *P.36* and *Pandora*, while another (*P.39*) was damaged beyond repair and beached; five tugboats; the Royal Fleet Auxiliary *Plumleaf*; one floating crane (which had been used to protect HMS *Illustrious* from low flying dive-bombers whilst under repair in January 1941 and the ex-German, Admiralty Floating Dock AFD *No.VIII*.

Malta's last surface striking force during the period of the siege arrived in November 1942, led by the *Dido* Class light cruisers HMS *Dido* and HMS *Euryalus* each of which carried ten 5.25in guns in five twin mountings and two sets of triple 21in torpedo tubes. Supporting them was the 14th Destroyer Flotilla which was led by HMS *Jervis* with *Javelin*, *Kelvin*, *Nubian*, *Pakenham*, *Paledin* and *Petard*. Of these ships, HMS *Petard* is best remembered for its involvement with *U-559* off Port Said, Egypt, on 30th October 1942, when members of *Petard*'s crew recovered items which subsequently helped to decode the German Enigma cipher from which *Ultra* intelligence was obtained, albeit at the cost of the lives of two of her crewmen who were still inside the U-boat when it finally sank.

Other Malta-based naval personnel included an unsung yet vitally important band of seamen, many of whom were locally recruited Maltese sailors, who manned the minesweepers and other smaller craft that assisted in keeping the approaches to Malta's harbours clear of mines in the face of an extensive mining campaign conducted most nights by Axis E Boats (analogous to British motor torpedo boats) and aircraft. This unglamorous role was extremely dangerous and several such vessels were lost, both to exploding mines or from marauding Axis aircraft. Minesweeping was of course essential and without them no vessel, be it merchantman, submarine or warship, could safely enter or leave harbour – the implications of which speak clearly for themselves.

A large number of sailors and Wrens (Women's Royal Naval Service) were also Malta-based who, generally speaking, were able to keep their feet firmly on dry land and included shore based radio operators and HQ personnel in addition to the previously mentioned FAA personnel stationed at Hal Far.

OTHER MALTA-BASED UNITS AND THEIR CONTRIBUTION

Malta's continuing survival was an accomplishment achieved by all who found themselves on the beleaguered islands – irrespective of traditional Service or unit rivalries. It is fitting therefore to include a brief mention of the other combatants – civilian and military, without whom the battle for Malta might conceivably have been brought to a very different conclusion!

The British Army

The British Army was well represented during the Battle of Malta and played a vital role, their most visible and obvious contribution to Malta's defence being that made by the anti-aircraft artillery whose role was crucial, especially if defending fighters were either unavailable or simply outnumbered. They are probably best remembered for the 'box barrage' which they maintained over HMS *Illustrious* whilst that badly damaged carrier was undergoing emergency repairs in Grand Harbour during the so called *Illustrious Blitz* of 1941.

Royal Artillery units based in Malta during the siege

Headquarters	Headquarters
Royal Artillery Malta	10 Heavy Anti-Aircraft Brigade
Fixed Defences	7 Light Anti-Aircraft Brigade
Units	**Units**
2nd Light Anti-Aircraft Regiment	12th Gun Operations Room Regiment
4th Coastal Regiment	26th Defence Regiment
4th Heavy Anti-Aircraft Regiment	65th Light Anti-Aircraft Regiment
7th Heavy Anti-Aircraft Regiment	74th Light Anti-Aircraft Regiment
10th Heavy Anti Aircraft Regiment	107th Light Anti-Aircraft Regiment
12th Field Regiment	

In addition there were Searchlight Batteries and Coastal Observation Detachments

Royal Malta Artillery units based in Malta during the siege

1st Coast Regiment (1-4 Coast Batteries)
2nd Heavy Anti-Aircraft Regiment
  (5, 6, 7 & 9 HAA Batteries)
3rd Light Anti-Aircraft Regiment
  (10, 15, 22 & 30 LAA Batteries)
4th Searchlight Regiment (8 Searchlight Battery)
5th Coastal Regiment (11, 12 & 13 Coastal Batteries)
11th Heavy Anti-Aircraft Regiment (TA)
  (20, 21 & 23 HAA Batteries)

As indicated by the table above, gunners of the Royal Artillery and Royal Malta Artillery were also responsible for the coastal artillery protecting the coastline at emplacements around the islands, the most famous of which must surely be Valletta's Fort St Elmo situated at the mouth of Grand Harbour. Here the first fatalities of Malta's war occurred during the very first air raid experienced by the islands, when a stick of three bombs killed six members of the Royal Malta Artillery. Fort St Elmo would later play a major role in helping to resist a seaborne attack mounted against a convoy inside Grand Harbour by Italian motor torpedo boats and explosive speedboats during the early hours of 26th June 1941. Today the fort houses the National War Museum of Malta.

Infantry

The original strength of the Army's Malta garrison at the start of World War Two stood at just five infantry battalions within the peacetime establishment of the Malta Infantry Brigade. This total would eventually grow to include numbers 231, 232, 233 and 234 Infantry Brigades containing 15 infantry battalions, plus all of their supporting arms, which included the: Royal Army Medical Corps (RAMC); Royal Army Service Corps (RASC); Royal Engineers (RE); Royal Signals (R.Sigs), and the Corps of Military Police (CMP) amongst others.

Between them the infantrymen and their supporting arms were involved in a variety of vitally important jobs which included manning defensive positions, protecting specific vital areas and beaches, airfields and radar sites and mounting round-the-clock guard duties. Additionally, they were required to assist on the airfields where the 'squaddies' worked alongside both RAF and RN ground crews by helping to refuel and re-arm aircraft, as well as providing teams to fill bomb craters whilst others constructed revetments to protect the aircraft.

Revetments became an iconic feature of Malta's war where they were known as aircraft pens. It was the British Army that built the majority of them, and they were designed to protect an aircraft from anything but a direct hit by a bomb whilst on the ground and could be constructed from almost any material that came to hand, although scaffolding and sandbags, scavenged stone masonry and earth-filled 4-gallon petrol tins or oil drums were the most commonly applied materials; by April 1942, 358 such pens had been built. Their numbers comprised: 27 large pens for Wellingtons; 67 for the medium-sized Marylands, Baltimores, Beaufighters and Beauforts; 205 small pens for fighters and 34 smaller pens for Swordfish or Albacores (which had folding wings). Aircraft apart, the overall figure also included 25 further shelters built to house irreplaceable steamrollers and fuel bowsers – which were perhaps better protected than the aircraft themselves! To emphasise the amount of work required, it took 3,500 tons of rubble to build a single large pen capable of holding a Wellington, most of which was shifted by horse and cart which, generally speaking, was the only transport available.

Whilst filling in bomb craters the Army repair teams became particularly adept at that type of work and went on to construct an additional network of taxiways that stretched for over twenty-seven miles around Malta's airfields, thus enabling aircraft to be dispersed in protective pens dotted around the Maltese countryside. The number of taxiways were so extensive that they helped link Malta's airfields, thus an aircraft landing at Hal Far could taxi to Luqa and then take off again, a great benefit when one of the airfields had been put out of action. In fact, by 1942, the link between Hal Far and Luqa became an airfield in its own right and was known as Safi Strip, while another was built at Qrendi which lay opposite Filfla Island, a rocky outcrop off the southern shore that was often used for target practice. On average approximately 1,500 infantrymen could usually be found working on the airfields at any one time, although this often rose as high as 3,000 when needed – with some battalions affiliated to particular airfields.

A testament to the Army's handiwork remains to this day as many of the taxiways that the soldiers built have since been incorporated into the road network of modern day Malta.

Infantrymen also took their turn alongside any spare manpower, be they service or civilian personnel, that could be mustered to act as stevedores to unload ships which had arrived in Grand Harbour. They usually continued in this vital role, despite air raids, in order to complete the task as quickly as possible and unloading only ceased, and the ship evacuated, if it was deemed at risk of receiving a direct hit. This was indicated in a rather haphazard but quite effective manner by a red flag hoisted on the roof of the Combined HQ in the *Auberge de Castille*. From this prominent vantage point directly behind the Upper Barracca Gardens in Valletta, which was visible throughout Grand Harbour, a duty officer would follow the direction of attacking aircraft through binoculars and order the flag to be hoisted if he thought they were approaching the vessels being unloaded; the judgement of some officers however proved to be better than others!

On 12th January 1942, the red flag was raised whilst B Company, 8th Battalion, The Manchester Regiment was unloading SS *Ajax* in Grand Harbour with SS *Clan Ferguson* close by. Each soldier wore plimsolls rather than their more usual hobnailed boots in order to prevent them slipping on the ship's decks and which doubtless assisted them greatly in evacuating the vessel within 12 minutes, bare moments before both ships disappeared in a deluge of spray caused by near misses. Although *Ajax* was spared a direct hit, damage was inflicted upon the superstructure and bridge but, nevertheless, in just two days, the 180 or so men of B Company unloaded thousands of tons of grain, chilled meat, margarine, petrol, anti-aircraft ammunition, bombs – including eighteen 4,000 lb 'Cookies' for the Wellington bombers, four Cruiser tanks, four lorries and six Bofors guns – all from one merchantman.

Infantry Battalions based in Malta during 1940-43:

1st Battalion (Bn). Cheshire Regt.
1st Bn. Dorsetshire Regiment (Regt) *
1st Bn. Durham Light Infantry
1st Bn. Hampshire Regt.
2nd Bn. Devonshire Regt.*
2nd Bn. Queens Own Royal West Kent Regt.*
2nd Bn. Royal Irish Fusiliers*
4th Bn. The Buffs (Royal East Kent Regt.)
8th Bn. Kings Own Royal Lancaster Regt.
8th Bn. Manchester Regt.*
11th Bn. Lancashire Fusiliers
1st Bn. Kings Own Malta Regt.
2nd Bn. Kings Own Malta Regt.
3rd Bn. Kings Own Malta Regt.
10th Bn. Kings Own Malta Regt.

* Formed part of the original Malta Infantry Brigade in 1940, but later became the Southern Infantry Brigade (August 1940); 1st (Malta) Infantry Brigade (July 1942); then 231st Infantry Brigade (April 1943) and served throughout the siege.

Tanks

Supporting the infantry in their defensive role was the Royal Armoured Corps, the first unit of which to arrive in Malta being No.1 Independent Troop, RTR, manned by three officers and 65 men drawn from two units 7th RTR and 3rd (Kings Own) Hussars of the UK-based 1st Army Tank Brigade. They sailed from the Clyde to Gibraltar in October 1940 aboard the *Louis Pasteur* where, upon arrival, the men transferred to the destroyers HMS *Faulkner*, *Greyhound*, *Gallant* and *Griffon* prior to continuing their journey to Malta. The tank crews reached Malta during November and were followed by their four Matilda Mk.II Infantry Tanks and two Vickers Mk.VIC light tanks which arrived a week or so later. The Matildas were named in honour of the four destroyers that had conveyed their crews, although the ex-cavalrymen left their Vickers tanks unnamed.

With the threat of invasion high, further tank reinforcements were sent from Alexandria in January 1942 in the form of A Squadron (redesignated X Squadron), 6th RTR, equipped with 13 A9 and A13 Mk.IIA Cruiser tanks; however, the convoy they were travelling in was hit hard by the enemy and only five A9s, three A13s and 85 men actually made it to Malta. On 27th January 1942, the newcomers were amalgamated with the Independent Troop to become the Malta Independent Tank Squadron, RTR, and was split into four independent troops and one HQ troop. As with most military vehicles on the island the tanks all wore distinctive and highly effective Malta Rubble or 'stone wall' camouflage.

In April and May 1943, four Valentine tanks also arrived in Malta from Egypt, of which two were Mk.IIs equipped with a 2-pounder gun mounted in a two-man turret, while the remaining pair (Mk.IIIs) retained the same weapon albeit in a more effective three-man turret. The Valentines were usually deployed in defence of the airfields and, alongside Matildas, were often used to remove crashed aircraft from runways in order to keep them open.

As previously mentioned, several of the soldiers based in Malta were specialists from supporting arms who performed various unsung, yet critical roles, as signallers, medics, mechanics and engineers etcetera. While it was the concern of RAMC personnel, alongside their RN and RAF equivalents, to attend to those who were wounded, sick or injured, it was the job of the RE 'sappers' to help prevent casualties. To this end, the Engineers enabled the Island's population to take refuge in large public air raid shelters which, in the main, were hewn out of the living rock by specialist mining units containing British miners who had been called up from civilian life especially for this task.

One of the most dangerous jobs in any Army is bomb disposal and this was especially so in Malta, one of the most heavily bombed locations on earth. The Army's bomb disposal squads operated alongside ad hoc RAF and Royal Navy units carrying out the same role and between them defused over 2,500 tons of unexploded ordnance. Army bomb disposal squads were drawn from the Royal Army Ordnance Corps (RAOC) and the RE, many of whom came from 24 (Fortress) Company Royal Engineers. Malta's original pair of bomb disposal officers, Captain (later Colonel) Robert Llewellyn Jephson Jones and Lieutenant (later Brigadier) William Eastman, both of the RAOC, had little formal training in this role and whose courage in dealing with over 275 UXBs in 1940 alone was said to be 'beyond all praise and it was a miracle that they both remained alive'. For their outstanding bravery they became two of the earliest recipients of the George Cross when both were gazetted for this gallantry medal on 24th December 1940, soon after it had been instigated by King George VI.

Malta's civilians
Although thrust into a situation quite beyond their making, the Maltese civilians were the quiet heroes of the epic of Malta and played their part by remaining resolute in the face of a starvation diet, Axis bombs, threat of invasion and, for most, the necessity of being forced to live underground for much of the time in bomb shelters. An example of the amount of time that might be spent in shelters is illustrated by the fact that between 1st January 1942 and 23rd July 1942, only a single twenty-four hour period passed without any form of bombing raid taking place. For their steadfast courage and bravery in the face of adversity, Malta and its inhabitants were appropriately awarded the George Cross by King George VI on the 15th April 1942; the only recorded instance of an entire population receiving such an award for bravery, although the actual presentation by the Governor Field-Marshal Lord Gort VC, in Palace Square, Valletta, had to wait until the 13th September 1942 due to enemy bombing. Today the medal can be seen in Fort St Elmo, whilst its image still proudly adorns the Maltese national flag.

IN SUPPORT OF MALTA: NON MALTA-BASED PERSONNEL

Royal Navy
Countless British and Commonwealth sailors served aboard the scores of warships engaged in the battle for Malta and they participated in some of the fiercest naval engagements of World War Two. Providing their own organic aerial protection in the face of airborne attack were the men of the Fleet Air Arm who proved so vital throughout, and especially so during Operation *Pedestal* in August 1942.

Apart from escorting convoys, aircraft carriers were also used to ferry replacement aircraft to within flying range of Malta, for which the carriers HMS *Argus*, *Furious*, *Ark Royal* and *Eagle* were utilised and which at times represented almost all of Britain's carrier assets. Of these the two last named ships were sunk by U-boats during operations in support of Malta; *Ark Royal* slowly sank within sight of Gibraltar in November 1941, having earlier despatched Hurricanes during Operation *Perpetual*. Whereas *Eagle* sank within four minutes of being hit by a spread of torpedoes fired by *U-73* on 11th August 1942 when part of the escort for *Pedestal*. The American carrier USS *Wasp* was also later employed to ferry vitally important Spitfires at a time when no suitable British carriers were available to deliver them in the numbers required. Although all played their part in saving Malta, it was *Ark Royal* and *Eagle* that provided the majority of Malta's fighters, having launched over 350 aircraft between them thereby materially assisting in the battle for Malta.

The Royal Navy's contribution to the island's survival was further enhanced by its transportation of supplies directly to Malta itself, often when it was too dangerous for merchant ships to do so. Amongst the warships so used were the distinctive three-funnelled *Abdiel* Class fast minelayers HMS *Welshman* and *Manxman*, both of which made lone unescorted trips to Malta utilising the high speed for which this class was renowned and which was perhaps their best means of defence in such contested waters. They were able to sustain speeds of 35 knots for extended periods, a little more with a clean hull; not quite the 40 knots that wartime propaganda proclaimed and which many post-war commentators have perpetuated. To sow confusion amongst the enemy, they were also known to adopt a disguise by erecting a fourth 'funnel' and painting false deck levels on the side of the hull to resemble Vichy-French *contre-torpilleurs* (super destroyers).

Both vessels could accommodate up to 200 tons of cargo within their relatively spacious internal mine-stowage deck which might include aircraft engines and spares, ammunition, dried food (the latter taking less space than fresh or canned food) and other vital equipment or goods plus any additional personnel and their equipment en route to Malta. Many RAF ground crew and Army anti-aircraft gunners were conveyed by these ships, both of which performed similar duties for besieged Tobruk, where *Welshman* succumbed to torpedoes fired by *U-617* with the loss of 151 of her crew as well as several soldiers and airmen who were on passage at the time.

The Navy also possessed a number of large submarines dating from the early 1930s, several being minelayers, which were soon employed to slip supplies into Malta as part of Operation *Tube*, although this quickly came to be referred to as the 'Magic Carpet Service'. This vital service ran from August 1940 until the siege was finally lifted in 1943, with a submarine arriving in Malta every 12 days so carrying an average load of 12 passengers, 140 bags of mail, two tons of medical supplies, 62 tons of aviation spirit and 45 tons of kerosene. Both the latter commodities could be carried in some of the vessel's diesel tanks in lieu of its own fuel and, in some instances, even within sections of the submarine's ballast tanks. Additional space could be found by removing spare torpedoes (reloads) when necessary.

Merchant Navy

Despite their best efforts the Royal Navy could never have delivered enough supplies by its self to victual Malta, so it fell upon the civilian sailors of the Merchant Navy to deliver, in bulk, the necessities required to both sustain the people and maintain a military capability. Because the passage to Malta, whether from Gibraltar or Alexandria, proved to be so dangerous for all vessels, only the faster merchantmen could be considered for inclusion in the Malta convoys. Their relatively high speed notwithstanding and with the protection of a powerful naval escort for much of a convoy's passage, the merchantmen suffered appalling losses and, of the 86 merchantmen involved, 31 were sunk while several others suffered serious damage.

A typical convoy was MW10 which ran in March 1942 and, although three of the four merchantmen arrived in Malta, the supplies they carried could not, even then, be regarded as having arrived safely. Whilst within Grand Harbour one of the ships, *Pampas* was sunk by bombing before it had been fully unloaded; another, *Talabot*, having been set on fire, had to be scuttled to prevent its load of ammunition from exploding, while the third vessel, *Breconshire*, which had had to be towed the last few miles into Malta sank in shallow water before it could be unloaded. Of the 26,000 tons of supplies aboard these three ships, only 5,000 tons was actually salvaged!

There is little doubt that the most famous merchant ship ever to enter Malta's harbours must be the American 16 knot oil tanker *Ohio*, which boasted both high speed and a larger oil-carrying capacity than any other such vessel in the world when built, and whose British crew battled their way through to Malta as part of the *Pedestal* convoy in August 1942. En route the vessel was extensively damaged by an Italian torpedo, several bomb hits and a direct hit by a Stuka dive-bomber which actually crashed onto the ship's deck. Despite all, *Ohio* survived long enough to reach Malta and discharge its cargo to become the embodiment of all that the battle for Malta stood for. Grievously damaged, *Ohio* never sailed again. Many other ships played an equally vital role too, including: *Brisbane Star*; *Sydney Star*; *Melbourne Star*; *Breconshire*; *Clan Ferguson*; *Ajax*; *Port Chalmers*; *Almeria Lykes*; *Rochester Castle*; *Waimarama* and many others besides, all manned by brave crews who well understood the meaning of danger.

Transport Aircraft

Initially Coastal Command Sunderland flying boats were employed on an ad hoc basis to convey urgent cargos and passengers to Malta, a practice which in fact continued throughout the siege, with many of the sorties being flown by 10 Squadron Royal Australian Air Force (RAAF) based at Mountbatten, Plymouth in the south-west of England.

However, it was recognised that organised regular flights to Malta on a consistent basis were called for and, in order to fulfil this requirement, both the RAF and the British Overseas Airways Corporation (BOAC) organised flights to Malta using Lockheed's Hudson and Lodestar transport aircraft from both the UK and Egypt. The RAF unit chiefly involved was 24 Squadron based at RAF Hendon near London. From here its aircraft flew to Portreath in Cornwall to top up their tanks prior to crossing the Bay of Biscay en route to Gibraltar, from where, during the following night – weather permitting – they would continue to Malta.

Flights were sporadic at first, conveying VIPs or urgent cargos as necessary, but on 12th April 1942, Hudson V, AM717, from 24 Squadron flown by Flying Officer (F/O)

From 1942 onwards, Consolidated Liberators began to make their appearance on the UK-Gibraltar-Malta supply flights to convey priority freight and personnel. Liberator C.I and C.II variants were employed by Lyneham-based 511 Squadron and in this instance one of their C.Is is illustrated and is painted in the standard night bomber scheme of Night Black with Dark Earth and Dark Green upper surfaces. They were completely unarmed and relied upon the cover of darkness to hide their nocturnal activities. Author's collection

Matthews instigated a regular shuttle service to Malta from Gibraltar. This service departed every three or four days and the return trip was usually undertaken on the same night using the darkness for protection. Hudson III, AE533 'Spirit of Washington', was also employed on the shuttle, but it was destroyed on the ground at Gibraltar, the victim of a rare Italian air raid on 28th/29th June 1942, the Rock's assailants being four Piaggio P.108B four-engined bombers.

As well as Hudsons and Lodestars, BOAC also introduced converted Whitley V bombers to the UK-Egypt route via Gibraltar and Malta as well as the company's sole Curtiss CW-20T Commando, G-AGDI, which proved particularly useful for transporting bulky cargo. Excluding the Sunderlands, all of the transports utilised thus far had only been twin-engined aircraft, however, as of April 1942 a significant boost in capability was enjoyed when four-engined Consolidated Liberator C.Is were introduced to the UK-Gibraltar-Malta route whilst being trialled by 1425 Flight based at Lyneham, Wiltshire. At first only four such aircraft were available, but four Liberator C.IIs were added during October 1942 which were then forward-based to Gibraltar's North Front airfield to undertake the second leg of the Malta-bound journey. Trials with the Liberators proved highly successful, it being faster with a greater payload than the other types and 511 Squadron, as 1425 Flight became on 10th October 1942, settled into a regular shuttle service.

Number 511 Squadron was to operate Liberators for over two years, albeit not without incident, one of which occurred during the early hours of 1st November 1942, when Liberator C.II, AL516, crashed whilst landing at Gibraltar.

Always a difficult place to land given the combination of turbulent winds generated around the 'Rock' itself, Spanish AA artillery – ready to open fire if their nearby airspace was violated, plus the darkness and atrocious weather conditions pertaining at that particular time, AL516 landed too far along the already short runway. In attempting to lift off and go around again, the aircraft stalled near to the ground and ran off the end of the runway into the sea. Aboard were six crewmen and 34 passengers, including 24 pilots who were returning to the UK following the end of their tours in Malta or for treatment to wounds, as well as 10 civilians (including two young children with their mothers) and the wives of British servicemen in Malta, one of whom was on board with her husband. Amongst the pilots in transit was the famous Canadian ace George Frederick 'Buzz' Buerling, Malta's highest scoring fighter pilot with 28 victories to his credit who was returning to the UK for treatment for wounds received following a combat on 14th October 1942.

Upon hitting the sea 100 yards from shore, the Liberator broke in half behind the mainplane and immediately sank in shallow water killing several of the passengers. Amongst the fatalities were eight of the civilians including both of the young children and their mothers, plus the married couple; many of the survivors suffered injuries of varying degrees and it was perhaps fortunate that the crash occurred so close to shore as help was immediately on the scene, including several soldiers who, billeted nearby, swam out to their rescue.

Another 511 Squadron Liberator which crashed into the sea at the end of Gibraltar's runway during March 1943 was C.II, AL523, in which the Polish Premier, General Wladislaw Sikorsky, was flying during a tour of the Middle East. On this occasion it was daylight, the conditions were clear and the incident, which resulted in the death of Sikorsky, has always been shrouded in mystery and the strong possibility of sabotage.

These two accidents apart, 511 Squadron ran a very successful service although it ought not be assumed that the smaller aircraft types had immediately been made redundant by the advent of the Liberators, when actually BOAC and 24 Squadron both continued to despatch Hudsons and Lodestars to Malta; in fact, it was a 24 Squadron Hudson which carried Malta's famous George Cross to the island, albeit under a veil of secrecy.

When Field-Marshal Lord Gort, VC, replaced General WGS Dobbie on 7th May 1942 as Governor of Malta, he should have had the medal with him during the handing-over ceremony as the King himself had ordered that he, Gort, should take it personally to Malta. However, as Viscount Gort waited to board the Sunderland of 10 Squadron RAAF which was to fly him from Gibraltar to Malta and the time of departure drew closer, there was still no sign of the George Cross – so he had to fly without it. The medal was in fact still at the Air Ministry in London where somebody had forgotten to despatch it. Instead it was secretly put in the care of F/O Victor Betty who, as the Armament Officer at RAF Luqa, was due to return to Malta following a brief visit to the UK to discuss future Spitfire requirements. He flew to Malta on the next scheduled 24 Squadron flight from Hendon on the night of 7th/8th May 1942, aboard Hudson III AE533 (mentioned earlier) which bore the name Spirit of Washington on its solid nose alongside its mission markers. Following this hushed-up top-secret adventure the George Cross was finally awarded to the people of Malta by Lord Gort during a lull in the bombing on 13th September 1942.

'NO PLACE FOR BEGINNERS'

Having discussed at some length each of the elements that combined to successfully allow Malta to remain in Allied hands as a base from which to prosecute the war in the Mediterranean, the reader will have appreciated that one further prime element remains untold. It is there then that the principle focus of this book now turns, to Malta's fighter pilots, without whom all would have been for nought.

For most of the time these men were greatly outnumbered and had to fly aircraft which were often inferior in performance to those flown by their Italian and German opponents. Worse, they also had to endure precisely the same privations as suffered by everybody else in Malta including the relentless bombing, a lack of food and sleep and the infamous 'Malta Dog', a vicious form of dysentery prevalent there at that time. Despite all, the fighter pilots never gave up in their attempts to defend the island and, even when there were only a couple of serviceable fighters left, they still went aloft to contest raids which often numbered over 150 enemy aircraft.

BOAC and 24 Squadron, RAF, made extensive use of the Lockheed Hudson and the similar but larger Lodestar for transport duties into Malta and a BOAC Lodestar is seen here nestling inside a rather large aircraft pen at Luqa constructed from 4-gallon petrol cans. It was unusual for transport aircraft to remain in Malta during daylight hours as they usually flew in and out during the same night; perhaps it had become unserviceable and was forced to remain until repaired during daylight! Malta's George Cross was delivered by a courier flying aboard a 24 Squadron Hudson. Walter Gillman (ex-RAF fitter)

A Spitfire PR.IV photographic-reconnaissance aircraft on detachment to Luqa from 2 Photographic Reconnaissance Unit (2 PRU) in Egypt seen inside its lair of earth-filled petrol cans. Some Spitfire PR.IVs, as with this one, could be identified by their faired-over gun ports, as the early PR.IVs (R7029-R7044 and R7055-R7056) were converted Mk.I fighters. Those serving in the Middle East theatre were generally equipped with a Vokes tropical filter and painted a dark blue colour known as Royal or 'Bosun' Blue (BS381C Colour No.6 Royal Blue). The first two Spitfires to arrive in Malta were PR versions on detachment from the UK and wore a PRU Blue colour scheme. Author's collection

In order to demonstrate perhaps just how dangerous the skies over Malta were between 1940 and 1943, an anonymous Malta-based fighter pilot who had also taken part in the Battle of Britain stated that 'The Battle of Britain was a piece of cake compared to this', while Air Commodore Forster HM Maynard, AFC, the Air Officer Commanding Malta from January 1940 until 1st June 1941 (when he was promoted to Air Vice-Marshal and replaced by Air Commodore Hugh Pugh Lloyd) pleaded with Winston Churchill and the Air Ministry not to send pilots with limited operational experience to Malta as it was 'no place for beginners'. That remark was made in response to the fact that many UK-based fighter squadrons were ridding themselves of their most troublesome or inexperienced pilots by 'volunteering' them away when a posting to Malta was promulgated, and who, upon arrival, were simply shot down in alarming numbers as were the invaluable fighters in which they flew. To try and prevent this from occurring, Malta-based fighter squadrons began to closely scrutinize the flying history of all newly arrived pilots and, if they were not considered to be experienced enough, they were sent straight back home for their own safety, greatly assisting Malta's fighter force in becoming a potent weapon and one to be reckoned with.

Air Commodore Maynard was an aggressive leader and one of very few senior officers able to perceive Malta's potential for offensive operations prior to the declaration of war with Italy, and it was he who pushed for the all-weather airfield at Luqa to be built during the lead up to war. Despite extremely limited resources during his 16 months in office as AOC Malta, Maynard, a New Zealander, helped lay the foundations for the excellent work carried out by his successor, Hugh Pugh Lloyd. He, in turn was replaced during 1942 by another successful New Zealander Air Vice-Marshal Sir Keith Park, who was finally able to break the siege of Malta.

In sum and to clarify a cardinal point, it was the efforts of the fighter squadrons, ground crews and some of the most skilful ground controllers within the RAF, that allowed Malta-based strike forces to attack the Axis in the Mediterranean around the clock. It speaks volumes for their tenacity therefore, that when Rommel's forces in North Africa suffered their worst defeats, Malta was at its strongest!

BRISTOL BLENHEIM IV, V5872 'XD-V', 139 SQUADRON, LUQA, MAY-JUNE 1941

Based at Horsham St Faith, Norfolk, within No.2 Group, 139 Squadron sent a detachment of Blenheims to serve in Malta during May and June 1941. Number 2 Group deployed several Blenheim units to Malta to conduct much the same type of daylight bombing and anti-shipping operations as those in which they were engaged across the North Sea, only now their heavily defended targets ran between Italy, Sicily and North Africa. Casualties in both theatres were exceptionally high and from 1940 to 1942 Blenheim crewmen experienced the lowest life expectancy in the entire RAF. Most of the deployed Blenheim units received replacement aircraft which had been specially tropicalised receiving Vokes filters under their engines (to protect the carburettor intakes from sand), additional air intakes (to cool the back of the engine), plus additional fuel tanks which were installed in the wing leading edges. However, as with 139 Squadron, some of the earlier detachments seem to have retained a number of their original aircraft, such as V5872 seen here, and had no filters fitted. This unit's deployment of five aircraft and seven crews was led by Wing Commander EW Pepper DFC and, although he and his crew were shot down, the unit's casualties proved otherwise to be relatively light, so once the detachment was ended, the aircraft were left behind and the crews returned to the UK by 11th June 1941. Later, V5872 served with 203 Squadron, the Communications Flight AHQ Western Desert and finally 84 Squadron, the latter being subsequently transferred to the Far East where V5872 was written off in a forced-landing near Mingaladon, Burma on 24th December 1942. Although the standard colour scheme for most Blenheim bombers at this time was Dark Green and Dark Earth with Sky undersides, many of No.2 Group unit's operating from the UK had been experimenting with more suitable over-water camouflage and V5872 appears to wear the Temperate Sea scheme of Dark Slate Grey and Extra Dark Sea Grey, with either Sky or Sky Blue undersides, the latter having been depicted here. This aircraft is shown fitted with a single rear-facing .303in Browning mg under the nose with a single .303in Vickers K mg in the dorsal turret. A photograph of this Blenheim appears on page 173.

FAIREY SWORDFISH I, (POSSIBLY K5945) 'M' OF 830 NAS, HAL FAR, 1940-41

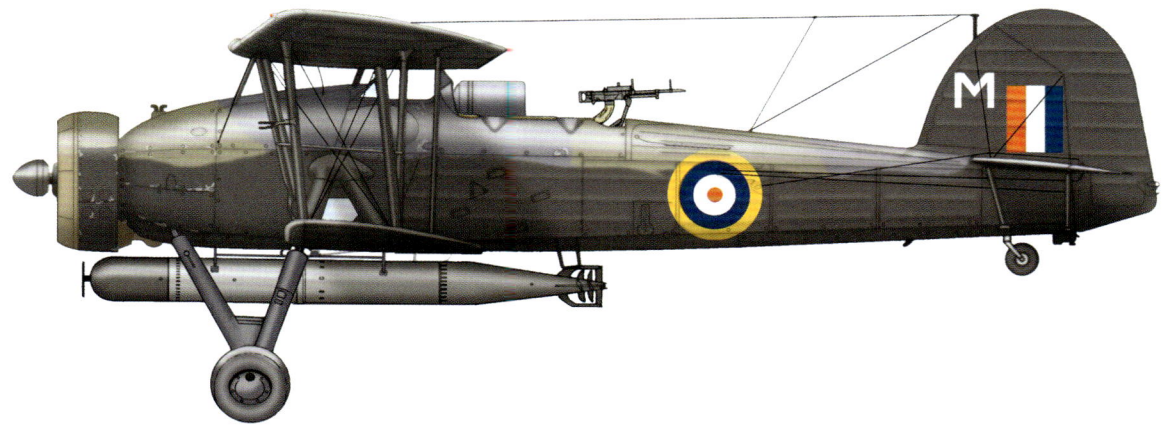

In order to reach the main Axis shipping routes from Malta the range of torpedo-carrying Swordfish had first to be enhanced by the installation of a long-range tank fitted into the observer's position as illustrated here. This meant that the crew of three was reduced to two, although bomb-carrying and ASV radar-equipped Swordfish could retain all three crewmembers by utilising a cylindrical Hurricane-style, long-range tank fitted to the torpedo crutches. Despite the black camouflage obscuring its serials, this aircraft is thought to have been K5945 which arrived with 830 NAS during September 1940 and variously wore the codes B, N & M prior to being shot down on the night of the 21st-22nd November 1941 whilst attacking an enemy convoy South of Cape Spartivento. Lieutenant PE O'Brien was killed but S/Lt (A) AJ Griffith was picked up by the escorting Italian destroyer *Emmanuel Pessagno* to become a POW. Although they had arrived in Malta wearing the naval daylight S.1.E. scheme comprised of Extra Dark Sea Grey and Dark Slate Grey with Sky Grey undersides, the Swordfish of 830 NAS soon received Night Black undersides to better camouflage them for their nocturnal strike role.

VICKERS WELLINGTON IC, T2838 'R', OF 148 SQUADRON, LUQA, DECEMBER 1940

Malta-based Wellington bombers made night attacks as far afield as the Italian mainland, Sicily and North Africa, concentrating mainly on ports and airfields and contributed considerably to the islands offensive effort. Whilst participating in a raid against the Libyan airfield at Mellaha, east of Tripoli on 7th December 1940, Wellington Ia, T2838 'R' from 148 Squadron flown by F/O PW de B Forsyth was attacked by an Italian CR.42 night fighter and badly damaged but succeeded in returning to Malta. Unfortunately whilst trying to land at Luqa the runway was already blocked by another Wellington which had suffered damage at the hands of the same CR.42 over the target area and T2838 ended up overhanging a quarry with its back broken. As illustrated here T2838 wore the standard bomber colours of Dark Earth and Dark Green on its upper surfaces with Night Black on the fuselage sides and undersurfaces, while the fuselage roundel had been converted by simply over painting the white portion (possibly) with red. The code 'R' is either Medium Sea Grey or white while the serial is Medium Sea Grey. The long fuselage windows on this aircraft had blackout curtains fitted which were vital on night operations but, as these were never opened, the windows were eventually deleted on later bomber variants of the Wimpey (as the type was affectionately known).

MARTIN 167F (MARYLAND I) No.114, CODED '2', (EX-VICHY-FRENCH), 69 SQUADRON RAF LUQA, MALTA, MAY 1941

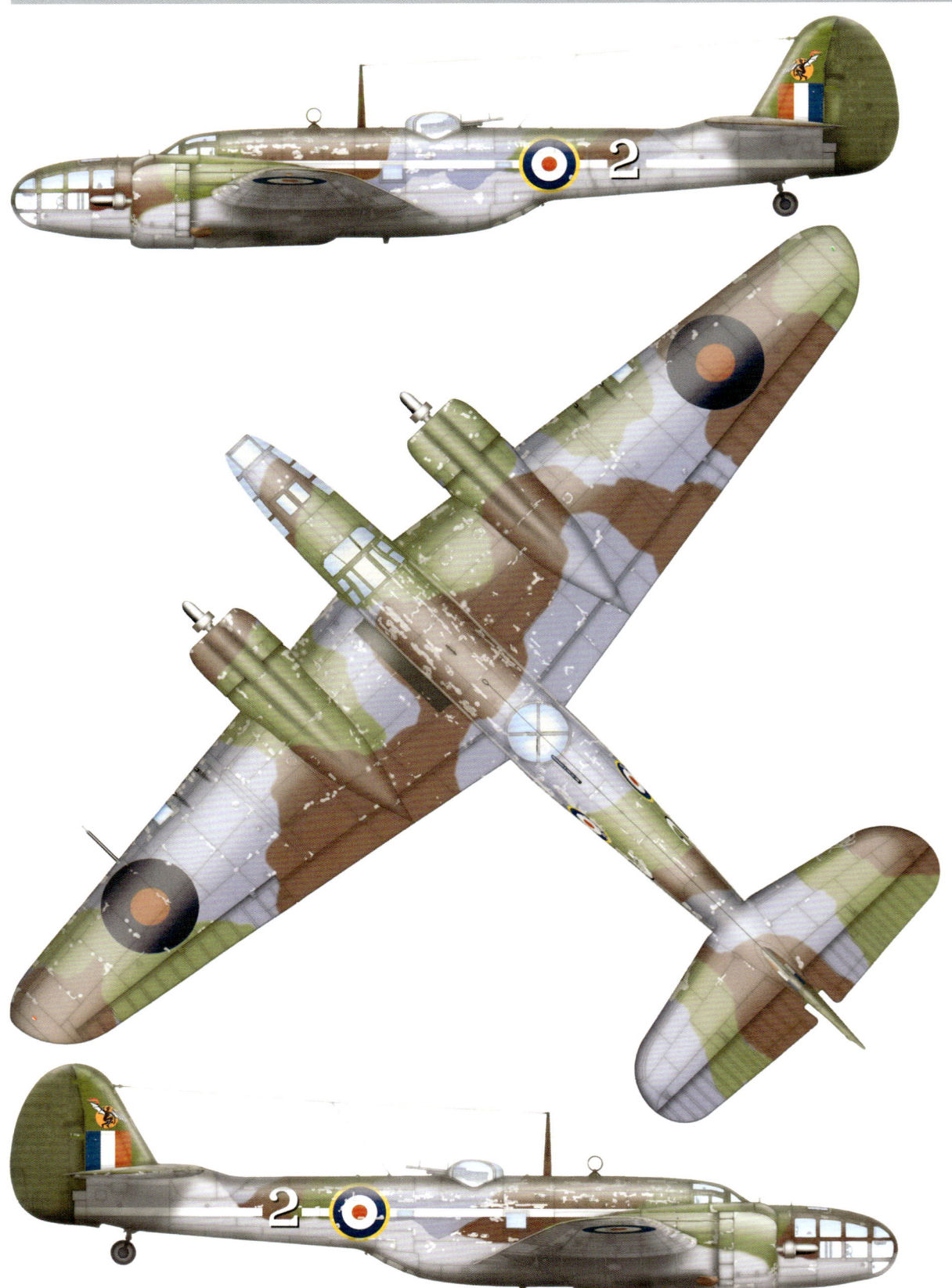

Martin 167F, (French) serial number 114 coded '2'.(The serial had originally been applied to the rudder but this, along with the French tricolour fin stripes were subsequently painted over.) No.114 was one of two ex-Vichy-French Martin 167s to be flown to North Front aerodrome in Gibraltar during early 1941 by crews defecting to join the Free French forces and had previously belonged to GR1/22; its defecting crew comprised of Sgt Brugere, Lt Giradon and Sgt Varrasseur. The French Martin 167F was essentially the same aircraft as the RAF's Maryland I which was itself diverted from French orders. Due to a dire shortage of RAF Marylands in early 1941 the two ex-French Martins were swiftly allocated to 69 Squadron for service in Malta, but, before No.114 left Gibraltar it was pressed into service to fly two reconnaissance sorties over Vichy-French ports in North Africa in the hands of the future reconnaissance ace P/O Adrian Warburton and his crew: Sgt's Frank Bastard (navigator) and Paddy Moren (gunner), who had been flown from Malta to collect the aircraft. On 3rd June 1941 they were intercepted by Vichy Dewoitine D.520 fighters at 3,000 feet over Casablanca, although these were easily outpaced and, on 8th June, they finally flew the aircraft to Malta. It would appear that Warburton made regular use of this aircraft although other than the fact that Moren later fitted twin Vickers K mgs into the dorsal cupola in lieu of the standard single gun, little else is known about No.114 because it was flown to Heliopolis in Egypt on 17th July 1941 by Warburton, who returned to Malta two days later in a standard RAF Maryland (BJ423) which had arrived via the Takoradi Route. Despite joining the RAF, No.114 retained its heavily weathered and peeling French camouflage scheme of Dark Brown, Dark Blue-Grey and Khaki with Light Blue undersides which had been applied without a primer directly onto a bare metal finish after it was delivered from the USA. Its serial number and code '2' were also retained but British roundels were applied over the previous French markings, namely: B-Type roundels above the wings, A-Type below, with an interpretation of the A1-Type roundel applied to the fuselage matching the proportions of the original French roundel with a narrow yellow band added to the outer circumference. The French rudder stripes and the serial 114 were obscured with what appears to be RAF Dark Green, while RAF fin flashes were added beneath the GR1/22 unit markings which were retained as was the white fuselage stripe.

2 | HOLDING THE FORT: 1940
Sea Gladiators and the First Hurricanes

Prior to service with the RAF, Malta's Sea Gladiators had previously served with 802 Naval Air Squadron whose aircraft are seen here lined up at RNAS Dekheila, Egypt, prior to embarking on HMS *Glorious*. All were delivered with aluminium-doped fabric surfaces with the metal panelling painted silver as opposed to the usual Cerrux Grey used on other inter-war naval aircraft and each was fitted with a three-blade Fairey-Reed metal propeller. When this image was taken in June 1939, these aircraft had yet to receive their unit markings and codes. The nearest aircraft, N5521, later returned to the UK aboard *Glorious* in February 1940 but was lost on 8th June 1940 when the carrier was sunk during the Norwegian campaign. RAF Museum (RAFM) P20012

THE ROAD TO WAR IN THE MEDITERRANEAN

Following the outbreak of war with Germany on 3rd September 1939, Britain's Committee of Imperial Defence (CID) issued a report concerning the state of Malta's defences – such as existed, and concluded that Malta should receive adequate defences in order that the islands might function as a staging post and as a forward base from which to operate if required. The CID further concluded that a new all-weather RAF airfield should be constructed at Luqa, that four fighter squadrons should be deployed to Malta as soon as possible and that the establishment of the heavy anti-aircraft (AA) artillery be raised to 172 guns. It continued by stating that Malta was also to receive radar, which ultimately resulted in No.241 Air Ministry Experimental Station (No.241 AMES) being despatched and stationed on the high ground above Dingli Cliffs. Thus No.241 AMES became one of only three such units to have been despatched overseas from Britain so far, the other two being sent to Alexandria and Aden.

Unfortunately, and irrespective of the report's conclusions, Malta received little of material benefit and remained something of a military backwater with few ships in Grand Harbour and just a small peacetime Army garrison on land. The RAF was represented by the occasional detachment of Short Sunderland and Saro London flying boats to Kalafrana seaplane base, which also hosted the float-fitted, target-towing Swordfish and Queen Bee target drones of B Flight, No.3 Anti-Aircraft Co-operation Unit; while A Flight operated the same types fitted with wheels from nearby Hal Far airfield, as well as a miscellany of ex-station flight aircraft that included Miles Magisters, a pair of Fairey Seals and at least one De Havilland Moth.

As the so-called Phoney War in Europe continued into the new year of 1940, the Royal Navy was able to use the Mediterranean as a vital training area where its ships could work up in comparative safety as, at this juncture at least, Britain was only at war with Germany and, beyond a single sortie east of Gibraltar by *U-26* in November 1939, the Sea was free of their submarines. The war's strategic picture altered abruptly during early April 1940 with the Nazi invasion of Norway which necessitated many of the RN's ships being recalled for service with the Home Fleet in North Atlantic, North Sea and Norwegian waters. It was there that the carrier HMS *Glorious*, once a familiar part of the Mediterranean Fleet and a regular visitor to Malta, met her end. The events leading up to her loss need not be repeated in detail here. Suffice it to say that on 8th June 1940 whilst on the open sea en route to the UK from Norway with just two escorting destroyers, and with none of her aircraft aloft or in readiness on the flight deck, they were intercepted by the German battleships *Scharnhorst* and *Gneisenau* and all

802 NAS Sea Gladiator, N5527, shared the same fate as N5521 but is seen here in June 1939 following a forced-landing near RNAS Dekheila. It wears 802 NAS's distinctive diamond markings across the upper wing which are often described as being blue in colour, although they were in fact yellow. At the time that this image was taken a yellow fuselage band had yet to be applied to this aircraft; yellow being *Glorious*'s identifying colour. The dark appearance of the yellow markings is a consequence of using orthochromatic film. It may also be noticed how much lighter the outer ring of the national roundel appears, which of course is known to have been blue! Fleet Air Arm Museum

Aluminium-doped Sea Gladiator N5519 '6GA' of 802 NAS landing on its parent carrier in July 1939 displaying yellow diamond markings across the upper wing and a yellow band around the fuselage denoting HMS *Glorious*. The code '6GA' (just identifiable within the fuselage band) is painted black, as too it appears is the fin and horizontal tailplane suggesting that it was either the CO's or a Flight Commander's mount. It seems that in this instance the aircraft may be fitted with a Watts two-bladed wooden propeller. Later stored at Kalafrana, N5519 became part of the Hal Far Fighter Flight and was coded 'R' until it was shot down over Malta on 21st July 1940 while being flown by P/O Peter Hartley who, though badly burned, survived. RAFM PO12201 via Ian Gazeley

three British vessels were sunk with few survivors. This tragedy occurred simply because the carrier's captain had sought and received permission to sail back to Scapa Flow a day early without the protection of the rest of the fleet as he was intent on returning as soon as possible in order to court-martial the ship's Commander (Air)!*

The sinking of *Glorious* had a profound effect on the air defence of Malta because caches of stored Gloster Sea Gladiators had earlier been established around the Mediterranean to act as a ready source of spares for her embarked 802 NAS, with the main cache being located at Kalafrana in Malta. It was established in April 1939 when 24 crated Sea Gladiators (N5512 to N5535) arrived at Kalafrana from the UK aboard the MV *Nailsea Court* and a number of these nimble biplane fighters were re-erected to join 802 NAS, although two were subsequently lost in accidents. After operating from the carrier and deploying in turn to the FAA shore base at Dekheila, near Alexandria and the French airfield at Hyères near Toulon, most of the surviving Sea Gladiators from this batch were returned to Kalafrana once more where they were dismantled, crated and held in storage as in-theatre reserves. Seven of them, N5512-N5517 and N5535, were later removed to Dekheila for use by the resident units and at least three, N5512, N5513 and N5517, were briefly re-embarked on *Glorious* for service with 802 NAS. Later, N5512 and N5517 went on to experience action flying from HMS *Eagle* as part of the ship's surprisingly effective ad hoc fighter unit known as 813F Flight while later still, N5517 was to become embroiled in the fighting over Crete with 805 NAS based at Maleme – as did N5513 and N5535.

Following its recall to northern latitudes, *Glorious* first made a brief visit to Malta to re-embark eight of the Sea Gladiators held at Kalafrana, namely: N5518, N5521, N5525, N5526, N5527, N5530, N5532 and N5533, which, once re-erected, were flown aboard the carrier from Hal Far airfield by pilots from 802 NAS. This left seven crated Sea Gladiators at Kalafrana which the Navy, for the time being at least, seemed to forget all about!

The 24 Sea Gladiators shipped to Malta aboard MV *Nailsea Court* in April 1939 and stored at Kalafrana seaplane base were:

N5512	Transferred to Egypt, 1939, HMS *Eagle*, then to HMS *Glorious*, lost 8.6.40.
N5513	Transferred to Egypt, 1939, HMS *Eagle*, then to HMS *Glorious*, lost 8.6.40.
N5514	Transferred to Egypt, 1939, HMS *Eagle* 813 NAS fighter Flight.
N5515	Transferred to Egypt, 1939, no further details.
N5516	Transferred to Egypt, 1939, returned to UK.
N5517	Transferred to Egypt, 1939, HMS *Eagle*, then to HMS *Glorious*, lost 8.6.40.
N5518	802 NAS, HMS *Glorious*, Feb 1940, lost 8.6.40.
N5519	Original Hal Far Fighter Flight a/c, coded 'R' shot down pilot injured.
N5520	Original Hal Far Fighter Flight a/c, coded 'S'.
N5521	802 NAS, HMS *Glorious*, Feb 1940, lost 8.6.40.
N5522	Original Hal Far Fighter Flight, no known code, crashed 21.6.40. Major sections of this aircraft were used to rebuild N5524.
N5523	Stored for Hal Far Fighter Flight. Later 813F Flight, HMS *Eagle* Nov 1940.
N5524	Hal Far Fighter Flight from June 1940, crashed 21.6.40.
N5525	802 NAS, HMS *Glorious*, Feb 1940, lost 8.6.40.
N5526	802 NAS, HMS *Glorious*, Feb 1940, lost 8.6.40.
N5527	802 NAS, HMS *Glorious*, Feb 1940, lost 8.6.40.
N5528	802 NAS Crashed in Egypt 11.10.39, pilot killed.
N5529	Hal Far Fighter Flight from June 1940.
N5530	802 NAS, HMS *Glorious* from May 1939, lost 8.6.40.
N5531	Original Hal Far Fighter Flight, no known code. Crashed and badly damaged 23.6.40.
N5532	802 NAS, HMS *Glorious*, Feb 1940, to 804 NAS June 1940.
N5533	802 NAS, HMS *Glorious*, Feb 1940, to 804 NAS June 1940.
N5534	802 NAS, HMS *Glorious*, crashed off Alexandria 19.5.39.
N5535	Taken to Egypt, operated over Crete with 805 NAS, later to UK.

TENSION BUILDS IN THE MEDITERRANEAN

Following the 1939 recommendations presented by the CID, Malta's fighter defences were supposed to consist of four squadrons of Hurricanes. However, due to commitments elsewhere and the fact that the Air Ministry in

Footnote

* For further details of this debacle as well as the experiences of FAA aircrew during the early-war period and Norwegian campaign see this publisher's title *Flying Sailors at War* Volume 1, by Brian Cull.

London still privately considered Malta to be untenable and therefore a waste of precious resources, none of these aircraft had ever materialised. Additionally, by late-May 1940, the Battle of France was going badly and large numbers of Hurricanes had been lost or abandoned there, and so it seemed unlikely that any could be spared for overseas service elsewhere because, with a French defeat looking likely, all available modern fighters would be required for the defence of Britain and the battle that must surely follow.

The Italians meanwhile had several hundreds of aircraft at their disposal, yet, despite Mussolini's increasing bellicosity toward Britain and France, Italy continued to make commercial flights into Kalafrana and Takali, their crews dutifully keeping Italy's military intelligence fully informed of the state of Malta's defences in the process. Luckily, as tensions between Britain and Italy increased, Flight Lieutenant (F/Lt) George Burges, the Aide de Camp (AdC) to Air Commodore FHM Maynard, the Air Officer Commanding (AOC) Malta remembered that a few Sea Gladiators existed in crates at Kalafrana, prompting the RAF to quickly place a request with the Mediterranean Fleet's headquarters in Alexandria for permission to use them, which was granted. Thus, as the possibility of war with Italy loomed, preparations commenced during March 1940 to form a unit that could operate the newly acquired Sea Gladiators and led to the appropriately named Hal Far Fighter Flight becoming officially established on 19th April 1940.

Having obtained the dismantled aircraft, the Aircraft Repair Section at Kalafrana, commanded by Flying Officer (F/O) Collins, immediately set about erecting six of them, to form the Flight's initial complement; the seventh remained in its crate initially as a source of spares. Of the six erected two were held in reserve, leaving four nominally available to the Fighter Flight although the fourth was always classed as an on-line spare, and so no more than three ever flew at any one time in accordance with the then standard RAF practice of flying in 'Vic' formations. Once their undercarriage had been fitted, each aircraft was wheeled uphill along the narrow road leading from Kalafrana to a hangar at Hal Far airfield where their wings were attached and rigged, on completion of which most of Collin's men stayed on with the Flight to serve as ground crew.

Possessing a handful of fighters was one thing of course, but, who was to fly them? With no trained fighter pilots stationed on the island a call for volunteers was made to help man the new Flight and, in very British fashion, an extemporised group of staff officers, station flight personnel, Swordfish and Queen Bee pilots gathered to answer the call. Without delay, the chosen few immediately commenced training for their new role of defending Malta against the might of the Italian *Regia Aeronautica*.

Original Pilots of the Hal Far Fighter Flight

Squadron Leader Alan 'Jock' Martin
Station Commander of the almost completed RAF Luqa and OC of the Hal Far Fighter Flight

Flight Lieutenant George Burges
AdC to the AOC Malta, (i.e. staff officer) and also a trained flying boat captain

Flying Officer William 'Timber' Woods
Hal Far Station Flight

Flight Lieutenant Peter Keeble
Hal Far Station Flight

Flying Officer John Waters
3 Anti-Aircraft Co-operation Unit (Swordfish)

Flying Officer Peter Hartley
3 Anti-Aircraft Co-operation Unit (Swordfish)

Flying Officer Peter Alexander
DH Queen Bee (Drone) Experimental Flight

Of the seven men, only John Waters possessed any previous fighter experience and even that amounted to a mere week-long attachment to 802 NAS flying Sea Gladiators from *Glorious*, and it is perhaps worth mentioning at this point that many of the aircraft operated from British carriers before World War Two were flown by RAF pilots. This was because the Air Ministry maintained control of naval aviation until 1937, with the Admiralty belatedly regaining full control of its air arm in May 1939. During the lead up to war the Navy tried hard to entice as many pilots as possible to transfer from the RAF to the Naval Air Branch, more commonly known as the Fleet Air Arm and this was most likely the reason for John Waters detachment to 802 NAS.

While the Hal Far Fighter Flight organised itself, the Admiralty in London, having heard of the unofficial transfer of Naval property (the Sea Gladiators) to the Junior Service, delivered a signal to the RAF in Malta instructing them to dismantle the aircraft immediately and return them to Kalafrana, from where they would be collected and sent to Egypt for use aboard HMS *Eagle*. Reluctantly, F/O Collins and his team set about dismantling the aircraft, yet no sooner had they completed their task when a new order arrived instructing that the Sea Gladiators be assembled once again! This *volte-face* was thanks to the Mediterranean Fleet's C-in-C, Admiral Sir Andrew Cunningham, who had made a private and semi-official deal with his friend and colleague Air Commodore Maynard as, without doubt, it was in everyone's best interest for Malta to possess some form of aerial defence. So, once again, the Sea Gladiators were unpacked, partly assembled and wheeled back up to Hal Far where their wings were re-attached and airframes re-rigged. As related in Chapter 1 (qv), Cunningham's battle with Admiralty bureaucrats over his allocation of naval 'stores' to the RAF simmered on for some time!

Believed to be 'The Bleriator', this Sea Gladiator has had its Bristol Mercury VIIIA engine adapted to accept an ex-Blenheim variable-pitch propeller, thereby greatly improving its climb performance. Once converted it received the nickname 'Bleriator' – an obvious contraction of the two aircraft names. Spare Blenheim engines and propellers were probably held at Malta for any visiting Blenheims that might require them; or, they may have been salvaged from Blenheims that had been damaged or destroyed in Malta while in transit. Although some sources state that Blenheim *engines* were also fitted to the Sea Gladiators (in addition to their propellers), this is in fact incorrect. There are persistent rumours however, that at least one Sea Gladiator was fitted with an ex-Blenheim Mercury engine on a trial basis towards the end of that aircraft's service. Although N5520 appears at first glance to be finished in an overall silver scheme, the strong Mediterranean sunlight has caused the photograph to become over exposed thus making the naval S.1.E shadow shaded colour scheme all but disappear. Frederick Galea

Having received their aircraft a second time, the pilots of the Fighter Flight continued to learn how to fly and fight them using N5519, N5520, N5522 and N5531, while N5524 and N5529 formed an immediate reserve in the event of the non-availability of any of the first four; the seventh, N5523, remained in its crate to initially act as a source of spares. As 'Jock' Martin resumed command of the reconstituted Hal Far Fighter Flight, and as they reached operational efficiency, he split his six pilots equally into A and B sections, which between them would be responsible for covering the period from dawn to 20:00hrs using a shift system that took into consideration the hot weather conditions. This system split the day into watch periods lasting from dawn until mid-morning, mid-morning until lunch, lunch to 16:00hrs and 16:00hrs to 20:00hrs, in this fashion one of the sections would cover the first and third periods, whilst the other covered the second and fourth. Even so, the RAF still expected these officers to continue with their usual jobs between watches!

On 10th June 1940 Italy declared war on Britain and France, a time when the Sea Gladiators were all that stood between Malta and 140 Savoia Marchetti SM.79 *Sparviero* trimotor bombers based in Sicily or on the nearby Italian mainland, as well as 66 Sicilian-based fighters comprising 40 Fiat CR.42 *Falco* biplanes and 26 Macchi MC.200 *Saetta* monoplanes. All three Italian types outclassed the Gloster Gladiator, while the two fighters were each armed with two large calibre machine-guns which possessed both a longer range and greater destructive power than the four rifle calibre weapons of the Sea Gladiator.

All but one of Hal Far's Sea Gladiators were initially fitted with wooden two-blade, fixed-pitch, Watts propellers without a spinner, while the exception, N5519, still retained its original metal three-bladed, fixed-pitch, Fairey Reed propeller – naval pilots in general preferring the attributes of the Watts design over the Fairey Reed product as too, generally speaking, did the RAF's Gladiator units in the Middle East. Given their forthcoming land-based employment, the Flight's Sea Gladiators had their belly-mounted dingy packs and arrester hooks removed as they were now superfluous. Also, courtesy of the Command Engineering Officer, Squadron Leader (S/Ldr) Louks, the four original aircraft had armour plating fitted behind the pilot's seat which was specially manufactured by the Admiralty Dockyards in Grand Harbour using a template that he had provided. Later, and in order to obtain a little more power from engines straining in the climb, Louks also devised an emergency override control which provided an additional 10 lb of boost from the Bristol Mercury VIIIA powerplant, although caution had to be exercised because if this was used for too long, the service life of the engine could be drastically affected.

Further improvements commenced with N5519 on 22nd June 1940 when it received an ex-Blenheim, three-bladed, De Havilland (DH) two-position, variable-pitch propeller, fitted to the suitably adapted crankshaft of its original 830hp Mercury VIIIA engine. Thereafter the Flight's surviving Sea Gladiators also received this modification which enabled them to climb faster than the original combination of engine and propeller had allowed. Indeed Louks continued his attempts to improve the biplane's performance throughout the summer of 1940 as related in his own words 'Experimentation with the Gladiator became more complex with each successive day. A Mercury XV Blenheim engine was brought out of storage from Kalafrana then painstakingly converted into a Mk.VIII and installed to [Sea] Gladiator N5529, to which a three-bladed variable-pitch propeller was fitted in place of the Gladiator's original two-bladed fan.' This would indicate that parts from both the Blenheim and Sea Gladiator engines were actually combined to produce a hybrid powerplant and suggests that the engines of the other previously modified Sea Gladiators could just as easily have been 'upgraded' later using parts from a Blenheim engine – particularly the propeller gearbox. Louks went on to say he 'tested the first one, Sea Gladiator N5529, on 21st September 1940 [achieving] 10,000 feet in a shade under 5 minutes.'

The exact source of these propellers and their relevant crankcase parts is unknown, but the likelihood is that they came from Blenheims from the Overseas Air Delivery Unit (OADU) which had been damaged or wrecked in Malta while en route to Egypt, or from stocks of spares already held in Malta, or even a combination of both. Certainly there were no Blenheims actively based in Malta for offensive duties at this stage of the war.

To further assist Malta's defences, a second radar unit, No.242 AMES, had arrived in Malta during late-1939. It was co-located alongside No.241 AMES on the high ground above the Dingli Cliffs in order to form an Advance Chain Overseas High unit which provided high-level radar coverage. Low-level radar cover of the approaches between Malta and Sicily would have to wait until October 1940 when No.504 AMES arrived at the same site. At a later date, the arrival of Nos.501 and 502 AMES plugged the remaining gaps by providing full Advance Chain Overseas Low radar coverage around the Maltese islands by operating from other sites situated around the coastline The advanced warning of approaching hostile aircraft that these stations could provide was essential to Malta's air defence as they allowed defending fighters to scramble much earlier, thereby increasing their chances of reaching the height of incoming raids. Radar also provided ranging information for the Royal Artillery's existing 34 heavy (far less than the 172 stipulated by the CID), and eight light anti-aircraft guns, although, with time, the Army would receive its own purpose-designed ranging radars which worked directly in conjunction with the AA guns. The Royal Artillery also operated 24 searchlights which were of course vitally important after dark.

ITALY DECLARES WAR:
THE LEGEND OF 'FAITH, HOPE AND CHARITY' IS BORN

In June 1940, the *official* RAF fighting or battle formation still consisted of three aircraft flying together in a V-shaped formation known as a 'Vic'; therefore, the fourth Sea Gladiator which was nominally available was only held as a serviceable spare which could not be flown anyway as only three pilots were on watch at any one time. With no more than three of the fighters ever seen flying together at any given time, and irrespective of which three they actually were, the Sea Gladiators of the Hal Far Fighter Flight have since gone down in history under the collective term 'Faith, Hope and Charity'. The originator of the term, in the context of Malta at least, is thought to have been Corporal Harry Kirk (RAF) who worked in Valletta and who told his story to Malta veteran and author Tony Spooner after the war. He saw three aircraft flying over the city during late 1940 or early 1941 and, in his own words, thought that they 'looked rather like the three silver hearts on a brooch belonging to his mother, named Faith, Hope and Charity.' This was passed by word of mouth and appears to have finally reached the *Times of Malta* newspaper who published a famous article about Malta's Sea Gladiators. Although highly appropriate, it is thought that the term was not actually applied to the Sea Gladiators when they served with the Hal Far Fighter Flight and indeed Corporal Kirk recalled that the aircraft that he saw in the sky above Valletta were Hurricanes! One of the units most famous pilots, F/Lt George Burges, only ever remembered the Sea Gladiators being collectively nicknamed by RAF servicemen as 'Freeman, Hardy and Willis' in joking referral to the long-standing UK shoe retailers!

Individually speaking, although the names 'Faith', 'Hope' and 'Charity' appear not to have been used when flown operationally as fighters, thanks to the *Times of Malta*'s patriotic article, the name 'Faith' was later ascribed to N5520 in the log book of Pilot Officer (P/O) Charles Pallister from 249 Squadron on 27th November 1941, following a meteorological reconnaissance flight when other pilots and ground crew were also known to have used the names 'Hope' and 'Charity' at around the same time. However, the name 'Charity' was used retrospectively in reference to N5519, which was lost in action during 1940, whilst 'Hope', *thought* to have been N5531 was no longer in a flyable condition. It would appear therefore that the last two surviving airframes, plus the one that was known to have been shot down were randomly named by personnel, again retrospectively, many of whom were probably not even based in Malta during 1940.

To this day the story of 'Faith, Hope and Charity' endures, being synonymous with Malta, the Siege and a fight against daunting odds; yet very obviously their eponymous existence has allowed ample scope for confusion and the full story, despite the best efforts of so many authors, will probably never be adequately resolved. Perhaps for many, particularly the devout people of Malta, it is best left at that!

THE FIRST AIR RAIDS

Italy's first attack against Malta was conducted on 11th June 1940, when 89 Italian SM.79 bombers from 34° *Gruppo* of 11° *Stormo* CT and 60° *Gruppo* of 41° Stormo based at Catania, Sicily, escorted by 18 C.200 fighters from 79ª *Squadriglia* of 6° *Gruppo* conducted a seven-wave attack that continued throughout the day. Their main targets were Hal Far airfield, Kalafrana seaplane base and Grand Harbour itself, although several bombs went astray and fell on civilian areas. The first wave of 10 SM.79s arrived overhead at 6:55am and despite prior warning from the radar unit located at Dingli Cliffs, the Sea Gladiator pilots on watch led by George Burges flying N5531, (allegedly the fastest of the Flight's aircraft) were still climbing when the first bombs began to fall.

Because the Sicilian airfields were so close to Malta the RAF fighters had insufficient time to climb high enough and engage the approaching bombers which were at

15,000 feet. The root of the problem lay in the fact that Gloster's biplane was obsolete by 1940 and outclassed by contemporary monoplane fighters and several types of bomber too; only the barest handful of Gladiators would remain on Fighter Command's Order Of Battle during the forthcoming Battle of Britain for instance. Its rate of climb averaged approximately 2,300 feet per minute, thus it

The first modern monoplane single-seat fighter to appear over Malta was the Italian Macchi MC.200 *Saetta*, the early versions of which featured the original sliding canopy shown here. This aircraft belonged to 6° *Gruppo CT*'s 81ª *Squadriglia*, based at Catania-Fontanarossa from summer 1940 until June 1941. Although 6° *Gruppo* was an autonomous (*Autonomo*) unit at the time, its Macchis still retained the 'Archer' unit insignia of 1° *Stormo*, their previous parent unit. The pilot wears a back-mounted parachute that resembled those used by balloon observers during World War One and must have seemed uncomfortable and cumbersome compared to the seat-type used by most other countries. Italian official image

An SM.79 trimotor bomber from 253ª *Squadriglia*, 104° *Gruppo*, 46° *Stormo* based at Pisa San Giusta, Italy, in summer 1940. Used in conjunction with Sicilian-based units in operations against Malta until November 1940, the unit then transferred to Albania for operations against Greece. '253-5' appears to be finished in one of the earlier camouflage schemes in use consisting of yellow, green and brown, diagonally applied, irregular bands using Italian paints: *Giallo Mimetico 3*, *Verde Mimetico 3* and *Marrone Mimetico 53193* with *Grigio Mimetico* undersides. It has yet to receive a white theatre band around the fuselage but still has a white disc applied behind the under-wing *Fascio* national marking; the individual aircraft number '5' is also repeated in white on the wing leading edge. Italian official image

would require at least nine minutes to reach 20,000 feet, an altitude which might then confer upon the defenders a small height advantage over the attackers. Nevertheless 'Timber' Woods did manage to engage in combat during this first scramble one of the escorting MC.200s, but only after it had dived down to attack him as he was still labouring in the climb towards the SM.79s. After being 'jumped' by the diving Italian, Woods managed to turn the tables on it, due to his biplanes tighter turning circle, and fired at his attacker which he claimed as probably destroyed. His claim was based upon his observation of puffs of black smoke emanating from the Italian's engine as it dived away; however, unbeknown to him at the time, the black smoke seen issuing forth was a feature common to the MC.200 caused when the pilot opened his throttle quickly. In this instance, the Italian returned to Sicily unharmed. The Flight's section leader, George Burges, also scored a number of hits along the fuselage of one of the SM.79s, but he had to fire at extreme range as the faster bombers pulled away from the British fighters and returned to Sicily.

Although the first section of Sea Gladiators had been unable to reach the Italian's altitude or prevent them from dropping their bombs, the next section did manage to get airborne much more quickly. To achieve this the pilots had remained at cockpit readiness, strapped into their aircraft, saving vital minutes, and on this occasion they managed to drive off a single SM.79 reconnaissance aircraft which had appeared later that morning. During the afternoon however, 34 SM.79s raided Malta without a fighter escort and went unchallenged by the Sea Gladiators, although the Army did claim to have damaged eight of them with anti-aircraft fire.

So far, despite the Fighter Flight's best efforts, its pilots had been unable to prevent the Italians from bombing their targets relatively unmolested, and the first raid of the war brought about Malta's first casualties when seven Maltese gunners from the Royal Malta Artillery including a 16-year old boy soldier called Philip Busuttil were killed by a stick of bombs dropped on Fort St Elmo in Valletta. The fatalities occurred very close to the current home of Malta's last surviving Sea Gladiator situated in the National War Museum that now occupies part of Fort St Elmo and a commemorative plaque now stands at the spot on the roof where the bombs fell that day. Civilian casualties also occurred during the day resulting in 11 deaths with 130 persons injured. Additionally, six Maltese naval personnel were killed during a so called 'friendly-fire' incident when their motor launches were shelled by coastal artillery units stationed at Forts St Elmo and Ricasoli on either side of the entrance to Grand Harbour after they were mistaken for enemy torpedo boats. The incident was concealed at the time to avoid poor morale!

Over the ensuing few days bad weather reduced air activity to a few single incursions which were 'chased off' by the Sea Gladiators, but on 15th June, 10 SM.79s escorted by nine MC.200s were successfully intercepted which resulted in damage to one of the bombers, although the Italians stated that this damage had in fact been caused by anti-aircraft fire. On the next day though there was no such doubt as to the cause of damage, when a Sea Gladiator managed to hit an SM.79 – to which the Italians admitted upon their return to Sicily; the Hal Far Fighter Flight was now 'getting its eye in.'

Unfortunately, a combination of damage and serviceability problems was beginning to take its toll on the Flight's aircraft, which meant that it soon became rare for more than two of the fighters to be available at any one time and, on occasion, only one took off. By a stroke of good fortune, for Malta at least, the Italians ignored the islands for the next three days as they turned their unwanted attentions against their French neighbours.

With a measure of fighter cover in place over Malta, plans were put in hand to equip the island with an airborne strike force which materialised in the form of twelve old Swordfish I torpedo-bombers from 767 NAS – a deck-landing training unit that had previously been based near Toulon which worked in conjunction with the elderly training carrier HMS *Argus*. Despite its second-line status (as delineated by its 700 series squadron number), this unit had already attacked the Italians when nine of its Swordfish had crossed the Franco-Italian border and bombed Genoa on 13th June 1940 using converted French 12in artillery shells bound onto their bomb racks with wire as no compatible British bombs were available. Unfortunately, the French

Italian ground crewmen re-arming the 12.7mm nose-mounted guns of a MC.200 belonging to 88ª *Squadriglia*, 6° *Gruppo CT*. This is an earlier variant with its original sliding canopy which proved so unpopular with Italian pilots who were used to open cockpit CR.32 and CR.42 biplanes. Italian official image

SM.79s over Valletta's peninsular and Grand Harbour. From bottom left of this image and in ascending order may be seen: Rinella Creek, Kalkara Creek, Dockyard Creek and French Creek with its two dry docks appearing like a pair of fingers and where HMS *Illustrious* would be berthed in January 1941. To the right of Valletta is Marsamxett Harbour and Sliema with Manoel Island just visible at the bottom centre of the image; the oval of Marsa racecourse can be seen at centre-right, with a portion of Luqa airfield and its all-weather runways just above. At top left is Marsaxlokk Bay containing Kalafrana seaplane base on its right-hand side, while Hal Far airfield is visible directly above the nearest aircraft near to the coastline and appears as a (roughly) rectangular clearing. Author's collection

Above: This image depicts SM.79s from Sciacca-based 193ª *Squadriglia*, 87° *Gruppo*, 30° *Stormo* during the summer of 1940 flying along the Sicilian coastline. The nearest aircraft wears the code '193-2' in black shadowed in white and also displays the initial style of under-wing, 1,800mm wide, *Fascio* national markings employing a black disc with white details as was common practice earlier in the war, while the white theatre band which later became commonplace has yet to be applied – confirming this to be an early wartime image.
Italian official image

Below: Four SM.79s from 194ª *Squadriglia*, 90° *Gruppo*, 30° *Stormo* seen flying over the Mediterranean coastline in June 1940 when the unit moved from Albania to Sciacca in Sicily to commence operations against Malta. The unit operated the SM.79 until September 1941 when it re-equipped with the Cant Z.1007*bis*. The three nearest aircraft are wearing a three-coloured mottled camouflage scheme which most likely consists of a base coat of *Verde Mimetico 2* with *Bruno Mimetico* and *Gialo Mimetico* mottling, whilst the furthest SM.79 has a lighter coloured mottling which may be a two-colour scheme of *Verde Oliva Scuro* with large *Nocciola Chiaro* mottles.

took a dim view of this attack fearing that it might provoke a response from the Italians (which it did) and, with France's impending surrender making 767 Squadron's situation increasingly untenable the entire unit and its 18 Swordfish departed for French North Africa and landed at Bône, Algeria on 18th June 1940. Upon arrival, the unit split into two parts and six Swordfish and most of the ground staff and trainee aircrew left for Gibraltar where the aircraft were absorbed into *Ark Royal*'s air group and most of the personnel returned to the UK to re-establish 767 NAS once more at Arbroath, Scotland.

Meanwhile, the 12 Swordfish at Bône, crewed by instructors and some of the more advanced trainees, flew to Malta on 20th June 1940, but, due to a miscommunication, their arrival at Hal Far was unexpected and they were forced to land in between cars and other objects that had been scattered about the airfield as an anti-invasion measure. Thanks to their deck landing skills, all of the pilots were able to land safely, including the CO who was carrying his motor bike between the torpedo crutches of his Swordfish. Shortly after their arrival the unit was renumbered to define its new frontline role and became 830 NAS, although additional aircrew in the form of observers had to be posted in from the UK as, in its previous pilot training role it had had no requirement for aircrew belonging to that branch.

Based at Hal Far alongside the Sea Gladiators, 830 NAS commenced a period of torpedo training flights around the Maltese coastline in their elderly early production (1936) Swordfish Is which unfortunately lacked blind-flying panels and accurate altimeters. Their altimeters were calibrated in multiples of 100ft, as opposed to the multiples of ten used in more modern instruments a critical consideration when launching torpedoes at night, although the crews quickly became adept at flying 'by the seat of their pants.' A batch of modern blind-flying instrument panels complete with accurate altimeters were flown into Hal Far in a Swordfish sent from HMS *Illustrious* during the late summer of 1940, where, having been offloaded, they were stacked in the corner of a hangar and remained there gathering dust for at least a year until a new commanding officer discovered them and swiftly had them fitted! Operational proficiency was achieved during August 1940 and the Swordfish soon conducted their first offensive mission – a night-time dive-bombing attack on oil storage tanks in Sicily.

REINFORCEMENTS ARRIVE: MALTA'S FIRST AERIAL VICTORY

When considering the fighting over Malta, wartime propaganda might easily convince its audience that a trio of old biplanes named 'Faith, Hope and Charity' had held out against overwhelming odds until the famous Spitfire arrived to save the island. Yet, as with the Battle of Britain, the aircraft that shouldered much of the burden over Malta was actually that doyen of British fighters, the Hawker Hurricane, the first of which arrived within days of Italy's entry into the war. At first they were few in number and they fought alongside the tiny force of Sea Gladiators but, as further examples arrived, they had become by the end of 1940 Malta's primary fighter.

In fact, even before war broke out in the Mediterranean on 10th June 1940, Hurricane reinforcements were already on their way to the Middle East, staging through France, Tunisia and Malta, the intention being that they would initially help to defend the naval base at Alexandria. Here they would join L1669, an early fabric-winged, unarmed, Mk.I – the only Hurricane then present in the entire Middle East.

Having been used for tropical trials at Khartoum in the Sudan, L1669 had been modified to accept a three-bladed, De Havilland, variable-pitch propeller in lieu of its original wooden two-bladed, Watts, fixed-pitch unit, presumably by fitting a Merlin III engine. It was known as 'Collies Battleship' after the World War One, RNAS ace, Air Commodore R Collishaw, DSO and Bar, OBE, DSC, DFC who was now the AOC of No.202 Group in Egypt. This single Hurricane had been constantly moved around Egyptian airfields in order to deceive the Italians into believing that a sizeable number of Hurricanes already existed in the Middle East where, following the arrival of fully operational Hurricanes, L1669 was presumably used as a conversion trainer.

The first six operational Hurricane Is intended for the Middle East were each equipped with two experimental long-range, non-droppable, 44 gallon underwing fuel tanks in order to increase their range which had initially been conceived to assist with the delivery of Hurricanes to Norway. This was as an alternative to using aircraft carriers which were urgently required for other tasks, but the campaign in Norway ceased before the tanks could be employed. Therefore this would be the first time that the tanks were to be used in earnest, having been fitted by 10 Maintenance Unit (MU) at RAF Hullavington, Wiltshire, from where the delivery pilots collected their mounts. The pilots were:

Hudson Is involved in the first ferry flight

Flying Officer Davies	N7324 (Retained in Malta)
Flying Officer Stacey-Smyth	N7357 (Returned to UK)

Hurricane pilots from the first ferry flight

Squadron Leader C Ryley (Officer in Command)
Squadron Leader CWM Ling
Flight Lieutenant TM Lockyer
Flying Officer Eric Taylor *
Pilot Officer DT Saville
Pilot Officer HAR Prowse
Pilot Officer T Balmforth* (spare pilot in Hudson N7324)

* These pilots remained in Malta to serve with the Hal Far Fighter Flight.

Hurricane Is despatched – with final destinations

P2627	Arrived in Egypt
P2638	Arrived in Egypt
P2639	Arrived in Egypt
P2641	Retained briefly with Hal Far Fighter Flight, then sent to Egypt
P2644	Crashed en route at Marignane Airfield, France
P2645	Retained in Malta

Providing the very necessary navigational support for the journey was a pair of Hudson Is detached from RAF Leuchars, Fife, consisting of Hudson N7324 (as recounted in Chapter 1) from 233 Squadron which was flown by F/O Davies and F/Lt Cooper, and N7357 from 224 Squadron flown by F/O Stacey-Smyth and F/O Potter. Each Hudson led three Hurricanes apiece and to further extend their range the fighters had their eight machine guns removed to save weight. These were loaded aboard the Hudsons so that each carried 24 guns per aircraft plus any essential spares which may be needed en route; additionally, P/O Balmforth (the spare pilot) rode in the lead Hudson, N7324. Strangely there is no reference to any ground crew being included, however air gunners were mostly volunteer ground personnel at this stage of the war so they presumably could have carried out light repairs if nec-

Above: The first Hurricane ferry flight was led across France by a pair of Hudson Is from 233 & 224 Sqns based at Leuchars, Scotland. They are represented here by an anonymous Hudson I with black undersides which is being serviced inside one of Leuchars 1918 vintage Belfast Truss hangars. Martin Derry

Below: Never previously published, this rare image shows Hurricane I, P2644, (flown by P/O Prowse) which had lost its port undercarriage leg at Marignane airfield in France, on 8th June 1940 during the first Hurricane ferry flight across that country. The aircraft had run over a recently filled bomb crater which had not been compacted properly and the leg was snapped off, causing the Hurricane to be abandoned to the Germans once they had overrun the area, as witnessed in this image – the missing panels and fabric having presumably been taken as trophies. The aircraft's finish appears to be Dark Earth and Dark Green with black and white halved undersides. A Vokes tropical filter can be seen beneath its nose and experimental long-range tanks are in evidence beneath each wing – a concept which had originally been developed for the aerial reinforcement of Norway. P2644's DH propeller lies in the foreground with part of the gear housing still attached. Ian Simpson

essary and at least two gunners were included in each crew.

The two formations left Hullavington on 6th June and flew to RAF Tangmere, Sussex, where they refuelled and awaited favourable weather conditions before commencing the first leg of their journey which would take them across France to the airfield at Marignane on the Mediterranean coast of southern France. They departed Tangmere on 8th June and, after reaching the French coast at Brittany, both groups crossed the Brest peninsula at Rennes and followed the Atlantic coastline south-west as far as the Gironde estuary, where they turned left and flew up the Gironde valley, thereby crossing France at its narrowest point and avoiding any high ground. Upon reaching the Mediterranean coast near Beziers they skirted the Gulf of Lion prior to landing at Marignane airfield where they were to refuel. However, bad luck struck Hurricane P2644, flown by P/O Prowse, when it fell into a bomb crater during its landing run and ripped off its port undercarriage leg. The damage was so bad that the Hurricane had to be left behind in the hope that a repair party would reach it in due course. In fact it was still there when German troops arrived following the French surrender.

Having refuelled, the remaining aircraft commenced the next leg of their journey across the Mediterranean to Tunisia. Here they refuelled again prior to following the North African coastline to a point where they would be able to 'nip' across the Mediterranean to Malta in order to refuel once more and prepare for their final leg to Egypt. All five remaining Hurricanes and both Hudsons reached Tunisia safely, but the electric fuel pumps in the Hurricane's new long-range tanks were proving to be so unreliable that two of the fighters, P2641 and P2645, accompanied by Hudson N7324, had to remain at Al Aouina airfield near Tunis for ten days until an engineer from Hawker could arrive from the UK and repair them. Hudson N7324 remained with them.

The three remaining Hurricanes, P2627, P2633 and P2639, led by Hudson N7357, carried on as planned and reached Malta on 13th June 1940, where they were refuelled again prior to departing for Egypt. Having successfully shepherded these three Hurricanes to their destination, Stacey-Smyth and his crew remained in Cairo for a few days prior to flying N7357 back to the UK on 16th June – presumably following the reverse of their outbound route.

Sorry to see the Hurricanes leave for Egypt, Malta's AOC, AVM Maynard, requested that the Air Ministry provide Hurricanes for Malta's defence and, having consulted with the AOC-in-C, Middle East Command, Air Marshal Sir Arthur Murray Longmore, GCB, DSO, permission was granted for Hurricanes P2641 and P2645 to be retained in Malta as soon as they had arrived from Tunisia. The pair finally arrived on 21st June 1940 and were allocated to the Hal Far Fighter Flight to operate alongside the Sea Gladiators. Two of the delivery pilots, Taylor and Balmforth, were retained at Hal Far, as too was Hudson N7324 and its crew to become the island's first land-based photographic reconnaissance asset, one which would go on to complete 22 reconnaissance sorties from Malta prior to its untimely demise at the hands of a British Fulmar!

The newly arrived Hurricanes and their pilots were swiftly incorporated into the Hal Far Fighter Flight, but on the day they arrived disaster also struck the unit. During the morning of 21st June 1940, S/Ldr Martin crashed Sea Gladiator N5522 during take off, thankfully without being hurt, while in the afternoon F/O Hartley hit a packing case during take off in N5524 which wrecked the undercarriage and caused him to crash and turn over upon landing. In one day the fighting strength of Malta's fighter force had been drastically reduced without any assistance from the *Regia Aeronautica*. Neither aircraft was repairable, however, always resourceful, S/Ldr Louks was able to combine surviving components from each to repair N5524, or in his own words, 'a hybrid was born out of two corpses.'

THE SECOND FERRY FLIGHT ACROSS FRANCE

Modern aircraft were desperately needed in the Middle East so, having proved that the cross-continental route was viable, a second ferry flight to the region was organised, albeit that none of the aircraft were intended to be retained in Malta. This ferry flight was to be on a more ambitious scale than the first and consisted of 12 Hurricane Is fitted with 44 gallon underwing fuel tanks, and 12 Blenheim IVs garnered from MUs across the country and hastily assembled at 20 MU, Aston Down in Gloucestershire.

Unfortunately this operation would prove to be more unwieldy than the first and rather less lucky, particularly as the Hurricane pilots were not given any instruction with regard to their underwing tanks. They were, however, specifically cautioned to conserve fuel by cruising at approximately 160mph using a weak fuel mixture with their propeller kept in coarse pitch and with engine revs maintained at a low 1,200rpm. Unfortunately, cruising at these settings meant that the engine revs were too low for the aircraft's generators to function and consequently their batteries ran flat, which in turn meant that the electric pumps failed and prevented the pilots from being able to transfer fuel from their underwing tanks to their wing tanks. What the pilots (of both ferry flights) ought to have been told, but weren't, was that they needed to temporarily increase the engine rpm and change to fine pitch while transferring their precious fuel. This lack of technical information would have consequences later. More immediately however, their collective misfortunes were added to when, instead of employing Coastal Command Hudsons with their experienced navigators as lead aircraft, four of the Blenheims were assigned navigators instead, each of whom was, in theory, to have led a mixed formation consisting of three Blenheims and three Hurricanes and designated as A, B, C and D Flights. On 17th June 1940, with the situation in France deteriorating drastically and German forces advancing rapidly through Normandy, Brittany and the Loire region towards Bordeaux, the Hurricanes and Blenheims were at last ready to head for their departure point at RAF Tangmere.

During the period between the first and second ferry flights, Marshal Pétain had become the new French Prime Minister and the government had relocated its seat of power from Paris to Bordeaux from where politicians were actively seeking an armistice with Germany at a time when confusion reigned supreme. From the midst of this confusion a message was sent to the Air Ministry advising that a change be made to the Ferry Flight's intended route, although no specific reason was provided. Unfortunately this message was misinterpreted in London and, instead of planning an alternative route which avoided high ground as the first flight had done, the new plan was to simply fly in a straight south-easterly direction across France after crossing the coast at Brittany. This would take them into the region of the mountainous Massif Central where peaks rise to almost 6,000 feet and where potentially atrocious weather conditions are often encountered.

Upon arrival at Tangmere on the evening of 17th June, the ferry crews found the station to be extremely busy and overcrowded with a number of aircraft that had been evacuated from the fighting over Northern France, consequently there were insufficient ground crew available to refuel all of the Hurricanes and Blenheims in time for their planned early-morning departure next day. To add to their problems, the lack of manpower and available room on the airfield meant that the aircraft could not be marshalled into their specific take-off order which was vital for forming up into their individual formations without burning excessive amounts of precious fuel in the air.

Following much hard work, the last of the ferry flight aircraft were finally refuelled and ready to depart by midmorning on the 18th. However, rather than progressing as planned in their four orderly Flights each with a navigator in the lead aircraft, their delayed departure caused them all to head for France in one loose gaggle. Their 'formation' was acceptable at first as the weather over southern England and the Channel was perfect with bright sunny skies, but as they crossed into France the weather grew steadily worse and by the time the much-extended gaggle had reached the foothills of the Massif Central, they were flying in low cloud and driving rain. As conditions deteriorated further and with visibility not even extending beyond their own wingtips, aircrew became lost or disorientated in the low cloud causing five Blenheims to crash into high ground killing everyone on board. The remainder of the formation either turned around and returned to the UK or force-landed in the local area becoming scattered over a large part of the countryside in the process with some having landed at airfields and others on farmland.

For those whose machines had been damaged, enterprising aircrew quickly began to make arrangements to save their aircraft where possible – including P/O Hilton-Barber whose Hurricane, P2653, had damaged its tailwheel whilst landing in an alpine field. He arranged for it to be replaced with a makeshift skid fashioned from a spring taken from a motor vehicle's suspension courtesy of a helpful local blacksmith! Other force-landed aircrew had their experiences too of course, some of whom, having landed more or less intact were also able to summon local assistance, and fuel, before continuing their journey south; while others less fortunate had to abandon their aircraft to the Axis and then make their own way to safety.

For P/O George Maycock flying Hurricane P2584, the story was a little different in as much that having lost the formation in the thick cloud over the Massif Central, and being low on fuel, he had turned back towards Britain but was attacked by a Bf 109E over Loudun, western France. With his tail controls damaged by cannon fire he decided to land straight away, but his aircraft flipped over upon landing on soft ground and was wrecked. Emerging uninjured, Maycock set fire to the Hurricane as the Germans were only 8 miles or so away, and he returned to the UK via Bordeaux. Of the surviving Blenheims IVs, L9320, flown by F/Lt Cole was suffering from a faulty fuel-transfer system and making for the UK when it had to land on the beach near Sablons Finisterre, Brittany, where the crew were arrested by French troops. Having convinced the soldiers that they were allies, the crew made repairs to their aircraft's fuel system using rubber tubing provided by a local garage, but it took so long to transfer the fuel between tanks by hand that they were still there when the tide came in and swamped the aircraft. When the sea finally receded, the Blenheim was dug out of the sand, the engines started and the crew took off, landing at Tangmere at 23:00hrs on 18th June!

Most of those aircraft which did return to Britain waited at Tangmere for better weather prior to resuming their journey the following day and, whilst en route, they began to encounter a few of their colleagues who had force landed in France. Small groups joined up with each other as they progressed southwards, although losses continued to occur including Hurricane P2626, flown by F/O Smyths, which tipped onto its nose whilst attempting to take-off from a soggy airfield at Ussel, near Limoges on 20th June. The damage was such that it was abandoned in situ as was Blenheim L9300, flown by F/O Wood which was totally bogged-in and could not be moved. That evening witnessed a tragic loss when an entire flight of three Hurricanes and a Blenheim crashed upon reaching the Tunisian coast near Bizerte. Having reached Marignane airfield in atrocious weather conditions during the late afternoon, the French authorities were keen for them to leave so, against his better judgement, the formation's leader, S/Ldr 'Scotty' Pryde, who had earlier crashed his own Blenheim following engine failure, took control of Blenheim L9334. Prior to departing for Tunisia, Pryde had his six aircraft refuelled, the flight having originally included five Hurricanes although two of the latter had later returned to France prematurely because of problems with their long-range tanks once again. The remaining four reached the North African coastline in darkness amidst a raging thunderstorm. Lost in the darkness, with limited visibility due to the rain, the Blenheim crashed into the sea and, low on fuel, P/O Mansell-Lewis flying Hurricane P2648, gallantly ditched close to the Blenheim in order to assist any survivors, but in the darkness he missed the only person to emerge from the wreck before it sank: the gunner, whose body was later washed ashore. Another Hurricane pilot, P/O Sims, bailed out of P2642 after he became totally lost in the pitch darkness, while the third Hurricane, P2650, crashed on the beach near Bizerte, presumably whilst trying to land on the sand, killing P/O GDH Beardon. Thus only Sims and Mansell-Lewis survived the night following an exhausting swim of three miles in rough seas, following which they were rescued by Arabs and later returned to the UK via Gibraltar.

By the morning of the 21st, seven Hurricanes and three Blenheims had succeeded in crossing the Mediterranean to reach Medjez-el-Bab in Tunisia, where there they reorganised themselves prior to departing for Malta the following day. Although Hurricane P2625 crashed on take-off, the remaining six Hurricanes and three Blenheims arrived safely in Malta – just one day after the pair of delayed Hurricanes and their Hudson escort from the first ferry flight had arrived at Hal Far. The three Blenheims and Hurricanes P2544 and P2651 flown by Pilot Officers Carter and Glen had been the first to depart and all arrived in Malta by lunchtime to be followed, six hours later, by Hurricanes P2623 and P2614 flown by P/Os Collins and McAdam. Problems with the battery delayed the start up of Hurricane P2629, flown by P/O Sugden for most of the day but, accompanied by P/O Hilton-Barber in P2653, they were finally able to set off from Medjez late in the day which of course meant that their arrival over Hal Far would be equally late. Upon arrival the pair found the airfield festooned with old vehicles as an anti-invasion precaution and, although Sugden's wing struck a bus while landing in the growing darkness which caused some damage, both Hurricanes landed safely.

Three of the newly arrived pilots: Hilton-Barber, McAdam and Sugden also remained at Hal Far to join F/O Taylor and P/O Balmforth from the first ferry flight. (The remaining six Hurricanes from the two ferry flights had departed Malta for Egypt where they replaced a Flight of 80 Squadron's Gladiators which was tasked with the protection of Alexandria's naval facilities.)

In retrospect, and despite difficulties and losses along the way, the two cross-continental flights had provided urgently needed reinforcements for Egypt and Malta at a time when even small quantities of modern machines could impart a far greater impact upon the enemy than their lack of numbers might otherwise imply.

FIRST KILLS AND LOSSES

Even though Hurricanes had by now arrived in Malta, albeit in small numbers, the first confirmed victory to be claimed over Malta was scored by a Sea Gladiator during the afternoon of 22nd June 1940, when George Burges flying N5519, coded 'R', shot down a lone SM.79 bomber from 216[a] *Squadriglia* flown by *Tenente* Francesco Solimena over Valletta in plain view of everybody below. By maintaining cockpit readiness on the ground in the blazing sunshine he and F/O 'Timber' Woods were able to gain a height advantage of 2,000 feet over the incoming aircraft and then dived to attack it. Burges positioned himself behind the bomber and shot off its port engine, causing it to crash into the sea in flames off Kalafrana with the loss of all but two of the crew who managed to bail out and were rescued. Burges recalls:

' "Timber" Woods and I were on the 1600 hours to dusk watch when the alarm went off. We took off and climbed as hard as we could go, as was the custom. We did not attempt to maintain close formation because if one aircraft could climb faster than the other, then the additional height gained might be an advantage. Ground control as usual gave us the position and course of the enemy. The enemy turned out to be a single SM79 presumably on a photographic sortie. It came right down the centre of the island from Gozo, and on this occasion we were 2,000-3,000 feet above it. "Timber" went in first but I did not see any result. I managed to get right behind it and shot off the port engine. I was told this happened right over Sliema and Valletta and caused quite a stir in the population. The aircraft caught fire and crashed in the sea off Kalafrana.'

Hurricane pilots despatched to Malta and the Middle East in the second cross-France direct ferry flight

Pilot	Aircraft	Pilot	Aircraft
P/O R Hilton-Barber	P2653	P/O WP Collins	P2623
P/O AG Maycock	P2584	P/O WRC Sugden	P2629
P/O CR Glen	P2651	P/O C Haddon-Hall	P2625
P/O RWH Carter	P2544	P/O GDH Beardon	P2650
P/O MA Sims	P2642	P/O AG McAdam	P2614
P/O J Mansel-Lewis	P2648	F/O SC Smyth	P2626

In sum, the surviving aircraft from the second delivery flight to arrive in Malta were: Hurricane I; P2544, P2614, P2623, P2629, P2651 & P2653. Blenheim IV; L9316, L9319 & L9335.

Of the above, all of the Blenheims plus Hurricanes P2544 & P2651 accompanied by P2641 (from the first ferry flight) continued on to Egypt on 24th June, to leave five Hurricanes with the Hal Far Fighter Flight. They were: P2614, P2623, P2629 and P2653 (with a new tailwheel) plus P2645 (from the first ferry flight).

A rare close-up image of a 73ª *Squadriglia* Fiat CR.42 coded '73-7', the individual aircraft number '7' (scarcely visible) being red in colour whilst the *Squadriglia* number ('73') is black. The colour scheme employed is *Verde Mimetico 3* and *Marrone Mimetico 2* mottling over a *Giallo Mimetico 3* background and *Grigio Mimetico* undersides. The full colour *Fascio Littorio* marking, which was usually applied as a transfer can be seen in detail beneath the cockpit. Italian official image

Fiat CR.42, serial number MM.5633 and coded '80' with no individual number or insignia applied as yet. This aircraft is from 80ª *Squadriglia*, 17° *Gruppo*, 1° *Stormo seen* at Trapani-Milo in Sicily during the summer of 1940 at a time when it had had to hand back its brand new Macchi MC.200 monoplane fighters due to technical problems and temporarily re-equip with biplane CR.42s. It would appear that MM.5633's colour scheme was virtually identical to that of CR.42,'73-7' seen in the preceding image. Italian official image

On the following day Burges scored another kill when he set fire to an MC.200 whose pilot bailed out into the sea, but, upon returning to Hal Far, his wingman 'Timber' Woods in Sea Gladiator N5531 crashed into a parked DH Queen Bee, (a remotely-controlled variant of the Tiger Moth used for anti-aircraft target practice). N5531 was very badly damaged and in consequence Sea Gladiators N5523 and N5529 were uncrated and erected to become the next available replacements. Although N5529 did join the Hal Far Fighter Flight during June, N5523 never saw operational service over Malta and by November 1940 it is listed as having been transferred to the Fighter Flight of 813 NAS serving aboard HMS *Eagle* in the Mediterranean.

The Hurricane's first sortie in the defence of Malta occurred on 30th June with P/O Hilton-Barber at the controls of Hurricane P2614, while the type's first kill over Malta occurred three days later. On this occasion F/O John Waters, also in P2614, attacked a 259ª *Squadriglia* SM.79 from which the entire crew of five bailed out before it crashed into Kalafrana Bay and, although rescue boats were sent to assist, none of the crew were found. Whilst landing at Hal Far following this sortie, Waters was strafed by a CR.42 *Falco* (Falcon) biplane fighter and P2614 was written-off in the resultant crash-landing from which Waters was lucky to survive relatively unscathed. Upon returning to Sicily the victorious Italian pilot, *Maggiore* Ernesto Botto, a one-legged Spanish Civil War veteran and commander of 9° *Gruppo*, claimed Water's Hurricane as a 'Spitfire' – an early instance of 'Spitfire snobbery'. This was an affliction that had already become apparent amongst many *Luftwaffe* aircrew during both the Phoney War and Battle of France and would continue throughout the forthcoming Battle of Britain and long afterwards, into the desert campaign and even over Burma against the Japanese.

During the early morning of the following day, 4th July, a force of 24 Fiat CR.42s from 9° *Gruppo* based at Comiso in Sicily, swept in low and unopposed across the Sicilian Narrows to carry out a surprise strafing attack on Hal Far airfield. Their intention was to neutralize the island's troublesome fighter force once and for all and, although they claimed to have destroyed seven fighters and one bomber, they in fact only slightly damaged two FAA Swordfish belonging to 830 NAS.

Further Hurricane victories would follow in the days to come, but not before another one was lost on 16th July during an air-to-air combat, as opposed to being strafed whilst landing. Fighter Flight veteran, F/Lt Peter Keeble took off in Hurricane P2623 in company with fellow 'original' F/Lt Burges – who was flying a Sea Gladiator, in order to intercept a force of 12 CR.42s from 23° *Gruppo* (see 'Italian Air Force Units' appendix) and during a fierce dogfight Keeble succeeded in downing one of the nimble high-performance Italian biplanes only for his own Hurricane to be attacked by two further CR.42s. Their gunfire set Keeble's aircraft on fire and his Hurricane was last seen diving vertically, in flames, before crashing into the ground near Rinella, close to where Keeble's last victim had crashed moments earlier. Peter Gardner Keeble was the first fighter pilot to lose his life defending Malta during World War Two and he was buried in Officer's Plot E, Grave 2 of the Capuccini Naval Cemetery near Kalkara. Three days after Keeble's death, George Burges became the first Malta-based pilot of the war to be decorated when he received a well deserved Distinguished Flying Cross (DFC) which was gazetted on the 19th July 1940, his citation reading: 'Although normally a flying boat pilot, and only transferred to fighter duties since the commencement of war with Italy, Flight Lieutenant Burges has shot down three enemy aircraft and so damaged three more that they probably failed to reach their base. He has shown great tenacity and determination in seeking combat, usually in the face of superior numbers.'

Not content with merely being on the defensive, the Swordfish of 830 NAS had mounted their first offensive sortie against Sicily at dusk on 30th June 1940 against the oil refinery and oil storage tanks in Augusta harbour; unfortunately their bombs proved to be mostly duds and little damage was caused. Another raid was launched at dusk on 6th July when the Swordfish struck the airfield at Catania where this time most of the bombs behaved as intended Sub-Lieutenant (Air) Jimmy Garnett delivered his bombs directly into a hangar that was packed with aircraft and which 'went up with a whoosh of flame,' just one of four hangars that were hit. As they flew over Augusta harbour on their way back to Malta the crews noticed that it was full of warships, a superb target if only they been carrying torpedoes!

By July 1940, the new all-weather airfield at Luca was available for use allowing the Sea Gladiators to commence a transfer there from Hal Far and to become fully operational at the new location by the 28th alongside the few Hurricanes which were still airworthy. As previously related, all five of Malta's first Hurricanes had originally been intended for other destinations and as a consequence the island held no spares for them and so their serviceability began to suffer as a result; in fact, by the end of the month none of the Hurricanes were serviceable at all. This meant that the biplane Sea Gladiators had to take sole responsibility for the defence of Malta once again and, on the morning of 31st July, three of them flown by Flying Officers Hartley, Woods and Taylor were scrambled to intercept a lone reconnaissance SM.79 escorted by nine biplane CR.42 fighters from 75ª *Squadriglia*, 23° *Cruppo* led by *Capitano* Antonio Chiodi. In the swirling dogfight that followed, which was surely reminiscent of those seen above the trenches in World War One, Sea Gladiator N5519, flown by Peter Hartley, was hit in the forward fuselage by a burst of fire from the twin 12.7mm guns of *Sergente* Manlio Tarantino's CR.42 that immediately set fire to the fuel tank located directly in front of his cockpit. Surrounded by a blowtorch of flame, Hartley's burning aircraft dived vertically towards the sea as he struggled to release the metal pin of the Sutton Harness (securing him to his seat) so that he could bail out. Just as it seemed that he might never remove the pin the fuel tank exploded and he was thrown out of the open cockpit, the canopy of which was usually left open, and, although terribly burned he managed to pull the ripcord and deploy his parachute. He descended into the sea from where he was rescued 45 minutes later to be taken to Imtarfa military hospital. Peter Hartley, as with most Malta-based pilots had been dressed only in shorts and a short sleeved shirt, but he survived his

Savoia Marchetti SM.79,'192-2'of 192ª *Squadriglia*, 87° *Gruppo*, 30° *Stormo* based at Sciacca in Sicily during June 1940, with the waist gunner peering from his open window. This unit flew day and night bomber operations against Malta from Sciacca and Castelvetrano in Sicily from June 1940 until late August 1941 when it returned to the mainland to convert to the Cant Z.1007*bis*. Between January and March 1941, 30° *Stormo* remained as the sole Sicilian-based Italian bomber unit to operate against Malta alongside their German allies. Italian official image

terrible injuries and after months of treatment he was returned to the UK where the more temperate climate proved better suited to his wounds. Moments after Hartley had been shot down, F/O Woods shot down his aggressor *Capitano* Antonio Chiodi, the leader of the CR.42 formation whose fighter fell into the sea off Grand Harbour; Chiodi was subsequently and posthumously awarded Italy's highest honour: the *Medaglio d' Oro*.

N5519 would in fact prove to be the only one of its type to be shot down over Malta, and although other Sea Gladiators would succumb to bombs or other forms of damage, no more would be lost in air-to-air combat.

OPERATION *HURRY*: THE FIRST CARRIER DELIVERY FLIGHT. MORE HURRICANES ARRIVE

In Britain, following the fall of France, the RAF required every available fighter pilot and aircraft that it could muster as the battle for Britain was expected to begin at any moment. Despite this, Air Commodore Maynard approached the Air Ministry in London to request that more fighters be sent to Malta as well as enough spares to keep them operational – plus additional spares to restore Malta's grounded Hurricanes to airworthiness once again. Prime Minister Churchill and his Cabinet understood that Malta's survival was critical for the reasons already discussed in Chapter 1 (qv), and so 12 more Hurricane Is were released for deployment to Malta in July 1940 despite the threat at home where modern fighters were essential to the very survival of the UK. Obviously the delivery route across France could no longer be used and so the question was raised as to what alternative method of supply existed.

In fact both the answer and a precedent already existed. In May 1940, during the Norwegian campaign, an RAF unit (46 Squadron) had successfully flown their Hurricanes from the flight deck of HMS *Glorious* in an effort to supply much needed air support to Allied ground forces in Norway. (Even more notable was the fact that the unit's ten surviving Hurricanes had landed back onboard again during their subsequent evacuation, albeit using sandbags inside the rear fuselages to weigh their tails down in lieu of arrester hooks.) Naturally, the similar use of an aircraft carrier to convey Hurricanes within flying distance of Malta would prove to be a much faster method of supply than the alternative of disassembling, crating and freighting each aircraft to its destination. Aptly, the first Hurricanes to be delivered to Malta using an aircraft carrier would be given the name Operation *Hurry*, and its purpose was to ferry the twelve Hurricane Is to the island under the auspices of 418 Flight.

The pilot of an early production Macchi MC.200 waves goodbye to his dog at Catania, Sicily, in August 1940. Although this aircraft is from 81ᵃ *Squadriglia*, 6° *Gruppo Autonomo CT*, it still came under the control of 1° *Stormo* despite its temporary independent or *CT-* ('*Caccia Terrestre'*) status. In evidence is the fully enclosed sliding canopy fitted to early MC.200s, while the aircraft's colour scheme consists of *Verde Mimetico 2* with *Bruno Mimetico* and *Giallo Mimetico 4* 'poached-egg' mottling with *Grigio Mimetico* undersides. The elaborate 1° *Stormo* insignia is that of a white-painted archer on a black background and incorporates the motto '*Incocca, tende scaglia*' ('knock, bend and shoot'). On these very early Macchis the upper wing fasces national markings were black on a white background whilst those on the undersides were white on a black background. The white cross on the tail incorporates the insignia of the House of Savoy – the Italian Royal Family – and was introduced on 12th June 1940 and applied by the unit in lieu of their original green, white and red tricolour markings. In this instance it resulted in a non standard cross with its horizontal stripe placed lower than normal. Fresh camouflage can be seen applied to the rudder to cover the previous markings. Italian official image

The pilots selected for this flight were all RAF personnel who shared one particular quality: at an earlier point in their respective careers each of them had been attached to the Fleet Air Arm and all were carrier qualified. Amongst them, the officers had served on carriers before 1937 when the RAF was still responsible, in effect, for naval aviation, while most of the sergeant pilots were pre-war RAF Volunteer Reserve (RAFVR) personnel who had been detached to the Royal Navy upon the outbreak of war due to a shortage of pilots. The Navy hoped that their time aboard ship during their carrier qualification period might persuade some of them to transfer permanently prior to joining 804 NAS in the Orkneys flying Sea Gladiators. However, following heavy RAF fighter losses over France and Dunkirk, the sergeants were glad to revert to RAF control once more and they were dispersed amongst various operational fighter squadrons until, after only a month or so, they were all reunited at RAF Uxbridge, Middlesex, preparatory to Operation *Hurry*. Despite such a brief period of service with Fighter Command, one of the NCO pilots, Sergeant Fred Robertson, had already scored two kills whilst flying Spitfires with 65 Squadron.

Although the assembled personnel were not yet up to full strength, the sergeant pilots and the sole officer to have joined them so far left Uxbridge for Hullavington where their 12 Hurricanes had been prepared. Some were painted in desert colours using an experimental colour that would later become known as Middle Stone which was applied over the Dark Green paint of the usual temperate land camouflage, whilst leaving the areas of Dark Earth in place to form a disruptive pattern with the new colour. Other Hurricanes retained the usual temperate land scheme of Dark Earth and Dark Green but irrespective of which camouflage pattern was applied to their upper surfaces, all of these Hurricanes were painted half black and half white

underneath as this was standard practice at the time for fighters serving abroad even though it had been superseded at home. Its continuing employment as a recognition feature beyond the UK was because Identification Friend or Foe (IFF) transponder equipment was, as yet, unavailable for use in other theatres, thus leaving ground observation of these highly visible colours as the only means of readily identifying friendly aircraft. Only a few of these Hurricanes had Vokes tropical filters fitted and photographs confirm that the 44 gallon long-range tanks which are usually associated with carrier deliveries of this type to Malta were not fitted on this occasion as the plan was for the carrier to sail within 200 miles of Malta before launching; a distance well within the Hurricane's normal range.

The pilots, assisted by test pilots from 10 MU at Hullavington, flew all twelve Hurricanes to RAF Abbotsinch, (today's Glasgow Airport), where 418 Flight was officially formed on 18th July 1940. Three days later the Hurricanes were taken to Greenock docks and loaded aboard HMS *Argus* or 'the Flat Iron', as this elderly carrier was fondly known throughout the fleet due to their undeniably similar outlines! At Abbotsinch, 418 Flight was finally brought up to full strength with the arrival of more officers including F/Lt DW Balden who assumed command. Some of the officers had received their posting orders at very short notice and, indicative of this, was F/Lt John Greenhalgh, who had never flown a Hurricane before and had only found out about his posting the previous day whilst stepping out of his Photo Reconnaissance (PR) Spitfire following a sortie from RAF Heston, Middlesex, with No.1 Special Duties (SD) Flight. He was simply handed a letter ordering him to report to Euston Station in London from where he was given a one-way train ticket to Glasgow and, upon arrival, was directed towards HMS *Argus*. In addition to their Hurricanes, 418 Flight was also joined by a pair of naval Skuas from RNAS Donibristle, Fife whose task would be to lead six Hurricanes apiece from *Argus*' deck once the ship had reached its predetermined flying-off position west of Malta; each Skua carrying a navigating observer in the back seat. On 23rd July 1940, *Argus* departed for the Mediterranean.

Having first called at Gibraltar to offload 23 ground crew who had also been assigned to 418 Flight, plus a consignment of Hurricane spares that were to be conveyed to Malta aboard a Sunderland flying boat and by submarine, *Argus* slipped her moorings and headed east escorted by Force H which comprised of *Ark Royal*, three battleships, two cruisers and ten destroyers; such was the importance of the mission. Considering the effort expended in prosecuting Operation *Hurry*, it might easily have ended in disaster following an absurd error made by the Royal Navy who consulted performance figures based upon their own much longer-ranged Fulmar to calculate the flying off position for the Hurricanes intended for Malta, rather than

Familiar, but important nonetheless, is this image of Sea Gladiator N5519 'R' seen at cockpit readiness plugged into a trolley accumulator starter and fitted with a three-bladed Fairey-Reed propeller, unlike the neighbouring Sea Gladiator which is fitted with a two-bladed Watts design. By this time 'R' was showing some wear and tear to its finish with chipped paint around the cockpit and patched fabric on the rudder, although the existence of black and white finished undersides can be confirmed by the white paint showing along the lower part of the rear fuselage. The rest of the airframe is finished in the standard naval S.1.E colours of Sky Grey – applied to the fuselage sides and to the underside of the upper wing: Extra Dark Sea Grey and Dark Slate Grey on its upper surfaces: with lighter, shadow-shaded, Dark Sea Grey and Light Slate Grey paint applied to the top of the lower wings. Lost on 21st July 1940, N5519 was the only Sea Gladiator to be shot down over Malta. A colour illustration appears on page 79. Frederick Galea

sticking to the agreed 200 miles! Luckily, potential disaster was averted when the experienced pilots of 418 Flight realised that the Navy had got it wrong. However, rather than accepting their word regarding the Hurricane's range, the ship's captain inexplicably insisted on breaking radio silence in order to confirm what the RAF men had already told him. Unsurprisingly, this breach of radio discipline gave their location away and brought attacks from Sardinian-based Italian aircraft. Despite the large naval escort there was also concern that the Italian Fleet would also put to sea and attempt to intercept them, so, as a consequence, the Hurricanes were immediately prepared to be flown off at the extreme range of 380 miles, leaving their pilots with no margin for error at all.

418 Flight Hurricane Is comprised:

N2484	N2673	N2715	P3730
N2622	N2700	N2716	P3731
N2672	N2701	N2717	P3733

418 Flight's 14 ferry pilots were:

F/Lt DW Balden (ex-266 Sqn) F/Lt AJ Trumble (ex-264 Sqn)
F/Lt RN Lambert F/Lt John Greenhalgh (ex-No.1 SD Flt)
F/O HFR Bradbury Sgt Frank N Robertson (ex-66 Sqn)
Sgt Eric N Kelsey (ex-611 Sqn) Sgt OR Bowerman (ex-222 Sqn)
Sgt RJ Hyde (ex-66 Sqn) Sgt Roy O'Donnell (ex-19 Sqn)
Sgt Harry W Ayre (ex-266 Sqn) Sgt James 'Jim' Pickering (ex-64 Sqn)
Sgt Dennis K Ashton (ex-32 Sqn) Sgt WJ 'Bill' Timms (ex-43 Sqn)

Above: SM.79, '58-8', from 58ª *Squadriglia*, 32° *Gruppo*, 10° *Stormo* with a white theatre band in place. This unit briefly visited Catania, Sicily, during September 1940 whilst en route from North Africa to Greece and later returned to Sicily once more to operate from Chinisea in April 1941. It continued to operate against Malta from other Sicilian bases at Boccadifalco and Palermo until 1943. Italian official image

Below left: An interior view of an SM.79. The aircraft's bomb aimer is in position nearest to the camera in the ventral gondola with the air gunner at his rear. The latter was responsible for manning the pair of 12.7mm waist guns seen in their staggered positions as well as the ventral 12.7mm gun which he is manning; the cluttered fuselage and restricted views are readily apparent. The bags attached to the guns are for collecting spent cartridge cases. Italian official image

Bottom left: An SM.79's waist gunner aiming his 12.7mm mg at an attacking British fighter over Malta. Italian official image

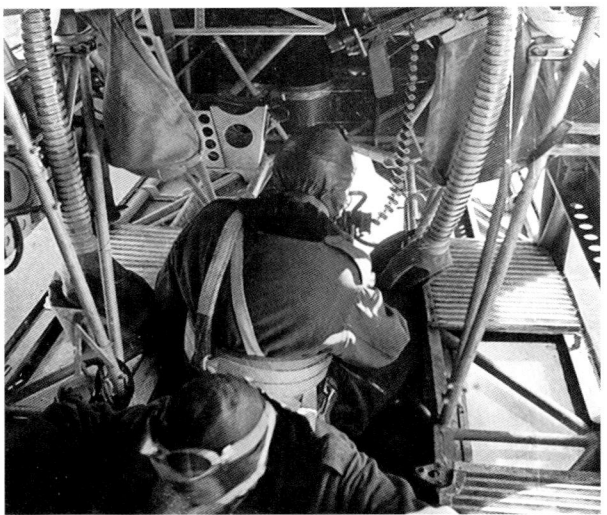

All 12 Hurricanes successfully departed *Argus* at first light on 2nd August accompanied by the two navigating Skuas which were flown by the spare Hurricane pilots together with naval observers in the rear seats. Sergeant Harry Ayre flew Skua L2911 with Captain KL Ford, RM (Royal Marines) as his observer after the young naval pilot who had originally been allocated to fly this Skua had the courage to admit that he lacked sufficient flying experience for the task. Flying Officer Bradbury flew Skua L2969 with naval pilot S/Lt WR Norwell acting as his observer.

Each Skua led its six assigned Hurricanes in loose formation during a flight which lasted approximately two hours and twenty minutes following which they all arrived safely over Malta, although two aircraft were subsequently written-off. The first was Skua L2969 which stalled upon landing at Hal Far and crashed into an air raid shelter near to the control tower, whilst the other, Hurricane N2700, flown by Sgt Fred 'Jock' Robertson, ploughed upside-down into the ground demolishing three stone walls after the engine cut due to a lack of fuel. Robertson had just completed a low-level 'beat up' of the airfield with two other Hurricanes when his engine cut out and, after he crawled out of the wreckage, he blamed a faulty fuel gauge for the resulting crash! Thankfully there were no serious injuries caused by either crash and Fred Robertson was fit to fly four days later suffering nothing more serious than

Top right: A study of SM.79, '258-6' from 258ª *Squadriglia* 109° *Gruppo*, 36° *Stormo,* based at Castelvetrano, during 1940. Featured prominently is the white theatre band which was introduced between late 1940 and early 1941, yellow engine cowlings, black spinners and the distinctive badge on the tail depicting the twin towers of Bologna dropping bombs on British paper boats! The camouflage probably consists of *Giallo Mimetico 2* upper surfaces with *Marrone Mimetico* and *Verde Mimetico 2* mottling and *Grigio Azzurro Chiaro* undersides; the codes are black and red. The Italian national insignia seen on the starboard wing incorporates the *fasces* – a bundle of rods with a protruding axe blade which was a symbol of authority in both ancient Rome and fascist Italy. Of added interest is the electrical generator mounted below the cockpit and the lowered fairings underneath the gondola for the bomb aimer's legs. Italian official image

Right: Looking significantly less ugly when viewed from this aspect, the trimotor configuration of the SM.79 is shown to advantage in this striking head-on view taken from the mid-upper gun position of the preceding aircraft whilst en route to Malta. A third SM.79 follows behind at a distance, although once they neared their target the formation would of course close up for mutual defence. Italian official image

Below: A view of SM.79 coded '253-4' of 253ª *Squadriglia,* 104° *Gruppo* which saw service over Malta as a bomber unit whilst part of 46° *Stormo* based at Pisa San Gusto on the Italian mainland. Later this unit became a menace to Malta-bound convoys when, after converting to the torpedo-bomber role, 104° *Gruppo* became an independent *Autonomo Aerosilurante* with detachments around the Mediterranean. The camouflage is a comparatively rare style which may consist of *Giallo* and *Verde Mimetico* in a wavy pattern although this particular *Squadriglia* was well known for employing a mix of different schemes. Author's collection

mild concussion. Of the remaining 11 Hurricanes, L3731 soon to be coded 'J', would prove to be one of the most successful and long-serving aircraft in Malta. This aircraft was flown against Italian and German opposition by a number of Malta's aces before leaving for North Africa in May 1941. It finally succumbed to a Vichy-French Dewoitine D.520 fighter when flying with 127 Squadron over Deir-es-Zor, Syria, in July 1941.

Most of the 23 airmen who had disembarked from *Argus* at Gibraltar also arrived in Malta during the day, along with the majority of their tools and some spares aboard two 10 Squadron RAAF Sunderlands that had followed the Hurricane and Skua formations as they flew to Malta in case any were forced to ditch. Bulkier spares, including engines and tyres, arrived a few days later aboard two large mine laying submarines, HMS *Proteus* and HMS *Pandora*. Before returning to the UK, each Sunderland made a return visit to Malta, one bringing extra stores from Gibraltar including two tons of ammunition and spares, whilst the other brought General Sir Archibald Wavell and his staff from

SM.79s from 193ª *Squadriglia*, 87° *Gruppo*, 30° *Stormo,* based at Sciacca, Sicily, during the summer of 1940 seen en route to Malta wearing a variety of colour schemes. Some bear the famous 'Electric Man' insignia emblazoned on the fuselage, that of the nearest aircraft (MM.22326 '193-6') being superimposed upon a blue disc with the motto 'Ardisco Colpisco Meninfischio' beneath. The red and black codes '193-6' are edged in white. Italian official image

This unfortunate Fiat tipped onto its nose whilst taxying at Monserrato Airport, Catania, Sicily. Other than the number '10' on the fuselage this CR.42 remains anonymous, but the image is included as it provides an excellent view of the type, especially the upper-surface camouflage pattern consisting of mottled *Verde Mimetico 3, Marrone Mimetico 2* and *Giallo Mimetico 3* with *Grigio Mimetico* undersides. Italian official image

Egypt for an inspection visit. One might wonder as to which was of more use or more welcome to Malta's garrison!

In sum, Operation *Hurry* worked so well that it would form the template for all future carrier reinforcement flights to Malta.

NUMBER 261 SQUADRON: A NEW UNIT EMERGES

Although they were expecting to return to the UK aboard the Sunderlands that had conveyed the ground crew to Malta, the newly arrived ferry pilots were surprised to find that the AOC Malta had decided to retain them instead. And so the welcome influx of 11 Hurricanes, 14 pilots and 23 ground crew from 418 Flight resulted in their amalgamation with the Hal Far Fighter Flight to become an enlarged 418 Flight on 6th August 1940. The surviving Skua, L2911, was also retained in Malta to join the lone Hudson operating in the reconnaissance role from Malta and, on 6th August 1940, Sgt Ayre and Captain Ford flew the Skua to the Sicilian ports of Catania, Augusta and Syracuse looking for a convoy which was thought to be forming. Although several merchantmen and an Italian cruiser were seen in harbour, no convoy was found.

Sufficient Hurricanes were now available to allow a dedicated night-fighting section of two to operate which was initially manned by F/O 'Eric' Taylor and P/O 'Jock' Hilton-Barber who would co-operate closely with the anti-aircraft and searchlight crews to help combat the increasingly common Italian night raids. It was this section which claimed the next Hurricane kill over Malta on the night of 13th/14th August 1940, when an SM.79 of 259ª *Squadriglia*, 109° *Gruppo*, having been illuminated by searchlights, was shot down by F/O Barber in Hurricane N2715, reputedly becoming the first successful Allied night-fighter engagement of the war to have occurred outside of Western Europe!

Hal Far's expanded 418 Flight was initially commanded by S/Ldr 'Jock' Martin who organised a three flight rota based upon the well-tried shift system that had worked so well with the Hal Far Fighter Flight since the start of hostilities over Malta, but this time allowing one flight per day to be off duty, leaving the other two flights to share the four separate watches.

Initial complement of 418 Flight, Hal Far, early August 1940

CO – Squadron Leader 'Jock' Martin*

A Flight	B Flight	C Flight
F/Lt DW Balden	F/Lt AJ Trumble	F/Lt John Greenhalgh
F/Lt George Burges*	F/Lt RN Lambert	F/O FF 'Eric' Taylor
F/O R 'Jock' Hilton-Barber*	P/O T Balmforth	P/O AG McAdam
Sgt RJ Hyde	Sgt Jim Pickering	Sgt OR Bowerman
Sgt Eric N Kelsey	Sgt Dennis K Ashton	Sgt Harry W Ayre
Sgt Roy O'Donnell	Sgt Frank N Robertson	Sgt WJ 'Bill' Timms

Plus F/O HFR Bradbury, F/O JL Waters* and F/O WJ Woods* who were held in reserve and P/O Alexander* who was soon posted.

* Original Hal Far Fighter Flight members.

Due to its increased size, officialdom soon caught up with the newly enlarged Flight which formally disbanded on 16th August 1940 and reformed the same day as 261 Squadron with the identifying codes 'XJ', although in

A poor quality but rare image which includes P3733 and an unidentified Hurricane (whose serial commences with the letter 'N') also from 418 Flight aboard *Argus* during Operation *Hurry*. The contrast in camouflage between P3733 and the unidentified Hurricane is noteworthy as the latter appears to wear a Dark Green and Dark Earth scheme with black and white undersides, yet the Vokes filter appears to be unpainted. Both aircraft have fin flashes covering the full width of the fin. The object between the cockpit and engine exhausts was one of a pair fitted to make night flying somewhat easier by protecting the pilots eyes from the direct glow and flames created by the exhausts. Author's collection via the late J Pickering

practice these codes were never applied to its aircraft and were only ever used by 13 OTU in the UK. The Squadron may have used the single code letter 'X' for a time in Malta combined with an individual aircraft letter, while the code 'FJ' was applied to the unit's P-47 Thunderbolts much later on in the war in Burma. Just as in pre-war days, it was still common practice in Malta for the AOC to appoint officers into positions of command due to their seniority rather than taking their combat experience, ability or local knowledge into account. Thereby, S/Ldr Martin was posted to AHQ Malta in Valletta while the newly arrived F/Lt DW Balden, who had gained operational fighter experience flying Spitfires with 266 Squadron in the UK, was promoted to the rank of squadron leader and became the first CO of the newly reformed unit.

Upon taking command, Balden reconfigured his squadron by adopting the same two flight system commonly employed in the UK, rather than retaining the existing three flight system employed up until this point which was better suited to the local operational conditions. Rather than selecting at least one of Malta's veteran pilots as a flight commander, whose experience and local knowledge would certainly have proved very useful, Balden chose instead to employ two newly arrived pilots based solely upon their seniority in rank. Therefore the new commander of A Flight was F/Lt Trumble, who had previously flown Boulton Paul Defiant turret fighters with 264 Squadron, while command of B Flight went to F/Lt John Greenhalgh, the former PR Spitfire pilot from No 1 SD Flight. It is worth noting that even at this relatively early stage of the war, UK-based RAF commanders were beginning to abandon (albeit unofficially) the peacetime hierarchical system of promotion through seniority. This was in order that relatively junior, yet operationally experienced aircrew might obtain positions of authority whereby the benefit of their hard-won knowledge might be shared by others with less operational experience. Such well-established hierarchies and systems are of course notoriously resistant to change and, for RAF personnel in Malta, for

the time being at least little would change in that regard; indeed, it was similar too with most overseas RAF Commands where the proportion of regular servicemen was generally much higher than in the UK, especially during the war's early years.

261 Squadron, August 1940

CO – Squadron Leader DW Balden

A Flight	B Flight
F/Lt AJ Trumble	F/Lt John Greenhalgh
F/Lt RN Lambert	F/Lt George Burges*
F/O JL Waters*	F/O HFR Bradbury
F/O FF Taylor*	F/O WJ Woods*
F/O R Hilton-Barber*	P/O AG McAdam*
Sgt Frank Robertson	P/O T Balmforth*
Sgt Eric Kelsey	Sgt RJ Hyde
Sgt Bowerman	Sgt Bill Timms
Sgt Harry Ayre	Sgt Ashton
	Sgt Jim Pickering

* = Original Hal Far Fighter Flight member

Unfortunately, the new two flight system adopted by 261 Squadron led to an overall drop in efficiency caused, presumably, by longer periods of duty spent sitting at cockpit readiness under the hot Mediterranean sun, just as Hal Far's original Fighter Flight pilots had discovered several weeks earlier! Thankfully, August proved to be a relatively quiet month and the time gained was usefully employed to

better train the fighter pilots, several of whom had little or no experience of modern monoplane fighters and whose presence in Malta, it will be recalled, was due to their having had previous carrier experience – none of it in monoplanes! Time was therefore spent learning to fight in Hurricanes and to become acquainted with their surroundings; a luxury that many of their successors would not live long enough to receive.

Towards the end of the month incursions by Italian aircraft intensified slightly and, in his first operational sortie over Malta on 20th August 1940, Sgt Fred Robertson flying Hurricane N2715, was scrambled with three others and inflicted damage upon a CR.42 from 23° *Gruppo*. Sixteen of the nimble fighters had been provided as escort to six SM.79 bombers belonging to 105° *Gruppo*, 46° *Stormo* which had flown from their base at Pisa San Guisto, on the Italian mainland, to bomb Malta's airfields. The net result

The old carrier HMS *Argus*. Known colloquially as the 'Flat Iron', particularly when viewed from above, *Argus* was responsible for conveying the first two carrier-borne deliveries of Hurricanes within ferry range of Malta under Operation's *Hurry* (2nd August 1940) and *White* (17th November 1940). Operation *Hurry* was successful and all 12 Hurricanes reached Malta, although one crashed on arrival, whereas *White* ended in disaster when eight of the dozen despatched were lost en route due to a lack of fuel. *Argus* is seen here turning into wind with a pair of Fulmars on deck waiting to take off while exercising with destroyers – possibly off the western coast of Scotland. The black paint around the stern was applied to hide stains created by the exhaust gasses which were ducted aft in lieu of vertical funnels. Author's collection

of their efforts left one Blenheim IV (in transit to Egypt) totally burnt out at Luqa, while two others were damaged but whose undamaged engines would at least prove useful later on. Two Swordfish from 830 NAS were also damaged at Hal Far, whilst the CR.42s, which were often a match for the Hurricane Is and much more manoeuvrable, claimed a Hurricane probably shot down – although none were shot down or even damaged on this occasion.

On 24th August, six 30° *Stormo* SM.79s attacked Hal Far airfield and the seaplane base at Kalafrana, escorted by seventeen 23° *Gruppo* CR.42s and were intercepted by a section of four Hurricanes led by the veteran F/Lt Burges flying N2730. Burges was able to damage three of the tri-motor bombers but was immediately assailed by fighters and *Tenente* Mario Rigatti from 75ª *Squadriglia* caused enough damage to his Hurricane for the undercarriage to collapse on landing. After attacking Burges, Rigatti was himself attacked and seriously wounded by P/O Balmforth who claimed the CR.42 as a probable, but the badly damaged biplane was able to reach Sicily and Rigatti was awarded the *Medaglia d'Oro* after recovering from his wounds. Flying Officer Taylor was able to claim a definite

A Hurricane I of 261 Squadron with a 'Z' series serial sitting at dispersal fitted with a late-type Rotol constant speed variable-pitch propeller which gave a greater climb performance and was highly prized in Malta. This Hurricane wears a Dark Earth and Dark Green camouflage scheme although the colour of the spinner – which appears to match the Dark Green areas of camouflage – is unknown. The undersides appear to be Sky Blue and are devoid of roundels. Author's collection

kill however when he downed a 75ª *Squadriglia* CR.42 flown by *Sergente* Maggiorre Bocconi who bailed out over the sea and was rescued to become a prisoner of war. On the ground the only damage inflicted by the raid was upon a single Swordfish which was slight and easily repairable.

During the last raid of the month which occurred on 29th August 1940, a sleek new shape appeared in Malta's skies when 10 Cant Z.1007*bis* trimotor bombers from 106° *Gruppo Autonomo BT*, based at Trapani in Sicily, conducted a high-level raid against Luqa airfield accompanied by 25 Fiat CR.42s from 1° *Stormo CT*. Four Hurricanes were scrambled to intercept, but they were unable to reach the altitude of the streamlined wooden Cants in time and were caught in the climb by the CR.42s, albeit without loss on either side. One bomber and a CR.42 were in fact hit by accurate anti-aircraft fire however and another bomber suffered a landing accident on return to Sicily in which the entire crew was injured in the resulting fire.

PICCHIATELLI: Ju 87s APPEAR OVER MALTA

In September 1940, the tempo of air raids against Malta increased and a succession of round-the-clock raids occurred during which, on the 4th of the month, Italian flown Ju 87B and R Stuka dive-bombers were introduced into the fray when they bombed Fort Delimara, situated opposite Kalafrana seaplane base. Known as *Picchiatelli* in Italian service, the Ju 87s were operated by 96° *Gruppo* whose component 236ª and 237ª *Squadrigli* were then based at Comiso in Sicily and on Pantelleria island respectively. They were escorted by 6° *Gruppo*'s newly returned MC.200 fighters (which had been out of action for some time having required very necessary structural repairs), plus more of the seemingly ubiquitous Fiat CR.42. On the

Cant Z.1007*bis*. This type first arrived in Sicily for operations against Malta during August 1940 with 106° *Gruppo*, 47° *Stormo*, and was based at Trapani-Milo and Chinisia, although the one seen here was in fact photographed on the island of Rhodes, the image being included as it serves as an excellent example of its type. For the sake of completeness this Z.1007*bis* belonged to 204ª *Squadriglia*, 41° *Gruppo* which was only briefly equipped with the type in the Aegean, yet it wears the stylised 'M' tail insignia of long-term user 95° *Gruppo*, indicating that there was every likelihood of it having been received from the latter unit, neither of which operated their Z.1007s against Malta. It still employs the initial underwing insignia with a black centre and white detail too. The Cant Z.1007's first raid against Malta was against Luqa airfield on 29th August 1940 and, as a medium bomber (constructed mostly of wood), it could carry a larger bomb load than either the contemporary SM.79 or Fiat BR.20. Italian official image

following day, six more *Picchiatelli* returned in the afternoon to bomb shipping in Grand Harbour, and according to one British Army officer who witnessed the attack some of them still retained their previous owner's black *Balkenkreuz* markings beneath their wings. Protecting the Ju 87s on this occasion was a large escort of CR.42s against which the four intercepting Hurricanes of 261 Squadron's A Flight, led by F/Lt Greenhalgh, became embroiled in a twisting dogfight over Grand Harbour. New Zealander, Sgt RJ Hyde, managed to shoot down a pair of CR.42s while Greenhalgh and Hilton-Barber were credited with one each; one of which was seen to fall into the sea five miles off Grand Harbour. However the fourth Hurricane, N2717 flown by Sgt Ayre, was attacked by up to 17 CR.42s and he was forced to make an emergency landing at Luqa after his engine blew up during a steep evasive dive in which oil was spewed across the windscreen, (probably caused by the DH variable-pitch propeller being over revved while at the wrong pitch setting, something easily accomplished during the stress of

A close-up of a Ju 87R-2 Stuka, or *Picchiatelli* (dive-bomber) to the Italians, which can be identified as a 97° *Gruppo BaT* aircraft by the somewhat indistinct bomb-carrying 'diving duck' insignia on its wheel spat; the white flecks representing loose feathers. In November 1940 this unit assumed the Malta commitment from 96° Gruppo's shorter-ranged Ju 87Bs and was usually escorted by CR.42s from 23° *Gruppo* until, in December, it returned to Italy for operations over Greece. Italian official image

combat.) The *Times of Malta* reported that there were 'thousands of eyewitnesses who were thrilled to the core' by the dogfights which they described as 'some of the most thrilling air battles of the war over Malta, so far.'

Grand Harbour and Valletta were targeted at midday on 7th September 1940 in a raid carried out by 10 SM.79s from 36° *Stormo* and escorted by 17 Fiat CR.42s, while in opposition, 261 Squadron was able to scramble a relatively large force of three Hurricanes and three Sea Gladiators. In the ensuing combat, British fighters shot one SM.79 into the sea (from where the surviving crew members were rescued), but this did not prevent some of the remaining bombers from getting through to the Naval Dockyard where they caused superficial damage to shore installations, sank the naval tug *Hellespont* and wounded five civilians. Two of the CR.42s from 23° *Gruppo* claimed to have shot down a pair of Hurricanes during this raid and indeed two Hurricanes were hit, but they suffered only slight damage and were soon repaired. The next air raid was conducted by seven SM.79s from 34° *Stormo* on 14th September, with both Valletta and Kalafrana seaplane base – which was also the island's principal aircraft and engine repair facility, being targeted. Unfortunately, Malta's fighters failed to make contact with the Italians who dropped their bombs and departed unscathed.

Italy's Ju 87s returned to Malta again on 15th September, although this time they switched their attention to Malta's airfields. On this day 12 Ju 87B and Rs, almost the entire strength of 96° *Gruppo*'s two constituent *Squadrigli*, were accompanied by a single Savoia Marchetti SM.86W, an ungainly Italian-built dive-bomber with two inline engines.

This sole SM.86W prototype was attached to 236ª *Squadriglia* for trials and was flown by the company test pilot Elio Scarpini, while the fighter escort for the 13 dive-bombers consisted of 18 CR.42s from 23° *Gruppo* and six MC.200s from 1° *Stormo*. Although 261 Squadron intercepted this raid there were no aerial losses on either side. On the ground it was a different matter however as Hal Far airfield was hit by approximately 60 bombs which damaged the guard room, motor transport (MT) garage and ration store, yet surprisingly the only casualties were two wounded Maltese servicemen.

Whilst in the process of shaking Italian fighters off of his tail during this raid, Sgt Bill Timms' Hurricane suffered a catastrophic engine failure which broke a conrod that penetrated the crankshaft of his Merlin. This, the second such failure in a fortnight, is said to have been caused by overboosting the engine while the De Havilland propeller was still in fine pitch; akin to driving a motorcar at maximum revs in first gear! Despite the very real risk of undershooting the runway and ending up in one of Malta's many stone-walled fields (making any crash-landing in Malta a highly dangerous if not lethal affair), Timms was just able to squeeze enough power from the crippled Merlin to allow his fighter to reach Luqa and land safely.

De Havilland's two-position variable-pitch propeller required the pilot to manually select either fine or coarse pitch (there being nothing in between) which needed to be changed at different power settings – loosely akin to driving a car fitted with a manual two-gear gearbox – which was often impossible during the stress of battle. Much preferred by fighter pilots was the Rotol (a contraction of *Ro*lls and Bris*tol*) constant speed propeller unit that automatically changed propeller pitch settings, thus relieving the pilot of that necessity and allowing him to better concentrate on flying his aircraft. Rotol's constant speed propellers were fitted with wooden Jablo covered blades with a refined hub that included a third intermediate pitch setting which helped to increase the rate of climb; however, as desirable as such improvements were the Rotol units were in short supply and, ultimately, only a mere handful of Malta's Hurricane Is received them at this time. It was imperative that Rotol's propeller be retrofitted to as many aircraft as possible and some arrived in kit form courtesy of the submarine 'Magic Carpet Service', or by flying boat but, as stated, there were simply not enough to go around. Ever resourceful, S/Ldr Louks addressed the matter and applied himself to the problem whereby, as a temporary and (very) unofficial measure, he managed to improve the climb performance of the DH propellers by altering the pitch of their metal blades, albeit at the expense of an increased take-off run. This was a most agreeable swap insofar as the fighter pilots were concerned for whom the mantra 'height is might' was just as valid then as it is today.

A further dive-bombing raid was launched on 17th September by the *Picchiatelli* of 96° *Gruppo*, although this time the 12 aircraft from its two *Squadriglia* attacked Luqa airfield and were escorted by 21 CR.42s from 23° *Gruppo* and six MC.200s from 6° *Gruppo*. In response, 261 Squadron scrambled three or four Hurricanes but they were unable to prevent extensive damage from being inflicted upon Luqa airfield which included the destruction of a visiting Wellington Ic and Sgt Timms' engineless Hurricane, the latter being under repair inside a hangar which received a direct hit. Two of Luqa's ground crew: Corporal Joe Davis and Aircraftman 1st Class Tom McCann, were each awarded a British Empire Medal following this raid in reward for entering the burning Wellington to retrieve four Vickers machine guns and six pans of ammunition. Meanwhile, in the skies above, intercepting Hurricanes caught up with the Italians and *Tenente* Malvezzi, who was flying one of the Ju 87s, described being attacked by eight Hurricanes and five Gladiators, having presumably mistaken some of the Italian biplane fighters for British aircraft. *Tenente* Brezzi, also flying a Ju 87, reported that he strafed a twin-engined aircraft on the ground – which could have been the visiting Wellington, and he also claimed to have shot down a Gladiator, although CR.42s were the only biplanes airborne at that time! Brezzi's Ju 87 was in turn attacked by a pair of Hurricanes which killed his gunner and badly damaged his aircraft which received eleven bullet holes courtesy of F/O Hilton-Barber in Hurricane N2484, despite which Brezzi successfully returned to Sicily. Hilton-Barber also attacked another Ju 87, flown by *Sergente* Maggiorre Catani, but this one ditched in the sea eight miles off Filfla island from where the wounded pilot was rescued by an RAF launch from Kalafrana, while his dead gunner was later buried at St Andrews Military Cemetery. A further kill was claimed by F/O 'Timber' Woods who opened fire on a 70ª *Squadriglia*, Fiat CR.42 which inexplicably performed a loop directly in front of him and then dived to the ground in flames, its pilot, *Sottotenente* Franco Cavalli managed to bail out and was captured by Maltese civilians. Following this mauling the *Picchiatelli* of 96° *Gruppo* made one more (ineffectual) foray over Malta prior to departing for Italy to participate in operations against Greece.

ITALIAN RAIDS CONTINUE: RECONNAISSANCE RECEIVES A BOOST

Further Italian incursions into Maltese airspace continued through the remainder of September 1940, including a fighter sweep by seven CR.42s on 18th September, which was intercepted by three Hurricanes and a pair of Sea Gladiators during which P/O Balmforth in Hurricane N2715 claimed one of the Fiat biplanes shot down. In the process Balmforth was attacked from the rear and a single bullet entered his cockpit and continued forward to smash through the instrument panel and into the coolant header tank behind the engine, causing the boiling hot contents to spray over him resulting in painful burns to both hands as they gripped the controls. As previously mentioned, given the hot Mediterranean weather, several of Malta's pilots flew wearing only short sleeve shirts and shorts offering no protection from the terrible burns that pilots could expect to receive from scalding liquids or a burning cockpit. Only much later in the war would a one-piece flying overall be introduced which was cool enough for pilots serving in hot climates to wear, and even then it was not classed as fire resistant.

On 25th September, three Hurricanes and two Sea Gladiators were scrambled to intercept six MC.200s from 79ª *Squadriglia* which were carrying out an armed-reconnaissance over Malta, one of which was lost to the guns of F/O Eric Taylor's Hurricane and which crashed near to St Thomas Bay, severely injuring the Italian pilot who later died. During the same action another MC.200, flown by the formation leader *Capitano* Giacomelli, was claimed as a probable by Sgt Fred Robertson in Hurricane N2484, but it in fact managed to limp back to Sicily with a large section of its right wing missing. Unfortunately, Sgt Jim Pickering in the third Hurricane (P3731) drew no success on this occasion.

It is worth reiterating at this point that despite the lessons learnt during the fighting in France and during the Battle of Britain regarding the *Luftwaffe*'s and *Regia Aeronautica*'s proven tactic of operating fighters *in pairs*, Fighter Command had yet to pass this knowledge on to the RAF on Malta and other overseas commands. Therefore, British fighters were still employing the outmoded, restrictive and inherently dangerous 'Vic', a close V formation of three aircraft in which the two wingmen were constantly looking inwards towards their leader in order to maintain station and avoid collision, rather than looking outwards for the enemy!

September 1940 brought significant changes to Malta's reconnaissance potential despite a disastrous start on the 1st of the month when F/O Davies and his crew, in Hudson N7324, were attacked in error by a naval Fulmar from 806 NAS embarked upon the carrier HMS *Illustrious* which had only recently arrived in the Mediterranean. The attack on the Hudson left two of its crew seriously wounded and with the aircraft itself so badly damaged that Davies had no option but to head for the nearest landfall – in Vichy-French Tunisia, where he carried out a successful crash-landing at El Aouina airfield and where all four men were interned. The pilot of the offending Fulmar was 43 year old Lieutenant Commander Robin Kilroy, who was not a trained fighter pilot but an ex-Swordfish pilot who was just 'keeping his hand in and simply helping out' whilst aboard *Illustrious* during his passage to Egypt prior to commencing a new posting! Amazingly, he continued to carry out his attack despite the fact that Malta's pair of Skuas were flying alongside the Hudson as fighter cover and that both the Skua leader and the Hudson had confirmed their friendly status by firing off the correct colours of the day, not to mention each aircraft's national markings which were clearly visible!

The Hudson's loss left only the pair of Skuas with which to conduct aerial reconnaissance from Malta, however, reinforcements were en route in the form of a detachment of Martin Maryland Is sent from 22 Squadron based at North Coates, Lincolnshire. Equipped with Bristol Beauforts, this unit had raised a new C Flight equipped with Marylands which was intended to be deployed to Malta as 431 (General Reconnaissance) Flight. The first of these American-built aircraft arrived in Malta on 6th September 1940, their serials being AR705, AR707 and AR712 which, with the two Skuas, formed the initial equipment of 431(GR) Flight under the leadership of Australian F/Lt 'Titch' Whiteley. A fourth Maryland, AR713, would follow soon afterwards. AR713 was externally distinguishable from the first trio by virtue of the bulbous, drag-inducing Avro Anson-type mid-upper gun turret with which it had been equipped that sat much higher than those fitted to the others and made AR713 slightly slower as a result. Additionally a pair of Blenheim IVs had also arrived in Malta en route to Egypt from the UK but, due to the high workload placed upon 431 (GR) Flight and the limited number of Marylands then available, both Blenheims were 'hijacked' by the Flight. One of the aircrew who arrived with the Marylands was the acclaimed Adrian 'Warby' Warburton who had been posted to the Flight as a supernumerary pilot and navigator. However, following an outbreak of 'Malta Dog' – a particularly debilitating form of dysentery commonly caught by newcomers to Malta at this time, Warburton was pressed into service as a pilot despite the fact that he had never flown the Maryland before. At first he had problems mastering the type which was especially demanding during take-off and landing due to the amount of torque produced by its powerful engines which, on one occasion, caused him to ground loop when landing and wipe AR712's undercarriage off. Even with his extrovert personality and outlandish methods, Warburton would go on to become the most famous reconnaissance pilot in the RAF and, despite countless close calls while flying from Malta, he would later die flying a USAAF Lockheed F-5 Lightning (the PR variant of the P-38 fighter) over Bavaria on 12th April 1944 where his remains were eventually located in 2002.

Making the most of any intelligence obtained by the reconnaissance aircraft, the Swordfish of 830 NAS were also busy searching for Italian convoys themselves with single aircraft covering designated patches of sea, whilst the rest of the squadron remained at Hal Far ready to take off at a moments notice. Sadly, most were to no avail

Blenheim IV N3589 landed by accident on the Italian-held island of Pantelleria on 11th September 1940 during its ferry flight from Gibraltar to the Middle East via Malta. Axis radio operators frequently tried to mislead unwary Allied aircrew into landing on this small island which could easily be mistaken for Malta and the Overseas Air Delivery Unit (OADU) aircrew flying this ex-40 Squadron Blenheim were deceived. The image below shows N3589 after it was repainted in Italian markings following its unwitting arrival at Pantelleria. The bombproof hangar beyond has been built into the hillside. Italian official image

despite frequently flying to within 20 miles of the Sicilian coastline. Land-based targets in Sicily were also attacked with Augusta harbour continuing to be a popular target as this was one of the main assembly ports for Italian convoys sailing to North Africa. At least one Swordfish was lost in the darkness whilst skimming over the water in Augusta harbour to deliver a torpedo attack having struck the water because of the ineffective altimeters fitted to these early-production Swordfish; although on occasion the wheels hitting the water could provide an impromptu indicator that they were as low as they could possible be and that it was time to gain a little height…quickly! A further Swordfish role was to conduct air-sea-rescue searches and it was during one such search in September 1940 that an unusual combat occurred when pilot, Petty Officer Charles Wines and his two crewmembers, telegraphist air-gunner (TAG) Leading Airman Pickles, and observer Lieutenant Brookes Walford, happened across an Italian Cant Z.501 single-engined, parasol-winged, flying boat. Wines dived into attack with his solitary forward-firing .303 in mg mounted in World War One fashion directly in front of the pilot, while Pickles swung his .303 Vickers K mg around and joined in as they passed over the Italian aircraft. Circling, both aircraft fired away at each other until the Cant made a break for Sicily and the Swordfish returned to Hal Far with only ten minutes worth of petrol in its tank, neither aircraft appearing any the worse for their tussle.

NEW ARRIVALS: SUNDERLANDS, WELLINGTONS AND CLANDESTINE FRENCHMEN

October 1940 started peacefully enough until the Italians returned on the 4th with nine MC.200s from 6° *Gruppo CT* carrying out another armed reconnaissance sortie. During a perfect interception, the principal camera aircraft, serialled MM4585 and flown by *Tenente* Mario Nosaoni, was shot down by Sgt Reg Hyde in Hurricane N2715, who saw the Italian dive into the sea off Ghan Tuffieha, while Sgt Fred 'Jock' Robertson in Hurricane P2653 managed to damage one of the others. Following this reconnaissance flight, five SM.79s from 36° *Stormo* based at Castelvetrano, Sicily, conducted a night raid against Kalafrana seaplane base, but, with the aid of searchlights, F/O Taylor was able to shoot a 257[a] *Squadriglia* aircraft down in flames. Additionally, he damaged another SM.79 so badly that it barely managed to return to Comiso where it landed with three wounded crewmembers on board. A further SM.79 was shot down on 16th October by F/Lt Waters in Hurricane P2645, although this proved to be the last aerial engagement for several days until, on 27th October, six Hurricanes and two Sea Gladiators scrambled to intercept nine MC.200s from 6° *Gruppo* led by their CO *Maggiore* Mezzetti In the combat which followed the Italians claimed to have shot down two Hurricanes whilst the British claimed a pair of Macchis damaged, whereas in fact one of the Italian pilots was forced to bail out from his badly damaged aircraft over Sicily, while no British fighters were lost at all.

There were no further actions over Malta for the remainder of October although the month did bring forth a number of reinforcements and additions to the island. Amongst these were Sunderland Is from 228 Squadron which had been based at Alexandria since Italy entered the war and had always been regular visitors to Kalafrana. Despite operating overseas their major servicing continued to be undertaken in the UK at far-distant Pembroke Dock in Wales, so it was decided to transfer this operation much nearer to Kalafrana, a move which was completed during October. Although the Squadron's main *operating* base would continue to be Alexandria, despite its poorer facilities, this new arrangement ensured that a steady stream of Sunderlands would need to call into Malta and therefore be on hand if needed.

Another aircraft 'adopted' by 228 Squadron was an ex-Vichy French Latécoère 298B floatplane whose crew had defected to Malta and who, since their arrival, had been dutifully employed taking agents to North Africa, as well as dropping leaflets. They were joined on 15th October by an ex-Vichy Loire 130 flying boat numbered '73' from the French battleship *Richelieu* flown by *Deuxiéme-Maître* Georges Blaize who had diverted to Malta during a ferry flight from Bizerte to Dakar in French West Africa, (modern Senegal). Also, as recorded earlier, 830 NAS were the recipients of ex-No.3 AACU Swordfish during this month following the disbandment of the latter unit, thus allowing its RAF personnel to transfer to 431 (GR) Flight to help fly and maintain the Marylands. Later the Flight would also include Georges Blaize and his crew.

Importantly, October also saw the arrival of a dozen Wellington Ic bombers which began to arrive at Luqa on temporary detachment from the Bomber Command stations of Marham and Mildenhall located in East Anglia. Officialdom ultimately caught up with this detachment on 9th November 1940 when it became known as the Malta Wellington Flight (MWF), although it was soon to become a squadron in its own right. Its arrival was to prove a tremendous fillip to the night offensive, although, as no ground crew had arrived it meant yet more work for Malta's hard-pressed ground staff.

From the commencement of hostilities on June 10th, until mid-October 1940, Malta's fighter force had recorded 72 daylight interceptions plus two by night, resulting in claims for nine SM.79s, seven CR.42s, four MC.200s and two Ju 87s destroyed; others were claimed as probably destroyed or damaged. Of course the quantities claimed are best viewed as a guide because the actual Italian losses were in fact lower and over claiming was the norm for all sides; a genuine consequence of 'the fog of war.' Against this the island lost two Hurricanes and one Sea Gladiator in aerial combat: two other Hurricanes were destroyed on the ground, as was a Swordfish, two Blenheims, a Wellington and a Maryland. Additionally, one further Swordfish and Hudson N7324 had also been lost in the air.

NOVEMBER 1940

November 1940 started badly. On the very first day of the month a Wellington from the Bomber Command detachment (the as yet to be named MWF) failed to return from a night raid over Sicily, leading to the despatch of two 228 Squadron Sunderlands to look for survivors during which both aircraft were attacked. One of these, N9020, flown by S/Ldr Menzies, was shot down in the Sicilian narrows by MC.200s from 88ª *Squadriglia*, 6° *Gruppo* with no survivors, while Sunderland L5806 'Q', flown by F/Lt Ware, was attacked and badly damaged by two more 6° *Gruppo* MC.200s and a sole CR.42 whilst flying 32 miles off the Maltese coastline; fortunately L5806 managed to reach Kalafrana although two of its crew were wounded.

On the following day a 431 (GR) Flight Maryland, flown by P/O 'Warby' Warburton, was almost lost during a seven hour reconnaissance flight to Taranto when it was intercepted by three CR.42s. Warburton was hit in the chest by a bullet that had entered through the aircraft's nose, the force of which rendered him unconscious and caused him to slump over the controls putting the aircraft into a dive. Thankfully the Maryland was equipped with an additional set of controls in the nose compartment for precisely this kind of emergency, allowing navigator Sgt Frank Bastard to retrieve the extra control column from its stowed position, correctly assemble it, then pull out of the dive and level off. Meanwhile, in the cockpit, Warburton had regained consciousness to find that his instrument panel had been destroyed by the round which had hit him, however, it had also absorbed most of the bullet's force in the process leaving him with only a superficial wound. Warburton was able to resume control and fly back to Luqa where Frank Bastard was immediately awarded a well deserved DFM for his immensely cool actions.

Due to the increased number of twin-engined aircraft at Luqa, ground staff were despatched from there during October to prepare the old civilian airport at Takali for fighters and by November 261 Squadron was ready to move across with its mixed force of Sea Gladiators and Hurricanes. The unit was soon in action and on the same day that Warburton was wounded, two Sea Gladiators were sent aloft alongside six Hurricanes from B Flight to intercept a raid on Valletta and Takali by 20 SM.79s from 34° *Stormo*. The bombers were escorted by five CR.42s and 11 MC.200s from 71ª and 72ª *Squadrigli* of 17° *Gruppo*, 1° *Stormo CT* which were still operating a mixed

Bereft of bombs, a 'diving duck' Ju 87R *Picchiatelli* of 97° *Gruppo BaT* crosses the Italian coastline during November 1940, possibly en route to Comiso, Sicily, after having left its previous base at Lecce on the Italian mainland. A narrow white theatre band has been applied over the standard German camouflage colour scheme consisting of RLM 70 *Schwarzgrun*, 71 *Dunkelgrun* and 65 *Hellblau* while its four-figure serial number appears on the top of the fin although *Squadriglia* codes have yet to be applied. The gunner/radio operator is facing forward, presumably attending to his radio with his sliding hood partially open. It was rare for Italian Ju 87s to wear national insignia on their upper wings and all retained German camouflage colours although Italian paint was used to obscure German national markings, despite which their form can still be identified. Italian official image

complement of aircraft due to structural weakness problems that had earlier beset their monoplane fighters. During the ensuing dogfight which occurred above the eastern corner of the island, F/Lt Burges in Sea Gladiator N5520, bearing the code 'S', claimed one Fiat as probably destroyed and another as damaged, whilst P/O Allan McAdam in a Hurricane accounted for a 72ª *Squadriglia* Macchi flown by *Sergente* Lanzarini and sent it down in flames to crash near to Zeitun (modern Zejtun). Although there were no British losses on this occasion the Italians, upon returning to Sicily, claimed to have shot down five Hurricanes although they did leave in their wake a demolished hangar at Luqa as well as four civilian houses in Zabbar which had all been destroyed by bombing.

November's run of poor luck continued into the third night when tragedy struck the Wellington force once more. On this occasion two Wellingtons crashed while taking off from Luqa to raid Naples and, on striking the ground, both burst into flames with full fuel and bomb loads on board. Amazingly, all but one of the crewmen in one of the Wellingtons survived when its pilot, Sgt Raymond Lewin, carried out a near-miraculous crash-landing in the dark; then, with his surviving crew clear of the burning wreck, he re-entered the aircraft to retrieve the body of his dead co-pilot P/O David Allen. Lewin later received the George

Cross for his actions. Conversely, all bar one crewman was killed after the second bomber, R1094, crashed on top of a house in Dun Mario Street, Qormi with the forward section breaking away and coming to rest in a nearby quarry. Maltese police constable Carmel Camilleri was lowered into the quarry to enter the Wellington's forward fuselage amid fire, exploding bombs and ammunition to rescue the badly injured wireless operator Sgt Arthur Smith, although, sadly, despite the constable's heroic efforts, Smith died of his wounds. Of the Maltese family living in the house, Alfred and Delores Agius died in the inferno but their children were rescued by three officers from the Queens Own Royal West Kent Regiment: 2nd Lt Lavington, Lt Flint and Lt Buckle who were assisted by Royal Engineer Joseph Zammit. Amazingly, air gunner Sergeant D Palmer survived the crash. For his bravery in entering the bomber to rescue Sgt Smith, Carmel Camilleri earned a well deserved George Medal.

A particularly audacious sneak attack was conducted by a lone CR.42 on 6th November which inflicted damage upon a Sunderland of 228 Squadron which was strafed at its mooring in Marsaxlokk Bay, while on the following day, P/O Warburton was flying a Maryland over Taranto when he was intercepted by seven MC.200s which, by fully utilising the Maryland's startling turn of speed, he was eventually able to outrun. The Malta Wellington Force (as it became on this day) was temporarily reinforced on the night of the 9th November when seven Mk.Ics from 37 Squadron arrived from Feltwell, Norfolk, four of which then bombed Taranto harbour during the following night. However, as implied, their stay at Malta was brief and, having completed a few further raids, these Wellingtons continued on to Fayid in Egypt on 21st November.

On November 10th, Fiat CR.42s carried out an early morning strike against Hal Far, sweeping in at low level at 06:00hrs to strafe the airfield, although the only damage incurred was to a Swordfish which was easily repairable. Interestingly the Italians had taken advantage of Wellingtons returning home from their night raids to approach Malta without being identified by radar, as individual transponders which distinguished a friendly from a hostile plot were not as yet available for Malta's aircraft.

The reason for 431 (GR) Flight's ongoing interest in Taranto became apparent on the night of 11th November when Swordfish from HMS *Illustrious* launched their famous attack upon Mussolini's battlefleet which was moored there. The 21 Swordfish from 815, 819 and 824 Squadrons, each fitted with overload fuel tanks and variously carrying torpedoes or bombs and flares, left three of Italy's six battleships crippled, a heavy cruiser and several destroyers damaged with yet further damage inflicted upon a nearby seaplane base and oil storage tanks. All for the loss of two aircraft and one two-man crew who were never found; the other crew became POWs. As a result of this raid the remaining Italian capital ships were ordered north to Naples, restoring to Britain, literally overnight, the balance of naval power in the Mediterranean and further undermining the confidence of Mussolini's admirals. Photographs revealing the results of the raid were obtained on the following morning by 431(GR) Flight's CO, F/Lt 'Tich' Whiteley while making his eighth sortie over Taranto.

Hurricanes of 261 Squadron seen at Luqa during November 1940, prior to moving to Takali but then back to Hal Far. They are fitted with a mixture of both De Havilland and Rotol propellers. Closest is Hurricane I, V7474, coded 'A' which appears to be wearing a Dark Earth and Dark Green colour scheme with black-and-white halved undersides with smaller than normal roundels near the wingtips and either a black or red spinner. This aircraft arrived in Malta on 17th November 1940 via HMS *Argus* when it was flown by F/Lt 'Mac' McLachlan who went on to score eight kills over Malta before losing his arm in combat during February 1941. As 'One Armed Mac' he resumed flying after treatment in the UK but was later killed on operations flying a Mustang I. A number of other Malta aces also flew this Hurricane including Fred Robertson who damaged a CR.42 and shot down a Stuka while at its controls, but V7474 was shot down by a Bf 109E on 26th February 1941 and its veteran pilot P/O Langdon was killed. RH Barber via Frederick Galea

On the 12th, six MC.200s from 6° *Gruppo* CT flew an armed-reconnaissance over Malta but their formation was broken up by accurate anti-aircraft fire. Pilot Officer Balmforth, flying a Hurricane, took full advantage of this by shooting one of them down and killing *Tenente Giueseppe* Volpe who crashed into the sea in flames near to St Thomas Bay, the Italian's body being duly recovered from the sea and buried in Malta. Two days later, five Hurricanes managed to become airborne in time to intercept two SM.79s, escorted by eight CR.42s, before they reached Gozo, whereupon F/O Hilton-Barber in Hurricane N2622, who had become separated from the others due to an overheating engine, made several lone diving attacks on a number of CR.42s, one of which he claimed as probably destroyed.

DISASTER AT SEA: OPERATION *WHITE*

Despite their successes a steady attrition of Malta's Hurricanes was inevitable and so, in mid-November 1940, the decision was taken to reinforce the islands fighter force with a further 12 Hurricane Is. Virtually the same procedures that had been used so successfully in August 1940, (Operation *Hurry*) utilising a Skua navigational aircraft to lead a group of six fighters from the deck of HMS *Argus* would again be employed, this time under the codename Operation *White*. Changes were made of course one of which was perhaps something of a concession by the Air Ministry whereby all twelve Hurricane pilots were to be experienced Battle of Britain veterans. A further change was that the Hurricanes involved in Operation *White* were to take-off from a point further west than those in *Hurry*, leaving them with a distance of over 400 miles to cover. For this, each Hurricane would be fitted with two, wing-mounted, 44 gallon auxiliary fuel tanks in order to provide the necessary additional range needed to reach Malta. Unfortunately, the operation would prove to be an unmitigated disaster!

As with Operation *Hurry*, the aircraft involved in Operation *White* were again ordered to take off prematurely, at extreme range, by Admiral Somerville, due to concerns that Italy's surviving battleships were at sea, and, although *Argus* enjoyed the protection of Force H, the latter only comprised the battlecruiser *Renown*, carrier *Ark Royal*, three cruisers, and seven destroyers. Despite their being ordered off earlier than intended, and although the distance to Malta was now at the very limits of the fuel carried, it was still just feasible for the aircraft to reach Malta, if flown using the correct engine and propeller settings at the optimum speed and altitude. For the Hurricane I, the optimum was approximately 120mph at 10,000 feet, leaving them with a possible 45 minutes worth of spare fuel. Unfortunately such statistics only applied where navigation proved to be faultless and if the weather behaved impeccably!

1st Formation: Operation *White*
S/Lt WR Norwell (pilot)* / S/Lt Smith (observer) Skua L2882
F/Lt JAF MacLachlan   Hurricane V7474
P/O CE Hamilton   Hurricane V7370
P/O HW Eliot   Hurricane V7548
Sgt JK Norwell   Hurricane V7346
Sgt RA Spyer   Hurricane V7413
Sgt WG Cunnington   Hurricane V7374

2nd Formation: Operation *White*
Petty Officer WEJ Stockwell (pilot) / S/Lt RC Neil (observer) Skua L2987
F/O EG Bidgood   Hurricane (Serial unknown)
F/O PW Horton   Hurricane (Serial unknown)
F/O JR Walker   Hurricane (Serial unknown)
F/O RW Clarke   Hurricane (Serial unknown)
P/O FJ Boret   Hurricane (Serial unknown)
P/O JM Horrox   Hurricane (Serial unknown)

* Sub-Lieutenant Norwell had navigated a Skua used in the first flight and had been sent to Gibraltar especially to fly this second sortie.

The first flight of six Hurricanes, led by F/Lt James Archibald Findlay MacLachlan, DFC, accompanied by the flight's navigational Skua, departed *Argus* at 06:15 on 17th November 1940. However, digressing momentarily, it is worth noting that the 21-year old MacLachlan had previously earned his DFC while flying Fairey Battle light bombers in France and had later converted to fighters in time to participate in the Battle of Britain, following which, he volunteered for overseas duty and later went on to make a name for himself over Malta where he shot down eight Italian and German aircraft. Unfortunately he fell prey to the *Luftwaffe* ace *Oberleutnant* Joachim Muncheberg and, although he escaped from his doomed Hurricane by parachute, he had received a cannon shell through his left arm which was consequently amputated. Just 16 days after the operation he was airborne from Takali in a Miles Magister, but was subsequently returned to the UK where he received an artificial limb and the nickname 'One Armed Mac'. He eventually became CO of 1 Squadron flying Hurricane IIcs in the night-intruder role and, by the end of 1942, had shot down five more German aircraft (all night bombers), receiving the Distinguished Service Order plus a Bar to his DFC as well as the Czech Military Cross. Following a six-month tour of the USA he joined the Air Fighting Development Unit and began flying long-range daylight intruder missions in North American Mustang Is with which he shot down six German training aircraft in one day. Sadly, with his score now standing at 19 kills, he was shot down by flak whilst crossing the French coast and died of his injuries on 31st July 1943.

Returning to Operation *White*: Having taken-off, MacLachlan's flight then spent 15 minutes forming up correctly and thus burnt into their precious fuel reserves. When they set course for Malta they did so at 2,000 feet and approximately 150mph, which, as explained earlier, was

Skua L2987 led the second flight of six Hurricanes from HMS *Argus* during the ill-fated Operation *White*. It is seen here after it had crash-landed on a beach near Syracuse, Sicily and shed its entire engine; a common occurrence with Skuas. Flown by Petty Officer Stockwell and his observer Sub Lieutenant Neil, their bad luck began when the Sunderland flying boat which was supposed to lead them to Malta was late leaving Gibraltar. Unable to wait, the formation pressed on alone but, as the weather grew worse, they became lost and as the radio receiver proved to be faulty they were unable to hear the replies to their requests for a 'fix'. One by one the Hurricanes dropped out of formation due to fuel starvation, leaving the Skua, which had a greater endurance, to carry on alone in driving rain to reach the Sicilian coastline just as its engine too spluttered to a halt. Despite Italian AA fire, Stockwell conducted a successful forced-landing on the beach and the two crewmen were taken prisoner; none of the six missing Hurricane pilots from the second flight were ever seen again, despite an extensive search of the entire area by a Malta-based Maryland. A colour illustration of this aircraft appears on page 83. Ian Gazeley

The second carrier-born delivery of Hurricanes to Malta was the ill-fated Operation *White* that consisted of 12 Hurricane Is led by two Blackburn Skua navigational aircraft – each Skua leading a flight of six Hurricanes – of which just one Skua and four Hurricanes survived to reach Malta. An early delivery of Hurricanes can be seen here ranged upon deck, all of which are fitted with DH two-speed propellers, though none appear to have Vokes tropical filters fitted. In contrast to the black-and-white halved undersides witnessed in other Hurricane images, the lead Hurricane here displays a non-standard demarcation line on its nose where the underside colour, most likely Sky Blue, extends upwards onto the side of the engine cowling, while its upper surfaces would appear to consist of Dark Earth and Dark Green, despite the apparent lightness of the Dark Earth painted areas. Carl Vincent

far from ideal for the distance to be covered and perhaps indicates that a proper briefing on how to handle their aircraft over such long distances was not supplied to the pilots. As the flight continued, the weather grew progressively worse with low cloud building and, as the wind became stronger it veered to leave all seven aircraft negotiating a headwind. Thankfully, Sub-Lieutenant Smith's navigation (in the Skua) was excellent and, despite being 25 minutes behind schedule, they reached their first landfall at Galite Island where they rendezvoused with a 228 Squadron Sunderland as planned which then led them to Malta. Unfortunately, with just 30 miles to go, Hurricane V7413, flown by Sgt Spyer, ran out of fuel and he was forced to bail out although thankfully he was rescued almost straight away by the accompanying Sunderland. While Spyer was being recovered from the sea, the Skua and the remaining Hurricanes continued onward but, after entering cloud, they emerged to find that the Hurricane flown by Sgt Cunningham was missing. Presumably he too had run out of fuel as, with a wave to his wingman, he bailed out and by the time the Sunderland reached Cunningham's position there was no sign of him to be seen despite an extensive search. The five remaining aircraft reached Malta at 09:20 and landed at the first airfield they found, which was Takali, with a bare four gallons of petrol remaining in MacLachlan's tanks, two in Norwell's Skua, fourteen in 'Chubby' Eliot's Hurricane and three in Sgt Norwell's; while P/O Hamilton, who actually ran out of petrol in the landing circuit managed to make a safe cross-wind, dead-stick landing. Having refuelled and taken breakfast, the pilots then flew across to Hal Far, their original destination, which is where 261 Squadron was now based having departed Takali after only a few weeks because the airfield was still somewhat basic and prone to flooding during the winter due to it being situated on a dry lake bed.

The second flight of Hurricanes and their lead Skua took off from *Argus* precisely one hour after the first at 07:15, and immediately faced problems. A Sunderland which was conveying the Hurricane's ground crews from Gibraltar to Malta was to have rendezvoused with the flight and escort them but it failed to leave on time forcing the second formation to fly on alone. Unfortunately the weather had grown worse by the time the second flight took off, causing them to miss their landfall at Galite Island where a Wellington from Malta was waiting to rendezvous and guide them to the island. The Skua's observer, Sub-Lieutenant Neil, radioed for help to assist him in locating their position by using radio direction finding in order to obtain a 'fix' but, although his transmitter was working the receiver was not, preventing him from hearing the replies that were sent. The formation became hopelessly lost. One by one the six Hurricanes ran out of fuel and dropped into the sea taking their highly experienced pilots with them until the Skua was left to carry on alone in driving rain.

Finally, the Skua's engine faltered then stopped too at which point the Sicilian coastline hove into view from out of the gloom, so, with its propeller windmilling and Italian AA fire trying to shoot him down, Petty Officer Stockwell brought the Skua down for a successful forced-landing on the beach near Syracuse. The two crewmen were taken prisoner but none of the six missing Hurricane pilots from the second flight were ever found despite an extensive search of the entire area by S/Ldr Whiteley and his crew in a 431 Flight Maryland.

The result of this flawed mission which had necessitated the inclusion of much of Force H as escort, was the arrival in Malta of just four Hurricanes and a Skua for the loss of seven highly experienced Battle of Britain veterans, two Skua crewmen taken prisoner, and nine sorely needed aircraft lost. A board of enquiry was convened at Gibraltar in which, as so often happens, the blame was laid squarely at the feet of the missing aircrew. This, despite the fact that they had been ordered off at extreme range, into a headwind and in poor weather; undoubtedly other circumstances also prevailed against the airmen, not least of which was the use of incorrect power settings and altitudes. However, the primary cause of the tragedy has to be the order issued by Admiral Somerville for the two flights to be flown from *Argus* earlier than planned due to fears that the Italian fleet had put to sea. All four Hurricanes and the five surviving Hurricane pilots from Operation *White* were allocated to 261 Squadron where they were joined by a further two experienced pilots, both of whom had arrived aboard the Sunderland which had eventually arrived from Gibraltar carrying the ground crew. Following them was Sgt Cyril S Bamberger, the spare pilot on board *Argus*, who already had two kills to his credit while flying Spitfires with 41 Squadron in the UK and who eventually arrived from Gibraltar aboard the destroyer HMS *Hotspur*. According to Sgt Jim Pickering, who was by now one of the more established pilots in 261 Squadron, these newcomers 'brought in ideas and tactics that had been evolved during the Battle of Britain' and their operational experience was to prove invaluable. As for the surviving Skua (L2882), both it and its crew were retained in Malta and were later posted to join the Marylands of 431(GR) Flight for reconnaissance duties.

1940 DRAWS TO AN END

All of the fighter interceptions carried out over the Maltese islands were made under radar guidance, initially from a temporary control room located in the control tower at Takali, but mostly from the underground headquarters in Lascaris Bastion known colloquially as 'The Hole'. Surprisingly perhaps, the first fighter controllers were two civilians named Mr Ryan and Mr Tomkins who were both employees of Imperial Airways and whose 'plotters' were mainly civilian women. RAF personnel were soon despatched to take over, the most famous of whom must surely have been the inimitable Group Captain AB 'Woody' Woodhall of Battle of Britain fame who arrived from the UK during early 1942 and is widely regarded as being the greatest fighter controller of the entire war. The civilian plotters though remained throughout the siege, one of whom was Christina Rathcliffe who became romantically linked with Adrian Warburton and, in company with other off-duty plotters, she formed part of the 'Whizz Bangs' cabaret troupe who did so much to sustain morale in Malta. Incredibly, unbelievably even, the underground headquarters was also the scene of a daily exchange of telephone communications which occurred each evening between RAF Intelligence staff at Lascaris and *Regia Aeronautica* staff in Sicily in order to discuss casualties and survivors from lost aircraft. Unsurprisingly this cosy arrangement failed to survive the arrival of the Germans in 1941.

THE LULL BEFORE THE STORM: ITALIAN ATTACKS CONTINUE

Due to the British Mediterranean Fleet's activities during November, which included the bombarding of Italian shore defences and escorting convoys, the month proved relatively quiet over Malta due to the *Regia Aeronautica*' need to concentrate the bulk of its efforts on anti-shipping operations. To maintain pressure on the Italians, Luqa's Wellingtons continued their night raids although in the process another of its bombers was lost during a raid against Bari.

The consequent lull enabled the previously unserviceable Hurricanes to be repaired using the spare parts that had been brought in by Sunderland, which in turn allowed eight Hurricanes to scramble on the morning of 23rd November to contest a raid against Takali by 10 S.79s from 34° *Stormo* escorted by 18 CR.42s from 23° *Gruppo Autonomo*. There were no losses on either side, despite claims to the contrary, and although Sergeant Robertson in newly arrived Hurricane V7474 was attacked by six CR.42s, he managed to turn the tables on them and fired at four, one of which was badly damaged when much of the fabric on its top wing was shot away. Hal Far Fighter Flight veteran, George Burges, (who had earlier made his last ever flight in a Sea Gladiator over Malta in N5529 during an uneventful patrol on the 20th), also participated in the same scramble flying Hurricane V7548; he fired at five of the bombers, causing one of them to lose height and 'shot pieces off another.' In contrast, three of the Italian pilots claimed a Hurricane each while all of the pilots from 75ª *Squadriglia* claimed to have shot another Hurricane down between them, when in fact only F/Lt Bradbury's Hurricane was hit and he managed to force-land safely at Luqa.

Small formations of Italian fighters began to carry out reconnaissance or strafing sorties over Malta towards the end of the month, one of which took place on 24th November 1940 when six CR.42s from 75ª *Squadriglia*, 23° *Gruppo*, attacked Luqa airfield. Coming in at low level, they destroyed a single MWF Wellington Ic on the ground but made claims for three upon their return. Although no interception was made on this occasion such raids were usually met and dogfights often broke out. The same Italian unit sent three aircraft on an armed-reconnaissance over Malta two days later, the 26th, and this time they were intercepted by a pair of 261 Squadron Hurricanes, one of which, N2701, flown by Sgt Dennis Ashton, shot *Tenente* Beccaria's CR.42 down into the sea in flames, killing the pilot. Moments later however, Ashton was himself shot down and killed when a CR.42 flown by *Capitano* Bobba got onto Ashton's tail and, after a short burst from his twin 12.7mm guns, Hurricane N2701 was also sent crashing into the sea. While death in war is always tragic, Dennis Ashton's was particularly poignant as he had received news, that very day, informing him that he had become a father for the first time!

On the 28th, HMS *Illustrious* was operating in the Sicilian Narrows whilst its Swordfish carried out a series of strikes against Italian-held islands in the Aegean. In order to provide additional fighter protection, six Fulmars from 805 NAS, which was usually shore-based in Egypt at the time, were embarked in addition to those of 806 NAS. The Fulmar Is of 806 NAS, which would later be based in Malta, made their first direct contribution to the island's defence when three of them, accompanied by three from 805 NAS, were directed against a formation of six CR.42s from 23° *Gruppo* flying 30 miles out from the Sicilian coast – towards Malta. Although they found the nimble Italians hard to deal with the heavy Fulmars gave a good account of themselves, the experienced 806 NAS trio proving to be far more capable than the inexperienced 805 NAS crews. In fact Sub-Lieutenant Stan Orr of 806 NAS shot one of the biplanes down into the sea killing the pilot *Sergente Maggiorre* Sala, whilst Orr's wingmen damaged two more. However the Fulmars did not have it all their own way and N1935, flown by Sub-Lieutenant Clisby, was hit and his TAG, Leading Airman Phillips, was slightly wounded. The remainder of the Italians were forced to turn and head back to Sicily.

During December many of the Sicilian-based air units were redeployed to North Africa in order to bolster their forces in Libya so, in an attempt to interfere with their lines-of-supply and logistical build-up, Malta's Wellingtons and Swordfish made an all-out effort to interdict enemy vessels and aircraft. On the night of 7th December 1940, Wellingtons from 148 Squadron, which had been formed out of the MWF at Luqa six days previously, bombed Castel Benito airfield near Tripoli whilst eight Swordfish from 830 NAS dive-bombed Tripoli

Harbour on the 10th, hitting three ships. In the weeks which followed the tempo continued, with the Wellingtons causing major damage to Castel Benito airfield before they too shifted their attention to Tripoli Harbour. At the same time the Swordfish began to lay mines around the harbour entrance as others made diversionary bombing attacks against the moles, shipping and seaplane base.

Because the presence of the Hurricanes made it so dangerous for enemy aircraft to fly over Malta in daylight, the Italian flyers who remained in Sicily elected to approach Malta mostly by night. Even then they were not safe. On 18th December 1940, a 30° *Stormo* SM.79 was coned by searchlights at 15,000 feet over Marsa Racecourse and was promptly intercepted by Sgt Fred Robertson in Hurricane P3731, coded 'J', who fired three bursts from directly astern and sent the Italian bomber diving into the sea in flames off Marsaxlokk Bay. It was Fred Robertson, it may be recalled, who had crashed at Hal Far at the conclusion of Operation *Hurry* due to a lack of fuel. Despite his poor start, Robertson would go on to become the leading exponent of the Hawker Hurricane in Maltese skies, achieving 10 kills in addition to the two he had already obtained while flying Spitfires in the UK. He also became the island's top scoring pilot during the first year of the war.

Above: A poor quality but rare image of Maryland I, BJ421, photographed alongside a 216 Squadron Bristol Bombay in early 1941 at Takoradi, Gold Coast, (present-day Ghana) in western Africa. BJ421 was later flown across Africa to Egypt and then on to Malta to join 69 Squadron at Luqa and was subsequently struck off charge on 29th January 1942, possibly as a result of bomb damage. This was one of eight Marylands delivered to the RAF in January 1941, all of which were intended for 69 Squadron although only three arrived as one had crashed in Nigeria, one was retained in Egypt, while the remainder were all lost at sea prior to arriving at Takoradi.

Adding to this image's rarity is the fact that it illustrates the Armstrong Whitworth 'Anson style' birdcage turret as fitted to a few Marylands (AR713 was another) which did nothing whatsoever to enhance the aircraft's sleek lines and even less for its top speed! Author's collection

Below: Seen at Luqa, this 431 Flight Maryland is also fitted with the comparatively rare birdcage turret and is believed to be AR713 the fourth Maryland to join the Flight, and the slowest, courtesy of the drag created by the turret's high profile. AR713 was struck off charge on 18th June 1941. Author's collection

Another exponent of the Hurricane was 'Timber' Woods, one of the initial band of extemporised Sea Gladiator pilots who had formed the Hal Far Fighter Flight. His personal score of victories now stood at five with one probable, which he achieved whilst flying both types – a remarkable achievement when it is recalled that he was *not* a trained fighter pilot. In December he became the second fighter pilot in Malta to be awarded a Distinguished Flying Cross, but shortly afterwards he was posted to Greece on the orders of the deeply moral Governor of Malta, General Sir William GS Dobbie, KCB, GCMG, DSO for allegedly having had a relationship with the wife of a serving naval officer. He duly became a flight commander within the highly experienced 80 Squadron which was in the process of converting from Gladiators to Hurricanes. Woods was placed in the company of other expert fighter pilots such as S/Ldr Marmaduke 'Pat' Pattle, DFC – the leading Commonwealth ace of World War Two, with at least 50 kills to his credit; P/O 'Bill' Vale with 30 kills, and Sgt CE Casbolt with over thirteen. Woods quickly raised his score to nine, but when the Germans joined the Italians in Greece the RAF found itself fighting against massive odds and 80 Squadron was all but decimated during the withdrawal through Greece to Crete. Almost overcome with fatigue, the Squadron's surviving pilots became embroiled in a massive dogfight against German Bf 109Es and Bf 110s over Eleusis Bay, near Piraeus, on 20th April 1941, in which both 'Timber' Woods and 'Pat' Pattle were shot down and killed.

On Christmas Day, a lone CR.42 from 72ª *Squadriglia*, 17° *Gruppo*, 1° *Stormo*, dropped a metal cylinder over Malta containing a cartoon entitled 'A Christmas Greeting To The Boys Of Hal Far And Kalafrana.' The card depicted a large cartoon of an Italian pilot in his CR.42 who was clubbing down RAF Hurricanes using his massive fists while downed British pilots queued up on a cloud outside Heaven's pearly gates…not the most festive of scenes!

The RAF's final kill of the year occurred on 29th December; however, rather than falling to a fighter's guns, it instead fell to a 431 (GR) Flight Maryland flown by F/O Warburton who shot a lone SM.79 down in flames over the Bay of Naples whilst en route to conduct a reconnaissance of Naples' harbour. Another Maryland participated in the final combat of the year when it scored hits on the port engine of a Savoia Marchetti SM.75 transport on 31st December whilst F/O Boys-Stone was returning from a reconnaissance of Taranto and Brindisi harbours.

By the end of 1940, RAF fighters had shot down approximately 20 Italian bombers and 11 fighters over Malta since the outbreak of hostilities with Italy. The strength of 261 Squadron then stood at 16 Hurricanes and four Sea Gladiators, meaning that on paper at least that Malta's fighter capability was obviously significantly better than had been the case just six months earlier. However, serviceability was becoming an issue once again, particularly with the Hurricanes which were low on spares of all types, especially tyres. Such spares as existed were having to be salvaged from wrecked aircraft, or were brought in at great risk by Royal Navy submarines or fast surface vessels. By the end of 1940 the Sea Gladiators were considered to be well past their prime and were used in the fighter role only when there were insufficient Hurricanes available; their principal role from this point was to fly daily meteorological flights instead. These usually took place early in the morning in order to obtain the upper air temperatures and barometric pressure settings for the day, by taking regular measurements right up to 25,000 feet.

British Airpower in Malta by December 1940

Unit	Type	No.	Location	Reserves
261 Sqn	Sea Gladiator I	4	Luqa/Takali/Hal Far	crated spares
261 Sqn	Hurricane I	16	Luqa/Takali/Hal Far	4
148 Sqn	Wellington Ic	16	Luqa	4
228 Sqn(det)	Sunderland I	4	Kalafrana	2
431 Flight	Maryland I	5	Luqa	2 Blenheim IV
830 NAS	Swordfish I	12	Hal Far	0

BUILD-UP OF GERMAN STRENGTH

Despite having sent reinforcements to North Africa, matters were not proceeding well for Mussolini's troops in the Western Desert, where much smaller British Commonwealth forces were making great strides and had captured Italian soldiers, by their hundreds of thousands, during Operation *Compass*. Elsewhere, *Il Duce*'s campaign in Greece was going no better than that in Africa, and his *Mare Nostrum* was rapidly becoming a fanciful echo from the past now that the Royal Navy had obtained virtual mastery of the Mediterranean following their raid on Taranto. All of this convinced Hitler to go to the assistance of his fellow dictator, the results of which would be twofold: the deployment of a German expeditionary force to Libya in February 1941 to be known as the '*Deutsches Afrikakorps*' led by General Erwin Rommel, (but which would later evolve into the much larger *Panzerarmee Afrika*); and a German invasion of Yugoslavia and Greece, via Rumania and Bulgaria by Field-Marshal List's 12th Army on 6th April 1941 called Operation *Merita*. A further result of German intervention in the Mediterranean theatre would be the transfer of the *Luftwaffe*'s anti-shipping specialists of *Fliegerkorps* X from their bases in Norway to Sicily in order to safeguard the Axis supply lines across the Mediterranean. Their essential aim was the obliteration of Malta as an Allied strike base, plus the destruction of British warships, especially the aircraft carrier HMS *Illustrious*, whose removal became an Axis priority following Taranto.

GLOSTER SEA GLADIATOR, N5519 'G6A', 802 NAVAL AIR SQUADRON, HMS *GLORIOUS* 1939

N5519 is seen here in its pre-war silver livery worn whilst serving with 802 NAS aboard HMS *Glorious* in 1939 and fitted with a wooden, two-bladed, Watts airscrew as suggested in an accompanying photograph. Watts propellers were often preferred by Sea Gladiator pilots in the Mediterranean as they produced a shorter take-off run than the metal Fairey Reed three-bladed, single-pitch units with which they were delivered. Unlike most inter-war carrier borne aircraft, the metal airframe panels of the Sea Gladiator did not receive a coat of anti-corrosive Cerrux Grey paint but were painted Aluminium instead – although the fabric covered areas were still doped silver. Here, *Glorious'* yellow carrier band has been applied to the fuselage and contains the code 'G6A' in black, while above the wings the 802 NAS diamonds were also applied in yellow *as opposed to blue* – as is so often misconstrued elsewhere, due no doubt to a misinterpretation of the original photographs which were obtained using orthochromatic film. The black fin indicates that this was the CO's aircraft at this time. Some Sea Gladiators had black under-wing serials applied on the production line but most appear not to have retained these in service and, as with N5519, many had the fuselage serial removed too and retained only the rudder serial. This aircraft went on to become a Malta veteran and is included here to show how most of the stored examples at Kalafrana would have looked prior to being repainted in the S.1.E. camouflage scheme upon the outbreak of war.

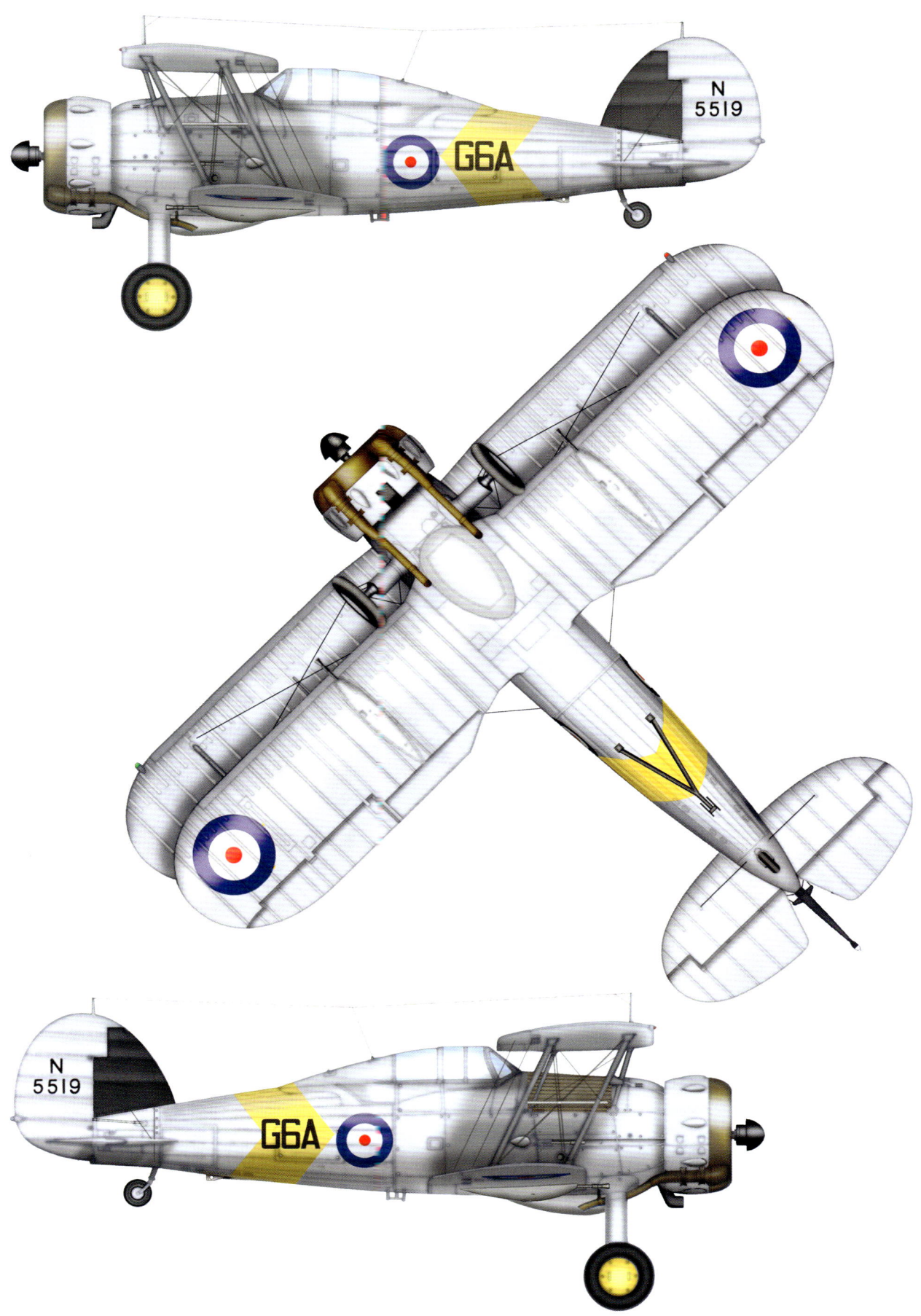

GLOSTER SEA GLADIATOR 'S' PRIOR TO ITS SERIAL BEING RE-APPLIED: HAL FAR FIGHTER FLIGHT, MALTA, SUMMER 1940

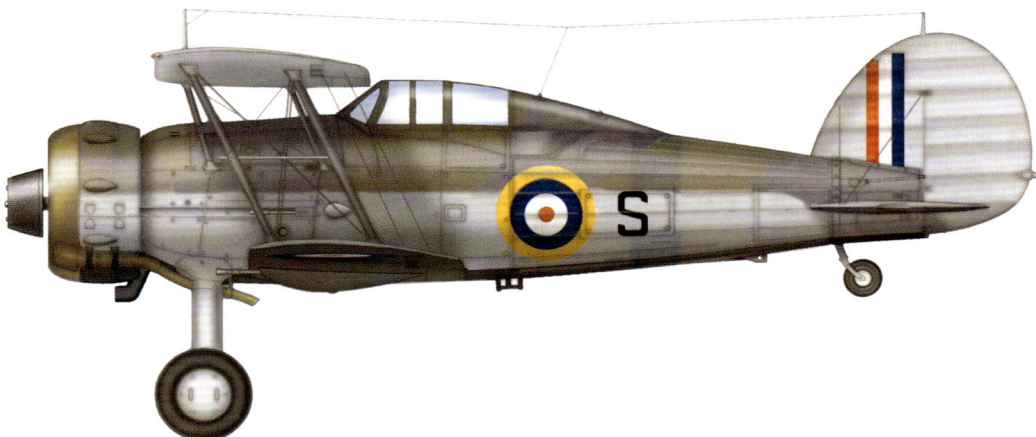

Although minus its serial number, the presence of the code letter 'S' strongly suggests that this is N5520. It is shown with a Watts propeller although its dinghy pack and arrester hook have been removed in order to lighten the aircraft. All three of the Sea Gladiators initially selected for operational use by the Hal Far Fighter Flight, including this one, received a sheet of armour plate fitted behind the pilot which was manufactured specifically by the Malta Dockyard – although this modification did not extend to the remaining (uncrated) Sea Gladiators. As with the others that were brought out of storage, this Sea Gladiator wore the naval S.1.E. camouflage scheme of Dark Slate Grey and Extra Dark Sea Grey on the top surfaces of the upper wing and upper fuselage, Light Slate Grey and Dark Sea Grey on top of the lower wings with Sky Grey applied to the lower-fuselage sides and fin. The underside of the fuselage and lower wings were then painted half black and half white to comply with the RAF's recognition regulations in the Mediterranean area. No serials were applied whilst in storage but doubtless the appropriate serial was applied in the style used on the other Sea Gladiators as time permitted.

Three Sea Gladiators of the Hal Far Fighter Flight in Malta at the start of hostilities in the Mediterranean. All are fitted with wooden two-bladed Watts propellers rather than the three-bladed metal type seen in other images. They have been repainted in the naval S.1.E camouflage scheme; no serials have been applied. Having been removed from their packing cases at Kalafrana, presumably wearing their new colours, the RAF applied black and white paint to the undersides of the Sea Gladiator's fuselage and lower wings, split equally with black on the left side and white on the right, but left the bottom of the upper wing in Sky Grey. Fighters in RAF overseas service continued to use this black-and-white colour division of the lower surfaces as a ready means of identifying friendly aircraft from the ground prior to the adoption of IFF equipment. Although the nearest two aircraft bear no identification letters the one furthest from camera appears to have the letter 'S' applied to the fuselage albeit that it is substantially obscured by the tail of the leading aircraft.
J.Pickering via Frederick Galea

GLOSTER SEA GLADIATOR, N5519 'R', HAL FAR FIGHTER FLIGHT, MALTA, SUMMER 1940

As related in detail earlier in this chapter, this biplane was being flown by F/O Peter Hartley during a swirling World War One-style dogfight when it was shot down in flames by a CR.42. Hartley, enveloped in flames, struggled to release the metal pin of his Sutton Harness in order to escape, however, before he could do so his petrol tank exploded and threw him out of his cockpit. Despite terrible burns, Hartley managed to open his parachute in time to descend into the sea and was rescued 45 minutes later. Hartley was taken to Imtarfa military hospital and ultimately survived his injuries. History would later show that N5519 was to become the only Sea Gladiator to be shot down over Malta, although others succumbed to bombing and ground attack.

N5519 is possibly the world's most famous Gladiator and is shown wearing the colour scheme in which it fought over Malta to provide a comparison to the inter-war livery shown previously. Unlike the other Fighter Flight Sea Gladiators, N5519 now possessed a three-bladed, fixed-pitch, Fairey Reed propeller instead of a Watts unit and it too had had its dinghy and arrester hook removed prior to receiving a sheet of armour plate behind the pilot's seat. N5519 still wore the S.1.E. colour scheme shown at the time of its demise. A photograph of this aircraft appears on page 57.

GLOSTER SEA GLADIATOR, N5567 '6-C', 813 FIGHTER FLIGHT, HMS *EAGLE* AND HMS *ILLUSTRIOUS*, SUMMER 1940

Although never a Malta-based aircraft, N5567 offers a useful comparison between those Sea Gladiators operated at Hal Far with those still in use with the FAA which were used to assist with the defence of Malta-bound convoys. As with several Sea Gladiators deployed aboard carriers during World War Two, and despite the risk, it appears that N5567 has had its dinghy pack removed whilst operating from HMS *Eagle* when it was part of the vessel's semi-official Fighter Flight which was manned by Swordfish pilots from 813 NAS and led by the ship's Commander Flying, Commander CL Keighley-Peach. For a few months, until *Illustrious*' arrival in August 1940, these Sea Gladiators were the only British naval fighters embarked throughout the Mediterranean where, despite their antiquity, they established an excellent record against Italian opposition. Later, *Eagle's* Fighter Flight (or 813F Flight) operated on detachment to *Illustrious* in order to augment 806 NAS's Fulmars. Like so many Sea Gladiators and RAF Gladiator IIs in the Middle East, N5567 was retrofitted with a Watts propeller to provide a shorter take-off run. The camouflage pattern is the S.1.E. scheme with black and white halved undersides.

FIAT CR.42 FALCO (FALCON) '4-70', 70ª SQUADRIGLIA, 23º GRUPPO, 3º STORMO, COMISO, SICILY, JULY 1940

Following the premature (albeit temporary) withdrawal of the Macchi MC200 from operations over Malta in mid-1940 due to technical problems, they were replaced by CR.42 equipped units that included 23º *Gruppo* which was transferred to Comiso, Sicily, from Northern Italy. The Fiat CR.42 was faster than the Sea Gladiator and, although still a biplane, it was a match for the Hurricane being almost as fast, more manoeuvrable, and equipped with twin 12.7mm (0.5in) mgs that out- ranged the British .303in mgs. As shown here, '4-70' is finished in the standard *Verde Mimetico* 3 and *Marrone Mimetico* 2 camouflage over a *Giallo Mimetico* base coat whilst the undersides are *Grigio Mimetico*. The national markings on the wings employ a white backing and the Fasces symbol appears as was usual beneath the cockpit with the House of Savoy coat of arms of the Italian Royal Family mounted within the white tail cross.

FIAT CR.42, MM.5024 '385-1', 385ª SQUADRIGLIA, 157º GRUPPO, 1º STORMO CT, TRAPANI-MILO, SICILY, 1940

Although often flown by the 157º *Gruppo* Commander, *Maggiore* Guido Nobili, MM.5024 was actually the personal aircraft of *Capitano* Aldo Li Grecis, the CO of *385ª Squadriglia* and it wears his *Squadriglia* commander's pennant and personal lightning flash on the fuselage. MM.5024's mottled camouflage consists of the same colours as those applied to CR.42 '4-70', while the national markings remain identical too; however, in this instance the aircraft's serial number, MM.5024, appears below the tailplane painted in white with black shadowing – a practice commonly applied to many Italian aircraft, dependent upon manufacturer, although individual styles might vary somewhat!

SAVOIA MARCHETTI SM.79 *SPARVIERO* (SPARROWHAWK), '254-2', 254ª *SQUADRIGLIA*, 105° *GRUPPO*, 46° *STORMO*, SUMMER & AUTUMN 1940

Amongst the first SM.79s to raid Malta was this 254ª *Squadriglia* example whose identifying MM number remains unknown. The trimotor SM.79 was of all metal construction with a fabric covered rear fuselage and tail, and was surprisingly fast; it could easily outrun the Gloster Gladiator and possessed a top speed comparable with the contemporary Fairey Fulmar fleet fighter. Bombs were carried vertically within a compartment behind the dorsal gunner's position and the bomb aimer occupied the gondola under the rear fuselage. This aircraft wears an early camouflage scheme which is believed to consist of *Giallo Mimetico* 3, *Marrone Mimetico* and *Verde Mimetico* with *Grigio Mimetico* or even painted aluminium undersides. The unit code '254' is black while the less visible '2' was most likely red with the national insignia on the wings being superimposed upon a white disc.

SAVOIA MARCHETTI SM.79, '193-6', 193ª *SQUADRIGLIA*, 87° *GRUPPO*, 30° *STORMO*, SICILY, SUMMER 1940

Wearing the famous 'Electric Man' insignia of 193ª *Squadriglia*, 87° *Gruppo*'s SM.79 bombers were based chiefly in Sciacca, Sicily (excluding a few days at Castelvetrano), between June 1940 and August 1941 when the *Gruppo* returned to Italy to convert to the Cant Z.1007. As with most Italian units of the period, the aircraft of 193ª *Squadriglia* wore a variety of camouflage schemes with this one wearing a base coat of *Giallo Mimetico* 2 with randomly applied *Marrone Mimetico* 2 and *Verde Mimetico* 2 mottling. The undersides are *Grigio Azzuro Chiaro*, as are the spinners and the codes are black and red with white shadow shading. The so called 'Electric Man' insignia is on a blue background in this instance with the Italian-language legend *Ardisco Colpisco Meninfischio* rendered in stylised characters which, loosely translated, means 'I dare, I hit and I don't care about it.' A photograph of this aircraft appears on page 60.

MACCHI MC.200 *SAETTA* (LIGHTNING), MM.5797 '88-9', 88ª *SQUADRIGLIA*, 6° *GRUPPO*, 1° *STORMO*, COMISO. FLOWN BY *SERGENTE MAGGIORE* MARSEILLE GIANLINO BASSCHIROTTO, AUGUST 1940

The Macchi MC.200 was in many ways comparable to the Hurricane despite its somewhat antiquated and rotund appearance. This is an early *Serie I* variant with the fully-enclosed sliding canopy that proved so unpopular with Italian pilots who were used to open cockpits, and, as a consequence, often flew with their canopy open. MM.5797 was flown by Italian ace Maresciallo Gianlino Basschirotto. It wears a typical three-toned camouflage consisting of *Verde Mimetico* 2 with *Bruno Mimetico* and *Giallo Mimetic* 'poached egg' *mottles* and *Grigio Mimetico* undersides with a standard Aermacchi-applied white tail cross projecting onto the fin. The elaborate 1° *Stormo* insignia appearing on the rear fuselage is that of a white-painted archer on a black ground which incorporates the motto *Incocca, tende, scaglia* ('knock, bend, shoot.'), while the colours of the underwing national markings are the reverse of the more usual style but quite common at this time. The fin displays the 'information table' commonly worn by Aermacchi-built aircraft and contains the company logo and weight information with the serial number below displayed as M.M. 5797.

JUNKERS Ju 87B, *PICCHIATELLI* (DIVE-BOMBER) MM5794, 236ª *SQUADRIGLIA*, 96° *GRUPPO BAT*, COMISO, 1940

The Italians referred to their Ju 87s as *Picchiatelli*, the first of which to appear over Malta being the Ju 87B variant belonging to 236ª *Squadriglia*, 96° *Gruppo BaT* whose aircraft wore a cartoon diving-bird insignia on their wheel spats. (The abbreviation *BaT* stood for *Bombardamento a Tuffo*, meaning land-based dive-bomber unit.) Although the Italians retained the standard German RLM 70 *Schwarzgrun*, 71 *Dunkelgrun* and 65 *Hellblau* camouflage scheme, German national markings were over painted using Italian *Verde Oliva Scura* paint on the upper surfaces with *Grigio Azzuro Chiaro* below. In lieu of the German insignia, comparatively small Italian national insignia were added to the bottom of the wings as well as above in most, although not all, instances, whilst a small white cross was applied to the tail albeit minus the House of Savoy coat of arms. The original German *Werk Nummer* has been replaced on the top of the fin by the crudely applied Italian MM number 5794, while a narrow white band has been applied to the fuselage.

HAWKER HURRICANE I, P3731 'J', 418 FLIGHT, (LATER 261 SQUADRON), HAL FAR, AUGUST 1940

The 12 Hurricanes of 418 Flight that were delivered to Malta by HMS *Argus* during Operation *Hurry* on 2nd September 1940 were the first to arrive there via aircraft carrier, with P3731 being one. Upon arrival it had its code 'J' applied either in white or a light grey such as Medium Sea Grey. A number of aces flew P3731 over Malta including Malta's top scoring Hurricane pilot – Sgt Fred Robertson, as well as Sgt Harry Ayre and P/O John Pain amongst others. P3731 survived operations over Malta and was later flown to Egypt following 261 Squadron's departure from Malta in May 1941, but, as related elsewhere it later joined 127 Squadron for service over Syria where it was shot down by a Vichy-French Dewoitine D.520 near to the River Euphrates on 3rd July 1941. This Hurricane was fitted with a De Havilland two-position, variable-pitch, metal propeller with its short spinner as well as a Vokes filter. Along with P3733, this was one of the Hurricanes received during Operation *Hurry* that wore a desert camouflage scheme comprised of Dark Earth and an experimental colour that would later become known as Middle Stone which was applied to obscure the previously existing areas of Dark Green. As a visual identification measure for ground forces, P3731 received black and white painted undersides split equally along the fuselage centreline with its left-hand side being black. The national markings consisted of 49in B-Type roundels on the top surfaces of the wings, with 45in A-Type below (although the roundel on the black wing probably had a yellow outline) and 35in A1-Type roundels on the fuselage with a large red, white and blue fin flash covering the entire fin. The serial and spinner are black, but it appears that the spinner may have been later repainted red.

BLACKBURN SKUA L2987, HMS *ARGUS*, OPERATION *WHITE*, 17th NOVEMBER 1940

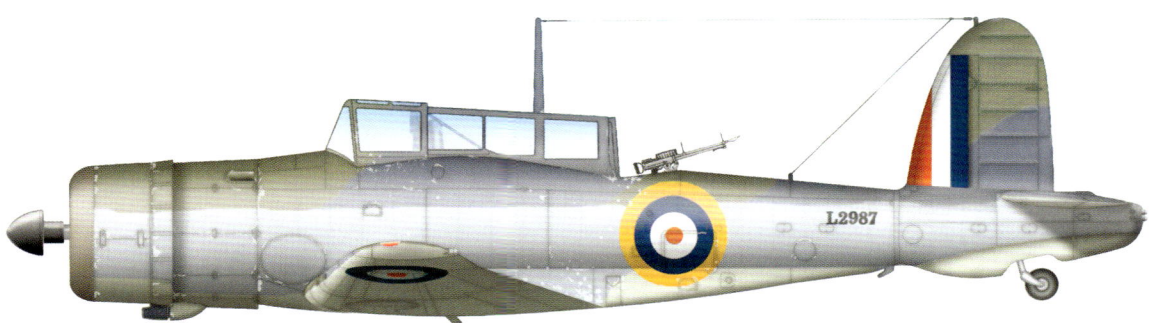

This Skua was the navigational leader of the second flight of Hurricanes to leave the deck of *Argus* during Operation *White* on 17th November 1940 and became the only aircraft of that flight to make a landfall, albeit on a Sicilian beach: all six accompanying Hurricanes were lost at sea. L2987 had previously enjoyed a distinguished record serving with 800 NAS aboard *Ark Royal* when it had been coded '6G' and had shot down two enemy aircraft. It was painted in the naval S.1.E. scheme of Extra Dark Sea Grey and Dark Slate Grey upper surfaces with Sky Grey lower fuselage and undersides, which it still retained at the time of Operation *White*, though no evidence of the code '6G' is apparent in the photograph seen on page 71. Many Skuas had a Sky Grey rudder but, as seen in the photo (qv), the rudder appears to be darker as if finished in upper-surface colours, however, the dark appearance might be explained by the fact that it is deflected and in shadow. Some Skua's had black and white halved undersides but these were often repainted using either Sky or Sky Blue (Sky is illustrated here). The carburettor intakes on all Skuas were black, while the black serial was applied using old-type British stencils.

3 | THE HURRICANE TAKES THE STRAIN

A contrast in style (and performance). Seen at Hal Far, after having moved there from Takali and Luqa during November 1940, this image helps to highlight the differing appearance of the Hurricane Is serving with 261 Squadron. The nearest aircraft has a Rotol constant-speed propeller identified by its wooden Jablo blades and a longer narrower spinner as commonly found on Mk.IIs but which was retrofitted to many Mk.Is including some in Malta due to the increased climb performance it bestowed. In contrast, the two furthest aircraft are equipped with the earlier two-speed De Havilland propeller as 'tweaked' by S/Ldr Louks, Malta's Command Engineering Officer who altered the pitch of the blades to give a slightly improved climb rate albeit at the expense of a longer take-off run. They are both fitted with a Vokes tropical filter too. Other more subtle differences are apparent in so far as the nearest Hurricane has light-coloured undersides, probably Sky Blue, while the others have black and white halved undersides. All three appear to have Dark Earth and Dark Green upper surfaces which tended to fade rapidly in the Mediterranean sunlight and also have black spinners.

1941: A NEW YEAR COMMENCES AND THE GERMANS ARRIVE

During the last days of 1940 the first units of the *Luftwaffe*'s anti-shipping specialists, *Fliegerkorps* X (10th Air Corps), made preparations to leave Norway. They were bound for the warmer climes of Sicily and the Mediterranean where their object was to achieve the thorough neutralisation of Malta.

Equipped with Heinkel He 111H twin-engined bombers and torpedo bombers, Junkers Ju 88D twin-engined bomber/reconnaissance aircraft and the Messerschmitt Bf 110C *Zerstorer* (destroyer) – a long-range, twin-engined fighter, this force of 10,000 men were to be joined by two *Gruppen* each of Junkers Ju 88A twin-engined and Junkers Ju 87R *Stuka* single-engined dive-bombers from *Luftflotte* 3 in France.*

The speedy Ju 88A-4s and A-5s would form the main strike force of *Fliegerkorps* X in Sicily and were provided by *Lehrgeschwader* 1, (LG 1) which was originally conceived as a training and evaluation unit although its function was now more synonymous with a standard *Kampfgeschwader* or bomber group.

Based in France, the *Stab* (HQ) plus II and III *Gruppen* would be the units deploying to Sicily after having previously been engaged in the night blitz against Britain with II/LG 1 based at Orleans-Bricy, and III/LG 1 at Chateaudun. The Ju 87 units were based on the Channel coast and had been re-equipping with the latest variant of the *Stuka*, the *Reichweitenausfuhrung* (long-range) Ju 87R which was provided with additional fuel and oil capacity plus provision for a pair of 300-ltr under-wing tanks to endow it with a very useful still air range of 1,255 km. Under the operational control of *Stab Stukageschwader* 3 (StG 3), the Ju 87R units that joined *Fliegerkorps* X were I/StG 1 and II/StG 2 whose crews were eager to restore the reputation of this dive bomber (following the debacle of the Battle of Britain) and were specifically assigned the task of attacking vessels of the British Mediterranean Fleet wherever possible. To help them train for their precision bombing attacks a full scale wooden mock-up of their prime target – the 23,000 ton carrier HMS *Illustrious* – was reportedly under construction off the Sicilian coast near to their new base at Trapani.

The original intention of *Luftwaffe* High Command was to subjugate Malta by means of blockade by closing the Sicilian Narrows to Allied shipping from both Gibraltar and Egypt thus starving the island into submission; hence the need for their anti-shipping specialists. *Fliegerkorps* X was also assigned more distant duties which included the mining of the Suez Canal in order to disrupt Allied supply lines to Egypt via the Cape, which became the main focus of the longer ranged He 111s. Added to this was a requirement to support the Italian forces in Libya prior to the arrival of General Rommel's *Afrika Corps*. However, the primary task of *Fliegerkorps* X, and the reason it was sent to the theatre, was to secure the Axis shipping lanes taking supplies to North Africa from Italy. Far better equipped and with more modern aircraft than the Italians, the German crews were also battle hardened and would prove to be a much more determined and deadly foe for Malta's fighter pilots during the months to come, although much of the fighter cover would still be provided by the *Regia Aeronautica*.

In early January 1941, Malta-based Maryland reconnaissance aircraft began to notice a build-up of German aircraft in Sicily where over 65 Junkers Ju 52/3m transports were involved in moving the men and supplies of *Fliegerkorps* X to their new bases on that island. Previously, on 29th December 1940, the first combat aircraft had arrived in the form of four Ju 88s from LG 1, although the remaining aircraft were strung out across the entire width of Europe routing across the Alps and down the leg of Italy to cross the Straits of Messina to Sicily. As the build-up continued, the unit's commander, *General der Flieger* Hans Geiesler set up his headquarters at the Hotel Domenico in the coastal resort of Taormina north of Catania.

Despite this build up the first few days of 1941 remained quiet over Malta and the first air attack of the year was an all Italian affair. This occurred on the 9th January 1941 when a combined raid was launched against Luqa airfield and Kalafrana seaplane base. The seaplane base, which was also the main deep repair and engineering facility for aircraft in Malta, was dive-bombed by nine Italian Ju 87Bs from 96° *Gruppo Autonomo* which was once again based in Sicily, albeit temporarily, as the unit was in fact due to move to North Africa. They were escorted by ten Fiat CR.42 biplanes from 156° *Gruppo*, while 16 Macchi MC.200s from 6° *Gruppo Autonomo* strafed Luqa. To counter this incursion five Hurricanes from 261 Squadron were scrambled and F/Lt MacLachlan claimed a pair of MC.200s shot down and F/O Taylor claimed another, while F/Lt Waters in Hurricane I, V7474, managed to hit and badly damage a further Macchi. In fact only two Macchis were lost on this raid: MM.5787 flown by *Mareschiallo* (Warrant Officer) Zanandrea who was killed; and MM.4586, flown by *Capitano* Armanino who, despite being wounded, was able to bail out over the sea to become a prisoner of war. The Italians' claimed to have shot down a Hurricane and damaged five Wellingtons on the ground at Luqa, but all of the Hurricane's returned unscathed and only three Wimpeys had been hit and dam-

Footnote

* *Stuka* is an abbreviation of **stu**r**zka**mpfflugzeug, a generic German term used to describe *all* dive-bombers. However, historically speaking the word has come to represent the Ju 87 virtually exclusively with the abbreviation becoming its name. Therefore, with this point in mind, where *Stuka* appears in this narrative it is in specific reference to the Ju 87.

Pilots of 261 Squadron on standby at Takali during the winter of 1940/41 in 'winter order' wearing their usual RAF Blue uniforms as opposed to the khaki-drill clothing worn in the summer months. Known identities amongst the assembled pilots are, from the left: Sgt Fred Robertson who became Malta's top-scoring Hurricane pilot; second left, Sgt Len Davies; third left, Sgt RA Spyer. Sgt CS Bamberger is seen in the centre with sunglasses; he too was a successful pilot and claimed a pair of Ju 87s during January 1941. The other pilots currently remain unidentified. Of interest is the ever-present RAF issue 'Lloyd Loom' wicker chair so common to RAF fighter airfields in World War Two, particularly during the Battle of Britain. Beyond the Malta bus which appears to be in use as a mobile dispersal hut is one of the unit's Hurricane Is which sits plugged into a 'trolley acc' with the pilot's parachute perched upon the tailplane in readiness for the next scramble.

Opposite page:

Part of the air group assigned to HMS *Illustrious*, an unidentified Fulmar I from 806 NAS, coded 'X', (with a Swordfish beyond) is probably seen while operating from RAF Aboukir, Egypt, circa December 1940, at a time when a press photographer had arrived to obtain images of this unit. A little earlier, 806 NAS had been shore-based at RNAS Dekheila, near Alexandria, where, for whatever reason, their Fulmar's tyres had suffered a number of blow-outs as a consequence of which they were moved to Aboukir, the principal RAF maintenance base. This Fulmar's colour scheme is interesting as it wears the basic S.1.E. naval scheme of Extra Dark Sea Grey and Dark Slate Grey upper surfaces with Sky Grey sides and undersides, but has a black lower left wing. Presumably, its lower right wing was painted white in order to comply with RAF recognition practices. It also has non-standard, Italian-style camouflage around the nose and wing leading edges, probably using a base coat of desert yellow (possibly Middle Stone) with green or dark brown mottling. Known as 'Spaghetti' style camouflage, it was quite common on 806 NAS Fulmars from 1940. During 1941, RAF-operated Hurricanes in both the Western Desert and Greece also began to adopt this scheme which was designed to fool enemy air and ground-based gunners into thinking that an approaching aircraft was Italian until it was too late! 806 NAS Fulmars proved to be extremely successful over the Mediterranean during 1940 and after their carrier was damaged by Stukas in January 1941 the survivors continued the fight from Hal Far, Malta. Ian Gazeley

aged. The fact that the Wellingtons of the newly formed 148 Squadron were the main target of this attack on Luqa indicated that they had been making quite a nuisance of themselves since the start of the year by mounting bombing raids upon the harbours at Palermo, Tripoli and Naples.

None too impressed by their Italian allies failed attempt at demonstrating their prowess however, the Germans would fly their first operational sorties in the Mediterranean theatre the following day, although they were not directed against Malta. This was because their prime target, HMS *Illustrious*, was off the Maltese coast and well within striking range of Sicily along with the rest of the British Mediterranean Fleet.

HMS *ILLUSTRIOUS* AND THE *ILLUSTRIOUS BLITZ*: THE BUILD-UP

The Germans were able to attack the Royal Navy because a convoy of four ships had been despatched from Gibraltar on 6th January 1941 bound for Greece under the codename Operation *Excess*, with a fifth ship, the SS *Essex*, instructed to break off en route and head for Malta. On board *Essex*, as deck cargo, were 13 crated Hurricane Is, while the holds were loaded with 4,000 tons of ammunition, bombs and torpedoes plus other vital supplies that included 3,000 tons of seed potatoes and (possibly) two Chain Overseas Low Type 5 radars. The latter were intended to augment Malta's original radar and be deployed at Ta Silch and Fort Maddalena to the north-west of Valletta. A heavy escort was provided for the first part of the convoy's journey through the Mediterranean by Force H from Gibraltar which included the battlecruiser HMS *Renown*, battleship HMS *Malaya* and the carrier *Ark Royal* aboard which were two fighter units embarked to provide air cover. The first unit, 808 NAS, was equipped with the almost brand-new Fairey Fulmar I, having become only the second operational unit to employ the type, and 800 NAS, now the only operator of the veteran Skua aboard *Ark Royal*. The (slightly) faster Fulmar assumed the role as the principal interceptor fighter aboard the carrier which had in fact been offered *two* Fulmar squadrons, however, the Skuas were retained because of their ability as dive bombers should the Italian Fleet come within range, though in this the Skua crews were seriously out of practice having been used mainly as fighters up until this point. Upon reaching the Sicilian Narrows Force H was to retire to Gibraltar and hand the convoy over to the protection of the Mediterranean Fleet sailing from Alexandria accompanied by HMS *Illustrious*.

After leaving Gibraltar, *Ark Royal*'s Fulmars had been kept particularly busy repelling shadowing Italian aircraft flying from bases in Sardinia and the commanding officer of 808 NAS, Lieutenant Commander Tillard added to his personal score by downing two SM.79s in one sortie. This brought him up to 'ace' status and resulted in the award of the Distinguished Service Cross for himself and his observer. Also aboard *Ark Royal* was 821X Flight consisting of six volunteer crews from the recently disbanded 821 NAS who were to fly six replacement Swordfish to Malta to bolster 830 NAS at Hal Far. These Swordfish were flown off during the early hours of 9th January from a point 25 miles north of Bizerta and were absorbed by the Malta-based unit upon arrival. As soon as the Swordfish had been despatched, the majority of Force H turned back for Gibraltar before they reached the large minefields off Pantellaria, whereby, as planned, the protection of the *Excess* convoy passed to the Mediterranean Fleet during the night.

During their passage from Alexandria to their rendezvous with the convoy, the Mediterranean Fleet was accompanied by the naval transport HMS *Breconshire* which broke away to run supplies into Malta, while at the same time a group of empty fast-merchantmen, which had been trapped in Malta, took the opportunity to put to sea and gain the protection of the *Excess* convoy. A further convoy comprised of slower merchantmen, coded MS.5, also left Malta at the same time bound directly for Alexandria, while the Town class cruisers HMS *Southampton* and *Gloucester* which had arrived to strengthen convoy MS.6's escort, were also used to deliver troops and airmen from Egypt to Malta before leaving once again.

With so many shipping movements and a large number of capital ships at sea there was every likelihood that fierce air attacks would be mounted, especially against the *Excess* convoy and its new escort bound for Greece. Therefore, the 15 Fulmar Is of 806 NAS embarked aboard *Illustrious* (less its CO, Lt Cdr Charles Lamb, who was ill) were joined by a detachment of three Fulmars from 805 NAS which was more usually based ashore at Dekheila, Egypt. Considering the hornets nest that they were undoubtedly sailing into, this reinforcement was a wise precaution although it meant that the three Sea Gladiators from HMS *Eagle*'s Fighter Flight, that had also been embarked on *Illustrious* as supernumerary fighters in the past, were left behind this time, no doubt because the Admiralty was aware of the possibility of Sicilian-based German opposition.

Whilst under the protection of Force H, *Excess* had already suffered sporadic air and sea attacks and had been constantly shadowed by Sardinian-based Italian aircraft but, when the Mediterranean Fleet assumed the escort role on the morning of 10th January, it coincided with the arrival in Sicily of the most feared anti-ship weapon in the world at the time. This was of course the Junkers Ju 87 *Stuka* dive-bomber and, as luck or bad luck would have it – depending on your point of view, the *Stukas* of I/StG 1 and II/St.G 2 were just in the process of arriving at their new base at Trapani-Milo in Sicily following their staged journey across the Alps from Northern France. After word reached Sicily from shadowing Italian aircraft that the convoy and its escort, including *Illustrious*, were only 100 miles west of Malta a large force of 43 Ju 87Rs from both I/StG 1

Many hands make light work! With its next bomb load waiting in the foreground, this 30° *Stormo* SM.79 is being manhandled around its dispersal at Sciacca in Sicily. Although it wears the 194ª *Squadriglia*, 90° *Gruppo* code '194-5', it also wears the 'Electric Man' insignia of 193ª *Squadriglia*, 87° *Gruppo*, both *gruppo*'s belonging to 30° *Stormo*. The engine cowlings have all been removed for work and the white tail cross, containing the House of Savoy's coat of arms, extends onto the fin. Italian official image

and II/St.G 2 was assembled from amongst those aircraft that had arrived so far. These were immediately refuelled and armed to their maximum capacity with PC 1000 (1,000kg) armour-piercing bombs and sent on their way.

Leading the I/StG 1 contingent was *Hauptmann* Werner Hozzel with *Major* Walter Enneccerus leading II/StG 2, while in addition a number of Italian SM.79s were sent from Sicily to continue shadowing the convoy. Another

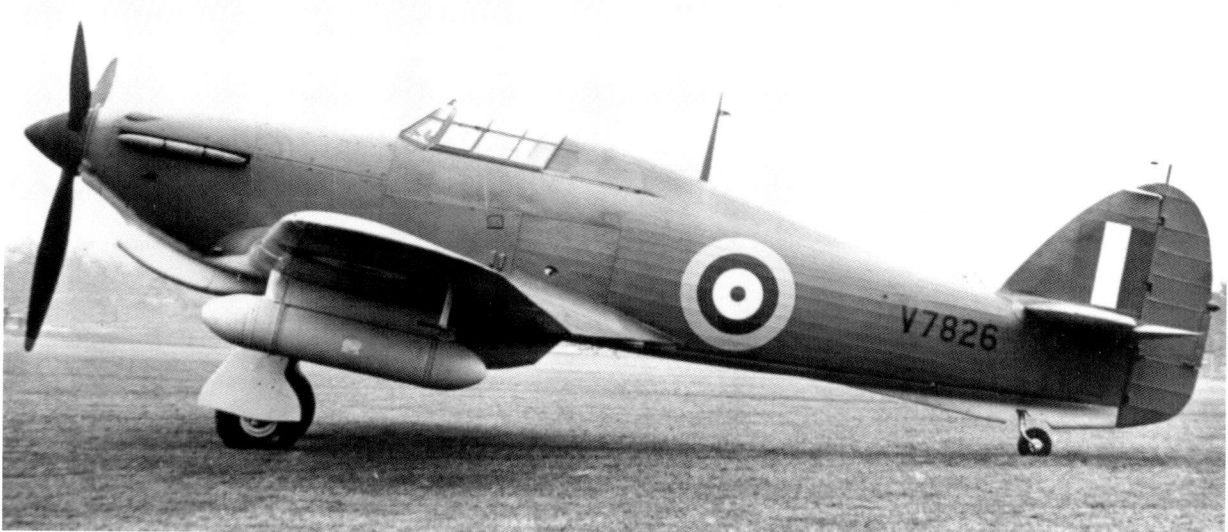

Tropicalised Hurricane I, V7826. A familiar photograph, but one which illustrates the necessary additions fitted to Hurricanes that operated in Malta. V7826 is equipped with a Vokes tropical filter that prevented dust from entering the carburettor, but which also restricted the aircraft's maximum speed, range and rate of climb; yet without the filter an engine's service life could be severely curtailed in arid, dusty climes. A removable 44-gallon long-range tank is fitted beneath the port wing (a second was fitted to the starboard wing) and is fully representative of those used to ferry Hurricanes to Malta. When photographed, V7826 was being used for trials at the Aircraft & Armament Experimental Establishment, Boscombe Down. Later it went to the Middle East and could perhaps have flown into Malta en route to Egypt. Sadly, beyond knowing that V7826 was struck off charge somewhere in the Middle East on 20th May 1941, nothing else appears to be known of its service life. V7826's colour scheme appears to be standard Dark Earth and Dark Green with Sky Blue undersides as applied to fighters destined for overseas service, and it is fitted with a De Havilland two-speed propeller. Author's collection

important contribution to the forthcoming attack came in the form of two torpedo-equipped SM.79*sil* (*Aerosiluranti* i.e. torpedo bombers) from the recently created 279[a] *Squadriglia Sil* at Catania, which would mount a low-level diversionary attack upon *Illustrious* although some reports state that they actually attacked the battleship HMS *Valiant*. This dedicated anti-shipping unit had originally been the experimental torpedo training unit with six specially modified SM.79*sils* and had arrived at Catania on 28th December 1940 from Goriza in Italy. Although each of these aircraft could mount a pair of torpedoes under their belly they usually carried only a single weapon during operations. Some accounts have stated that Ju 88 bombers also took part in the attack on *Illustrious* but, insofar as can be determined, the only aircraft of this type involved were three Ju 88As from III/ LG 1 which were intercepted by Hurricanes and driven off much later during the afternoon, although Ju 88D reconnaissance variants may have been present in a purely observational role.

That very same morning, whilst the Ju 87s were in the process of being armed in Sicily, *Illustrious* was recovering her own strike force of Swordfish after 815 NAS had mounted an early morning bombing attack against an Italian supply convoy. Four of the Swordfish were rapidly turned around and sent aloft straight away to conduct anti-submarine patrols while the rest were quickly struck below to the hangar deck. Little did the Swordfish crews realise that they would soon be on the receiving end of a devastating attack themselves.

THE FULMARS OF 806 NAVAL AIR SQUADRON

Before dealing with the attack on *Illustrious* it may help to pause at this stage to make mention of the 806 NAS Fulmars she had aboard and the success that this carrier had enjoyed following its arrival in the Mediterranean the previous year. The two-seat Fulmar was designed by Marcelle Lobelle and was the first monoplane eight-gun fighter to enter Royal Navy service. Powered by a Rolls-Royce Merlin – specifically the moderately supercharged, low-level, 1275hp Merlin VIII – the Fulmar was developed from the Fairey P.4/34 and was essentially a smaller and lighter derivative of the Fairey Battle light bomber. The first operational unit to convert onto the Fulmar was 806 NAS in June 1940 having previously operated both the Skua and Roc. Fulmar deliveries were slow at first and consequently the Squadron joined the Navy's brand-new armoured fleet carrier *Illustrious* equipped with a mixture of Fulmars and Skuas in addition to the Swordfish Is of 815 and 819 NAS the carrier's strike component. There followed a work up cruise to Bermuda on completion of which 806 NAS could only boast of having four Skuas and a single Fulmar on charge, however, upon their return to the UK the unit received its full complement of 15 Fulmars plus four

A Fulmar I from 806 NAS which was embarked aboard HMS *Illustrious* seen low over the sea while on patrol flown by S/Lt Jackie Sewell, an ace, during late 1940 or early January 1941. This Fulmar also has Italian-style 'Spaghetti' camouflage applied around its nose and wing leading edges, but is otherwise finished in the standard naval S.1.E colour scheme. The lower part of the left wing is painted black, with the opposite side presumably painted white. Author's collection

spares. Some sources maintain that when 806 NAS later departed for the Mediterranean, the Skuas were retained because there were insufficient Fulmars available but that was untrue, a fact made clear in the diary of Sub Lieutenant (S/Lt) Graham Angus Hogg (an 806 NAS pilot and the Squadron Supply Officer) who confirms both the quantity of Fulmars on charge and that *all* four Skuas were left in the UK.

With the Battle of Britain at its height, *Illustrious* departed for the Mediterranean on 22nd August 1940 escorted by the cruisers HMS *Sheffield* and *York*. Two days later, on the 24th, a pair of Fulmars crewed respectively by S/Lt Angus and PO Gould and Midshipman Day and Naval Airman Newton, were both lost in a mid-air collision without survivors. Thankfully there were no further incidents before the carrier docked in Gibraltar on Thursday 29th August to refuel before departing early the following morning bound for Alexandria accompanied by the battleship *Valiant* which was also on its way to join the Mediterranean Fleet. To ensure that the two vessels reached their destination safely Operation *Hats* was set in motion with elements of Force H providing an escort part-way across the Mediterranean. On 31st August, 806 NAS flew the first operational sorties undertaken by the Fulmar when fighter patrols were maintained overhead and on Sunday 1st September, while sailing between Majorca and Algiers, they claimed the fighter's first kill when Blue Section downed a shadowing Cant Z.501 flying boat, with a second shadower being shot down a few hours later. That night Force H turned back for Gibraltar to be replaced during the morning of the 2nd by the Mediterranean Fleet which included battleships HMS *Warspite* and *Malaya*, cruisers *Orion* and *Sydney*, and attendant destroyers.

Two Italian air attacks were beaten off by the Fulmars and anti-aircraft gunners during the afternoon and evening as the ships passed near to Malta. Taking advantage of their close proximity to enemy bases as they sailed south of Crete, *Illustrious* launched a dawn raid by eight Swordfish on the morning of the 4th against an Italian seaplane base on Rhodes, although one 'Stringbag' crashed into a pom-pom while taking off and fell into the sea killing the observer. The remaining seven carried on to the target and left hangars, aircraft and buildings burning in their wake for no further loss to themselves. At 09:15hrs that same morning the Italians carried out another high level bombing raid but it proved to be ineffectual and did nothing to prevent the carrier's arrival at Alexandria 24-hours later.

Over the next four months *Illustrious* and her aircraft proved to be particularly successful, a period in which the pinnacle of their success was reached on the night of 11th November 1940 with the attack on Taranto that devastated the Italian battlefleet as previously related. The Fulmars had played their part in this operation by ensuring that the carrier arrived at its flying-off point near Cephalonia without being discovered; in fact between August and the end of 1940 the fighters shot down 26 Italian aircraft and damaged a similar quantity in the process. Their success was all the more remarkable given that the Fulmar's climbing performance was poor and that it was actually slower than the Italian SM.79 bomber it was often sent to intercept. Even so, at least four of 806 NAS's pilots achieved ace status during this period despite the fact that at the time of the carrier's departure to the Mediterranean, most of the Fulmar pilots (with the exception of the CO and senior Pilot) had little or no previous operational experience with many having only recently completed their training.

While no one would wish to detract from the abilities of the Fulmar aircrews, the skilful use of shipboard radar by the Fighter Direction Officers (FDOs) aboard *Illustrious* played an essential role in determining both the altitude and direction of an incoming aerial threat by ensuring that the Fulmars were in the right place at the right time and thereby helped to compensate, wherever possible, for the fighter's poor performance. Indeed the top speed of the Fulmar I never exceeded 260mph (246mph at sea level) and took over 30 minutes to reach its operational ceiling of just 20,000ft. In its favour though, the Fulmar carried a battery of eight .303in Browning machine-guns in the wings with an ammunition capacity fully three times that of the similarly armed Hurricane and Spitfire, with each ammunition box holding over one thousand rounds. Usefully, the Fulmar also had an effective endurance of up to five hours – a valuable asset for any naval aircraft.

During the fighting which took place over the Mediterranean during 1940 many of the men who occupied the Fulmar's rear cockpit be they NCO ratings trained as telegraphist-air-gunners (TAGs), or officers trained as observers had expressed an opinion that they would like some form of weapon with which they could defend their aircraft from the rear. Therefore, a Very pistol or a Thompson 'Tommy Gun' sub-machine gun was often carried for this purpose although the most remarkable 'weapon' employed by Fulmar 'back-seaters' was perhaps naval issue toilet paper! With an enemy aircraft on the Fulmar's tail, bundles of toilet paper were thrown out of the side window by the man in the back, and when the tightly bound wads of waxy paper squares exploded into the slipstream, some enemy pilots instinctively swerved to avoid the large cloud of 'solid' debris exploding in front of their windscreen.

10th JANUARY 1941: *STUKA* ATTACK ON *ILLUSTRIOUS*

Returning to the morning of 10th January 1941, by 11:15hrs the *Luftwaffe* formation of 43 Ju 87Rs was rapidly approaching the ships of the British Mediterranean Fleet which had just reached the most vulnerable point of their journey where there was little room to manoeuvre in the relatively shallow water of the Sicilian Narrows with large enemy laid minefields strewn around the islands of Pantellaria as well as Malta itself. The FDOs in the fighter control room aboard *Illustrious* were usually 'on the ball', but today they were late to spot the approaching Germans, probably because they had been inundated throughout the morning by the large number of contacts on their screens made by Italian aircraft which were continually conducting feint attacks or probes against the fleet from every conceivable direction. As those Fulmars already aloft on Combat Air Patrol (CAP) were directed against one or more threats, the Italians would simply pull away to safety and another feint would be made from a totally different direction instead, overwhelming the FDOs and causing the CAP to chase around the sky to no avail. To have accomplished this so successfully the Italians must, presumably, have been listening in to the radio frequency used between the FDOs and the Fulmars on CAP, maybe from nearby Pantellaria and then skilfully directing their forces in the air accordingly.

During this hectic morning there had been five Fulmars on CAP, flying in two separate sections. The first section had taken off at 10:15hrs and consisted of two fighters with S/Lt Stan Orr and his TAG Leading Airman (L/Air) Douet flying in N1884 '6K', and S/Lt Graham Angus Hogg with L/Air Oakes in Fulmar '6Y'. The second section of three had taken off later than the first and was led by Lt Robert Henley with his TAG, Midshipman (Mid) Cullen, flying in '6F', accompanied by S/Lt Jackie Sewell and L/Air Denis Tribe in '6Q', and S/Lt Griffith and L/Air Stevens in N1881 '6H.' To avoid confusion it must be mentioned at this stage that although the codes on these Fulmars are replicated here as they appear in official records with the prefix '6', this number was not actually applied to the Fulmars themselves which only wore their respective code letters on the fuselage. This is because 806 NAS was the only fighter unit based aboard the carrier. Had there been two fighter squadrons on board, then the senior unit would adopt the number '6' ahead of its code letters and the other unit would wear the number '7' to differentiate their aircraft – both numbers being reserved to identify fighter units on board. To reiterate therefore, when only one fighter unit was embarked it was common practice for its aircraft to drop the use of the number on the aircraft, although the number prefix, in this case '6', was retained within written reports and other paperwork to avoid confusion later on if a second fighter unit joined the ship.

Lieutenant Henley's section had had an encounter with an enemy aircraft earlier that morning which briefly joined their formation before making off at high speed and was described as resembling a Bf 109; however, as no Bf 109s were in theatre at this stage the exact type remains unknown. At 10:30hrs Henley's section attacked a pair of shadowing SM.79s and shot one of them down jointly with S/Lt Sewell during which Sewell's aircraft, '6Q', was damaged by enemy machine-gun fire and he was forced to return to his carrier, leaving only two pairs of Fulmars on CAP.

At around 11:20hrs Henley's section was directed down to sea level to intercept the pair of 279[a] *Squadriglia* SM.79*sil* trimotor torpedo bombers described earlier, this lone formation was now rapidly approaching *Illustrious* (or perhaps *Valiant*) at wave top height. Along with the ships, gunners who put up a wall of flak, the two Fulmars managed to disrupt the bravely executed attack causing the torpedoes to miss whichever ship they were aimed at and both Henley and Griffith chased after the two SM.79s and succeeded in damaging them using their last few rounds, having expended most of their ammunition earlier in the morning. Despite their success the two Fulmars were now at low level, miles from their carrier, and without ammunition while at 12,000 feet the *Stukas* were minutes away from tipping into their dives directly above *Illustrious*. The *Aerosiluranti* crews had succeeded in luring half of the defending fighters away from the approaching German airmen.

The other section of Fulmars on CAP led by Stan Orr had also been busy chasing SM.79s around the sky during the morning. After Henley's section had been sent down after the low-flying *Aerosilurantis* it appears that Orr's section too was inexplicably ordered to sea level to chase after the same torpedo bombers and finish them off, even though they were no longer a threat to the fleet and were now flying back towards Sicily. Due to their similarity in speed at low level, it took an age for the Fulmars to gain upon the SM.79s as Orr's wingman, S/Lt Hogg, describes in his diary. 'We chased a pair of SM.79s but could not catch them so we strafed an aircraft on an island,' implying that they had seemingly chased them all the way back to Sicily! Most official accounts state that Orr and Hogg shot down one of the SM.79s, but this is untrue and the claim would appear to refer to the aircraft which was strafed on the ground and, in doing so, they had expended most of their remaining ammunition. Worst of all, the low-level chase now left them at wave top height too – and a long way away from their ship.

After directing both of the CAP patrols away from the fleet the FDOs must have finally become aware of an approaching enemy formation on their screens and belatedly realising their mistake, now attempted to scramble more fighters. By the time the approaching *Stuka* formation hove into sight five Fulmars were in the process of being swiftly ranged on deck. The first section of two comprised of S/Lt Sewell and TAG, L/Air Dennis Tribe, in either '6Q' (assuming that it had been repaired in time following its earlier battle damage) or N1860 '6M'; plus S/Lt Ivan Lowe with TAG, Naval Airman (1st class) Kensett in N1935 '6Z'. Both Fulmars became airborne at 12:30hrs even before the carrier had swung into wind.

The second section of three Fulmars was to be led by Lt Bill Barnes in '6A' who, as Senior Pilot, was the Squadron's second-in-command while his observer, acting-CO, Lt Desmond Vincent-Jones, rode in the rear seat. They were leaving it very late however, because even as he climbed into the rear cockpit while the wings of his Fulmar were still being unfolded Vincent-Jones recalled seeing what he described as 'a gigantic swarm of bees approaching from astern.' They were to have been joined by S/Lt Marshall and PO Tallick in '6G' and S/Lt Roberts and his crewman in '6C', however, '6G' failed to start and caused a delay as it obstructed the path of the Fulmars behind. Eventually the 'dud' was moved to one side allowing Bill Barnes to become airborne swiftly followed by Fulmar '6C'. Yet even as the last three fighters became airborne, the first bombs were already starting to fall on and around *Illustrious*.

One of the first bombs to find its target landed directly on top of '6G' the 'dud', whose crew were still in their cockpits, just as it was being lowered to the hangar via the aft lift. The armour-piercing bomb totally obliterated '6G' and sliced through the steel deck of the half-lowered lift before exploding underneath, the blast of which threw the lift upwards off its rails, buckled it, and killed the entire deck party who, along with Marshall and Tallick, were never seen again. The same blast then continued to travel along the full length of the fully enclosed hangar deck causing widespread carnage and damage amongst the men and closely packed, fully fuelled aircraft. At least 30 ratings from 806 NAS who had been working in the hangar were listed amongst the dead and five Fulmars (including the three from 805 NAS) and 12 fully-armed Swordfish lay totally destroyed amid a jumble of wreckage and gore.

Sixty-eight years later, while stood on the hangar deck of the present-day *Illustrious* one of the veterans of that day in 1941 graphically described to the author how the walls and floor of the hangar deck resembled an abattoir with human remains scattered amongst the twisted wreckage of burning aircraft and other debris. Leading Air Fitter Ted Whitley of 819 NAS was also inside the hangar and vividly recalled his own memories of this attack 'that first hit [was] like an earthquake, the whole ship lifting up and slamming down again. The PO with his intestines sticking out saying "my stomach hurts", feet hot, shoes steaming, the deck red-hot, the hose with nothing coming out of it.' Another bomb pierced the armoured deck on the centreline near to the carrier's island and travelled straight through the hangar deck, wrecking an ammunition conveyor and severing petrol pipes as it continued on to the decks below before exploding in the officers' wardroom where many of the Swordfish pilots were sheltering after their early morning raid. Eight of these men were killed and two others were very seriously injured – most had been veterans of the raid on Taranto and, although they couldn't know it, the *Stuka* crews' had gained the revenge the Axis sought.

While the *Luftwaffe* busied itself with the ships below, the two Fulmars flown by Sewell and Lowe had clawed their way up to 2,000 feet and immediately set about attacking the Ju 87s as they dived all around them. Sub Lieutenant Lowe in '6Z' scored hits on one *Stuka* and swiftly shot it down but his Fulmar was hit almost immediately by machine-gun fire from another *Stuka* following behind which killed Kensett in the rear cockpit and wounded Lowe in the shoulder. His engine was also hit and Lowe was forced to ditch in the sea, although luckily he was rescued later in the day by the destroyer HMS *Jaguar*. This just left Sewell and his TAG, Dennis Tribe from the first section and they continued climbing to 7,000 feet before attacking and shooting down a *Stuka*. They then moved onto another and damaged it but in the process of attacking and damaging a third dive-bomber they were hit by return fire from its rear gunner which damaged the fighter.

While the first two Fulmars busily engaged the Germans, the Fulmars from the second section were well behind, far below and desperately climbing for height. At around 200 feet they were suddenly surrounded by *Stukas* as they pulled out of their bombing dives and, as there were so many targets around them, the Fulmar pilots just fired at one dive-bomber after another without having time to check for results in most cases. An exception was S/Lt Roberts in '6C' who did at least observe a *Stuka* that he had shot at hitting the sea. While the Fulmars were busily shooting at the enemy they in turn received fire from German rear gunners as well as the forward firing guns from the other *Stukas* following behind although, unlike Sewell's section, they were lucky to get away with only superficial damage to their aircraft.

By this stage the four Fulmars from the original morning CAP had also managed to reach the mêlée though the section led by Robert Henley was forced to make feint attacks due to their lack of ammunition. Flying in the other section Graham Hogg subsequently wrote in his diary, 'we came back to the fleet in time to attack scores of Junkers 87s which had just finished dropping bombs on the *Illustrious*.' And also that she had ' been hit by four bombs.' Using their remaining few rounds Orr and Hogg went in to 'attack around twenty Junkers' and between them they claimed to have shot down another *Stuka* while causing damage to a further two. Unfortunately these late arrivals had been on CAP for a considerable time and were almost out of fuel so, as *Illustrious* could no longer receive them due to the damage inflicted upon her, the four Fulmars from the original CAP were ordered to proceed to Hal Far airfield in Malta to refuel and re-arm. By the time they landed they had been airborne and in almost constant action for at least three hours and forty minutes, with Hogg reporting only five gallons of fuel remaining in his tanks. Their arrival was the first indication for many in Malta of the drama that was unfolding just over the horizon.

Despite the best efforts of the Fulmars and anti-aircraft gunners aboard *Illustrious* and other warships, the divebombers had hit the carrier with a total of seven bombs (one of which did not explode) leaving her badly damaged with smoke belching out and with all eight of the aft 4.5in anti-aircraft guns knocked out with many of their crews being killed or wounded. A number of near misses had also caused substantial underwater damage and this, plus a direct hit in an aft steering compartment forced the crippled carrier to sail in circles until the rudder could finally be freed and centralised. The damage inflicted would have sunk most ships yet, despite being penetrated, the armoured flight deck had served its purpose and while the damage control parties fought desperately to fight the fires below, the captain decided to make for the relative safety of Grand Harbour 75 miles away. It was a journey in which, due to the damaged rudder, all manoeuvring would have to be achieved by using the ship's engines to vary the power applied to the propeller shafts and in which the ship would remain vulnerable to further attack throughout.

Following the Germans' departure, the three surviving Fulmars of the five that had been hurriedly ranged on deck during the *Stuka* attack were also ordered to Hal Far to join the four from the original CAP and to refuel and re-arm. However, when it came to turning the naval fighters around quickly to allow them to head back to sea and protect their ship there were problems. The ground personnel at Hal Far had hardly any experience of working on the Fulmar as only a few of the type had visited in the past and because they lacked the specialist tools which were needed for loading and cocking the guns it took over an hour to make just one aircraft ready. Due to this delay the Fulmars

Seen carrying their characteristic long-range drop tanks, two Junkers Ju 87R-2s from 2/StG 3 fly over Trapani, Sicily, during May 1941 following a raid against Malta. The nearest *Stuka* wears the code 'S1+HK' and has a blue spinner-tip but no white theatre markings, while the other, 'S1+AK', has an additional white band on the spinner signifying a *Staffelkapitan*'s aircraft and it does have a white fuselage band. Both are finished in the standard Luftwaffe camouflage scheme consisting of: RLM 70 *Schwarzgrun* (Black Green), 71 *Dunkelgrun* (Dark Green) and 65 *Hellblau* (Light Blue). A colour illustration of S1+HK appears on page 146. EN Archive Collection

were unable to oppose a further attack against *Illustrious* by seven level-bombing SM.79s and three Italian Ju 87R *Picchiatelli* from 236ª *Squadriglia*, 96° *Gruppo*, led by *Tenente* Malvezzi. Luckily no further hits were scored thanks to an impressive anti-aircraft barrage, despite Italian claims to the contrary that they had sunk the carrier! The Fulmars were also unable to prevent a later attack by 13 *Luftwaffe* Ju 87Rs which scored another serious hit on *Illustrious* and which slowed the carrier down from 24 to just 15 knots. They did however arrive overhead at 16:50hrs just as this last attack was coming to an end and, in diving down to attack them, the Fulmars' claimed two *Stukas* shot down and left others limping back to Sicily damaged – including one which had been hit by S/Lt Stan Orr. Due to this latest bomb hit (which had entered via the open after lift) it was almost dark before the sanctuary of Grand Harbour finally hove into sight at which point another torpedo attack was made by Italian SM.79sil, although thankfully their torpedoes missed.

Amid all this, Italian fighters had mounted a number of sweeps over Malta to keep 261 Squadron's Hurricanes engaged all afternoon, a few of which were claimed by the RAF pilots. Later, during the night, the Royal Navy hit back at the Axis when it despatched ten 830 NAS Swordfish from Hal Far to bomb Palermo harbour, the Squadron having benefited by the welcome addition of several Swordfish that had been airborne when *Illustrious* was attacked and which in consequence made for Malta to become an unintended inclusion to the ranks of 830 NAS.

SAFETY OF A SORT: THE *ILLUSTRIOUS BLITZ*

At 21:00hrs HMS *Illustrious* finally limped into Grand Harbour smoking, listing, and with her stern low in the water to berth at Parlatorio Wharf in French Creek on the opposite side of the harbour from Valletta, where the modern Number 6 Dock can today be found. Of her crew, 126 were killed in the attacks whose remains were retrieved and transferred to a destroyer for burial at sea, while 91 others who had been injured were taken ashore for treatment at the Mtarfa Military Hospital. Even as this gruesome task was being conducted by other members of her crew, Maltese dockyard workers swarmed aboard to begin patching up the battered vessel in order to make her sufficiently seaworthy to sail for Alexandria where more substantial repairs could be made in relative safety. Everyone knew that the newly arrived *Luftwaffe* would undoubtedly unleash its bombers in an all-out attempt to finish the carrier as she lay at her moorings – so the work had to be done quickly and would continue around the clock for days to come. In an attempt to dissuade dive-bombers from pushing their attacks down to almost deck-level, as they had done at sea, the largest floating crane in the dockyard, Admiralty Crane Lighter *CL.IV* (known for obvious reasons as 'CLIVE'), was brought alongside *Illustrious* and its jib was swung protectively over the carrier's deck to provide an added deterrence. A more conventional method of overhead protection however, was the provision of a large 'box barrage' consisting of as many anti-aircraft guns as could be mustered. The guns were assembled around the area of Grand Harbour, mostly using mobile batteries equipped with the ubiquitous 40mm Bofors gun backed up by larger calibre weapons that were already in situ, plus those mounted aboard the vessels in Grand Harbour itself. HMS *Illustrious* alone was fitted with eight, twin-barrelled 4.5in gun mountings, plus four surviving eight-barrelled pom-pom mounts (at least two others having been damaged during the air attacks) and could therefore add substantially to a barrage. Any aircraft attacking *Illustrious* would have to fly through a veritable 'blanket of steel', while her surviving Fulmars at Hal Far would supplement the Hurricanes of 261 Squadron.

In summary, those Fulmars and crewmembers involved in the actions of 10th January 1941 are given below. Those marked * subsequently landed at Hal Far airfield.

Morning CAP
First section.
'6K'* N1884, S/Lt Stan Orr, L/Air Douet
'6Y'* S/Lt Hogg, L/Air Oakes

Second section
'6F'* Lt Robert Henley, Midshipman Cullen
'6H'* N1881, S/Lt Griffith, L/Air Stevens
'6Q' S/Lt Jackie Sewell, L/Air Dennis Tribe

(Sewell returned to *Illustrious* after receiving damage to his aircraft while on CAP duty. He and Tribe were launched again during the subsequent dive-bombing attack.)

Scrambled from *Illustrious*
First section scrambled
'6Q'* (**or** N1860 '6M') S/Lt Jackie Sewell,
    L/Air Dennis Tribe
'6Z' N1935, (shot down) S/Lt Lowe (wounded),
    L/Air Kensett (killed)

Second section
'6A'* Lt Bill Barnes, Lt Vincent-Jones (acting CO)
'6G' Failed to start, (destroyed by bomb while on lift).
    S/Lt Marshall (killed), PO Tallick (killed)
'6C'* S/Lt Roberts and crewman.

Note: In the weeks ahead, many of the Fulmar aircrews were swapped around and flew in whichever one was available and, for a time, they were supposed to have been flown without an occupant in the rear seat.

In addition to the known identities of Fulmars N1881 and N1884, it is possible that two of the otherwise unidentified Fulmars by now located at Hal Far could have been N1857 and N1865, as both are believed to have been present during this period.

On paper at least, a defending force of 14 Hurricanes and at least seven Fulmars seemed to be a substantial number of fighters for Malta, though in fact several of the Hurricanes were unserviceable due to an ongoing lack of spares while some of the Fulmars required repairs to battle damage before they became fully airworthy once more. The 13 crated Hurricanes delivered by SS *Essex*, (believed to have been Hurricane Is: V7072, V7101, V7102, V7114 to V7117, V7121, V7545, V7546, V7670, V7671 and V7672) would take some time to assemble and would not be available straight away; while the arrival of the Fleet Air Arm pilots allowed the four surviving Sea Gladiators from 261 Squadron (now mostly used for meteorological work), to be returned to naval control for use by 806 NAS.

The four Sea Gladiators were the last serviceable examples of those which had famously been found in crates at Kalafrana seaplane base before the start of the war with Italy. As related previously, the ever-resourceful Command Engineering Officer, S/Ldr Louks did all in his power to improve the Sea Gladiators' performance having fitted them with metal DH three-bladed, variable-pitch airscrews in 1940. Louks also experimented with different fuel octane mixes, enhanced armament (described later) and, in order to further increase the climb performance of the biplanes he also 'tweaked' the new propellers by slightly altering the pitch of their blades. As with the Hurricanes to which Louks also applied this last measure, the change of pitch came at a price: a greater take-off run – though the improvement in climb performance was worth it.

In order to service the Fulmars and Sea Gladiators of 806 NAS at Hal Far, fifty or so maintainers who survived the bombing of *Illustrious* were taken ashore with whatever equipment could be salvaged from the devastated hangar deck, several of whom later joined 830 NAS. Some sources state that a serviceable Fulmar was also retrieved and wheeled to Hal Far too, but this cannot be confirmed though, if it were true and if S/Lt Sewell had flown his damaged Fulmar '6Q' during his second sortie of 10th January, then the extra Fulmar could have been N1860 '6M', as this aircraft was almost certainly used by 806 NAS in Malta. There was also a damaged 806 NAS Fulmar already at Hal Far which had been there since 2nd September when Sewell had landed with a badly damaged engine and with his crewman, Dennis Tribe, wounded. If this aircraft had been repairable it may have resulted in nine available Fulmars, but firmly establishing a precise quantity remains elusive.

Just 60 miles away in Sicily, the Germans and Italians were assembling an armada of over 200 aircraft which were expected over Malta at any time in order to finish off the carrier. However, instead of fierce air battles overhead, the next few days were an anticlimax with hardly any enemy activity over Malta at all apart from the occasional high-altitude reconnaissance aircraft snooping overhead. Sergeant Bill Timms was sent up from Takali in Hurricane N2622 to intercept one of these reconnaissance aircraft on 11th January 1941, but his engine over revved and blew up at over 20,000 feet. This may have been as a result of hypoxia caused by faulty or frozen oxygen equipment which would have rendered the pilot unconscious, or unable to manually control his throttle and propeller settings. In diving towards the ground with a wrecked engine, the aircraft was seen to gain a measure of control after reaching a lower altitude suggesting that Timms might by then have regained consciousness, but, while trying to glide into Luqa as he had done in similar circumstances only recently, he presumably realised that he would not make it and turned the aircraft onto its back and bailed out over Siggiewi. Unfortunately the red-nosed Hurricane, which had arrived as part of 418 Flight (possibly coded 'B'), was too low – Timm's parachute failed to open in time and he was killed; his aircraft crashed four miles north-west of Luqa airfield.

In Malta full advantage of the unexpected lull was taken to ready the defences whereby the Fulmars usual naval radio fit of a T1115/R1116 W/T Morse set and a H/F TR9D R/T set were replaced by a more up-to-date RAF type TR.1133 VHF voice set allowing naval pilots to talk directly to the RAF fighter controllers in the Lascaris operations room. Another adaptation made to the Fulmar was to improve the pilot's rear view by removing wing mirrors from a number of lorries in the Hal Far Motor Transport pool and re-fitting them on top of the Fulmar's windscreen. Yet another attempt at improving its performance was via an official order to save weight by leaving the rear cockpit empty as the TAG or observer would not be needed on such short-range missions – which would help improve its poor rate of climb; however, the bond between pilot and observer was especially strong in 806 NAS and this order was often ignored as pilots felt more comfortable with their crewmen aboard.

The lull in action over Malta was caused by the continued build-up of *Fliegerkorps* X in Sicily as sufficient stocks of spares and munitions had still to arrive, as too had many of its aircraft with stragglers scattered the entire length of Italy. British signals intelligence including *Ultra* decrypts from Bletchley Park were following the movement of aircraft south and knew that at least some of these were located at Reggio nell Emilia, Pisa and Naples. Those aircraft which were available for use in Sicily had all been sent to search for the *Excess* convoy before it sailed out of range towards Greece, most particularly they were looking for the remaining ships of the British Mediterranean Fleet which were providing escort, including the battleships *Warspite* and *Valiant*. Although the *Luftwaffe* failed to find the capital ships, a formation of 12 Ju 87Rs from II/StG 2, led by a single Heinkel He 111 navigational aircraft, used their longer range to good advantage by finding slow convoy M.S.6 at the limit of their endurance as the ships headed for Alexandria and bombed the escorting cruisers *Gloucester* and *Southampton*. The attack took the convoy totally by surprise as they had presumed they were out of range of an air attack in which *Gloucester* was hit by a bomb that failed to explode, while *Southampton* was hit three times with damage so extensive that she had to be scuttled by torpedoes fired from the cruiser HMS *Orion*.

In an attempt to disrupt the continued build-up of aircraft in Sicily, ten Wellington from 148 Squadron at Luqa bombed Catania airfield on the night of 12th January 1941 and destroyed two Ju 88s from III/LG 1, two Ju 52/3m transports, an SM.79 and a Caproni Ca.133 as well as damaging six He 111Ps and eleven MC.200s.

THE *BLITZ* BEGINS IN EARNEST

On the same day that *Illustrious* was bombed, Malta's 431 (General Reconnaissance) Flight became 69 Squadron with an 'official' establishment of 12 Maryland Is and 12 Beauforts; however, the latter failed to materialise as they were in extremely short supply and those which were available were needed to equip torpedo bomber squadrons forming in the UK. The supply of Marylands was little better and the unit was always under strength, yet, following their successful contribution to the Taranto strike, the workload of the reconnaissance unit had increased tenfold with their services now being much sought after. Such Marylands as were available continually monitored the German build-up in Sicily as the main body of *Fliegerkorps* X continued to arrive, though for less demanding reconnaissance duties a few Blenheims that had been transiting through Malta were also pressed into service with the new unit.

For Malta the lull in enemy activity finally ended on 13th January 1941, thereafter, the period of Maltese history which will be forever remembered as the *Illustrious Blitz* began in earnest. Axis forces commenced the day with a raid by Ju 87Rs from I/StG 1 which dived upon the aircraft carrier to drop 1,000kg bombs from their ventral crutches and, although many of these weapons exploded harmlessly

Never previously published, Luftwaffe ground crew wearing greatcoats and woolly hats, push a Ju 87R-2 Stuka out of the hangar on a cold Sicilian winter morning ready for a strike against Malta. It has its long-range drop tanks in place, though they were hardly needed for the short hop to Malta. The rear gun has yet to be brought from the armoury to be fitted by the rear gunner who also doubled as a radio operator. James Payne

in Grand Harbour, the remainder fell onto the three medieval cities of Senglea, Vittoriosa and Conspicua which surround French Creek where *Illustrious* was berthed. The Germans caused widespread damage and civilian casualties were very high, though despite becoming airborne from Hal Far within two-and-a-half minutes of receiving the alarm, the Fulmars of 806 NAS saw nothing of the enemy and they remained on patrol over Grand Harbour for an hour before returning to Hal Far.

On 15th January the Ju 88s of II/LG 1 arrived at Catania and that evening 16 of them carried out the unit's first raid against Malta, but Grand Harbour was obscured by cloud and they failed to register any hits. At the same time Malta's Wellingtons repaid the complement to Sicily by bombing Catania airfield and were rather more successful, leaving four enemy aircraft destroyed on the ground plus human casualties that included two Ju 88 pilots killed and eight other personnel wounded. On the morning of January 16th, 17 Ju 88s from II and III/LG 1, escorted by 20 Bf 110s from III/ZG 26, swept in over Grand Harbour and recorded two near misses alongside *Illustrious* which exploded between the carrier and the dockside. As with most near misses of this nature they caused further underwater damage to both the keel and hull that had already sustained severe damage to a 100 ft long section of its port side below the armour belt. Additionally, the port bilge was described as hanging down like a 'kippers backbone'. Yet, even while the bombing took place, naval divers were busy in the water beneath the carrier making repairs at terrible risk to themselves from the concussive effect of underwater shockwaves while the dive-leader bobbed alongside in his small wooden rowing boat.

The Ju 88s were followed almost immediately by 44 Ju 87Rs which dove upon *Illustrious* while their escort of ten Italian MC.200s and ten CR.42 biplanes patrolled above, and although the *Stukas* scored two direct hits to cause further substantial damage, neither was as serious as those incurred at sea. Although *Illustrious* was the main target, other vessels in Grand Harbour also received unwanted attention including the submarine HMS *Upholder* (moored just 50 feet away), and the recently arrived merchantman SS *Essex* which received a direct hit that killed 18 members of her crew and seven Maltese stevedores in the hold. Although four Hurricanes and three Fulmars were scrambled to intercept the raids, only the Fulmar pilots managed an interception and claimed four Ju 88s from II/LG 1 destroyed with two more of each type probably so. Of these claims, S/Lt Orr and Lt Barnes each claimed a Ju 88, while S/Lt Hogg records in his personal diary that he and his crewman, L/Air Roberts 'shot down two Ju 88s before returning for ammunition.' Hogg was also responsible for one of the probables too. The anti-aircraft defences performed well, particularly in helping to disrupt the enemy attacks and by damaging a number of their aircraft. Although only one Ju 88 (L1+CT) flown by *Oblt* Kurt Pilcher from 9 *Staffel* was actually shot down, three other Ju 88s were so badly damaged that they were forced to crash-land on returning to Catania with dead or wounded crewmen aboard, while yet another crash-landed on the beach at Pozallo, Sicily, due to flak damage. To add insult to injury, two further Ju 88s were wrecked at Catania when an Italian aircraft ran into them on the ground.

After licking their wounds the attackers returned in force on the afternoon of Saturday 18th January with a preliminary attack against the airfields at Hal Far and Luqa by over 50 *Stukas* from I/StG 1 and II/StG 2 in an attempt to wipe out Malta's fighters on the ground so that future attacks upon Grand Harbour might go unmolested. However, they were met by five Hurricanes and four Fulmars. One *Stuka* was shot down by F/Lt George Burges, making him a confirmed 'ace', while an escorting MC.200 from 6° *Gruppo* was shot down into the sea, probably by S/Lt Arthur Griffith, although the identity of the victor cannot be confirmed for certain as Griffith's Fulmar failed to return having presumably been shot down too. The four Fulmars had initially intercepted a large formation of enemy aircraft further out to sea where the section leader, Lt Henley, shot down a Ju 88 which may have been L1+ER from III/LG 1 flown by *Leutnant* Horst Dunkel who was forced to ditch after reportedly being attacked by a Hurricane. Henley may also have shot down a *Stuka* in addition to damaging at least two other aircraft, but, as he prepared to attack another *Stuka* its rear gunner scored several hits on the Fulmar's engine causing it to stop dead. As N/Air AS Rush in the rear cockpit could not swim, Henley refrained from baling out over the open sea and instead attempted to glide back towards land. They made it to within a mile of Marsaxlokk Bay before they ran out of sky and Henley successfully ditched the Fulmar. Upon hitting the water a brave Maltese soldier named Sapper Spiro Zammit swam out to help the two crewmen to safety, which was just as well for Rush, and for his actions the Royal Engineer was awarded the British Empire Medal.

To demonstrate their determination to avenge the bombing of *Illustrious* another Fulmar, possibly flown by Jackie Sewell, was observed to follow hard-on-the-heels of a *Stuka* as it dived through the 'box' barrage over Grand Harbour during the same raid. As the bomber pulled out of its dive and flew at wave-top height across the harbour making for the perceived safety of the open sea, the Fulmar followed right behind and then shot it down when the *Stuka* was forced to climb to clear the harbour breakwater. Legend has it that after landing at Hal Far this same Fulmar pilot angrily telephoned the anti-aircraft desk at Lascaris HQ to express his unhappiness with the barrage due to the fact that the German had escaped it unscathed whilst his own aircraft was riddled with flak!

This, the heaviest raid that Malta had suffered to date, killed 57 civilians while hundreds more packed up their belongings and fled to the countryside. A total of seven Ju 87s and a Ju 88 were claimed as shot down with a further three *Stukas* and a Ju 88 damaged. Additionally, anti-aircraft gunners claimed three more enemy aircraft shot down too, however, as with most intense combat, the claims were inaccurate and the *Luftwaffe*'s losses were lighter than suggested. On the ground three Swordfish were destroyed at Hal Far and at Luqa a Wellington was burnt-out and a Hurricane seriously damaged; worse still, the hangars and runways at both locations were badly damaged too. Despite the devastation soldiers toiled to fill in the bomb craters while ground crews worked throughout the night to get as many fighter aircraft as possible patched and serviceable again ready for the morning. In the event they managed to prepare a small force of six Hurricanes, a Fulmar and a single Sea Gladiator, although by mid-afternoon the number of serviceable Fulmars had been increased to four.

Due to the damage inflicted upon the airfields, the Germans may have assumed the fighter menace had been quashed once and for all because on the following day, Sunday 19th, wave after wave of bombers were directed against *Illustrious* once more. The first raid of the day saw 40 *Stukas* and Ju 88s over Grand Harbour at 08:30 hrs to commence a relentless tempo of operations that continued throughout the day. Hurricane pilot Sgt Jim Pickering of 261 Squadron was one of those scrambled to intercept and he succeeded in damaging a Ju 88 and a *Stuka*. After landing to rearm and refuel, Pickering was sent straight off again and found an Italian Cant Z.506 floatplane circling off the coast with an escorting CR.42 and given that air-sea-rescue aircraft were considered fair game by the British (for reasons which will be explained later), he chased the floatplane away scoring some hits.

A Hurricane being re-assembled inside a hangar, possibly at Hal Far. Judging by the cleanliness of both the airframe and engine it is probable that it arrived in crated form such as those delivered by SS *Essex* as deck cargo on 10th January 1941. In that instance 13 Hurricane Is were received, the serial numbers of which are believed to have been: V7072, V7101, V7102, V7114 to V7117, V7121, V7545, V7546, V7670, V7671 and V7672). This aircraft's serial however remains unidentified. It has black-and-white undersides and a Sky fuselage band while the upper surfaces appear to be Dark Earth and Dark Green: all indicative of an early 1941 time frame. As mentioned previously, the Sky band was usually over-painted in Malta to avoid confusion with the white theatre bands worn by Axis aircraft and so serves to indicate that this is very probably a newly arrived airframe. Of interest is the stirrup behind the wing root seen in its lowered position, an action which automatically opened the handhold which is visible higher on the side of the fuselage.
Frederick Galea

The day's second raid arrived over *Illustrious* at 10:00hrs and comprised 20 *Stukas* escorted by 24 CR.42s. Defending fighters engaged once again, only landing to refuel and re arm and allow fresh pilots to take over where needed. During the morning George Burges in Hurricane P3730 shot down a pair of *Stukas* which both crashed into Grand Harbour. Later that day, while flying V7546, one of the crated Hurricanes delivered by SS *Essex*, he attacked a Ju 88 and set fire to one of its engines, however, return fire was accurate and a bullet pierced his canopy and hit him in the shoulder only to be deflected by the metal buckle of his parachute harness leaving him with just a bruise, albeit a big one. Sergeant Fred 'Jock' Robertson was busy on this day too. Starting at 10:00 hrs, he took-off in Hurricane V7474 with five others to intercept the second raid. By the time the British fighters reached them the dive-bombers were flying at 9,000 feet over Grand Harbour where Robertson shot one into the water as well as putting a good burst into the fuselage of a CR.42 as it attacked him head-on – which was claimed as probably destroyed, raising his tally to five kills and two 'probables' in return for which his Hurricane received a bullet through the wing. Changing aircraft to well-known Hurricane 'J', P3731, which had originally arrived with 418 Flight, 'Jock' Robertson and four other Hurricane pilots found another *Stuka* formation during his fourth sortie of the day. However, while chasing one of them over St Paul's Bay he was bounced by escorting CR.42s from 70ᵃ *Squadriglia* which led to a twisting dogfight in which he shot one of biplanes fighters down in flames and although its pilot, *Sergente Maggiorre* Ezio Iacone, was seen to bail out into the sea, he was never found despite a search. Robertson scored hits on another CR.42 which could be seen emitting smoke as it flew away but his Hurricane had also been hit a number of times in return, and a bullet was later found inside his parachute pack.

The Fulmar pilots were also busy this day, including Graham Hogg, who took-off in a solitary Fulmar at 13:15hrs to 'find scores of Ju 88s all round [me]' he 'attacked a formation of three, two went down in flames and one went on fire but did not go in. I attacked three more but with no results.' The star of the day however was F/Lt James MacLachlan of 261 Squadron who claimed four victories and became an 'ace'. His first two kills were *Stukas* which he shot down early in the morning when flying Hurricane V7546, but after his aircraft was hit in the wings and tail by a CR.42 he landed and switched to Hurricane V7545 to claim a controversial kill in the form of an air-sea-rescue Cant C.506B from 612ᵃ *Squadriglia* which wore Red Cross markings. (It should be explained that the RAF had refused to recognise the status of Red Cross-marked aircraft ever since similarly marked *Luftwaffe* floatplanes were reported to have abused their non-combatant status by radioing the locations of British shipping during the Battle of Britain.) MacLachlan recalled that 'at about 1,000 yards I opened fire. It was a huge three-engine job. I could hardly have missed if I tried. A sheet of flame burst from its starboard wing root, so I ceased fire. It didn't seem to be losing height, but instead flew calmly on with flames and smoke pouring from it. I gave it another short squirt but it was already doomed.' His last kill of the day was a Ju 88 from 8/LG 1 which crashed into the sea near Zonqor Point, Malta; only one of its crew members bailed out before it hit the water.

The tally of enemy aircraft claimed shot down during Sunday's battles totalled nine Ju 87s, two Ju 88s, one CR.42 and a Cant floatplane, all for the loss of a single Hurricane, P2629. The latter, flown by Sgt Eric Kilsey, was indeed shot down, though whether Kilsey fell to a Bf 110 from III/ZG 26 (flown by *Major* Karl Kaschka), or to one of four Italians who all claimed a Hurricane destroyed, or, that he fell foul of Grand Harbour's box barrage (into which he was last seen entering), has not been determined. Four other Hurricanes suffered varying degrees of battle damage during the day, two of which may account for some of the enemy claims. One of the Ju 88s lost was flown by *Hauptmann* Wilhelm Durbeck, the *Staffelkapitan* of 8/LG 1, whose aircraft suffered multiple hits and disintegrated when it dived through the barrage over *Illustrious*; while a third Ju 88 (from III/LG 1) was destroyed after it returned to Sicily with a burning engine to crash-land on the beach at Pozallo, which was by now beginning to acquire a number of wrecks as it was the nearest point

A view across Grand Harbour from Valletta showing *Illustrious* under attack in French Creek: even at this distance it is apparent that the carrier is down by the stern. 'Hovering' protectively above the ship's deck is the jib of Admiralty Crane Lighter *CL.IV* a massive floating crane referred to, unsurprisingly, as 'CLIVE'. It was brought alongside *Illustrious* to deter dive-bombers from pushing their attacks down to almost deck-level as they had done at sea. Most of Malta's anti-aircraft guns were redeployed to Grand Harbour, or its vicinity, in order to create a box barrage above the carrier through which all attacking aircraft, and many defending fighters had to fly. This image was taken from the vicinity of the World War One War Memorial at Floriana alongside the bus station outside the main gates of Valletta. Author's collection

of Sicily that aircraft returning from Malta could reach.

Despite the large number of raids *Illustrious* survived without receiving further hits, although the neighbouring three cities were less lucky as they received many of the bombs that had fallen wide of the mark. Even Valletta, on the other side of Grand Harbour, was badly hit. The events of Sunday 19th January had also witnessed the employment by the Germans of a very strange weapon: an experimental 'guided glider-bomb'. Obviously intended for *Illustrious*, it missed and demolished a convent in Vittoriosa instead. Despite the damage caused, the weapon had actually failed to explode so, after digging deep into the rubble to reach it the over-worked bomb disposal crews defused this odd weapon and sent it back to the UK for further examination. Might this have been an early prototype of the rocket-powered guided bombs which were used to such great effect by the Germans against Allied shipping at Salerno and other locations later in the war?

MALTA'S FIRST SPITFIRE: *ILLUSTRIOUS* LEAVES

On Malta's airfields the damage was just as extensive as it was in the cities with many of the hangars and buildings flattened while a number of aircraft which had been caught on the ground were either destroyed or seriously damaged. Nonetheless, the bomb craters were filled by gangs of soldiers using rubble from wrecked buildings and the runways were soon made serviceable again while essential buildings which had been destroyed were progressively replaced by tunnels excavated below ground level. During a brief lull in the day's fighting, a new shape appeared in the circuit above Takali – a Spitfire. This, the first of its type to arrive in Malta was not a fighter but a photo-reconnaissance Spitfire PR.ID, P9551, flown by F/Lt P Corbishley DFC from No.1 Photographic Reconnaissance Unit (PRU) based at RAF Benson, Oxfordshire. This unarmed long-range variant of the famous fighter had been flying a sortie from the UK to photograph Turin in northern Italy when a change in wind direction meant that Corbishley would have to face a headwind during his long return journey to the UK and, with fuel margins already minimal, he opted to continue to Malta and land there instead. Given its pair of vertically mounted F.24 cameras which were offset in an overlapping 'fan' in order to cover as wide an area as possible, high-altitude performance and 1,750 mile range, this new arrival was manna from heaven for Maynard (Malta's AOC), who sought to retain the Spitfire and its pilot for as long as possible before having to return them to the UK. Permission was granted for the aircraft and its pilot to conduct operations from Malta until weather conditions allowed a return flight to the UK, but unfortunately the Spitfire was lost to flak over Viareggio, Italy, on 2nd February 1941 during its second sortie from Malta and Corbishley was captured.

A Fulmar I of 806 NAS. Based at Hal Far, this unit remained in Malta following *Illustrious*'s departure for Alexandria, and remained throughout February 1941 until the arrival of Bf 109E-equipped 7/JG 26 made the skies over Malta far too dangerous for this two-seat fighter. The final straw for the unit came on 2nd March 1941 when three Fulmars were intercepted by Bf 109Es as they clawed for height over Hal Far to meet an incoming raid and were duly converted into flying colanders by the Germans; yet, by some miracle all three Fulmars and their crews returned safely. This unidentified Fulmar appears to be coded 'Z', has black paint applied beneath its lower left wing while the wing leading edges and spinner appear to be painted in a light brown colour prior to a mottle being applied in the Italian-style 'Spaghetti' scheme. Otherwise the airframe wears standard S.1.E. camouflage. *Author's collection*

Following the mauling both sides inflicted upon each other during the raids of the previous day, the 20th dawned quietly as poor weather brought a calm to the fighting while the combatants regrouped. This though did not prevent 148 Squadron Wellingtons from 'visiting' Sicily during the night to bomb Catania once again, the increasing regularity of which caused Catania-based Ju 88s to habitually take off at last light and fly to Reggio di Calabria on the Italian mainland in order to avoid any further attention from the nocturnal 'Wimpeys'.

Only a few daytime reconnaissance sorties and sporadic night raids occurred over the next few days, during which time the pilots of 806 NAS took the opportunity to visit Takali and learn how to fly Hurricanes with 261 Squadron. Sub Lieutenant Hogg recorded a 30-minute flight in a Hurricane on the afternoon of the 20th having learned the cockpit procedure during the morning, but, by the 22nd he was back at Hal Far flying a Sea Gladiator. This lull could have been caused by rumours which were circulating that *Illustrious* had actually been sunk and now sat on the bottom of French Creek in shallow water. Nothing could be further from the truth however as the work on her was completed by 23rd January 1941 and, as night began to fall, the battered carrier raised steam and slipped out of Grand Harbour at 18:00hrs heading for Alexandria, with a number of Maltese dockyard workers still on board and scaffolding still attached to the side of the hull. There had not even been time to completely cast off before sailing and mooring ropes were snapped as *Illustrious* pulled away from Parlatorio Wharf. After reaching Alexandria for further repairs the carrier sailed via the Suez Canal and South Africa to the USA for an extensive rebuild at Norfolk, Virginia, that would take the best part of a year to complete. During that time, the remains of some of the men who had been killed during the *Stuka* attack on 10th January were discovered amid the wreckage below decks – such was the devastation wreaked upon certain parts of the ship. Also aboard when she sailed from Malta were some of the aircrew and ground crew of 806 NAS who were to re-build the squadron in Egypt and receive new Fulmars prior to joining *Illustrious*' sister ship, the new armoured carrier HMS *Formidable*. Upon arrival at Dekheila however, some of these survivors were detached to 805 NAS at Maleme in Crete to participate in the fighting around Greece and Crete, while a third detachment of 806 NAS remained in Malta to continue operating the four surviving Fulmars at Hal Far. In typical naval fashion therefore, elements of the same unit were flying in three widely separated locations at the same time between January and March 1941.

This then was the end of the *Illustrious Blitz*, the carrier had survived to fight another day, albeit at a high price to the people and defenders of Malta. During the twelve-day blitz, the combined defences of Malta had claimed over 40 enemy aircraft destroyed with many more damaged, although the primary role of the defenders had less to do with their individual scores than to disrupt the enemy and spoil his intended aim literally. In this the defenders succeeded. The historic medieval cities of Senglea, Vittoriosa and Conspicua surrounding French Creek were almost levelled by bombing, while Valletta was heavily hit too, as also were the villages and towns bordering the three airfields. Over 2,000 civilian buildings were destroyed or damaged during this period and 60,000 people left the cities for the countryside with 11,000 leaving Valletta alone. This latter figure was around two thirds of the capital's population; a population deeply angered by the damage inflicted upon their city and whose feelings were summed up by a message scrawled across a plank on the window of a boarded up shop which read 'We will endure anything except the rule of these barbarous savages.' The message was directed towards the Italians who the Maltese have always blamed for the devastation inflicted upon their island during the war, whereas most of the damage was actually caused by the Germans who the Maltese maintain were acting at the behest of the Italians.

During a Meteorological flight on the morning of 24th January, S/Lt Jackie Sewell was flying a Sea Gladiator when he was attacked while climbing over Hal Far airfield by a lone Ju 88, thought to be L1+HM from 4/LG 1 flown by *Unteroffizier* Gustav Ulrich. Using the outstanding manoeuvrability of the biplane to his advantage, Sewell, who had previously flown the type aboard *Illustrious*, was able to rapidly turn the tables on his attacker which he then shot down into the sea off Filfla Island, the uninhabited rock off the coast near to Hal Far which was used as a bombing target in peacetime. The same rock was also the point where friendly aircraft approaching Malta were supposed to orbit before being cleared to land. One of the many people who witnessed Sewell's accomplishment from the ground was Lt Vincent-Jones who was at Hal Far at the time and is reported to have said in relation to the Sea Gladiator 'from the ground it resembled a terrier yapping at the heels of a mastiff.' On the same day a pair of Fulmars were airborne, possibly conducting an air-sea-rescue search, when they came across an Italian Cant Z.506B performing the same task and shot it down into the sea.

After sneaking out of Grand Harbour under the cover of darkness on the 23rd January 1941 HMS *Illustrious* left Malta for Alexandria to have further repairs carried out, but the damage was so extensive that the carrier had to sail to Norfolk, Virginia, USA for a major refit which lasted over a year. This view shows *Illustrious* leaving Alexandria on 10th March 1941 wearing new Paint but with the damaged quarterdeck plated over and the S2 Pom Pom anti-aircraft gun mounting removed. The new paint could not hide the devastation below decks however which was so bad in certain areas that the remains of men killed during the *Stuka* attack of 10th January 1941 were still being found by dockworkers in the USA as they removed debris. Ian Gazeley

Above: Just good friends! An Italian SM.79 has taxied into the back of a Ju 88A-5 from LG 1 at Catania in Sicily, breaking the back of the German aircraft in the process. Italian official image

Below: As they settled in to their Mediterranean surroundings LG 1's Ju 88s gradually adopted a more suitable camouflage scheme. This Ju 88, seen at Gela, Sicily, has a locally applied camouflage that used either German-manufactured paints RLM 79 *Sandgelb* (Sand Yellow) with RLM 80 *Olivgrun* (Olive Green) mottling and RLM 65 *Hellblau* undersides), or, most likely, similar Italian paints. The spinners appear to be painted in RLM 70 *Schwarzgrun* with white segments while the nose bears the unit's red Griffin in a white crest. Significantly, a forward firing MG FF 20mm cannon has been mounted in the nose-glazing and not the *Lofte* bombsight, the window for which has been blanked off. For low-level attacks the cannon proved very effective, particularly against shipping and is supplemented here with a cockpit-mounted 7.92mm MG81 mg. Frederick Galea

Above: Two Messerschmitt Bf 110D-3s from 9/ZG 26 in Sicily equipped with extended tail housings (for a dinghy) and 900-litre external drop tanks. The nearest aircraft has *Werk Nummer* 3406 in small white characters on the rear fuselage plus the cockerel marking of 9 *Staffel* and the ladybird insignia of ZG 26 on its yellow-painted nose. They are probably engaged on convoy escort duties on this occasion, however Sicilian based Bf 110s also flew bomber escort sorties over Malta as well as low-level fighter-bomber attacks against Maltese airfields. A colour illustration of this aircraft appears on page 156. EN Archive Collection

Below: A Messerschmitt Bf 110E-3 from III/ZG 26 being inspected inside a Sicilian hangar. It may be a new arrival as the 7 *Staffel* unit badge has not yet been finished and still requires the red quarters to be added to the black shield. Author via internet: www.military-aircraft.photos.com

Due to serviceability problems caused mainly by a lack of spares, there were periods when no Hurricanes were available, as was the case for much of the 26th. On such occasions the pilots of 806 NAS often stepped into the breach and, buoyed by their recent successes, two Fulmars and three Sea Gladiators were scrambled to intercept an incoming raid, although, as they climbed to intercept, the entire enemy formation turned around and headed back to Sicily before any contact was made. There was no explanation for the sudden *volte-face*, though in an inter-service dig at their RAF comrades the Navy men joked that the bombers must have been secretly tipped off about facing the Senior Service and fled in terror! Late in the day a pair of Hurricanes became available to intercept a sole reconnaissance Ju 88D, coded 7A+DH, from 1.(F)/121 flown by *Leutnant* Helmut Fund which was intercepted and shot down high over Malta. On the 27th, both 830 and 806 NAS, operating Swordfish and Fulmars respectively,

Above: Messerschmitt Bf 110D-3, 3U+ET from 9/ZG 26 in Sicily. The ZG 26 codes 3U have been applied over those of a previous unit and its individual code letter 'E' is in yellow outlined in black. Visible in this image is the fairing added to the D3's rear-fuselage extremity containing a dinghy for the crew on their long over-water flights. Also apparent is the pod fitted to the lower fuselage, aft of wing trailing edge, containing an extra 75 litres of oil, vital when carrying additional fuel in long-range tanks as seen fitted here. Mark Proulx

Below: Seen on a Sicilian airfield in 1941, this Bf 110E-3 from III/ZG 26 wears the cockerel emblem of this *Gruppe*'s 9 *Staffel* on its nose and belongs to *Major* Schulze-Dickow, *Kommandeur* of III *Gruppe* whose chevron insignia appears behind the cockerel. Seen from this aspect the massive proportions of a 900-litre drop tank becomes readily apparent. The code 'A' beneath the wing also appears in yellow on the fuselage. Frederick Galea

combined to conduct a daylight attack on an Axis convoy consisting of three escorted German freighters – an operation quite out of the ordinary for the usually nocturnal Swordfish crews. To carry out this strike six of the Swordfish were armed with torpedoes, one carried bombs and two Fulmars, flown by Lt Henley and S/Lt Orr, provided fighter escort. After searching for two hours the convoy was successfully located and attacked by the Swordfish which sank one of the ships and left another in flames while the Fulmars strafed the vessels in an attempt to suppress anti-aircraft fire. All aircraft returned safely. Throughout January, 830 NAS had continued to attack land targets and shipping by night but their losses were heavy, both operationally and as a result of the increasingly heavy bombing raids against Hal Far. A number of sorties were flown against the Axis supply port of Tripoli in Libya, bombing ships and installations and also mining the harbour entrance. To allow them to fly so far, the Swordfish had a long-range fuel tank mounted in the observer's position, reducing the crew from three to two with either an observer or TAG carried in the rear gunners cockpit. Without these tanks the Swordfish were unable to reach the Axis shipping lanes either, and so they had become a standard fit ever since they were delivered from *Illustrious* during September 1940.

THE SURVIVING SEA GLADIATORS

Soon after 806 NAS took charge of the four surviving Sea Gladiators (N5520, N5524, N5529 and N5531), at least three of them (N5520, N5524 and N5529) received a new camouflage finish which covered the Sky Grey-painted sides of the earlier naval S.1.E. Scheme. Using newly discovered photographs some enthusiasts have surmised that they were re-painted in Dark Earth and Dark Green in order to match the majority of Malta's Hurricanes, but, as they had been returned to naval ownership this argument does not appear to be logical. The ready availability of Temperate Sea Scheme aircraft paints and dopes at Kalafrana and the fact that the Sea Gladiators already wore naval colours would make it highly likely that the latter colours were used instead. Additionally, Hurricane pilot, F/Lt Jay MacLachlan, remarked in his diary entry of 19th January 1941, after having seen the Sea Gladiators at Hal Far a few days earlier, that they 'look very spick-and-span in their new Navy camouflage.' This seems to indicate that the new colours were simply the existing Extra Dark Sea Grey and Dark Slate Gray colours from the upper surfaces which had been extended down the sides of the fuselage, a modification which also applied to other Sea Gladiators serving in the UK and North Africa around this time. If this was the case then the top surface of the lower wings would most likely have remained in the shadow-shaded Dark Sea Grey and Light Slate Grey colours if the fabric covering was retained; what is known for certain however, is that the underneath of the upper wings retained the same Sky Grey colour as before and the bottom of the lower wings and fuselage were still half black and half white.

During the *Illustrious Blitz* naval pilots flew the Sea Gladiators in the fighter role alongside both Hurricanes and Fulmars and MacLachlan records that one of them scored a kill on 19th January 1941. Generally the biplanes were often held in reserve where possible although they did continue to fly daily early morning meteorological flights. In early 1941 the Sea Gladiators were damaged on the ground by bombing, however, unconfirmed reports state that they were also damaged during aerial combat too – and the *Luftwaffe* did report shooting down two Gladiators over Malta in 1941, though they might just as easily have been misidentified Swordfish. While undergoing repair the opportunity was taken to improve the firepower of at least two of the damaged fighters by adding two further .303mgs. One of the modified biplanes was N5531 which was referred to as 'Hope' by some and by others as 'The Battleship' because of its experimental six-gun armament for which a factory manufactured provision did actually exist enabling an extra pair of guns to be fitted under the upper mainplane if required, in an identical manner to those on the lower wings, by enclosing them in blisters. The additional firepower came at a price though, as flight trials in the UK had already indicated that the weight and drag penalty involved caused a drop in maximum speed to around 200mph. But, before it could be flown operationally in its new configuration, N5531 was destroyed inside a hangar at Hal Far during a bombing raid on 4th February 1941. According to Australian Hurricane pilot John Pain: 'Hope [N5531] which was in the throes of becoming a six-gun Gladiator received a bomb smack through the centre section and that was the finish of her.' Fleet Air Arm fitter, Ted Whitley, from 830 NAS worked on this aircraft and recalled: 'When I went to Malta from HMS *Illustrious* in January 41, a Gladiator was being fitted with two extra guns under the top mainplane...we worked on this between looking after 830 Squadron's Swordfish. Alas before it flew, along came the *Stukas*. No Glad, no hanger, no offices, no billets. I don't know if it was one of the famous three.'

The other six-gun Sea Gladiator has been variously quoted over the years as being the 'Bleriator', 'Bloodiator' and 'Bleareator' (the serial number for which remains unconfirmed) an aircraft which in addition to the fitting of extra weapons also received significant modifications to its powerplant as related in the photograph caption for 'The Bleriator' (a contraction of Blenheim and Sea Gladiator) in Chapter 2. It would seem that this aircraft was destroyed by bombing at Hal Far in March 1941 and that it flew at least once in its six-gun configuration.

AFTER *ILLUSTRIOUS*: THE ONSLAUGHT CONTINUES

Following the departure of *Illustrious*, small scale incursions by Italian and German reconnaissance aircraft continued over Malta, with a few small bombing raids usually at dusk. On 29th January 1941, six Hurricane Is flew in from Egypt as reinforcements led by a Wellington which was carrying the fighters' machine-guns plus three more pilots. The fighters had arrived in Egypt via the recently established Takoradi Route, having flown across Africa from Takoradi on the Gold Coast. For their final hop to Malta, each Hurricane retained its long-range tanks (which they had carried throughout their long journey) while the ammunition boxes in their wings were left empty to reduce the weight of the aircraft during the long over-sea crossing. As they approached Malta there was a raid in progress with a large force of Italian MC.200s blocking their way, however, fuel was by now critical and they had to land soon. Their only choice therefore was to deliver a series of feint attacks on the Italian fighters to try and drive them off, temporarily at least, which thankfully worked enabling the Hurricanes and Wellington to land safely. The six Hurricanes joined 261 Squadron to supplement the 13 crated Hurricanes which had arrived via SS *Essex*, to which HQ Middle East also offered to send additional aircraft; namely seven Fulmars and ten Brewster Buffaloes. All were politely declined.

An offer of another four experienced fighter pilots from Egypt on the other hand was another matter; they were eagerly accepted and resulted in the arrival, by Sunderland, at Kalafrana of Pilot Officers Worrall, Wyatt-Smith, Walsh and Currie. Additionally, another Sunderland brought a further six experienced Hurricane pilots to Malta, namely F/Lt Peacock-Edwards (an ex-Fairey Battle pilot who had flown fighters in the Battle of Britain); P/O Rippon; P/O Counter; and Sgts Davies, Todd and Dexter. With the ten new arrivals, George Burges, one of the Hal Far originals and an ace despite never having been trained as a fighter pilot, decided that it was time to leave fighters and return to his usual 'trade' as a qualified general reconnaissance pilot by transferring to 69 Squadron to fly Marylands. He continued to fly Marylands from the island as well as some high-altitude operations in a specially converted Hurricane until 5th June 1941 when he was posted home to the UK as a Squadron Leader within No.44 (Ferry) Group.

All of these changes and additions to the fighter force meant that there were 28 Hurricanes, three Fulmars and four Sea Gladiators nominally available by February 1941, although their exact numbers would vary day-by-day depending on serviceability. This was the largest fighter force that Malta had had to date and confidence was growing, yet the months ahead would prove to be one of the bleakest periods of the entire war for Malta's fighter pilots!

7/JG 26: THE MUNCHEBERG MENACE ARRIVES

Following their mauling at the hands of British fighters over Malta during the *Illustrious Blitz*, the Germans decided to deploy some of their own fighters to Sicily during February that would in turn present the defenders of Malta with a significant problem: namely, *Oberleutnant* Joachim Muncheberg and his elite 7/JG 26 equipped (predominantly) with the Bf 109E-7, a formidable aeroplane. Although 7/JG 26 never had more than 14 Bf 109Es on strength, usually with just eight available at any one time, every one of its pilots was a highly skilled Battle of Britain veteran, while Muncheberg himself was one of Germany's top aces who had already scored 23 victories against British, French and Polish opponents. All of their Bf 109Es were distinctively painted with yellow nose cowlings upon which was emblazoned the 7 *Staffel* insignia of a red heart, whilst the *Jagdgeschwader* 26 (JG 26) badge, consisting of the letter 'S' within a white shield, was positioned further aft underneath the windscreen. The later arrival of this small unit would ensure that the days of the Sea Gladiator and Fulmar as front-line fighters over Malta were all but over, while the Hurricanes would be severely stretched.

The first enemy aerial incursions of any significance following the departure of *Illustrious* occurred on 1st February 1941 was a morning reconnaissance flight by a single SM.79 from 193ª *Squadriglia* based at Sciacca, escorted by four CR.42s from 156° *Gruppo*. They were intercepted at 11:40hrs by three 261 Squadron Hurricanes flown by F/O Whittingham and Sgts Fred Robertson and Davies. The SM.79 was badly damaged by Robertson who riddled it, creating over one hundred bullet holes, to leave it with one engine stopped and two crew members wounded, although he then had to pull away and allow it to return to Sicily when the Italian fighters set upon him. In managing to avoid their first attack, Robertson turned the tables on the CR.42s and claimed one of the agile biplanes destroyed after his burst of fire raked the Italian's fuselage and probably killed the pilot as the CR.42 went into a spin from which it didn't recover and crashed into the sea. The other two Hurricanes engaged the fighters and Whittingham also claimed a CR.42 destroyed although 156° *Gruppo* only admitted to losing a single CR.42 whose pilot was killed. At dusk a large force of Ju 88s from LG 1, with a heavy fighter escort, bombed Luqa airfield and were intercepted by Hurricanes which claimed two of the bombers destroyed, one of which was last seen diving in flames towards cloud over Gozo. In fact all of the Ju 88s returned to Sicily although an aircraft from 6/LG 1 was so badly damaged that it crash-landed upon returning and was written off; perhaps this had been the aircraft seen in flames near Gozo.

On 2nd February, PR Spitfire PR.ID, P9551, which it will be recalled was on loan from No.1 PRU until it could return to the UK, was sent on its second sortie from Malta to photograph the Italian shipbuilding port of Viareggio in Tuscany. However, as related, it was shot down by flak and its pilot captured. There were no raids against Malta on this day but the Germans made up for it on 4th February when three large raids were mounted by over a hundred Ju 88s which tried to obliterate the airfields at Hal Far and Luqa once more, as well as Kalafrana. The bombers left buildings shattered, taxiways and runways cratered with a Swordfish and the six-gun Sea Gladiator N5531 being destroyed on the ground. Opposing the bombers were eight Hurricanes and two Fulmars that accounted for two Ju 88s, one of which was shared between S/Lt Stan Orr and wingman S/Lt Roberts. By now the Fulmars were regularly flying with a crewmember aboard once more and Stan Orr's 'passenger' during this combat was the acting CO of 806 NAS, Lt Desmond Vincent-Jones, who, being in the bath when the scramble came, swiftly dressed and took-off without the benefit of a parachute or Mae West life jacket and dressed only in his trousers, uniform jacket, flying helmet and a towel!

As well as operating against Malta, German units in Sicily were venturing as far as the North African coastline in an attempt to help stem the British advance towards El Agheila and Tripoli itself. An 'own goal' was scored off Tripoli when a Fiat G.50 fighter of 378ª *Squadriglia* flown by *Tenente* Galbiati, who was carrying out a standing patrol above the Libyan capital, came across an unfamiliar aircraft which he thought was a British Blenheim and, only after firing his first burst, did he realised that it was a German aircraft. It was in fact a Ju 88D reconnaissance aircraft from 1(F)/121 which, despite the damage inflicted, was still able to return to its base in Sicily although one of its gunners was seriously wounded. That night German He 111s from Sicily dropped mines at the entrance to Tobruk harbour while others carried out a bombing raid on the port to provide a distraction; the mines subsequently claiming a number of Allied vessels supplying the garrison stationed there.

Due to the increased strength of the fighter force in Malta, the *Luftwaffe* had reverted to flying night raids over the island just as the Italians had done only a few months earlier. Most of the Hurricane pilots who were on duty facing these raids flew 3 or 4 sorties per night working in close co-operation with Army searchlight units which on the night of 8th/9th February bore fruit when F/Lt MacLachlan added two more aircraft to his burgeoning tally of kills when flying Hurricane V7671. His first kill was an He 111 from 5/KG 26 which was intercepted over Rabat and Mdina during one patrol which ditched offshore; his second victory was against a Ju 88A-4 from II/LG 1 during a later sortie. Despite accounts by witnesses on the ground who claim to have seen the Ju 88 crash, it appears that it actually returned to Catania albeit in a severely damaged condition. It is probable therefore that the 'crash' might have been its bomb load being jettisoned. Unlike Italian night bombers which flew straight and level at all

Malta's first Spitfire. A change of wind direction meant that unarmed Spitfire I (PR Type D), P9551 from 1 Photographic Recconnaissance Unit at Benson, Oxfordshire, was unable to return to its UK base after photographing Turin on 19th January 1941, forcing its pilot F/Lt Corbishley DFC to divert to Malta instead. With its split F.24 cameras in the rear fuselage, high-altitude performance and 1,750 mile range this arrival was 'manna from heaven' for AOC Malta, Air Commodore Maynard, who sought to retain the Spitfire and its pilot at Takali for as long as possible until favourable weather conditions allowed it to return to the UK. Unfortunately this would not occur as it was shot down by flak over Viareggio on 2nd February 1941 during its second sortie from Malta and Corbishley was captured. Like most UK-based PR Spitfires, P9551 was painted overall PRU Blue with the unit codes 'LY' applied in Medium Sea Grey and it is seen here taxiying at Takali following its arrival on 19th January 1941 with Mosta's famous dome and 261 Squadron's Hurricane Is in the background. Author via Reg Fitzpatrick

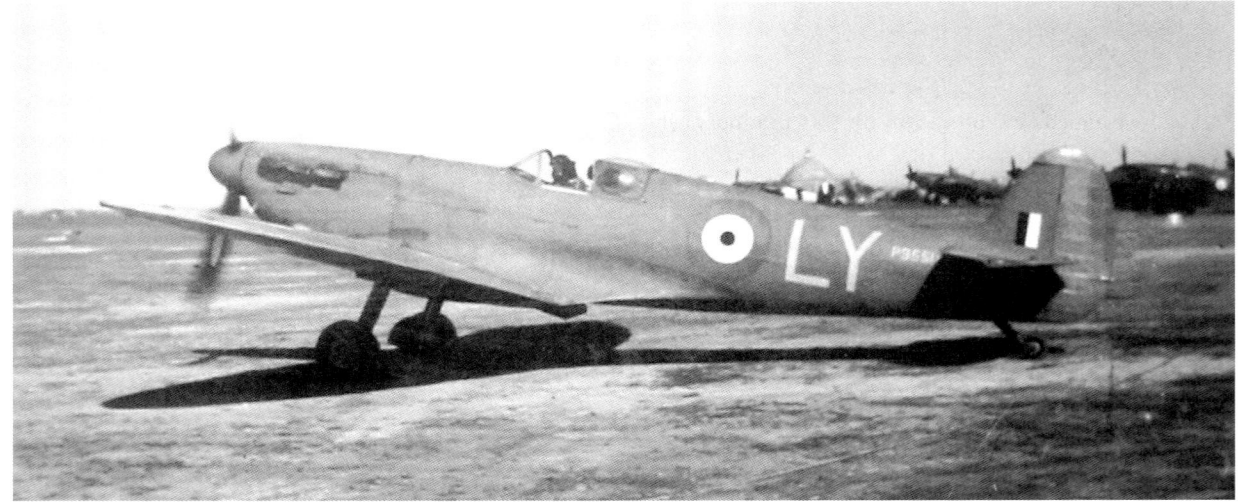

times, even after having been illuminated by searchlights, the searchlight operators found the Germans to be much harder adversaries – being far more difficult to locate as they constantly weaved and varied their height and direction in an effort to confuse Malta's defences.

When not on duty at night, most of Malta's servicemen now slept in air raid shelters for safety as did the civilians, and many veterans speak of the constant tiredness they felt while serving there due to a lack of sleep caused by the continual bombing. In addition, rations were cut to eek out the food supply whereby hunger became yet another part of daily life for all in Malta.

It was during this period too that British paratroopers were flown from Luqa to attack the Tragino Aqueduct on 10th February during Operation *Colossus* as related in chapter 1.

On 11th February the first ships carrying members of the German *Afrika Korps* docked in Tripoli, although it was the following day when Malta's fighter pilots witnessed, what was for them, a far more ominous arrival in the skies above the island in the form of Muncheberg and 7/JG 26. Their first mission took place on the afternoon of the 12th as escort to three high-flying Ju 88 'decoys.' The bait was taken when a flight of five Hurricanes scrambled from 261 Squadron's new home at Takali and it was as they laboured to gain height that the Bf 109s pounced. Muncheberg himself claimed a Hurricane destroyed, as did two of his pilots, but in return a Ju 88D from 3(F)/121 was heavily damaged and a Bf 109 was also hit and damaged. Incredibly, at this stage of the war, F/Lt Watson who was leading the Hurricanes in N2715 was not a trained fighter pilot but a Wellington bomber captain who was compelled to lead the flight by HQ Malta because, under pre-war service terms, he was the most senior Flight Lieutenant in respect of time served in rank on the island irrespective of his lack of appropriate fighter experience. When attacked, this unfortunate officer failed to take proper evasive action and his Hurricane dived straight into the sea after being hit, costing him his life. Flight Lieutenant Thacker in P3733 managed to bail out over St Paul's Bay and landed in the sea where he was saved by an ASR launch, while the third Hurricane claimed, V7768, flown by F/Lt Bradbury who was wounded, crash-landed at Takali in a substantially damaged state with most of the fabric removed from one side of the rear fuselage.

From the time of this initial engagement the Bf 109s would be encountered on an almost daily basis as they slashed down out of the sun and dived away to leave an ever-increasing number of burning Hurricanes in their wake. Unsurprisingly, this caused a detrimental effect on the morale of the men of 261 Squadron, as more and more of their colleagues were killed or maimed and, in an attempt to raise their morale, the most aggressive pilots in the unit together participated in an early morning scram-

Oblt Joachim Muncheberg, *Kommandeur* of 7/JG 26 and the scourge of Malta's Hurricane pilots. His small unit of Bf 109E-7s almost wiped out Malta's defending Hurricanes without loss to themselves. Thankfully for the Allies they moved to North Africa before this could occur. EN Archive Collection

ble on 15th February with the intention of shooting down one of the German fighters. Unfortunately the plan backfired badly and the anticipated victory did not occur; instead, F/Lt James MacLachlan, who was by now the leading scorer over Malta, with eight victories, was shot down and two other Hurricanes were damaged. Despite suffering severe wounds to his left forearm, as previously related, MacLachlan survived and recovered to later fight and fly again as 'One Armed Mac.'

Although the Hurricane I had fared quite well against the Bf 109E during the Battle of Britain, those flying from Malta in 1941 were usually functioning with a distinct operational disadvantage because their German opponents almost always had the advantage of height. The proximity of enemy airfields in Sicily left the Hurricanes with little time to scramble and gain sufficient height before meeting an incoming raid and, in most instances, were still clawing for height when the Bf 109s dove upon them. In addition, most of Malta's Hurricanes were quite worn-out with many having bulky Vokes tropical air filters fitted beneath the nose which protected the engine from the all-pervading dust, but seriously affected their top speed. Their climb rate was further affected by the fact that most were still fitted with old two-position, variable-pitch De Havilland propellers for which S/Ldr Louks devised a short-term fix by slightly altering the angle of the propeller's blades, albeit at the expense of a decreased take-off performance. The ideal solution lay in the combination of a more powerful engine fitted with a constant-speed, variable-pitch Rotol propeller unit to provide a much enhanced climb rate. As mentioned previously, some Rotol propeller units fitted with wooden Jablo-covered blades did arrive in Malta and were retrofitted to the Hurricane as a matter of urgency. Because they were so precious, a repair facility was created in Malta to refurbish Rotol hubs recovered from crashed aircraft, while replacement wooden Jablo blades were manufactured at the Naval Dockyard in Grand Harbour. The locally produced blades were so well made in fact that they were actually preferred to those sent from factories in the UK!

In short however, a better fighter was urgently required to counter the threat of the Bf 109E but, as the Spitfire was still not available for deployment outside of Britain, the

Ju 88A-4, 4D+AB, from Stab 1/KG 30 the HQ *Staffel* of KG 30 which was usually based in Denmark and Holland in 1941 and not Sicily. However, it is believed this image was taken in Sicily during 1941 to where 4D+AB is thought to have been despatched probably as a replacement aircraft (and has yet to have its insignia amended) to reinforce III/KG 30 during operations from Gerbini, Sicily. All three *Gruppe* of KG 30 wore the same 'diving eagle' insignia, albeit upon different coloured shields with III/KG 30 having a yellow shield, I/KG 30 a white shield, while II/KG 30's was red. The shield of the unit HQ had a combination of all three colours as seen here. Author's collection

only other option was the slightly improved Hurricane II. The Mk.II did at least feature a more powerful Merlin XX engine and was equipped with three differing weapon installations according to its sub-variant, namely the Mk.IIa (8 x .303in mgs), Mk.IIb (12 x .303in mgs), and Mk.IIc (4 x 20mm cannon).

Although Hurricane losses continued to mount during daylight operations, with poor results in return, those flying in the night-fighter role continued to score by shooting down a Bf 110C night-fighter from 1/NJG 3 on 17th February. Other Bf 110s appeared over Malta during daylight on the 21st – probably Bf 110Ds from III/ZG 26 of which P/O Hamish Hamilton claimed one while other Hurricane pilots shared another between them. Around this time S/Ldr Trumble, who had taken over command of 261 Squadron from S/Ldr Balden during December 1940, was posted to Crete. His replacement was the newly-promoted S/Ldr RN Lambert (who had arrived in Malta during August 1940 as a member of 418 Flight), which in consequence led to both flight commanders being changed too.

On 23rd February 1941, *Stukas* from III/StG 1 returned to Maltese skies possibly in the belief that the fighter defences had been all but eliminated – they hadn't, and, with no 109s in sight, the small flight of intercepting Hurricanes had a field day. Although only a single *Stuka* was actually shot down by the fighters, a number of others were damaged, one of which had to be abandoned over the Sicilian coast, while no less than three others fell to anti-aircraft fire. In response to the *Stuka* losses, Bf 109s returned to Malta on the 24th when four of them attacked a section of Hurricanes, although on this occasion the RAF pilots were lucky and they all returned home intact.

A small formation of Bf 110s appeared over Malta on the 25th, consisting of a reconnaissance machine from 2 (F)/123 escorted by two Bf 110Ds fighters from III/ZG 26. They were intercepted at 6,000 feet over St Paul's Bay by eight A Flight Hurricanes led by F/Lt Whittingham who swiftly shot one of the *Zerstorers* down into the sea. Sergeant Fred Robertson chased another out to sea and claimed it as damaged and other pilots made damage claims too, although it appears that only the reconnaissance machine failed to return to Sicily. During this combat the Hurricane pilots were surprised to see that 109s were flying top cover yet they did not come down to help their twin-engined charges. No doubt suitably chastised, 7/JG 26 was over Malta again later in the day and, at 15:45hrs, above St Paul's Bay, *Oberleutnant* Muncheberg shot down Hurricane V7346 flown by P/O John Walsh from Canada. Although he managed to bail out, Walsh must have struck the tailplane when exiting the aircraft as he suffered serious multi-fracture breaks to his arm and leg. He was soon rescued from the water by a warship and taken to hospital, though sadly, in recovering from his injuries he contracted pneumonia and died.

LG 1 was fully stretched at this time supporting operations in North Africa, consequently, reinforcements began to land at Gerbini airfield, Sicily, from 24th February onwards when the first Ju 88As from 7/KG 30 led by *Oberleutnant* Hajo Hermann, a Knights Cross holder who later went on to develop '*Wilde Sau*' night-fighter tactics, arrived from Holland having been involved in nocturnal operations against Britain. This was the advanced *Staffel* of III/KG 30 which was due to arrive five days later and the first task for the ground crew (who followed in a pair of Ju 52/3m transports) was to wash the black distemper night-camouflage from their undersides. Until their parent unit arrived, 7/KG 30 was subordinated to LG 1 and, wasting no time at all, they were told to prepare for their first operational sortie over Malta the very next day as there was to be a maximum effort involving Ju 88s from both II and III/LG 1, as well as 7/KG 30 plus He 111s, Ju 87s and Italian close-escort fighters protected by the Bf 109Es of 7/JG 26.

RAIDS CONTINUE: FULMARS DEPART

The all-out aerial assault against Malta commenced on 26th February 1941 when the *Luftwaffe* sent a force of 38 Ju 87s, 12 Ju 88s and ten He 111s to raid Luqa airfield with an escort of 20 to 30 fighters that included Italian MC.200s and CR.42s with Muncheberg's Bf 109Es providing top cover. Rising to face this veritable armada were eight Hurricanes whose pilots skilfully avoided the Italian fighters and immediately set upon the bombers, sending two Ju 87s down in flames in quick succession. The Bf 109s were soon amongst them however, with each Hurricane rapidly acquiring one on its tail. Within a short space of time five Hurricanes had been shot down and three pilots lost their lives, including F/O 'Eric' Taylor DFC, who had scored seven kills over Malta since having delivered one of the first Hurricanes to arrive on the island in 1940. Consequently the number of Hurricanes remaining in Malta was reduced to such a low level that on some days none were serviceable enough to fly, dictating that the Fulmars which had otherwise been relegated to air-sea-rescue patrols and night-intruder sorties over Sicily and possessing the climbing performance of a brick – were once again called upon to fly as daytime interceptors.

It was precisely these circumstances which existed on 2nd March 1941 when a small incoming raid was plotted on radar. With no Hurricanes available, three Fulmars flown by Lt Bill Barnes, S/Lt Stan Orr and one other pilot were sent aloft to intercept the raid instead, but the incoming raiders turned out to be a *Kette* (a finger four formation) of Bf 109Es led by Muncheberg himself. The 109s fell upon the Fulmars with a vengeance as they climbed slowly above Hal Far and riddled all three naval aircraft with bullets and cannon shells to literally knock chunks out of all of them. Miraculously, none were shot down and all managed to return and make shaky but safe landings at Hal Far with their crews in one piece, although it was the last time that Fulmars were used in the daylight fighter role over Malta. To celebrate their escape from almost certain death at the hands of the Germans, the Fulmar crews went out that evening for a party in Valletta, however, when driving back to Hal Far, Bill Barnes, who was an up-and-coming naval fighter leader and ace with six kills and two shared to his credit, was the tragic victim of a freak accident. When a jumpy Maltese sentry fired a warning shot at their car, his bullet ricocheted off a rock and hit Barnes through the back of his seat and killed him.

As soon as the three Fulmars had been made airworthy again they left Malta for Egypt carrying two passengers apiece, while the Squadron's remaining aircrew and ground staff sailed on a destroyer to eventually meet up with them again at RNAS Dekheila, where the rest of the unit it will be recalled was re-equipping with new Fulmars. At Dekheila, S/Lt Orr received a bar to his DSO in recognition of having achieved five kills over Malta. Although 806 NAS had gone, they had left behind the sole remaining airworthy Sea Gladiator and so N5520 rejoined the RAF once more to serve with the Hal Far Station Flight in its previous Meteorological role.

Returning to Malta, RAF fitters and riggers had been working tirelessly to salvage spare parts from crashed or bombed-out airframes and, by 5th March, had succeeded in making sufficient Hurricanes serviceable for eight of them to be sent aloft at 17:00hrs to meet a large incoming raid. This raid consisted of over 60 *Stukas* and Ju 88s

Fulmar I, N1860 'M' from 806 NAS seen at Dekhaila, Egypt in April 1941. This was one of the Fulmars that survived the bombing of *Illustrious* having served with the Squadron since 1st June 1940 and thereafter throughout Malta's *Illustrious Blitz*. It remained in Malta until being withdrawn from the island in March 1941 when the Bf 109s of 7/JG 26 made it impossible for Fulmars to continue to operate there. Unlike others in the unit it did not have black and white halved undersides and retained its roundels as seen here. The camouflage is the standard naval S.1.E. scheme of Dark Slate Grey and Extra Dark Sea Grey with Sky Grey undersides although by this point it had become very faded and worn. Only the seventh Fulmar built, N1860 would appear to have been struck off charge at some point in 1943. A colour illustration of this aircraft appears on page 147. Author's collection

escorted by a number of Bf 109Es from both 7/JG 26 and newly arrived I/JG 27, another unit which had been temporarily retained in Sicily while en route to North Africa. One of the intercepting Hurricane pilots was Fred Robertson flying V7116 who shot down Ju 88, L1+CM, from 4/LG 1 which crashed into the sea in flames off Filfla

Heinkel He 111H-6, 1H+DN, from II/KG 26 seen en route to Malta during early spring 1941. Because the He 111 could only accommodate small bombs internally, larger weapons such as the SC1000 'Hermann' 1,092kg demolition bomb had to be carried beneath the fuselage on external racks; the bomb's nickname stemming from British mockery of Hermann Goring's rotund figure. In theory two such weapons could be carried but, judging by the opened radiator doors below the engine cowlings, this single bomb is causing the twin Jumo powerplants to work hard enough already. 1H+DN is also armed with a forward-facing MG FF 20mm cannon in the ventral gondola (which was especially effective against shipping), while 7.92mm mgs were fitted in the other positions. EN Archive Collection

In a scene reminiscent of a modern day holiday resort the crew of He 111H-6, 1H+AN, also from II/KG 26, relax in the Mediterranean sun prior to a sortie. Their aircraft appears to carry a smaller external bomb load, possibly an SC 500. KG 26 was known as the *Lowen Geschwader* (Lion Wing) due to its insignia which was carried on the nose and depicted a sitting lion inside a coloured shield, the colour of which differed depending upon which *Gruppe* it belonged to; in the case of II *Gruppe* the shield was yellow with a black lion. Both this aircraft and 1H+DN (above) wear the Luftwaffe's standard European theatre colour scheme of RLM 70 *Schwarzgrun*, RLM 71 *Dunkelgrun* and RLM 65 *Hellblau* with a white Mediterranean theatre band. After some use over Malta in the daylight role, most He 111s reverted to nocturnal bombing raids and were used extensively to drop magnetic mines into the Suez Canal and the sea lanes around Malta, mostly using magnetic bar-mines. EN Archive Collection

The *Luftwaffe*'s principal bomber used against Malta was the superlative Junkers Ju 88. The model seen here is a Ju 88A-5, *Werk Nummer* 2352 (visible on the fin tip), coded L1+FF from 7/LG 1 of *Fliegerkorps* X based at Catania, Sicily, between January and May 1941. It has the early-style rear cockpit glazing with just a single rear-facing 7.9mm MG 15 mg and white-coloured panels in the top glazing which are in fact foldable sun screens. Camouflage is the *Luftwaffe* standard European scheme of RLM 70/71/65 with a white theatre band and (predominantly) white individual code letter 'F'. Apart from a pair of incendiary containers, a number of SC50 and SC500 bombs are stacked in the foreground, some with 'screamers' attached to their fins. The term SC in relation to German bombs was an abbreviation of *Spreng Cylindrisch* and referred to high-explosive bombs with a thin steel case: the numerals referred to the weight of the bomb in kilograms. Common too were bombs prefixed SD (*Spreng Dickwandig*) which were medium-case bombs whose heavier steel wall created both blast and heavy fragmentation. Included in the SD range were some that were designed to pierce armour and in their case the prefix SD was replaced by PC (*Panzer Cylindrisch*). These weapons were identified by coloured bands on their tail fins, or nose: yellow for SC weapons; red for SD; and blue for PC. Colour illustrations of this aircraft appear on pages 152-3. EN Archive Collection

island before he was set upon soon afterwards by 12 Bf 109s. Skilfully using the Hurricane's superior manoeuvrability, he managed to out-turn his assailants and even hit one of them which was last seen diving away streaming smoke. This fighter was later reported to have crashed into the sea by an artillery battery and was credited to Robertson as a kill, although as all of 7/JG 26's aircraft returned safely to base, his victim must presumably have come from I/JG 27. During this same combat *Leutnant* Willi Kothman from I/JG 27 scored his unit's sole victory over Malta when he severely damaged the Hurricane flown by Sgt Ayre who managed to conduct a successful crash landing. Lucky to survive injury or worse due to the abundance of small stone-walled fields that cover Malta, Ayre was soon airborne once more in a different Hurricane. During this single combat a total of nine German aircraft were claimed destroyed by 261 Squadron while others were claimed as damaged or probably destroyed for the loss of two Hurricanes. The increasingly effective anti-aircraft defences also claimed a further nine enemy aircraft including a Bf 110 that exploded when it was in a firing position just 100 yards behind F/Lt Whittingham's Hurricane. Although it was obviously a successful day for the British, the *Luftwaffe*'s losses this day were not so heavy as the RAF believed and on their way back to Sicily two Bf 109s strafed and damaged a Sunderland and a Free French Loire flying boat moored in St Paul's Bay.

Much needed reinforcements arrived in Malta on 6th March, when 12 Hurricane Is arrived in Malta from Egypt led by a pair of 148 Squadron Wellingtons and, better still, most were flown by experienced fighter pilots, seven of whom came from 274 Squadron which had served with distinction in the Western Desert. Importantly, some of the other pilots had recent operational service with Fighter Command and brought news of the latest methods and tactics with them.

In terms of tactics, one employed ruthlessly by 7/JG 26's fighters was to mount standing patrols over the island's airfields ready to attack any aircraft that took off or came into land – when they were of course at their most vulnerable. This gave them total control of an airfield's airspace, whereby the arrival or departure of Allied aircraft during daylight often led to a dogfight because, whenever possible, 261 Squadron sent its fighters up to cover them. One such example occurred on the 7th when 69 Squadron Maryland, AR706, flown by F/O Boys-Stones had been sent on a reconnaissance over Sicily. The crew had so far enjoyed a successful sortie by photographing the HQ of *Fliegerkorps* X at Taormina and, thanks to the Maryland's top speed of over 300mph, were able to outrun the Italian fighters sent to catch them. During their return journey over the sea they encountered and damaged a Cant Z.506B, but, when approaching Malta, the crew noticed eight Bf 109s patrolling over Luqa. Six of the German

Above: A major problem for Malta's fighters commenced from 9th February 1941 when 7/JG 26 and its Bf 109E-7 fighters arrived at Gela, Sicily. Led by *Oberleutnant* Muncheberg, this unit consisted of hardened veterans and although it rarely had more than eight or nine aircraft available at any one time its pilots downed a large number of Malta's Hurricanes for no loss to themselves. The Bf 109E shown here is said to be Muncheberg's personal aircraft coded 'White 12' with the red heart insignia seen on the cowling as was worn by all of the *Staffel*'s aircraft along with JG 26's stylised 'S' on a shield in front of the cockpit, although his triangular pennant is not apparent on the antenna post. Beyond is a Bf 110 belonging to 9/ZG 26 and beyond that an He 111 from II/KG 26 all the 26s in fact! Author's collection

Below: The old and the new. A Messerschmitt Bf 109E-7 from 7/JG 26 identified by the red heart on its cowling, taxies past an Italian Fiat CR.42 biplane fighter, serial MM.4427, which is having its pair of fuselage mounted 12.7mm guns harmonised at Gela in Sicily during the spring of 1941. Although the biplane fighter was already a relic of the past for many air forces, the Italians continued to operate this type until the end of the war. EN Archive Collection

fighters dived to attack the Maryland and during their first pass set fire to one of its engines and killed the gunner. As the stricken aircraft crossed Malta's coast 250 feet above the Dingli Cliffs the navigator bailed out of the nose section and his parachute opened just in time to save him, but by the time the pilot could follow suit the aircraft was even lower and Boys-Stones died of his injuries within minutes of hitting the rocky ground as his parachute hadn't time to fully deploy. As this took place, 261 Squadron had been making valiant attempts to protect the Maryland during which newly arrived Sgt Jessop, in Hurricane P2645, who was making his first flight over Malta since his arrival from Egypt the previous day, was shot down and wounded by *Feldwebel* Kestel of 7/JG 26, while several other Hurricanes were damaged. After these combats, two of the German pilots followed the coastline to St Paul's Bay once again where they strafed and destroyed moored Sunderland I, L2164 of 228 Squadron, and Sgt AS Jones was killed while firing a pair of machine guns from one of

the Sunderland's mid-upper gun positions. When flying low along the coastline the Bf 109s commonly strafed targets of opportunity, placing traffic moving along coastal roads at especial risk. Civilian buses were targeted and drivers kept a good lookout, particularly along the exposed north-eastern coastline between St Julian's and St Paul's Bay, and it was there that an Army dispatch rider endured a cat-and-mouse encounter with a marauding Bf 109. Taking cover behind rocks on the beach as it made a strafing run at him, he would then jump back onto his motorcycle as soon as the fighter passed overhead and ride a few hundred yards while the German fighter banked around for another pass before dismounting and taking cover again. After repeating the process a number of times he managed to reach safety inside one of the ancient stone lookout towers situated along that part of the coastline until the German finally flew off, probably short of fuel or ammunition or both.

During early March many of the *Luftwaffe*'s Sicilian-based aircraft were temporarily detached to participate in the fighting over Greece and the Balkans, thus making life comparatively quiet over Malta as it was left mainly to the Bf 109s of 7/JG 26 plus a handful of Ju 88s and Bf 110s to maintain pressure on the island by mounting sneak low-level raids. One of these occurred on 8th March 1941 when SS *Essex* in Grand Harbour, and already damaged by bombs, was hit once again. This time the damage inflicted was so great that a year later the vessel was still in Malta awaiting repairs until, on 12th April 1942, it was bombed once more and had to be beached at Rinella to prevent it from sinking.

Another sneak raid was mounted against Takali airfield next morning on Sunday 9th March by a single Ju 88 escorted by four Bf 110s, but, as they sped in at low level from the north across the neighbouring island of Gozo one of the Bf 110s flew a bit too low and crashed into a hill near to Nadur. The rest had reached Takali by 07:00hrs where, despite crossing Gozo, no air raid alert had been sounded and they took the defences by surprise leaving one Hurricane destroyed on the ground and two others damaged during a single pass before returning to Sicily. To try and make it harder for enemy aircraft to target serviceable aircraft on the ground, wrecked aircraft that had previously been taken to the Safi Strip (a dispersal area between Luqa and Hal Far) and dumped, were now returned to the airfields and placed inside aircraft pens to act as decoys. Additionally, obsolete types were also used as decoys, including at least one old Fairey IIIF at Hal Far with sagging wings, a dummy gun and a thin coat of camouflage paint with modern roundels applied in an attempt to make it at least vaguely resemble a Swordfish.

On the following day, the 10th, Bf 109s returned to strafe 228 Squadron Sunderlands moored in St Paul's Bay where they set fire to the damaged hulk of L2164, which now sank, and also damaged T9046. On the same day two Ju 88s from 5/LG 1 were badly damaged by flak over Malta and that night a Bf 110C night-fighter from 1/NJG 3 (L1+BH) was shot down by a Hurricane flown by P/O Tony Rippon who also damaged a second Bf 110C.

On 17th March, a convoy arrived in Malta from Alexandria escorted by the Mediterranean Fleet which by now included the brand-new armoured fleet carrier HMS *Formidable* carrying the newly reconstituted 806 NAS equipped with six new Fulmar Is and the similarly equipped 803 NAS. Together they escorted a raid against Tripoli harbour made by Fairey Albacores from 826 and 829 NAS which formed the remainder of the air group. The attack was mounted to help divert attention away from the convoy as it reached Malta and Grand Harbour. There was only one incursion over Malta as the convoy arrived and this was met by Hurricanes with P/O Noble reporting that he 'Intercepted five Ju 88s with escort. Fired head-on at leading bomber port engine smoked damaged.' To increase the number of Hurricanes on the island, a flight of seven Hurricane Is flown by pilots from 274 Squadron arrived in Malta on the 18th from Egypt led by a pair of Wellingtons aboard which were eight other Hurricane pilots. Amongst the newcomers was F/O 'Imshi' Mason DFC, who, with 15 kills over the desert was at that time the RAF's leading ace in the Middle East.

Recent events had helped improve morale amongst the men of 261 Squadron, though further welcome news came with the award of a Distinguished Flying Medal (DFM) to Sgt Fred Robertson – who had now scored eight victories to equal the record of the wounded F/Lt 'Mac' MacLachlan, while ground staff, working ceaselessly, had fully repaired eight damaged Hurricanes. To boost moral yet further, a combat took place on 18th March without a German aircraft to be seen anywhere as the opposition on this occasion amounted to 15 CR.42s from 23° *Gruppo* which flew an armed-reconnaissance sortie over Malta following their recent arrival in Sicily from Libya; two of their biplanes were shot down by P/O John Pain in well-known Hurricane P3731 'J' with no losses in return.

Unfortunately their feeling of wellbeing would not last long as 261 Squadron was to receive an unfortunate blow just a few days later on the 22nd. The day started well when four Hurricanes went up at around 08:30hrs to intercept a twin-engined aircraft flying at 21,000 ft which was carrying out a reconnaissance over Malta. Fred Robertson identified this as a Ju 88 and he fired a few bursts at it but it dived away and headed for Sicily. In fact the aircraft had been a He 111P from 5/KG 26 which returned to Sicily, despite being badly damaged, with two of its crew wounded. It must though have obtained photographs of the recently arrived convoy in Grand Harbour because by mid-afternoon a formation of ten Ju 88s escorted by 12 Bf 109Es had been despatched from Sicily bound for Grand

Harbour. In response, eight Hurricanes were scrambled to intercept and in the mêlée which followed 261 Squadron suffered the loss of five Hurricanes and all five pilots. They were F/O Terry Foxton (P2653), P/O Garland (V7493), P/O Knight (V7358), F/O Southwell (V7799) and Sgt Spyer (V7672). The survivors of the disaster were F/L 'Chubby' Eliot, P/O Hamish Hamilton and P/O Doug Whitney; the last named being credited with a kill against a Bf 109 which had just shot a Hurricane down, but, in fact, all of 7/JG 26s fighters returned safely to Sicily. Nevertheless, it is believed that a *Staffel* from JG 3 also operated briefly from Sicily around this time so the fighter that he claimed may well have come from that unit.

In relating his experiences to his diary, P/O Laubscher of 261 Squadron summed up the mood of the pilots when he wrote: 'Our losses were heavy and our successes few, as a Hurricane I was no match for an enemy who always had the advantage of height. Violent death for Malta's fighter pilots came under numerous guises. On one occasion a pilot's parachute caught on his aircraft's rudder and he was

Above: To provide the newly arrived *Fliegerkorps* X with air-sea-rescue support, *Seenotberichskommando* X, deployed its Dornier Do 24 flying boats and Heinkel He 59 seaplanes to Syracuse, Sicily. Seen here is one of the unit's Do 24 flying boats clearly displaying its impressively large 20mm cannon in the mid-upper turret. The Dornier's colour scheme represents the *Luftwaffe*'s standard maritime combination of RLM 72 *Grun* and RLM 73 *Grun* with RLM 65 *Hellblau* undersides while the otherwise conspicuous white theatre band has been over painted in black to avoid compromising its camouflage when flying low over the sea. Author via internet: www.military-aircraft-photos.com

Below: A pair of Bf 109E-7s belonging to 7/JG 26, the second of which is coded 'White 13'. Seen at their base at Gela, they both have yellow nose cowlings adorned with the units red heart insignia and each has had a white theatre band applied to the rear fuselage. EN Archive Collection

dragged to his death as the machine dived into the sea. Another parachuted into the sea, only to drown before the crash boat could get to him.' He continues...' Pilots were even lost during test flights, their aircraft going into sudden almost vertical dives from which they never pulled out. We could only assume that these men had not used oxygen, and lost consciousness at altitude.' Loss of consciousness may have led to the death of Bill Timms in Hurricane N2622 on 11th January 1941 and was probably caused by the type of oxygen tube employed with the 'D-Type' oxygen mask used by RAF fighter pilots at this time. This was a direct flow system without an economiser, which meant that the oxygen flowed all the time whether the pilot was breathing in or out, while the small-diameter smooth rubber tube, cased in cloth, was prone to kinking or becoming blocked by ice, especially during the rapid transition from the heat experienced at ground level to the cold of high altitude. This problem was eventually solved by copying the flexible and ribbed rubber hose as used by *Luftwaffe* pilots and applying it to the RAF's new 'G-Type' mask.

OPERATION *WINCH*: HURRICANE IIs FINALLY ARRIVE

Assuming perhaps that Malta's fighter defence was a spent force following the losses incurred on 22nd March 1941, several Ju 87Rs from III/StG 1, escorted by 15 Italian MC.200s from 6° *Gruppo* left Sicily on the afternoon of the 23rd to attack the airfields at Luqa and Takali as well as the recently arrived ships in Grand Harbour. To their surprise, nine (some sources state 14) Hurricanes rose to meet them led by S/Ldr Lambert. Considering the severity of their recent losses the sudden appearance of so many Hurricanes is surprising but might be attributed to the convoy's recent arrival – by either delivering crated Hurricanes, or spares that enabled unserviceable fighters to be rapidly returned to airworthiness.

Whatever the facts, without Bf 109s to contend with the Hurricane pilots enjoyed a '*Stuka* Party' and quickly claimed nine of them shot down, with anti-aircraft gunners claiming four more: a single Hurricane was lost in return. Fred Robertson in Hurricane V7495 destroyed two Ju 87s (bringing his score to ten), as did P/O Tony Rippon while S/Ldr Lambert, F/Lt Peacock-Edwards, P/O Doug Whitney, and Sgts Harry Ayre and Reg Hyde all claimed single victories, plus others damaged. The Hurricane that was lost was Sgt Fred Robertson's machine, V7495, which burst into flames after receiving multiple hits from a *Stuka*, although he managed to bail out safely over land near to Zebbug from which his only injury was a bruised knee inflicted upon landing. He was soon located by villagers who carried him shoulder high back to the village and in his combat report Robertson stated: 'I had just shot down one Ju 87 when I was attacked by another from ahead and got a bullet in my port main petrol tank. I followed the enemy aircraft around in a very steep turn and finally shot it down into the sea: next I found that my aircraft was burning fiercely and so I climbed from 700 feet over the sea to a position about a mile south of Rabat and bailed out.' Post-war records indicate that only four dive-bombers were actually lost during this raid, at least one of which was hit by anti-aircraft fire, though several returned to Sicily seriously damaged. Next day, 17 Hurricanes were available although the only raid to take place was a high-level dusk operation by He 111Ps from II/KG 26 escorted by seven 6° *Gruppo* MC.200s, however, their bombs proved ineffectual and no contact was made.

Since taking command of 261 Squadron, Lambert had proved popular with his pilots due to his tactical awareness and bravery and, as A Flight's new commander, F/Lt Whittingham wrote in his journal: 'Squadron Leader Lambert should go down in history for the calm courage and complete lack of side that he displays. He is a complete inspiration to every member of the squadron. This, despite the fact that he has neither the liking nor the inclination to be a fighter pilot.' Leading ace Sgt Fred Robertson also had a high regard for his squadron commander and credited the success of the 23rd to Lambert's leadership and positioning of the Squadron prior to attacking the enemy.

On 28th March, Muncheberg and his wingman *Oberleutnant* Mietusch claimed a pair of Hurricanes between them over Malta flown by Sgts Reg Goode, one of the transferees from 274 Squadron in V7430, and Jock Livingstone in V7297. Both pilots were able to carry out successful crash landings, although Reg Goode had been quite badly wounded. Two days later, on the 30th, Bf 110Ds from III/ZG 26 mounted a low-level attack on Takali dropping bombs amongst Hurricanes parked at dispersal, a number of which failed to explode – possibly because they had been dropped too low which prevented their fuses from arming properly. Nevertheless the Hurricanes were all pushed to safety while bomb disposal crews defused them, the only damage inflicted upon them being limited to a number of superficial fabric tears caused by flying stones.

Towards the end of the month the AOC, Air Commodore Maynard, was promoted to Air Vice-Marshal owing to the increased size of his command and he used his added authority to urge the Air Ministry to provide more fighters, by which time 261 Squadron reportedly had a total of 34 Hurricane Is on strength – not all of which remained serviceable. Following Maynard's representations, a consignment of 12 urgently needed Hurricane IIs arrived in Malta on 3rd April 1941 (led by a pair of Skuas), after having been flown from *Ark Royal* as part of Operation *Winch*. The Hurricanes were Mk.IIa variants fitted with Merlin XX engines featuring a new two-speed supercharger allowing the impeller-speed ratio to be altered by the pilot in response to the ambient air pressure,

Above and below: As Spitfires could not yet be spared overseas the best that Britain could provide to help counter the Bf 109Es over Malta was the Hurricane II. Fitted with a Rolls-Royce Merlin XX engine and a two-speed supercharger, its impeller-speed ratio could be altered by the pilot in response to ambient air pressure resulting in an improved power-to-altitude performance enabling them to climb faster than the Hurricane I. Twelve Mk.IIas were despatched from *Ark Royal* on 3rd April 1941 under Operation *Winch* and were led to Malta by a pair of Skuas. All the Hurricanes were finished in Dark Earth and Dark Green, with (most probably) Sky Blue undersides. As seen here, it is evident that some featured Sky bands and spinners while others had black spinners and no bands, while some had a wavy demarcation along the wing leading edges extending onto the nose. Included amongst these Hurricanes are some presentation aircraft, though the wording (below their cockpits) is unintelligible. These two images were taken at Gibraltar and show the Hurricanes aboard *Ark Royal* with 44-gallon long-range tanks fitted. The lattice masts are radio antennas which were folded down during flying operations. I B Westmacott via Frederick Galea

resulting in an improved power-to-altitude performance enabling them to climb much faster than the Hurricane I. All 12 Hurricane IIs arrived in Malta although one had lost its tailwheel and punctured a wing tank when taking off from the carrier, and another crashed upon landing. The arrival of these Hurricanes and their pilots meant that some of the veterans from 261 Squadron could now be rested, therefore, on 7th April 1941, Sgts Jim Pickering, Jock Norwell, Harry Ayre and Drac Bowerman were flown to Egypt in a Wellington of 148 Squadron. No doubt glad to see the back of Malta, F/Lt John Waters and P/O Allan McAdam departed for Gibraltar in a Sunderland the following day.

PHOTO RECONNAISSANCE HURRICANES

One of the pilots who could also have left Malta was George Burges, late of the Hal Far Fighter Flight, 418 Flight and 261 Squadron. Burges, it will be recalled, had elected to continue flying from Malta with 69 Squadron in his proper role as a fully trained reconnaissance pilot flying Martin Marylands, or, as they were known by their crews the 'Glenn' or 'Glen Martin' after the founder of the Martin company. In its day the type possessed an outstanding performance at low-to-medium altitudes (up to 15,000 ft and was capable of speeds of up to 309 mph, but, for high-altitude, photo-reconnaissance work over land something else was needed due to the Marylands' decreasing performance, hence increased vulnerability, at high altitude.

To fill this gap it was decided to convert one of the standard Hurricane Is which had arrived aboard the *Essex* with Burges being selected to fly it and, needless to say, the chosen fighter (V7101) would be stripped, converted and adapted by S/L Louks. First, it was lightened by removing its armour, guns, radio and radio mast, and then, in Louks' own words: 'By using [a] crashed Wellington's fuel tanks [it] enabled a further 150 gallons to be carried, along with an extra 25 gallons of oil in an extra tank in the [wing] leading edge, allowing a range of 1,500 miles with additional oxygen and two cameras completing the modification.' The cameras were a pair of F.24s placed in the radio compartment facing vertically downwards in an overlapping fan arrangement to cover a wider area. Conflicting with Louk's statement, George Burges has stated, 'there was no room for extra fuel.' He also mentions that the centre of gravity was too far back on the aircraft, probably due to removal of so much equipment, that the Hurricane could whip into a spin if you were not careful.' It remains open to speculation therefore as to whether such tanks were actually fitted or merely considered and then dismissed, particularly so given the lack of available room in a Hurricane's rear fuselage with its myriad of internal bracing wires and wooden formers which left barely enough room for the cameras in the empty radio bay. The only free space for additional fuel tanks would have been in the empty gun bays. It is not known whether the Hurricane was originally fitted with a Vokes filter, or, if it was, whether it was removed to help improve performance; it seems highly likely that a Rotol propeller was fitted due to the superior climb performance that it conferred and the only known photograph of this aircraft would seem to support this. In its converted state Hurricane PR.I, V7101, could achieve 35,000ft with an absolute ceiling of 39,000ft having been mentioned although it usually operated at 30,000 feet because, as Burges states: 'it was dangerously unstable above this height.' When asked about the dangers of hypoxia at such high altitudes Burges replied, 'we did not know much about those things in those days, I went a bit light-headed but that counteracted the frostbite and the bends!' Other conversion work is also said to have been carried out to improve visibility by Louks who recalled that the windscreen was replaced by a Blenheim 'astrodome', probably meaning the blister as fitted to the side windows of Blenheim cockpits, and that a clear-view panel was placed in the floor. However, as the latter would entail looking between the retracted wheels, the V-shaped fairing at the rear of the wheel-well may have been removed to provide a downward, but still rather limited view. Burges also described V7101 as being, 'painted overall blue as much for the benefit of our own gunners to recognise it as for purely camouflage purposes,' and is described as being mixed from, 'five gallons of De Lux Bosun Blue, seven pints of turpentine, 16 lb of zinc powder and 3 lb of De Lux Black' which would have made it very dark and similar to those Hurricanes operating with 2 PRU in Egypt. Burges flew V7101's first photo-reconnaissance mission on 4th May 1941, and, although most sorties were flown over Sicily where 'at 30,000 feet it could cover two or three targets,' some were flown as far away as Naples. Later, a second Hurricane, Mk.IIa Z3053, was similarly converted and modified to join V7101.

HURRICANE IIs GO INTO ACTION

Following their arrival all remained quiet for the next few days and the Hurricane IIs were not scrambled until the morning of 11th April 1941 when two of their number took-off to intercept a Ju 88D reconnaissance aircraft from 1(F)/121 escorted by CR.42s from 23° *Gruppo*, MC.200s from 17° *Gruppo* and Bf 109s from 7/JG 26 flying as top cover. Meanwhile, Hurricane I, P3978, flown by Sgt Bert Deacon, became embroiled in a tense dogfight with five of the CR.42s – which could easily turn inside a Hurricane, but was able to disengage safely and there were no losses on either side. Another incursion by a mixed formation of Bf 109s and MC.200s took place around 11:00hrs and eight Hurricanes were scrambled led by S/Ldr Lambert, but, at 10,000 ft they were bounced by the enemy. Sergeant

Deacon was again flying Z3978 and he managed to break away in time to engage three enemy fighters, one of which was seen to dive vertically into the sea (probably an MC.200), but then made the mistake of circling over his victim to watch it crash and was attacked by a pair of 109s which hit his Hurricane in the cockpit area. Fearing that a fire might break out Deacon made for Takali in order to land, however, the ground defences there opened up on him so he made for Hal Far instead where his undercarriage collapsed upon landing. Two other Hurricane II pilots, P/O Peter Kennett in Z3036 and Sgt Peter Waghorn in Z2904 found themselves alone over the sea north of Gozo when they spotted what they thought was a Ju 88 and attacked it, though in fact it was a Bf 110C, coded 4U+ZK, modified for reconnaissance duties from 2(F)/123 which they shot down nonetheless. Unfortunately both Hurricanes were then bounced by Muncheberg and Mietusch and Peter Kennett was shot down, although he was able to bail out into the sea. Peter Waghorn's Hurricane was severely damaged and he elected to crash-land soon after crossing the coastline of Gozo near to Bidnija, but unfortunately his Hurricane was smashed to pieces as it ploughed through a number of the stone walls that separated the small Gozitan fields. Waghorn was later found dead close to the wreckage of the forward fuselage having been thrown out while still strapped to his seat. Peter Kennett died in the water while swimming toward Gozo because the rescue launch, HSL 107, was unable to set sail until enemy aircraft had left the area – by which time he had drowned.

Still later in the day, another Hurricane I was shot down and two others were badly damaged with a Bf 110 and a Bf 109 being claimed in return, though yet again, all of 7/JG 26's aircraft are recorded as having returned to Sicily intact. To round the day off, Italian MC.200s and CR.42s strafed the airfield at Luqa destroying a Wellington on the ground. Despite the comparatively heavy losses incurred during this day a press statement was issued by the RAF in Malta that evening stating that since the start of the fighting over Malta, 132 enemy aircraft had been destroyed, 44 had probably been destroyed and 58 others damaged for the loss of 29 British fighters. That night another German aircraft was added to this score when P/O Hamish Hamilton, who was still wearing his pyjamas, shot down one of nine *Stukas* despatched by III/StG 1 to carry out nuisance raids over Takali – sadly, the doomed bomber crashed into a Maltese home and killed an 8-year old girl as well as injuring others in the house. The two occupants of the *Stuka* perished.

Over the next few weeks little of note occurred above Malta with only the odd skirmish taking place including one on the 13th, when newly promoted Flight Lieutenant 'Imshi' Mason was shot down and injured while flying Hurricane II, Z2838. He had been patrolling with his wingman, F/O Innes Westmacott, when Mason spotted four Bf 109s flying below them so, making the most of this extremely rare occurrence he dived out of the sun but, either because his radio was broken or he simply didn't announce his intention, he broke away from his wingman. Mason claims to have quickly shot one of the Germans down into the sea before being jumped in return by another Bf 109 flown by Klaus Mietusch, who registered hits all over the Hurricane's fuselage with cannon shells smashing into the instrument panel, controls and engine as well as Mason's elbow and wrist – severing an artery. Twisting and turning as best he could and with the Hurricane's engine losing power, Mason had no option but to ditch four miles from the coast. As he ditched the large radiator beneath the belly dug into the water bringing the aircraft to a sudden halt that projected Mason forward causing him to break his nose on the gunsight because he had released his straps too soon. Losing blood, Mason began to swim for shore and was soon rescued by HSL 107 where he received first aid and, once ashore, was taken to hospital. Although a witness on shore saw Mason's victim crash into the sea the Germans still didn't report any of 7/JG 26's fighters as missing to thereby leave the unanswered question: who or what was his victim?

On 14th April, Innes Westmacott and Bert Deacon were scrambled before dawn to intercept a low-flying aircraft reported to be approaching St Paul's Bay at speed and encountered a lone Ju 88 from 7/KG 30, which was now in the process of attacking Luqa, so they shot it down. Continuing to patrol overhead they noticed anti-aircraft fire over Hal Far airfield being directed towards a twin-engined aircraft so, assuming that it was another Ju 88, they dived, opened fire and set alight one of its engines before they realised that it was actually a British Maryland and broke off. The Maryland was AR735 from 69 Squadron flown by F/Lt Warburton who ironically had been taking advantage of the early morning darkness to perform an air test without fear of being 'jumped' by the enemy. With one engine on fire and the undercarriage damaged he returned to Luqa to make a successful belly-landing.

It was on this day that Prime Minister Winston Churchill signalled to AVM Maynard in Malta that: 'In order to control the sea communication across the Mediterranean sufficient suitable naval forces must be based on Malta. Protection must be afforded to these naval forces by the Air Forces at Malta, which must be kept at the highest strength in fighters of the latest and best quality that the Malta aerodromes can contain. The duty of affording fighter protection to the naval forces holding Malta should have priority over the use of the aerodromes by bombers engaged in attacking Tripoli.'

Despite this signal and the fact that fighter pilots were crying out for Spitfires to be sent in order to meet the Messerschmitts on equal terms, the Air Ministry bizarrely continued to regard the Spitfire as unsuitable for overseas

Above: Following combat with Bf 109Es on 11th April 1941, Sgt Deacon of 261 Squadron was slightly wounded and forced to land his damaged Hurricane I, P3978 in a hurry. With his windscreen smashed and a cockpit full of smoke he tried to land at Takali but was driven away by 'friendly' anti-aircraft fire. Landing instead at Hal Far, his aircraft tipped onto its nose when the left undercarriage leg folded. This was a bad day for the Hurricanes as two others were shot down by Bf 109s and both pilots were killed, while three, including P3978 were badly damaged. The Hurricane's colours seem very dark and AC Jack Paternoster, who served at Takali, remembers that some of them were Brown and Grey! To the rear of the Hurricane sits a damaged ex-806 NAS Fulmar I minus its rudder that probably served as a decoy but which presumably could also have served as a valuable source of spares for the Fulmars of 800X Flt following their arrival in Malta. Other types known to have been used as decoys at Hal Far included at least one ancient Fairey IIIF (which received a rudimentary coat of camouflage to make it look like a Swordfish) and a Fairey Gordon. Author's collection via AH Deacon

Below: A further victim of Bf 109s on 11th April 1941 was Hurricane I, V7116, flown by P/O PA Mortimer of 261 Squadron who was slightly injured during his subsequent crash-landing. V7116 was delivered by SS *Essex* and it appears to be wearing a Dark Earth and Dark Green camouflage scheme with black and white halved undersides with the Sky band on the rear fuselage painted over to avoid being mistaken in combat for the white band of an Axis aircraft. Frederick Galea

service due to its narrow track undercarriage! Further, Maynard did not specify which type of fighters he required and so Hurricanes continued to be sent.

Apart from some night-time activity over Malta the next daylight incursion occurred on the 19th when a pair of unescorted *Stukas* from III/StG 1 sneaked in low and sank a merchantman in Grand Harbour, only for both to succumb to anti-aircraft fire. It was during this month also, as a direct result of Churchill's wishes, that Force K, a Royal Navy surface flotilla, was formed to operate from Malta. This force would come to terrorise Axis convoys during the hours of darkness and helped to demonstrate Britain's resolve to use Malta as a true striking base. Their operations are considered in more detail in Chapter 1, (qv).

As the *Luftwaffe's* presence in Sicily had temporarily reduced due to other commitments, both in North Africa and as a result of Operation *Marita* (the campaign against Greece and Yugoslavia), the Italians returned to the fray above Malta. On 20th April, three SM.79s were sent to bomb Grand Harbour covered by nine CR.42s from 23° *Gruppo* and 15 MC.200s from 17° *Gruppo*. Two Hurricane IIs were scrambled from Takali in response flown by F/O Charles Laubscher and P/O John 'Tiger' Pain in Z3032 and, taking advantage of the Mk.II's superior climb rate, they both clawed for height in order to provide top cover for the rest of the squadron. At 11,000 ft Laubscher and Pain noticed the flak open up over Valletta but then spotted seven CR.42s flying 300ft or so directly below them. Surprised at seeing biplanes appear over Malta once more, they dived and made a near-head-on attack that took advantage of the biplanes' upper wings to mask their approach, following which Laubscher claimed two of the CR.42s destroyed and his wingman one other. They in turn were intercepted by the Italian top cover which they identified as Bf 109s but were most probably MC.200s which they evaded and then returned home. The anti-aircraft gunners around Valletta also claimed to have destroyed a number of Italian aircraft, though only one CR.42 was actually lost this day. More importantly for 261 Squadron, none of their Hurricanes were lost and this successful combat proved a boost to morale, even though the remainder of the unit, in Hurricane Is, had spent most of their time flying nervously in a defensive circle at a lower altitude. As if to remind the RAF fighter pilots that they were still about, the 109s returned that afternoon to damage a Hurricane and, next day, the 21st, another Hurricane was shot down by Muncheberg himself who was escorting a photo-reconnaissance mission. During this day the fast supply ship HMS *Breconshire* arrived in Malta once again loaded with canned aviation fuel, oil fuel and general supplies having been escorted most of the way by the Mediterranean Fleet which was on its way to bombard Tripoli. Always an important supply vessel, *Breconshire* departed Malta for Alexandria one week later.

ANTI-SHIPPING BLENHEIMS ARRIVE: AND SO DO FURTHER HURRICANES COURTESY OF OPERATION *DUNLOP*

The Italians re-commenced their night-time bombing of Malta's airfields during April in an attempt to both destroy aircraft and crater the ground in order to disrupt the following day's operations, although Army maintenance crews usually repaired any such damage with minimal fuss or delay. A further consignment of fighters arrived in Malta on 27th April 1941 courtesy of *Ark Royal* and Operation *Dunlop* when 23 Hurricanes, a mix of Mk.IIa and IIb variants, were flown off. They were led by three Fulmars and all but one of the Hurricanes arrived safely after a flight of three hours and twenty minutes. Unfortunately Sunderland L5807 from 228 Squadron which had ventured out from Kalafrana to guide one of the Hurricane flights into Malta was spotted by a *Kette* (pair) of Bf 109Es led by Muncheberg as it returned to base where it was strafed, set ablaze and sunk while the slipway crew struggled to fit its beaching gear and get it out of the water.

Another important arrival on this day was a detachment of six 21 Squadron Blenheim IV bombers that arrived at Luqa led by S/Ldr LV 'Attie' Atkinson. They had flown from their home base of Watton, Norfolk, via Gibraltar on, what was in effect, a fact-finding mission to see if Malta could support regular detachments of No.2 Group's Blenheims. The anti-shipping veterans of No.2 Group were definitely the best suited to the role of mounting daylight attacks upon Rommel's Mediterranean supply convoys at this early stage of the war – before dedicated maritime strike aircraft and tactics had been fully developed – given that they had been conducting regular operations against German convoys in the North Sea for some time. Daylight attacks would provide an ideal complement to the nocturnal ones already being conducted in the Mediterranean by the Swordfish of 830 NAS, although sadly, the Blenheim crews would incur appalling casualties in the process.

Until this time, Swordfish had operated mostly in the bombing or mine-laying role with just the occasional torpedo strike; however, by April, nocturnal torpedo strikes against convoys were becoming more common. Therefore, in order to maintain a continued supply of torpedoes for the Swordfish, the weapons were delivered to Malta by means of Sunderlands, the submarine 'Magic Carpet Service', or via the recently arrived 10th Submarine Flotilla, though the latter were understandably loath to sacrifice valuable space in their boats for torpedoes which they were unable to use themselves. (British submarines used 21in Mk.VIII** torpedoes weighing 3,452 lb each as opposed to the air-dropped 18in Mk.XII* torpedo which weighed 1,158 lb and was over 5ft shorter than the 21in weapon). Their high unit cost of £1,500 notwithstanding, each torpedo was considered to be precious in Malta because of the risks taken to get them there in the first

Of the 24 Hurricane IIs involved in Operation *Dunlop* (one was rendered unserviceable and could not fly) 23 are seen here on *Ark Royal*'s flight deck on 27th April 1941 as the ship turns into wind ready to launch them in three flights, each led by a Fulmar. All are fitted with DH propellers, Vokes tropical filters and 44-gallon long-range tanks. This was a further attempt at combating the Bf 109Es appearing over Malta and consisted of a mix of the Hurricane IIa (8 x .303in mgs) and IIb (12 x .303in mgs). The two nearest aircraft each have a strange white-coloured marking on their rear fuselage which might indicate that they were formation leaders. Otherwise, the colour scheme of these fighters appears to be the usual Dark Earth and Dark Green with Sky Blue undersides as applied to fighters serving overseas at this time. Author via Kev Darling

place, particularly during one period when submarine and flying boat losses were so high that only a few Mk.XII torpedoes remained on the island. The supply problem was eased though by the (re)discovery of a stock of 'geriatric' *18in* Mk.VIII torpedoes, of 1913 vintage, which had been found stored in a corner of the Malta Dockyard by personnel of the Hal Far torpedo section who pressed them into service with 830 NAS, despite having originally been designed for surface vessels and not aircraft. In order to adapt such ancient weapons for aerial use various fittings had to be filed off by armourers and others welded on before they would fit beneath a Swordfish, though dropping them from any height brought mixed results as their soft phosphor-bronze warheads and gyro controls were very fragile.

Due to the heavy losses being inflicted on Axis convoys during the hours of darkness by Malta's Swordfish, the Germans decided to maintain a round-the-clock presence above Hal Far which at night included one or two aircraft at a time intermittently dropping bombs in an attempt to disrupt operations. This of course could often make for a hazardous departure, despite which, operations continued nonetheless and naturally precluded the use of any lights. During daylight the standing patrols were conducted by Bf 109s and should a long nocturnal sortie overrun causing Swordfish or Wellingtons to return after dawn, then they often had to run the gauntlet of interception in which quite a few aircraft were either lost or damaged.

Towards the end of April, three more Hurricanes were shot down by Muncheberg's unit, two of which fell to the man himself, with the only claim in return being made against a Ju 88. On 27th April, 261 Squadron received a new CO when F/Lt Whittingham was promoted to take over from S/Ldr Lambert who was long overdue for a rest. Leaving also was Sgt Hyde and Sgt Fred Robertson DFM, the latter being one of Malta's 'star' pilots who concluded his tour with 12 victories to become Malta's top-scoring Hurricane pilot, 10 of which were scored over the island. Upon returning to the UK Robertson was posted as an instructor to 60 OTU at East Fortune, Lothian, where he instructed Boulton Paul Defiant night-fighter crews. Later however, having converted to Beaufighters, Fred Robertson was tragically killed when his Beaufighter collided with an American B-17 over Suffolk on 31st August 1943.

OPERATION *TIGER*: A VITAL CONVOY

May 1941 began badly for the RAF in Malta when two further 261 Squadron Hurricanes fell to the guns of Joachim Muncheberg on the morning of the 1st: one over St Paul's Bay and the other while landing at Hal Far, although their wounded pilots, Sgt Walmersley in Z3061, and P/O Innes Westmacott in Z2900 survived. Both casualties belonged to the unit's recently raised C Flight which was based at Hal Far under the command of F/Lt Mould, while the

Squadron's other two flights were each based at Luqa and Takali in order to maximise the dispersal of their aircraft. Battle of Britain veteran, F/Lt Peter William Olber 'Boy' Mould DFC, was already an ace with eight victories to his name prior to reaching Malta and became well-known during the Battle of France when he became the first pilot to score a kill in a Hurricane. The Germans returned in the early evening escorting Italian SM.79s against which six Hurricanes were scrambled to intercept, but, yet again, they were bounced by the Bf 109s with Muncheberg claiming his third kill of the day while another Hurricane was downed by *Unteroffizier* Kuhdorf. In between these combats Blenheims of 21 Squadron flew their first sortie from Malta and welcome reinforcements arrived in Malta when 13 Beaufighter Ic twin-engined long-range fighters from 252 Squadron arrived at Luqa having staged through Gibraltar from Aldergrove in Northern Ireland where they had been under the control of Coastal Command. Their ground crews and spares were conveyed aboard Sunderland I, P9600, from 10 Squadron RAAF. That night Force K sortied from Grand Harbour, but upon returning the next morning HMS *Jersey* activated a magnetic mine at 07:09hrs which had been laid by aircraft in the harbour entrance and sank immediately. The wreck effectively blocked the harbour entrance causing the cruiser *Gloucester* and destroyers *Kipling* and *Kashmir*, which were following astern, to divert to Gibraltar instead, leaving the destroyers *Kelly*, *Jackal* and *Kelvin* bottled up in Grand Harbour until *Jersey*'s wreck could be cleared.

The Beaufighters of 252 Squadron had been detached to Malta as part of Operation *Temple* to provide long-range air cover for the merchantman SS *Paracombe* which had been despatched, on its own, from Gibraltar on 1st May without any escort whatsoever bound for Malta carrying 21 crated Hurricanes amongst other vital items. Ultimately, by hugging the North African coastline the experienced master of SS *Paracombe* somehow managed to reach Cap Bon without being detected by Axis aircraft, but the lone merchantman's luck ran out shortly afterwards when she struck a mine and sank, taking the crated Hurricanes and many of her crew with her. Thus ended Operation *Temple*: hardly the best conceived plan to have emanated from the Admiralty by a considerable margin. Despite *Paracombe*'s loss, 252 Squadron was retained in Malta because an extremely vital eastbound convoy was due to pass very shortly on its way to Alexandria. Unfortunately the Squadron had suffered its first casualty within days of arrival when, on 3rd May, Beaufighter Ic, T2337, was badly damaged after it was mistaken for a Ju 88 by a 261 Squadron Hurricane pilot – thankfully, F/Lt Riley was able to crash-land safely at Luqa despite having been wounded. Not so lucky was Hurricane pilot Sgt Ottey

Bristol Beaufighter Ic long-range fighter, T3317 'XK-?'. The first examples of this type to operate from Malta arrived during May 1941 when 15 were sent on detachment from Coastal Command's 252 Squadron (coded 'PN') in order to help protect a vital convoy and remained at Malta until June before departing for Egypt. This image shows T3317 at Luqa and although it is often described as being one of 252 Squadron's aircraft, the partially visible letter on the fuselage bears no resemblance to 'PN'. It is in fact K, of 'XK' i.e. 272 Squadron's code, a unit that arrived in Malta during June 1941. This aircraft 'the CO's Query' (hence the code '?') was flown by Canadian, S/Ldr AW Fletcher, whose command pennant appears on the aircraft's nose. On 28th July, Fletcher led a most successful attack on Borizo airfield in Sicily where, by using the Beaufighter's four 20mm cannon and six wing-mounted mgs to full advantage he destroyed four SM.79s and two CR.42s. Another raid was launched two days later against Cagliari airfield in Sardinia where he destroyed three more SM.79s. Identifiable as an early Mk.Ic by virtue of its early-style heavily framed cockpit canopy, non-dihedral tailplane, propeller spinners and a DF Loop inside a Perspex dome behind the cockpit, it wears a Dark Earth and Dark Green camouflage with Sky undersides and white or very light grey codes; its individual code '?' is repeated on the nose. T3317 was lost on operations on 8th December 1941 when it force-landed south of Tmimi, Libya. Paul Lazell

whose aircraft dived straight into the ground from high altitude at the beginning of May; once again the culprit was thought to be hypoxia as the same type of fabric-lined oxygen tubing was still in use with 'D-Type' masks.

OPERATION *TIGER*

From Britain's perspective, her future prospects with regard to the war in general and the Middle East in particular appeared grim by May 1941, particularly following the fall of Greece and Yugoslavia during the previous month. General Sir Archibald Wavell's British and Commonwealth forces in North Africa had been considerably weakened to support the disastrous Greek campaign and Rommel had taken full advantage of this to attack and push the British back across the Egyptian border. In doing so, the 9th Australian Infantry Division had remained behind in Libya to hold the besieged port of Tobruk which was seen as a crucial objective for the enemy. The Axis advance across the desert had only ground to a halt due to a lack of supplies, thanks largely to the efforts of Malta's strike forces in attacking Axis southbound supply convoys. To try and redress the situation in the Middle East a convoy, codenamed Operation *Tiger*, was assembled in the UK to convey vital reinforcements to the Western Desert, which included 53 crated Hurricane IIs and an entire armoured division containing 295 tanks and 180 other vehicles. Rather than taking the circuitous Cape route to Suez, which would have taken months, and because the situation was considered so dire by the British, the decision was made that the convoy of five large transport vessels would be routed through the Mediterranean to Alexandria via Gibraltar. In order to protect this convoy during its hazardous journey across the entire length of the Mediterranean, its western escort would be provided by Force H which included: *Ark Royal*, battlecruiser *Renown*, battleship *Queen Elizabeth*, cruisers *Sheffield*, *Gloucester*, *Fiji* and *Naiad*, plus the 5th Destroyer Flotilla. Upon reaching the vicinity of Malta, the Mediterranean Fleet would replace Force H and escort the convoy to Alexandria.

To help provide air cover for this essential convoy as it passed Malta, 252 Squadron's Beaufighters were to fly long-range fighter patrols in conjunction with *Ark Royal*'s Fulmars, while Malta's Swordfish and Blenheims were ordered to increase their offensive operations to tie down or destroy as many Axis assets as possible. This, it was expected, would result in increasingly heavy raids being conducted against Malta in the days ahead in an attempt to neutralize the island's strike force, which, by extension, meant that Malta's Hurricanes would become deeply embroiled too – particularly as those *Luftwaffe* units which had recently been engaged in the Balkans were staging through Sicily on their way back to Germany. The latter would provide *Fliegerkorps* X with a significant (albeit temporary) boost as it launched attacks against both the convoy and Malta.

The expected onslaught began in earnest on 6th May 1941, just as the *Tiger* convoy left Gibraltar, and commenced at midday when a formation of four Heinkel He 111Hs from II/KG 26 was intercepted by Hal Far's C Flight. The Heinkel's enjoyed a combined fighter escort of between 20 and 30 Bf 109Es from both 7/JG 26 and III/JG 27 *Jabo*, the latter, a fighter-bomber *Gruppe*, was temporarily based in Sicily as it passed through en route from the Balkans to Germany. Despite the heavy escort, the Hurricanes were able to break through to the bombers though each rapidly acquired at least one Bf 109 on its tail. Hurricane IIb, Z3060, flown by P/O Gray, and Z3059, flown by Sgt Branson, fell to the guns of Muncheberg, but both were able to bail out with minor injuries. *Oberleutnant* Erbo Graf von Kageneck from III/JG 27 also claimed a Hurricane for his 14th victory of the war so far which is believed to have been Mk.IIb, Z3057, flown by P/O Dredge who tried to bring his badly damaged aircraft back to Hal Far. Unfortunately he was unable to keep control of the Hurricane when landing and overshot, causing it to crash and burst into flames and Dredge was badly burned as a result. Another Mk.IIb, Z3034, flown by P/O Peter Thompson, was also badly damaged during this combat but he was able to land safely with shell splinters in his leg. At 18:00hrs a further raid by He 111s from II/KG 26 reached Malta and C Flight's three remaining Hurricanes took off to intercept. Bf 109s were as ever in attendance but F/O Innes Westmacott in a Hurricane IIa was able to dodge them long enough for him to open fire on one of the bombers which he claimed as a probable as it was last seen heading for Sicily emitting smoke and losing height. Thought to have been He 111H, coded 1H+FM, it crashed on landing in Sicily killing the crew. This combat was watched from the ground by the AOC who congratulated Westmacott on his persistence in attacking the bomber when he was under attack himself while S/Ldr Whittingham, who was also on the ground, noted that there were a number of Germans on his tail as he opened fire on the bomber.

During the day's fighting Beaufighter Ic, T3294, from 252 Squadron was damaged beyond repair by bombs, while eight others suffered superficial damage. Later that evening, as dusk was falling, more bombers arrived over Malta in the gloom – but without a fighter escort. A pair of Hurricanes flown by Whittingham and his wingman P/O Pain were scrambled to intercept and they claimed a Ju 88A (4D+FS) from 8/KG 30 which crashed near to Floriana. Hits were also scored on at least two other aircraft, one of which must have been a He 111H from 4/KG 26 that returned to Sicily with a dead gunner on board. Later still, during the night, three Swordfish from 830 NAS left Hal Far to lay mines outside the entrance to Tripoli harbour of which one,

A colour view of a reconnaissance Ju 88D-2 from *Auflarungsgruppe* 123 based in Sicily during early 1941 seen with its lower engine access panels removed for maintenance purposes and with the tip of a long-range 900-litre fuel tank visible under the left wing root. It is fitted with later-style bulged panels in the rear cockpit transparency which allowed more room for the gunners manning a pair of rear-firing 7.9mm MG 15 mgs. A forward-firing MG 15 can be seen in the front of the cockpit while another is mounted in the glazed section at the rear of the ventral gondola which doubled as an entrance hatch. This aircraft wears an overall RLM 65 *Hellblau* (Light Blue) colour scheme as worn by many German reconnaissance aircraft, while the colourful unit insignia representing 2(F)/123 seen on its nose consists of an eagle carrying a telescope on a red and yellow quartered shield. EN Archive Collection

P4232 'A', flown by Lt Campbell with two other crewmen aboard, was hit by anti-aircraft fire and forced to ditch. Although the pilot and observer were rescued from the sea and taken prisoner the TAG, PO Welsh, appears to have been wounded by flak and did not survive.

Losses in action were one thing, but a tragic accident occurred the next day when two more Hurricanes were lost, albeit as a result of a collision in which one of the pilots was killed. The accident occurred when seven C Flight Hurricanes were scrambled from Hal Far to intercept a lone Ju 88D reconnaissance aircraft and the two Mk.Is involved (V7365, flown by Sgt Henry Jennings, and V7548, flown by Sgt Walker) struck each other. Whereas Jennings was unable to exit his aircraft before it struck the ground, Walker managed to bail out over the sea.

From the 8th, most Italian and German aerial activity centred upon the *Tiger* convoy as it traversed the Mediterranean, in which the Fulmars of Force H fought a series of running battles around the fringes of the convoy that would last for the next three days. The two Fulmar units aboard *Ark Royal*: 807 and 808 NAS, beat back wave upon wave of SM.79s, CR.42s, Ju 87s and Bf 110s on the 8th, and on the 9th. As the convoy crept closer to Malta, it came within range of the island's Beaufighters and although a number of Fulmars had been shot down or damaged, the only Beaufighter lost defending the convoy was Mk.Ic, T3239 'B', flown by F/Lt Lowe and Sgt Tranter on 10th May. It had been one of two Beaufighters that attacked a Ju 88D from 2(F)/123 and, although the Junkers was hit and damaged, it managed to reach Sicily whereas Lowe and Tranter, who had been hit in the exchange, failed to return.

Using *Tiger* as a diversion, two other convoys took advantage of its passage by sailing from Alexandria to Malta on the 6th. Convoy MW7A was a four-ship, 14 knot convoy consisting of the merchantmen *Amerika*, *Settler*, *Thermopylae* and *Talabot* escorted by the cruisers HMS *Calcutta*, *Dido* and *Phoebe* plus destroyers *Hereward*,

Hero, *Ilex* and *Isis*. Convoy MW7B, a 10kt convoy, consisted of the tankers *Hoeghhood* and *Svenor* escorted by cruisers HMS *Carlisle* and *Coventry* and destroyers HMS *Decoy*, *Defender* and *Greyhound*. The Malta-based Flower class corvette *Gloxinia*, which had been adapted to sweep for magnetic mines, was also attached to MW7B as was the conventional minesweeper HMS *Swona* in order to sweep a passage for the convoy through the extensive enemy-laid minefields surrounding Malta. Both convoys were covered by the Mediterranean Fleet as it sailed to meet *Tiger* and accompanying it was the fleet transport *Breconshire* which was to break off and return to Malta once again carrying RAF ground crews, fuel and general stores. All of those vessels intended for Malta arrived undetected by the Axis on 9th May, by which time the wreck of HMS *Jersey* had finally been cleared from Grand Harbour's entrance.

Having discovered that they had been hoodwinked, the Germans sent a formation of *Stukas* to Malta on the 9th in order to bomb the new arrivals but were intercepted by Hurricanes and two of the dive-bombers were destroyed. That night Force K sailed from Grand Harbour both to bombard Benghazi and act as a diversion for *Tiger* which was due to pass Malta during the night. Following this they joined the convoy's escort and returned to Malta once more before later departing for Crete. Despite the successful defence of *Tiger* from aerial attack so far, the merchantman *Empire Song* struck two mines whilst traversing the narrows off Malta during 9th May, killing 18 men. A fire then spread out of control and reached the stores of ammunition, following which the ship exploded and sank resulting in the loss of 57 tanks and ten crated Hurricanes. Prior to this however, all surviving personnel had already been taken aboard the appropriately named destroyer HMS *Foresight*.

On the afternoon of the 10th, Bf109s from 7./JG 26 appeared over Malta on a fighter sweep and became embroiled in a dogfight with intercepting Hurricanes. Although no losses were recorded on either side on this occasion, *Oberleutnant* Muncheberg broke off and elected to partake in what seems to have become a favoured pastime of his: 'Sunderland strafing,' because he descended alone to strafe Sunderland N9049 'RB-B' from 10 Squadron RAAF which had arrived at Kalafrana three days earlier with a cargo of 20mm cannon ammunition for the Beaufighters. N9049 had been on charge with the unit at its home base of Mount Batten, Plymouth, since 19th September 1939 according to the unit's records, records which describe its demise simply enough, namely, 'During an air raid on Malta on the 10/05/41 an ME 109 attacked 'B' with M/G fire setting it on fire. The aircraft then sank.' This Sunderland had been one of a small detachment of Australian-flown flying boats which were sent from the UK to Gibraltar in order to ferry ammunition, stores and personnel to Malta during the month in support of the Beaufighter detachment.

In order to give the Germans and Italians a taste of their own medicine, nine of 252 Squadron's Beaufighters made a low-level strafing attack on Catania and Comiso airfields on the 10th in which their heavy armament caused so much damage and confusion that the *Tiger* convoy was able to

Sunderland II, W3989 'DQ-L' from 228 Squadron on patrol. Although this photo was taken after 228 Squadron had been withdrawn from Kalafrana by May 1941, (having lost four Sunderlands in March and April alone at their moorings to marauding Bf109s), it does represent the little known use of 'stickleback' ASV Mk.2 radar by this unit while serving in Malta. The CO, W/C Nicholetts, had conducted trials with this equipment during April 1941 in Sunderland I, L5806 and had also trialled the use of twin-Vickers K mg mountings in the dorsal gun positions rather than the more usual single gun. W3989 served until finally struck off charge on 23rd February 1945. Author via Kev Darling

Above and left: For a short period of time 7/JG 26 was joined in Sicily by Bf 109E-equipped III/JG 27, one of whose Bf 109E-3s, 'Yellow 10', is seen here being fitted with a 500kg bomb at Gela in May 1941. Of interest is the early-style canopy used by this variant, the starting handle on the right-hand side of the nose cowling which is thought to be painted white, and, scarcely apparent, the plated-over mg ports inboard of each cannon. Frederick Galea

Below: Chalked in German on this bomb located under the centre section of a III/JG 27, Bf 109E is the legend (which translated reads) 'Malta, Malta, you vanished and took with you my happiness' taken from Act III of the Opera 'Martha' replacing the name Martha with Malta. Frederick Galea

Above: Improved Macchi MC.200s with semi-enclosed cockpits from 91ª *Squadriglia*, 10° *Gruppo*, 4° *Stormo* at Trapani, Sicily in 1941. This example, coded 91-6, features the famous 'prancing horse' insignia on the white theatre band while the pilot's cumbersome parachute pack sits on the wingtip. Unlike British seat-type parachutes, Italian fighter pilots had to wear their parachutes on their back and proved very uncomfortable and impractical. The camouflage is an intricately sprayed three-coloured mottle scheme of *Giallo Mimetico* 4, *Bruno Mimetico* and *Verde Mimetico* 2 (as often applied to aircraft built by the Breda company under contract), with *Grigio Mimetico* undersides. Italian official image

proceed largely unmolested for most of this day, the last that it lay within range of Sicilian-based air attack. A few night torpedo strikes were attempted by the Italians but these were warded off by intense anti-aircraft fire and the convoy reached Alexandria on 12th May having successfully battled its way through the Mediterranean. Although one had been lost, the remaining four merchantmen delivered their crucial loads intact including 43 crated Hurricanes, thousands of troops for the Western Desert, 238 tanks and 180 other vehicles with which to refit the 7th Armoured Division that had lost most of its tanks during Operation *Compass* the previous February. The tanks were urgently required for Operation *Battleaxe* which was to commence in June 1941 and which was intended to retake eastern Cyrenaica and relieve Tobruk, thus forcing the Germans onto the defensive for the first time since the war had begun.

Once the *Tiger* convoy had been shepherded beyond the range of Sicilian airpower, the Beaufighters continued to operate from Malta for some time and regularly flew escort to Malta's Blenheims during their anti-shipping strikes, often employing their heavy armament of four 20mm cannon and six .303in machine guns in the flak suppression role. Such an operation occurred on 7th May when three Beaufighters, flown by S/Ldr Yaxley, F/Lt Riley and naval pilot S/Lt Fraser escorted five 21 Squadron Blenheims against a convoy off Lampedusa. En route, the Beaufighters shot down an Italian trimotor transport which they came upon, then, having located the convoy, a Blenheim flown by P/O Dennis scored direct hits on a 5,000 ton transport which later foundered while another, flown by Sgt Osborne, bombed a destroyer which also later sank. Both Blenheim pilots went on to score direct hits in the course of two further strikes in as many days and were recommended for decorations as a result – receiving the DFC and DFM respectively. Having proved the concept of conducting Blenheim operations from Malta – by mounting six sorties for the loss of only a single aircraft – 21 Squadron's detachment returned to Britain in early May and preparations were put in hand to mount a continuous series of future detachments up to full squadron strength. In the event, Squadron Leader Atkinson's detachment proved to be the only one to return to the UK with its aircraft however.

'MALTESE GRIFFONS'
A NEW HURRICANE UNIT IS FORMED

By early May 1941, 261 Squadron had over 50 Hurricanes on charge spread between Hal Far, Takali and Luqa, so it was decided that a new unit would be formed using C Flight as its nucleus. The new unit, 185 Squadron, was reformed on 12th May 1941 (having previously been disbanded in 1940) at Hal Far under S/Ldr 'Boy' Mould DFC,

who had been promoted to take command. The Squadron's aircrew were a mix of veterans and newcomers, one of whom designed the unit badge consisting of a Maltese Cross superimposed by a winged griffin and bearing the motto (in Maltese) *Ara fejn hu* which, translated, means 'Look where it is.' Most of the ground crew on the other hand came from the recently disbanded 1430 (Army Co-Operation) Flight which had previously been based at Khartoum in the Sudan flying Gloster Gauntlet and Vickers Vincent biplanes during the East African campaign. They were joined by the nucleus of what was originally intended to have become 251 Squadron, but when the formation of this Squadron stalled in Palestine, those personnel already in situ were redeployed to join the ex-1430 Flight men aboard the fleet transport *Breconshire* bound for Malta where they docked on 9th May.

By the time 185 Squadron reformed, just one airworthy Sea Gladiator was left in Malta and although it had been on the charge of the Hal Far Station Flight since the departure of 806 NAS, the biplane now became the property of 185 Squadron which also assumed responsibility for the daily early morning meteorological flights. The Sea Gladiator concerned was N5520 which, according to Sgt FG Sheppard RAAF of 185 Squadron, was by now doped in a scheme similar to the Hurricanes but with 'Royal Navy' titles above its serial numbers. As most Hurricanes were camouflaged using Dark Green and Dark Earth the same colours were probably applied to N5520 following repair work to fix serious damage inflicted upon it following a ground loop, which occurred soon after it reverted to RAF control. During its meteorological flights N5520 occasionally encountered enemy aircraft and, in an earlier incident, at least three Bf 109Es tried to shoot it down. However, the unknown pilot at the controls managed to survive unscathed by using the biplane's excellent manoeuvrability to coolly turn inside each attack until they finally gave up and left, although Sgt Jim Pickering of 261 Squadron who had been monitoring the radio on the ground commented that the pilot was far from cool and that his transmissions 'graphically described his distress at their attentions.'

The first operational sortie by the new squadron occurred on 13th May when four Hurricanes provided top cover for 261 Squadron, but they were 'bounced' by a pair of Bf 109s from III/JG 27 and although they managed to break away before receiving the full brunt of the attack, Hurricane IIa Z2837, flown by F/Lt Innes Westmacott was hit – wounding the pilot in the elbow, despite which he managed to bail out. Hurricane I, V7115, of 261 Squadron was also shot down and unfortunately its pilot, P/O Thompson, was killed. Over the next few days repeat performances followed with 185 Squadron providing top cover for 261 Squadron in which a Hurricane was lost each time including Hurricane IIb, Z2901, flown by P/O

Hurricane IIb, BD702 'K', 185 Squadron at Takali in mid-1941 wearing Dark Earth and Dark Green camouflage with Sky Blue undersides and a Sky-coloured spinner without a corresponding band on the rear fuselage; its code letter 'K' was white. BD702's dozen doped-over mg ports are evident, each wing being equipped with a bank of four guns inboard and two outboard of the landing light thus identify it beyond doubt as a Mk.IIb. The quantity of scattered debris and rubble on the ground, caused by bombing, is remarkable. Frederick Galea

Hamish Hamilton, one of the most popular members of the squadron with five kills to his name, who died just days before his award of a DFC was announced. According to S/Ldr Whittingham: '[Hamilton was] one of the finest characters I have met. It was he who always took extra watches when things were hottest. Dear old Hamish you could almost smell the heather of Scotland when you spoke to him.' Although he had completed six months duty in Malta and was due for a rest he had volunteered to stay on until the new Squadron had settled in.

Bf 109s shot down two more Hurricanes between 15th and 20th May with only an Italian SM.79 being shot down in return. It was during this month that several German units began to leave Sicily for Germany in preparation for Operation *Barbarossa* which commenced on 22nd June 1941, and others left to reinforce units based in North Africa or Greece, while *Fliegerkorps* X eventually moved its HQ to Crete.

GERMAN EFFORTS WIND DOWN AND THE ITALIANS TAKE OVER: OPERATION *SPLICE* COMMENCES

The period of change seen during May coincided with an increase in the number of Hurricane IIs being sent to Malta as well as its use as a staging post for flights either destined for or returning from Egypt. For Operation *Splice*, 48 Hurricanes from 213, 229 and 249 Squadrons were embarked aboard the carriers *Ark Royal* and *Furious* from which they were due to depart for Malta on 21st May led by six Fulmar navigational aircraft from 800X Flight NAS. It was originally envisaged that all three squadrons would land in Malta, refuel, and then continue to Egypt to meet with their ground echelons who had departed long before aboard troopships sailing around the Cape to Suez. Of course, as was by now usual, there would be a slight change of plan once the Hurricanes arrived in Malta. On the 21st, the first Fulmars and Hurricanes commenced taking off as planned but there was confusion from the start when several Fulmars developed mechanical problems that caused them to fail to start, return to the fleet, or even ditch, and with strict radio silence imposed considerable confusion reigned among the Hurricane pilots who were supposed to follow them. Consequently, some were forced to orbit the carriers as they waited for their navigational leaders to join them, which in turn meant that they were expending their precious fuel.

The problem stemmed from the fact that each of the brand-new Fulmar IIs which had been issued to 800X Flight in the UK and then specially prepared for this mission, had been disembarked from *Furious* at Gibraltar and reallocated to the Fulmar units aboard *Ark Royal* instead – on the direct orders of Admiral Sir James Somerville of Force H. In their place 800X Flight received a motley collection of the worst duds that could be found amongst the *Ark*'s Fulmar Is and it took most of the transit time

Top right: A Bf 109E-7 from 7/JG 26 has its fuselage-mounted 7.9mm mgs loaded at Gela, Sicily, as its pilot, who would appear to be Muncheberg himself climbs out of the cockpit. If it is him, then this aircraft is most likely his personal aircraft 'White 12'. The cap at the tip of the spinner covers what would have been a gun port had production Bf 109Es been fitted with an engine-mounted cannon as originally intended. Instead, a 20mm cannon was eventually fitted into each wing, as seen here, adjacent to a now-redundant mg port protected with a leather cuff. EN Archive Collection

Right: Seen visiting 249 Squadron at North Weald, Essex, with 249 Squadron Hurricane 'GN-Z' in the background possibly V6728), this tropicalised Hurricane Mk.IIa (whose serial ends xxx33) was used for training purposes shortly before this unit left for Malta to allow pilots to become used to the 44-gallon long-range tanks seen here and the DH propeller. This would appear to be one of those which were sent to Malta during Operation *Splice*, for which the Hurricanes were flown to Abbotsinch, Scotland, loaded onto HMS *Furious* at Glasgow and then taken to Gibraltar where some were transferred to *Ark Royal*. Both carriers then sailed east and flew off Hurricanes belonging to 249, 213 and 229 Squadrons on 21st May 1941. The aircraft's gun ports have been sealed with doped fabric and painted over, while the guns themselves might very well have been removed. Ian Simpson

Above: Operation *Splice*. 800X Flight Fulmar Is and RAF Hurricanes being ranged on *Ark Royal*'s flight deck prior to departing for Malta. In this operation 48 Hurricanes from 213, 229 and 249 Squadrons, (all equipped with the Mk.IIa), were to be flown from *Ark Royal* and *Furious* in six formations each led by a navigational Fulmar. However, the plan began to unravel when the brand-new Fulmars intended for the task were instead allocated to *Ark Royal*'s resident squadrons, in return for which 800X Flight received *Ark Royal*'s barely airworthy discards, many of which failed to start in time to lead the Hurricanes and thus delayed the operation. Worse, it left formations of Hurricanes orbiting the carriers burning precious fuel as they waited for their leaders. The delays were such that the carriers themselves were forced to turn back for Gibraltar before all of the Hurricanes could take off to leave half of 229 Squadron still on deck. Of those which did depart for Malta, one Hurricane was shot down off Pantellaria by AA fire while a geriatric Fulmar, carrying the CO of 800X Flight, was lost due to engine failure and its crew captured by the Vichy French. The Hurricanes were not destined to remain in Malta however. The original plan had called for all three units to refuel and then continue to Egypt but the pilots of 249 Squadron were instead retained on the island and the veterans of 261 Squadron, who were long overdue for a rest, were ordered to fly 249's new Hurricanes to Egypt while 249 Squadron pilots remained in Malta to fly the aged Hurricanes 'bequeathed' to them by 261 Squadron. Ian Gazeley

Hurricane Z4544, an early production Mk.IIa which has been misquoted elsewhere as a Mk.I, possibly because it was fitted with a De Havilland propeller rather than the Rotol unit more often associated with the Mk.II. Having landed in Malta on 21st May 1941 during Operation *Splice*, it was refuelled and continued on to Egypt the next day where it later saw service with 806 NAS in late 1941 when that unit formed part of the Royal Naval Fighter Squadron in the Western Desert. It was written off at Helwan on 29th December 1941 after colliding with a car. A partially dismantled Beaufighter Ic from 252 Squadron stands in the background. Author's collection

required to reach the flying-off position just to make them reasonably airworthy. When the worst of the 'duds' gave-up-the-ghost and either ditched or failed to start, a number of *Ark Royal*'s own Fulmars had to be prepared at short notice and flown off as replacements. The delays incurred however, meant that half of 229 Squadron's Hurricanes had to remain onboard *Furious* as they could not be despatched prior to the fleet reaching its pre-determined point of return at which the fleet was compelled to head back to Gibraltar. Fortunately for the many Hurricanes orbiting the carriers, Fulmars began to appear and eventually all six separate formations began heading for Malta led by a Fulmar; each with a navigator on board. Unfortunately, as related in Chapter 1, the flight being led by Lt Cdr G Hare DSC – the officer commanding 800X Flight – had to navigate themselves to Malta when Hare's geriatric machine, N1994, ditched near Bône after its engine seized and both he and his pilot, Lt Pat Connolly, became prisoners of the Vichy-French.

En route to Malta, the combined Hurricane and Fulmar formations had to pass close to the Italian island of Pantelleria where one of the Hurricanes crashed into the sea, apparently a victim of anti-aircraft fire. The rest all reached Malta safely, although several were flying on fumes by then. Their problems didn't end there though as they had arrived in the middle of an air raid and, instead of circling out to sea until it finished, they were forced to land straight away while bombs fell around them. After such a dramatic arrival, the three Hurricane squadrons (less those which remained aboard *Furious*) were eager to refuel and be on their way to Mersa Matruh in Egypt, 100 miles east of the Libyan border. However, the pilots of 249 Squadron, ably led by Canadian Battle of Britain veteran S/Ldr Robert Alexander 'Butch' Barton, received new instructions and were ordered instead to remove their gear from their Hurricanes and told that they were to remain in Malta while the others continued on to Egypt. This left the pilots with only the clothes they stood in as their baggage was sailing around the Cape with the ground echelon and, worse still, they would not be able to retain the new Mk.IIs they had just brought into Malta either. Instead the veteran pilots of 261 Squadron, most of whom were utterly exhausted, were to fly them to Egypt instead. The newcomers would receive 261 Squadron's old Mk.Is plus a solitary Mk.IIa at Takali though some of these, including veteran P3731 'J', which had arrived during Operation *Hurry* in August 1940, were also being flown out as they were in urgent need of overhaul.

Upon arriving at Takali by Maltese bus (an eye-opener in itself for anyone who has ever experienced them, especially as the wartime buses had no glass in their windows), the pilots of 249 Squadron were shocked to see the state of the Hurricane Is they had inherited. They were described by the A Flight commander, F/Lt Tom Neil, in his book *Onwards To Malta*, as being: 'A motley collection of old Mk.Is, some with Vokes filters others without, which had a mix of different types of propellers, no code letters and were covered in patches whilst some even had their tailwheel [tyres] stuffed with straw, such was the lack of spares on the island'. One of the pilots later remarked that the Hurricanes left by 261 Squadron had had bullet holes patched by using *Players* cigarette tins, though ground crew who served on Takali's Hurricanes during this period and who were interviewed on this matter, robustly refuted that claim as a matter of pride explaining that there was always enough aircraft-grade aluminium available from wrecked aircraft to use for patches.

The 800X Flight airmen involved in Operation *Splice* had also expected merely to land at Malta, refuel, and then depart (in their case) for Crete, but the Germans had invaded the day before and had occupied the main airfield at Maleme. Consequently, the Flight's five surviving Fulmars were retained in Malta to conduct night-intruder sorties over Sicily. Under the leadership of its new CO, Lt DEC Eyres, 800X Flight (later to receive the unofficial title of Independent Night Fighting Unit) flew mostly against airfields, ports and rail targets armed with 20 lb bombs carried on Light Stores Carriers beneath their wings. Considering that no spares existed for the Fulmars and that they were in such an awful state, the unit was not expected to last long, so, to assist their colleagues in 830 NAS, 800X Flight aircrews converted onto the Swordfish to fly operations with this type too. Against all expectations however, the Fulmars *did* keep going, until 26th February 1942 in fact, when the last one, N1931, departed for El Adem,

Egypt, flown by tour-expired Swordfish pilot Lt Bill Garthwaite (a veteran of the *Bismarck* strike) with his observer S/Lt Tony Gillingham. Another 800X Flight Fulmar, N4001, had also been flown to Egypt a month earlier by S/Lt Cedric Coxon, which raises a question: how did the unit manage to remain operational without any spares? Some Fulmar spares must have remained in Malta following the departure of 806 NAS and some of their old wrecks would presumably have been cannibalised. But, in order to keep 800X Flight operational for so long, the maintainers must have had access to additional spares too. This in turn suggests that those Fulmars which had been damaged aboard *Illustrious* in January 1941 had been offloaded while the vessel lay alongside in Malta undergoing repair prior to sailing to Alexandria. Their hulks would have been left on the dockside no doubt, thus allowing 806 NAS to strip them of useable parts and these, combined with the other sources mentioned must have been enough to allow 800X Flight to operate for as long as it did.

The Fulmars of 800X Flight reportedly received anti-searchlight Night Black undersides when in Malta, though no photographs exist to confirm this, and at least one ('7H') was photographed with Hurricane long-range fuel tanks beneath its wings, though they were unlikely to have contained fuel as the type had a belly-mounted auxiliary tank for additional range if required. The most likely purpose for fitting the under wing tanks would have been to drop equipment and money to an agent who was then operating in Sicily and who regularly received such supplies. They were dropped onto the quiet slopes of Mount Etna from night-flying Hurricanes using converted long-range tanks and he even received a radio and (disassembled) bicycle in this fashion, so it seems logical therefore that night intruder Fulmars might also have been used for the same purpose. By using his bike, the agent was able to cycle around the various Sicilian airfields counting the number of aircraft as well as collating other useful information. Ultimately however, he was disturbed by a patrol on the perimeter of an airfield in 1942 and was captured when his bike chain snapped as he attempted to flee and he was later tried as a spy and executed.

Following the departure of 261 Squadron, 185 Squadron moved from Hal Far to Takali later in May 1941 to operate alongside 249 Squadron so that both units could pool their resources more efficiently. Their respective complements of Hurricanes stood at 10 Mk.Is and two Mk.IIas with 185 Squadron, and approximately 10 Mk.Is and a single Mk.IIa with 249 Squadron: a far cry from the 50 plus that had been available only a few months earlier.

As a postscript to Operation *Splice*, four 213 Squadron Hurricanes had turned back for Malta after leaving for Egypt on the morning of the 22nd when, according to the late Kenneth Cox an LAC serving with 185 Squadron, 'The fourteen Hurricanes that landed at Hal Far on the 21st May [the remainder having landed at Takali and Luqa in order to disperse them] were serviced during the day. Early next morning they were on their way to the Middle East four of them [from 213 Squadron] returned to the airfield some hours later. Two had developed technical problems and the other two had lost sight of the navigating leaders [four Beaufighters from 252 Squadron].' Following remedial work on the pair with technical problems all four Hurricanes were left on the airfield until 25th May when, as Cox continues, 'The long-range tanks fitted to the four that had turned back were removed and the fighters kept at Hal Far.' They made a very welcome addition to Malta's near extinct population of Hurricane IIs.

As a welcoming gesture to the newcomers of 249 Squadron, Joachim Muncheberg's Bf109s duly greeted them with a low-level strafing attack on Takali airfield on the 25th, leaving two of 249 Squadron's poorly dispersed Hurricanes in flames and a further three badly damaged with three airman and two pilots wounded. Luckily, this proved to be the Squadron's only engagement with 7/JG 26 because this elite unit left Sicily soon afterwards and moved to North Africa. During their time in Sicily, 7/JG 26, which rarely had more than eight aircraft available at any one time, had claimed 42 Hurricanes shot down over Malta, 19 of which fell to the guns of Muncheberg himself and whose personal score now stood at 43 in total. His rate of scoring would continue until he was killed on 23rd March 1943 over Tunisia when his 135th kill, an American-flown Spitfire of the 52nd Fighter Group, exploded directly in front of him bringing his own aircraft down too and although he managed to bail out, Muncheberg died of his injuries. Unlike most German aces with over 100 kills to their credit, he only served on the Russian Front for a short period of time (22nd July until end of September 1942), consequently 102 of his kills were scored against Polish and Western Allied pilots who were generally considered to be harder to defeat than Soviet pilots of the early war period at least, marking Muncheberg as a truly exceptional fighter pilot.

FURTHER BLENHEIMS ARRIVE: AND FRENCH MARYLANDS TOO

On 16th May 1941, a second Blenheim IV detachment arrived in Malta. Stationed at Luqa, the new arrivals were from 139 Squadron based at Swanton Morley, Norfolk, under the command of W/C EW Pepper DFC, whose detachment consisted of five Blenheims and seven crews. On the 19th, other Blenheim IVs arrived with A Flight of 82 Squadron led by newly promoted W/C LV 'Attie' Atkinson who, it will be recalled, had led the first Blenheim detachment to Malta while serving with 21 Squadron. As with all of the Blenheim reinforcement flights, the crews had departed individually from Portreath, Cornwall, in an

Above: The consequences of non-dispersal. On 25th May 1941, 249 Squadron's fighters were strafed at Takali by Muncheberg's Bf109Es which swept in to carry out a surprise attack leaving two Hurricanes totally burnt out and three badly damaged. Casualties were thankfully low as only three groundcrew and two pilots were injured: F/O Pat Wells was hit in the ankle by a bullet and Sgt MacVean broke both his legs as he hurriedly vacated his cockpit, the fighters having been manned pending a scramble. Flight Lieutenant Neil, the only pilot not in his aircraft, was on the phone demanding to know why the air raid sirens had just sounded yet they were still on the ground; while perhaps the luckiest man that day was F/O Harrington who was fortunate to survive unscathed when the parachute he was sitting on was wrecked by a cannon shell and the fuel tank in front of him was hit and erupted in flames. Fortunately for the Squadron (and the rest of the RAF in Malta), Muncheberg's unit, 7/JG 26, in common with much of the *Luftwaffe*, departed Sicily within days of this attack and further German incursions over Malta became a thing of the past: at least it did for the next six months! The two burning, broken-backed aircraft seen here (which had been manned by Wells and Harrington) reveal their black and white halved undersides to the camera, although the right-hand aircraft appears to have received a replacement wing finished in Sky Blue instead of white. Author, via T Fellows

Below: Members of 249 Squadron picking over the wreckage left in the aftermath of 7/JG 26's raid showing the two Hurricane Is that were burnt out. The wooden stringers and formers have burnt away in the rear fuselage leaving just the steel framework which has buckled due to the heat and broken the aircraft's back while much of the aluminium skinning has also melted. No doubt the intact Rotol propeller would be removed and fitted to another aircraft as they were in very short supply.
Author's collection

A rare image depicting a 249 Squadron pilot checking the cockpit of one of the Hurricanes taken over by this unit from 261 Squadron at Takali on 21st May 1941. It is fitted with a Rotol constant-speed propeller identified by its wooden Jablo-covered blades and characteristically long spinner. The latter is Sky-coloured, as is the fuselage band which was usually painted out and it wears the usual Dark Earth and Dark Green scheme, although the underside colours are indistinct and harder to determine. It is possible that this might be the unit's sole Hurricane IIa. In the distance a fully manned anti-aircraft position is evident containing a twin Lewis gun mounting and, further still, a crew bus and what appears to be an engineless Hurricane with a tripod over the nose. Author via R Rist

overloaded condition which obliged them to use the sudden drop over the cliff at the end of its runway in order to gain the required flying speed prior to hitting the sea! Inside each aircraft bomb bay was a pair of overload fuel tanks which had to be hand pumped by a fourth crewman (usually a member of the ground crew) who sat amid the crew's baggage in the tiny radio compartment situated between the wing spar and the turret. Having crossed the Bay of Biscay, a night stopover was usually had at Gibraltar where the crews made the most of the bright lights and lack of rationing before continuing their journey to Malta.

Also at Luqa, 69 Squadron's Marylands (and their sole high-altitude PR Hurricane), continued to perform their reconnaissance tasks despite the fact that their intended establishment of 12 Marylands had yet to be realised, while none of the 12 Beauforts originally envisaged had so far arrived. The supply of replacement Marylands had temporarily slowed to a trickle, probably because other RAF and SAAF units in East and North Africa were also receiving the type too. Therefore, when the crews of two Vichy-French Glenn Martin 167Fs defected to Gibraltar to join Free French forces in May 1941, bringing their aircraft with them, both machines were immediately allocated to 69 Squadron. The American-manufactured 167F was, in effect, identical to the British-operated Martin Maryland, quantities of which had been acquired directly from the USA as well as via undelivered ex-French contracts that were diverted to Britain's cause at the time of the Franco-German Armistice. As a consequence, 69 Squadron despatched F/Os Warburton and Bloxam with their crews to Gibraltar on 26th May to collect the two ex-Vichy machines and fly them back to Malta. Bloxam took-off from North Front airfield for Malta a few days later, however, Warburton remained behind for the time being as he was required to fly two reconnaissance sorties over the Vichy-French ports of Casablanca, Oran and Mers El Kebir in North Africa. In doing so, on 3rd June, he was intercepted at 3,000 feet over Casablanca by a pair of Dewoitine D.520s but the 167F or simply 'Glenn' as the Maryland was known to its British crews, easily outran them. Five days later, on the 8th, Warburton flew the machine to Malta and, despite the fact that it was now an RAF aircraft, no British serial was allocated to it at the time and it therefore retained its French serial number 114, the code '2' and its old Vichy unit insignia, GR1/22, on the tail fin. It was still finished in rather weathered French camouflage colours of dark brown, dark blue-grey and khaki with light blue undersides, though RAF roundels were applied over the French roundels whilst the tricolour-striped rudder was over-painted using camouflage paint with British stripes applied to the fin. Sergeant Moren is believed to have fitted twin .303in Vickers K Guns into the dorsal cupola instead of the standard single gun but, beyond that, little else is known about No.114 in 69 Squadron service as it was flown to Heliopolis in Egypt on 17th July 1941 by Warburton who returned to Malta two days later in standard RAF Maryland BJ423, which had arrived in Egypt via the Takoradi Route. Perhaps No.114 was ultimately re-allocated to Free French forces as this type remained in front line operational service with them as a light bomber well into 1945, although it is a fact that No.114 was allocated the RAF serial DD825 in London, but whether it was actually applied to the airframe is unknown.

Meanwhile, at Hal Far, the emphasis had now switched to night operations following the departure of 185 Squadron to Takali as the Fulmars of 800X Flight began their night-intruder sorties over Sicily and 830 NAS's Swordfish continued their nocturnal assault against Axis shipping and harbours. On 15th May, the minelaying submarine HMS *Cachalot* brought 76 tons of 'special stores' into Malta including vitally needed aircraft spares, ammunition and fuel. Prior to this the hugely successful 10th Submarine Flotilla had continued to grow with the arrival of HMS *Union* on the 4th, despite a near miss by an acoustic mine near to the harbour entrance, while the Flotilla's most famous and successful commander, Lt Cdr David Wanklyn of *Upholder* fame, sank four ships and damaged another from a southbound supply convoy off Sicily on the 24th. Amongst those ships was an 18,000 ton Italian liner, the *Conte Rosso*, laden with German troops bound for the *Afrika Korps* the loss of which represented a real blow to the Axis war effort. For this and other actions, Wanklyn was awarded the Victoria Cross.

ITALY ASSUMES THE OFFENSIVE ONCE MORE: A THIRD HURRICANE UNIT ARRIVES

Thankfully for Malta's defenders, the daylight bombing raids mounted by *Fliegerkorps* X *in* Sicily had reduced significantly by late-May 1941 as *Luftwaffe* combat units were transferred back to Germany to participate in Operation *Barbarossa*, or to reinforce either North Africa or the Balkans. The only German aircraft destined to remain in Sicily would be those Ju 52/3m transports involved in ferrying supplies between Sicily and North Africa; the Bf 110s of ZG 26 detailed to escort them; and possibly a few air-sea-rescue aircraft. As part of the deception plan for *Barbarossa* however, *Fliegerkorps* X's HQ was not officially withdrawn from Sicily until 22nd June (the day that *Barbarossa* commenced) when it transferred to Crete.

Since its arrival in the Mediterranean at the start of the year there had been a total of 2,741 offensive sorties mounted against Malta by *Fliegerkorps* X, despite which the British had just held on. Now the task of subduing the island fortress, its strike forces and air defences was left squarely in the hands of the Italians once more. A number of new units were posted to Sicily by the Italians to try and maintain the tempo of operations but in this the Italians would display far less vigour than the Germans, thus granting Malta's strike units a renewed opportunity to inflict heavy losses on the Axis supply convoys. For Malta's pilots this was the start of a much needed respite in which reinforcements would arrive and offensive operations could flourish once again as it became increasingly obvious to the British that, with the *Luftwaffe* seemingly absent, the Italians alone were wholly responsible for operations over Malta making it feasible to base greater numbers of offensive aircraft on Malta's airfields.

Following the losses and damage inflicted during 7/JG 26's strafing attack of the previous day, the pilots of 249 Squadron moved to Hal Far on 26th May to operate the

A colour image depicting Fiat BR.20M medium bombers from 242ª *Squadriglia*, 99° *Gruppo BT*, 43° *Stormo* based at Cameri during summer 1940 prior to deploying to Belgium for its ill-fated operations over England during the Battle of Britain. The unit returned to Cameri in January 1941 and four months later moved to Gerbini, Sicily for operations over Malta, mostly by night. This aircraft MM.22267, coded 242-3 was not one of them however as it was apparently lost during the latter stages of the Battle of Britain: nevertheless it is fully representative of those which operated over Malta and appears to be camouflaged in *Giallo Memitico* 2, *Marrone Mimetico* 2 with *Verde Memitico* 2 mottling. Italian official image

four ex-213 Squadron Hurricane IIs while their damaged aircraft were repaired. Meanwhile, returning briefly to early May 1941, (the 7th to be exact), 43° *Stormo* and its two constituent *Gruppo* had arrived at Gerbini and Catania equipped with Fiat BR.20M bombers and subsequently embarked upon a series of nocturnal bombing raids against Malta, to which 185 Squadron responded specifically by allocating one of its flights to deal solely with that threat.

The remainder of 185 Squadron however, in considering the *Luftwaffe*'s declining numbers (and very shortly of course its virtual departure from the theatre), was required to begin offensive operations from Malta in a similar fashion to those conducted by Fighter Command across the English Channel. Therefore Beaufighter bomb racks were fitted beneath the wings of their aircraft to create the first experimental Hurricane fighter-bombers or 'Hurribombers'. The racks, which could each carry bombs of up to 250 lb, were secured to the strongpoint under each wing which previously accommodated the long-range ferry tanks needed to fly to Malta. The fighter variants chosen purposely were the Hurricane IIa Series 2; Hurricane IIb; and, at a later date the Hurricane IIc, all of which employed specially strengthened wings. The 'Hurribombers' were to go onto the offensive over Sicily in daylight, for which the timely arrival of a further 42 Hurricanes (including the first official delivery of an unknown number of cannon-armed Mk.IIcs) on 6th June 1941 via *Ark Royal* and *Furious* as part of Operation *Rocket*, ensured that the new fighter-bomber offensive against Sicily would not unduly weaken Malta's air defence. The *Rocket* reinforcement comprised 24 aircraft from 46 Squadron led by Battle of Britain veteran S/Ldr Sandy 'Rags' Rabagliati DFC, along with the remaining aircraft of 229 Squadron which had previously been unable to take off during Operation *Splice*. This time though, instead of using Fulmars as lead aircraft, the Hurricanes were shepherded to Malta by nine Blenheim IVs from B Flight of 82 Squadron which flew over the carriers to rendezvous with the fighters during their journey to Malta. Upon arrival, the Blenheims joined with the survivors of their own A Flight who had earlier arrived on the island to further reinforce Malta's anti-shipping capability.

After reaching Malta, the pilots of 46 Squadron remained on the island though the ground echelon never did catch up with its pilots. 229 Squadron however, continued on to Egypt as planned to join with the rest of their unit, but, instead of taking their brand-new Hurricane IIs with them, they had to be surrendered instead and substituted for some of the island's remaining elderly Hurricane Is that needed to be flown to Egypt for long-overdue major servicing. The net result was that Malta now had three experienced fighter squadrons available with a reasonable number of Hurricane IIs between them to allow any enemy daylight incursions to be regularly met by up to 20 Hurricanes at a time, something utterly unheard of only months earlier. Given that the tempo of operations had dropped somewhat since the departure of the Germans, the three Hurricane squadrons found time available to apply their respective official code letters to their aircraft, namely: 46 Squadron 'PO', 185 Squadron 'GL', 249 Squadron 'GN'.

By Malta's standards this was a relatively substantial fighter force, one that soon began to claim victories against the Italians who had recommenced daylight sorties against Malta using SM.79s protected by Macchi MC.200s. A typical day's combat was recorded on 12th June 1941 which commenced when 18 Hurricanes from 46 and 249 Squadrons were scrambled against a lone SM.79 carrying out a photo-reconnaissance sortie escorted by 30 MC.200s. The Hurricanes claimed four Italian fighters shot down and also damaged the SM.79 for the loss of one Hurricane. Later in the day a further combat occurred during which two Cant Z.506B air-sea-rescue floatplanes were shot down in addition to a pair of escorting CR.42s, albeit for the loss of another Hurricane.

A NEW AOC ARRIVES: OFFENSIVE OPERATIONS MOUNT

On 1st June 1941 a new AOC was appointed to Malta to take over from AVM Forster Maynard in the form of Air Commodore Hugh Pugh Lloyd, MC, DFC, who was soon to be promoted to AVM. He had previously served as a Group Captain on the staff of No.2 Group, Bomber Command, where he was highly regarded by the Blenheim crews, many of whom were now deploying to Malta for anti-shipping operations. His simple brief from the Air Ministry was: 'Sink Axis shipping sailing between Europe and Africa'. In this respect he was an ideal choice for Malta as he was both fiery and offensively minded and, having realised just how small his forces on the island actually were, he was not shy of 'hijacking' aircraft bound elsewhere which earned him the nickname 'Sticky Fingers'. Lloyd's attitude was best summed up by a sign which he hung outside his office in the Lascaris operations room which read 'Less depends on the size of the dog in the fight than on the size of the fight in the dog' and he made a point of visiting the units under his command as often as possible whereby his distinctive sky blue-coloured Lincoln Zephyr car became a common sight. Being a died-in-the-wool 'bomber man', Lloyd had little grasp of modern fighter operations and while his fighter leaders were loud in their demands for Spitfires before German Bf 109s returned to Maltese skies, he continued to be happy simply asking for 'fighters' without specifying a particular aircraft type or version, as in his eyes as a 'bomber man', a fighter was simply a fighter regardless of name. In fact following a particularly arduous sortie later in the year (against the greatly-improved Macchi C.202), Hurricane pilot F/Lt Tom Neil of 249 Squadron was approached by Lloyd who enquired 'How are you doing?' Neil replied 'We're not doing very well. We simply cannot cope,' indicating that the Hurricane was now well past its best and needed replacing; upon which Lloyd pressed his face directly into Neil's and said: 'You know Neil. It isn't the aircraft, It's the men.' Like Neil, many of Malta's fighter pilots who had recently arrived from the UK could not understand why Lloyd was not pressing for Spitfires, nor, why the type was still not released for service abroad where they were sorely needed when so many were available back home with little to do other than conduct fighter sweeps over France. In his favour, one of the first decisions made by Lloyd (or 'Hugh Pugh' as he was known to the troops), was to instigate a massive building programme to disperse his limited number of precious aircraft away from their vulnerable airfields by constructing additional dispersal tracks and aircraft blast pens around the countryside. This was achieved by using the only labour available the Army, equipped simply with picks, shovels, wheelbarrows and horse-drawn carts rented from local Maltese farmers for four days a week. Little wonder then that Lloyd described the task as being akin to that of building the pyramids!

HURRICANE IIs FLOOD IN (AND OUT AGAIN!)

Further deliveries of Hurricanes were set to arrive in Malta on 14th June under the auspices of Operation *Tracer*, although in this instance all 20 aircraft from 260 Squadron aboard *Ark Royal*, plus 28 others from 238 Squadron aboard the new fleet carrier HMS *Victorious* were only supposed to be staging through Malta en route to Egypt. For the first time carrier-launched Hurricanes were led to Malta by four Hudsons flying from Gibraltar though some of the Hudson crews were fresh from training and were too inexperienced to lead such a flight. Irrespective of such considerations the Hurricanes were duly launched, though one failed to take off, another crashed into the sea and the pilot of another became disorientated and landed in Tunisia only to realise his error when unfriendly Vichy-French troops appeared on the scene whereby he took off again to finally reach Malta long after he had been given up as overdue. One of the lead Hudsons flew past Malta until its crew were informed of their mistake thanks to Malta's radar and turned back; but the error had bitten deeply into the fuel reserves of the following Hurricanes. Scotsman Robert McInnes Wilson was one of these Hurricane pilots and he described events thus: 'Of the four navigating Hudsons from 200 Squadron, one flew astray and by the time Malta was sighted the fuel gauges in each Hurricane were at their lowest mark. Soon one of the Hurricanes was abandoned and Saunders parachuted into the sea, from where he was later picked up. Briefed to land at Hal Far we used the airfield nearest to our approach – Luqa. Tanks now dry Sergeant Robert McPherson undershot the runway and crashed killing himself and writing off a fighter.' McInnes Wilson endeavoured to make a fast gliding approach to avoid stalling and spinning into the ground as McPherson had done but he was far too fast and overshot the end of the runway where, 'overshooting a slit trench I came to a stop against a wall, breaking up a third valuable fighter but coming away from the wreck without injury.' An enquiry was held into this fiasco and it was found that the pilot of the Hudson was obviously not experienced enough for such a demanding task and was unable to follow directions from the navigator, yet, in typical RAF fashion *he* was court-martialled rather than the person who had allotted him the task in the first place. Despite the losses the remaining 43 Hurricanes arrived in Malta safely, 34 of which were refuelled and sent on to Egypt over the next two days, though the remaining nine were retained, some of which (at least four according to a 46 Squadron combat report dated 23rd June 1941) must have been cannon-armed Mk.IIc versions, a type which had only entered RAF service earlier that month. In this instance the retention of the nine fighters might be viewed as a Hugh Pugh Lloyd-inspired 'windfall' as the first official delivery of the Mk.IIc *to*, as opposed *through*, Malta didn't occur until Operation *Railway I* later in the month.

Returning to the Blenheims of 82 Squadron once more, a third detachment of Blenheim IVs from 82 Squadron drawn from the remainder of B Flight in the UK arrived in Malta on 11th June 1941 to replace 139 Squadron's detachment whose CO had been killed on 3rd June during an attack which sank a 6,117 ton Italian munitions vessel and a 6,135 ton tanker. As well as the loss of the CO's Blenheim, four others had been damaged leaving the unit with just two serviceable bombers available. On 22nd June, six of 82 Squadron's Blenheims attacked a convoy of five merchantmen protected by two destroyers off Lampedusa. The leader of the first section of three, S/Ldr Harrison-Broadly flying Z6422, was shot down at low level by flak and, immediately afterwards, Z9545, flown by F/Lt Tom Watkins who led the second section, was also riddled by flak. As well as damaging his aircraft, the flak all but severed Watkins' leg and left him with other injuries too; then, to add to their problems, Z9545 was set upon by a CR.42 after the flak had ceased. Thankfully Sgt Chandler in the dorsal turret was a good shot and he was able to despatch the fighter while at the same time the observer, Sgt Sargent, leaned across to regain control of the aircraft as it skimmed along at zero feet. Tom Watkins was obviously in a great deal of pain and losing a lot of blood which caused him to pass in and out of consciousness but, with first aid and help from his observer, he was able to fly his damaged machine back to Luqa and make a successful landing before passing out once more as it rolled to a stop. The Squadron's CO, W/C Atkinson, immediately recommended Watkins for the Victoria Cross which was fully

endorsed by AVM Lloyd and also by the AOC of 2 Group in the UK, yet the only award authorised was a DSO while Sergeants Chandler and Sargent both received the DFM. More importantly for Tom Watkins the doctors at Imtarfa Military Hospital were able to save his leg and he was returned to the UK whilst his pock-marked Blenheim was written off as scrap.

Although No.2 Group's Malta-based Blenheim detachments strove to fulfil the day-bomber role, their losses and combat damage were sometimes so severe that there were occasions when non remained serviceable, with 28th June appearing to have been just such a day. On this date an Axis convoy was sighted off Tripoli and, as 82 Squadron were unable to respond, 69 Squadron despatched three bomb-laden Marylands instead. Led by F/O Bloxham, they executed a successful strike on the convoy leaving a 15,000 ton troopship on fire.

On 23rd June, S/Ldr Rabagliati led a dawn strike against Syracuse seaplane base using four cannon-armed Hurricane IIcs that had been allocated to 46 Squadron following Operation *Tracer*, for which their heavy armament was used to advantage to strafe six moored aircraft leaving substantial damage in their wake. Among those involved was one of the unit's longest serving pilots, F/Lt 'Pip' Lefevre, who had served with the unit since the Norwegian campaign and who recorded in his logbook that the raid took place at 04:45hrs and that he was flying Hurricane IIc Z3058. Next day, the Italians took their revenge when they in turn strafed Sunderland flying boats moored in Malta. The fighters responsible were described as Bf 109Es though they were more likely to have been Macchi MC.200s, a type which had been involved in increasingly daring fighter sweeps over Malta lately. They continued to do so on the 25th when a large incursion was made toward Maltese airspace by 48 of them acting as escort to a single SM.79 from 58ª *Squadriglia*, 32° *Gruppo*; a unit which had arrived at Chinisia, Sicily, on 29th April 1941. En route 12 of their number turned back toward Sicily with technical difficulties leaving 36 to face nine Hurricane IIs from 46 Squadron led by Rabagliati which tore into them. Rabagliati, a Scot with Italian ancestry who would become one of Malta's finest fighter pilots and leaders, headed straight for the SM.79, his gunfire causing the bomber's undercarriage to drop down leaving the Italian to be last seen heading for Sicily streaming oil and losing height. The rest of 46 Squadron latched onto the MC.200s and although many of them were fired at only three were claimed shot down, albeit without loss to themselves: a good result though considering the odds against them.

Yet more Hurricanes arrived on 27th June when 22 were flown from *Ark Royal* during Operation *Railway I* that included further examples of the hard-hitting Hurricane IIc. This time all of the Hurricanes were intended for Malta and although one was lost en route and the pilot taken prisoner, the remainder arrived over Malta where one subsequently crashed on landing. This delivery was swiftly followed by another on 30th June named Operation *Railway II* when *Ark Royal*, operating in company with the elderly *Furious*, ferried both Hurricane IIbs and IIcs toward the island. Unfortunately, a tragic take-off accident occurred aboard *Furious* when the tenth Hurricane to take off, flown by Sgt Hare, struck the ship's navigational platform and ripped off his long-range tanks which in turn caused a large petrol fire to spread across the deck that killed or injured many of the deck crew and pilots waiting to take off, including Hare, who later succumbed to his injuries. This prevented any more aircraft from departing *Furious*, leaving the nine Hurricanes already aloft (of the 16 conveyed) to join the 26 from *Ark Royal*, all of which were led to Malta by six Blenheims from Gibraltar.

On the same day that this latest batch of Hurricanes arrived in Malta there was a renumbering exercise involving two of the fighter units already based there. Having been unexpectedly retained in Malta, the pilots of 249 and 46 Squadrons had become separated from their ground echelons, baggage and personal effects, consequently, when their respective ground parties finally arrived in North Africa as planned they were assigned new pilots and aircraft. To prevent duplication however, i.e. two squadrons operating simultaneously while using identical numbers, it was decided on 30th June 1941 that Malta's 249 Squadron would remain in being and that its ground echelon in Africa would be broken up and posted to other units. For 46 Squadron the opposite occurred whereby the ground echelon in Africa retained the Squadron number while its pilots in Malta became part of a newly re-formed (having briefly existed in 1918) 126 Squadron operating from Takali and the newly constructed runway at Safi Strip. With squadron codes now the vogue in Malta, 126 Squadron applied the code 'HA' to its Hurricanes.

On 1st July 1941, 185 Squadron returned to Hal Far and had their bomb racks removed in order to resume daylight interception duties once more and also gained an additional 14 Hurricane IIas while their night-fighter responsibility was temporarily passed to 249 Squadron which established its own specialist flight. It was also around this time that the Fulmar intruders of 800X Flight picked up their unofficial title of the Independent Night Fighting Unit.

On 9th July, 126 and 185 Squadrons joined forces to attack the seaplane base at Syracuse with five Hurricanes, all of which were Mk.IIa variants, led by Squadron Leaders Rabagliati and Mould accompanied by F/Lt Pip Lefevre, F/Lt Jeffries and F/Sgt Mackey with Channel Islander Lefevre recording in his logbook: 'Attacked seaplane base, hangars, railway, trains etc. Three seaplanes set on fire.'

Meanwhile, the Blenheims continued to be active and, as well as attacking convoys out at sea, 82 Squadron also mounted a highly successful bombing attack on Palermo harbour at zero feet which destroyed three ships, (two were set on fire and burnt out while the third broke its back) and three others were damaged, one seriously.

The next Blenheim unit to be detached to Malta was 110 Squadron from Wattisham. They took 17 aircraft to the island and served throughout July losing seven of their number, including that flown by the CO, W/C Theo Hunt DFC, who was shot down by a CR.42 when attacking Trapani Power Station in Sicily. In return for these losses the squadron sank eight ships and were relieved during the last week of July by a 105 Squadron detachment from Swanton Morley, led by W/C Hughie Edwards VC. The detachment became operational on 22nd July, although only 10 of its Blenheims arrived in Malta as two were lost en route with one landing in neutral Portugal while the other crash-landed at Gibraltar. On their first anti-shipping strike from Malta, 105 Squadron attacked a convoy and sank two ships, the attack being duly followed up by a night-strike by five 830 NAS Swordfish which sank a tanker and damaged the two remaining merchantmen and an escorting destroyer.

OPERATION *SUBSTANCE*: ANOTHER VITAL CONVOY

On the same day that 105 Squadron became operational, the offensive capacity of 830 NAS was considerably enhanced by the arrival of a new consignment of six Swordfish. These were flown by volunteer crews from 825 NAS aboard *Ark Royal*, herself a component of a heavily reinforced Force H which formed the escort for Operation *Substance*, the convoy bound for Malta from Gibraltar consisting of six merchantmen and a troopship. This latest delivery of Swordfish was particularly important because two of them were equipped with ASV Mk.I (Air-Surface-Vessel) radar which was to prove such a boon to 830 NAS as the enemy convoys, hitherto virtually invisible by night, could now be located in the darkness and allowed the unit to change its tactics. The ASV-equipped aircraft became known in Malta as 'Special' or 'Ping' Swordfish and, ever since, any Fleet Air Arm aircraft which has carried search radar for use over the sea has been known as a 'Ping' or 'Pinger'. 'Ping' Swordfish always flew with a crew of three as the ASV set and radio were considered too complex for one man alone to operate. This in turn displaced the long-range fuel tank frequently carried by Malta's Swordfish in the rear cockpit in lieu of a third crewman. It was of course necessary to ensure that ASV Swordfish still possessed sufficient range to reach Axis shipping lanes and they therefore received a Hurricane-style, long-range fuel tank mounted beneath the fuselage on the torpedo crutches. In consequence this then displaced the torpedo and restricted any ordnance carried to bombs or flares beneath the wings. Normally, one ASV Swordfish would fly ahead alone to find and shadow a convoy utilising previously received intelligence derived via *Ultra*, or a sighting report from a Maryland or submarine to determine a rough search area and, once found, a sighting report would be sent by radio. The main Swordfish strike force would then be led to the convoy by the second ASV-equipped Swordfish, which usually carried the CO who was invariably an observer as opposed to a pilot in naval TBR squadrons. The CO would lead the strike component into an ideal attacking position before climbing to join the other ASV Swordfish, then, as the main formation dived to sea level prior to their attack, the ASV aircraft would drop flares beyond the target vessels to silhouette them for the torpedo bombers which would by now be running in towards the target at wave-top height out of the darkness.

In order to cover the arrival of the *Substance* convoy, long-range fighters were to be deployed to Malta once more as the Beaufighters of 252 Squadron had previously departed the island; thus a detachment of Beaufighter Ics from 272 Squadron was sent to Luqa from its base at Idku in the Western Desert. The Italians reacted strongly to *Substance* and a series of stiff running battles were fought at sea against Italian aircraft, submarines, MAS boats (Italian motor torpedo boat or MTB) which scored a number of hits on British warships with bombs and torpedoes. An SM.79sil torpedo bomber scored a hit on the cruiser HMS *Manchester* which caused such severe damage that it took almost a year to repair her, while the destroyer HMS *Fearless* was damaged by SM.79 bombers and had to be sunk by RN gunfire. Unsurprisingly, the two Fulmar squadrons aboard *Ark Royal* (807 and 808 NAS) were extremely busy and downed at least 12 enemy aircraft while protecting the convoy for the loss of six of their own shot down with six more lost to accidents, but, as importantly, many other enemy aircraft were driven off. Also damaged was the 11,000 ton *Sydney Star* which was torpedoed and crippled by MAS boats, though fortunately the Australian destroyer HMAS *Nestor* was on hand to take off some of the troops she was carrying and then assist her to Grand Harbour where the other five merchant ships had arrived on 24th July. Between them the ships brought 65,000 tons of stores to Malta including Merlin engines, anti-aircraft guns, torpedoes, 10,000 tons of ammunition, food, edible oils and, of course, tea; all of which would prove vital to the island's survival throughout the months to come.

Digressing briefly, one problem that did arise following the convoy's arrival was the matter of fuel storage, the bulk of which arrived in 4-gallon tins (known as flimsies due to their fragile nature) which were originally stockpiled in highly vulnerable outdoor fuel dumps. Protected only by barbed wire fencing, they contained Malta's entire supply of petrol, diesel and kerosene, yet to break them down into smaller caches presented awkward security problems for which an early solution was sought. Ultimately this was solved by storing the fuel underground for which a dedicated Command Petrol Pool was officially formed to administer this vital commodity, with each airfield receiving a dedicated 30,000 gallon bombproof bulk fuel installation which was dug into the Maltese rock.

The Beaufighters of 252 Squadron had played their part too in defending the convoy against waves of Italian bombers, dive-bombers and escorting fighters, but lost Sergeants Deakin and Jenkins in the process; their aircraft was shot down by MC.200s on 23rd July, albeit that it was claimed as a Blenheim. The Beaufighters though were not the only Malta-based twin-engined aircraft shooting at Italians as Adrian Warburton and his gunner, Sgt Paddy Moren, claimed a Cant Z.501 destroyed on 22nd July while flying a Maryland, then, a week later, Warburton claimed a Fiat G.50 (more probably a Macchi MC.200) with his front guns when it attempted an intercept over Palermo, Sicily.

Following the arrival of *Substance*, the Italians sent a lone Cant Z.1007*bis* trimotor bomber over Grand Harbour on the 25th to conduct a reconnaissance sortie in an attempt to obtain photos of the ships in preparation for a later attack, the solitary machine being escorted by no less than 47 MC.200s from 7º and 10º *Gruppo* which had arrived in Sicily on 25th May and 16th June respectively. The Italians were met by 22 Hurricane IIs from 185 and 249 Squadrons and, in the dogfight which followed, 185 Squadron headed for the Cant and shot it down into the sea while S/Ldr Barton and 249 Squadron engaged the escorting fighters. Both he and P/O Hill claimed a Macchi each while a third, claimed by P/O Matthews, crashed into Valletta's high street (then known as Kingsway but since renamed Republic Street) and although the pilot managed to bail out, his parachute failed to open.

THE ITALIAN SEABORNE ATTACK ON GRAND HARBOUR

On the night of 25th-26th July 1941, the Italians launched an audacious seaborne raid in an attempt to sink the newly arrived *Substance* vessels as they lay in Grand Harbour. Using MAS boats, two '*Miale*' 'human torpedoes' and eight '*Barchini*' explosive-filled motor boats; the latter were directed toward their target by a 'pilot' who would jump overboard at the last moment. Luckily for the British, news of this attack had already reached the Y-Service detachment in the HQ at Lascaris, which decrypted *Ultra*-derived intelligence sent from Bletchley Park in England. Consequently, this carefully planned attack was detected by the already alerted coastal defences and beaten off, though not before a steel bridge on the harbour breakwater adjacent to Fort St Elmo had been blown up by one of the explosive motor boats, creating a gap which was only re-spanned in October 2011. The *Regia Aeronautica* was to have supported this attack by bombing Grand Harbour at 01:45 on the 26th, i.e. before the motor boats attacked, in order to illuminate the target area and divert the defenders' attention inland, but they proved ineffective and although two raids occurred later in the night they were too late to be of any use. At first light, Hurricanes of 126 and 185 Squadrons were scrambled to intercept surviving Italian vessels as they returned to Sicily, and found three of them: the fast sloop *Diana*, (which, acting as a transport had conveyed the explosive motor boats involved in the attack), plus *MAS451* and *MAS452*. The Hurricanes commenced a series of strafing attacks on the Italian vessels but as they did so they in turn were 'bounced' by a formation of MC.200s from 7º *Gruppo*, which had been despatched to provide cover for the returning flotilla, and P/O Denis Winton from 185 Squadron was shot down in Hurricane IIa, Z4946 'GL-E'. In the ensuing dogfight two of the Macchis were destroyed, one of which was claimed by Australian Sgt Alan Haley from 126 Squadron who then shared the second with P/O Peter Thompson of 185 Squadron flying Hurricane IIc, Z3456 'GL-X'. One of the downed Italians was subsequently rescued, although the other, *Sergente Maggiore* Gallina of 76ª *Squadriglia*, 7º *Gruppo* was killed; two other MC.200s suffered damage. Having survived being shot down, Winton sat in his dinghy for a few hours until he noticed one of the MAS boats that he had earlier strafed lying immobilised on the water and which later turned out to be *MAS452*, (*MAS451* having blown up and sank). Clambering aboard, he found a scene of utter devastation and carnage with eight of its crew, including the captain, dead, no doubt due in part to the actions of the gunners from 3rd Battery RMA at Fort St Elmo, one of whom related, 'At 06:00hrs L/Sgt Bates drew my attention to the outline of a MAS that was just visible in the dawning light. It's rangewas 5,500 yards. We decided to test the accuracy of that figure. One round was fired & the shell fell about 500 yards short. What we did not know at the time was that the shell had ricocheted off the water and by a chance in a million had bounced about 500 yards to enter the cabin of the MAS. It exploded inside killing *Capitano* Moccagatta and the entire crew.'(In fact 11 survivors were taken aboard *Diana*). After signalling to passing aircraft that he was well Winton was eventually picked up by a Swordfish floatplane from the Kalafrana Rescue Flight and he took the boat's flag with him to use as a squadron trophy. Meanwhile, his war prize was jubilantly towed back to Malta by the converted trawler HMS *Jade*, following which *MAS452* was pressed into the Royal Navy and appropriately renamed *XMAS*. Believed to have been retained as a harbour launch in Malta, it was sold in 1945.

Having operated in support of Operation *Substance*, the Beaufighters of 272 Squadron remained in Malta to provide cover for Operation *Style*, in which warships of Force X, supported by those of Force H, departed Gibraltar on 30th July 1941 to convey 1,750 Army and RAF personnel, anti-aircraft guns and stores to Malta. While waiting for the ships to come within range and help cover their approach, the Beaufighters made a nuisance of themselves by carrying out a series of raids against Sicilian airfields, with Hurricane escorts, and on one raid alone claimed as many as 30 Italian aircraft destroyed on the ground. Longer-ranging unescorted sorties against Italian torpedo-bomber bases in Sardinia also proved successful, while the Marylands of 69 Squadron entered the fray when one of them strafed the airfield at Zuara leaving an SM.79 on fire and three more damaged. In retrospect, July 1941 had proved to be a successful month for Malta's forces during which the Italians had been attacked on and over their own soil. They had also lost heavily to Malta's defences as part of which the island's Hurricane pilots claimed 21 enemy aircraft destroyed, five probably destroyed and nine damaged. Just three Hurricanes were lost in return.

MALTA'S SUMMER OFFENSIVE

Earlier, in March 1941, the Wellingtons of 148 Squadron had left Malta for Kabrit, Egypt, as Luqa airfield became increasingly untenable for such large machines given their vulnerability to attack on the ground once the Germans had seized air superiority over Malta. However, by the summer of 1941, following the *Luftwaffe*'s withdrawal, the tactical situation had changed allowing the RAF to regain the upper hand once more and therefore plans were made to send a detachment of Wellingtons to the island again. Consisting of Mk.Ic and Merlin-engined Mk.II variants, the night bombers belonging to 38 Squadron would arrive at Luqa from North Africa during August to continue the nocturnal offensive against Sicilian and African targets. Equally, the nocturnal anti-shipping activities of Malta's Swordfish continued unabated being currently engaged in laying mines outside Sicilian and North African harbour entrances, while other Swordfish undertook diversionary raids using bombs. Sicilian airfields continued to be attacked during daylight hours by 252 Squadron's Beaufighters until they left Luqa for Egypt during August 1941 to make room for the Wellingtons. As for the Italians, their daytime activity over Malta itself was comparatively quiet for the most part, although disruptive Italian night raids still continued.

To counter such night raids the dedicated Malta Night Fighter Unit (MNFU), was formed at Takali in late July 1941 equipped with Hurricanes drawn from all three fighter squadrons that comprised eight Mk.IIc and four Mk.IIb variants. All 12 Hurricanes were painted overall black with red and blue 'B Type' roundels. Later, aircraft retained standard Dark Earth and Dark Green upper surface colours with black undersides as they could also be called upon to fly daylight sorties if required, though it would appear that they wore a mixture of roundels with either standard daytime, or, 'B Type' roundels being applied. The first CO was S/Ldr George Powell-Sheddon who had been brought back to Malta despite having only recently left, while the remaining pilots and ground personnel came from within Malta's Hurricane units. The two flight commanders were F/O Cassidy, who had flown night fighters in the UK, and F/Lt Don Stones, both of whom came from 249 Squadron, as did F/O Tommy Thompson, P/O Jack Mills and P/O Douglas Robertson. Pilot Officer Jack Grant and Sgt Alex Mackie hailed from 126 Squadron, while 185 Squadron sent P/O David Barnwell, P/O Denis Winton and Sgt Bob Branson, giving the MNFU a total of 11 pilots. Considering that the main effect of a night raid was to disrupt the sleep of everyone in Malta, military and civilian alike, the new unit adopted the particularly apt motto 'We Fight So That You May Sleep' and, working in close co-operation with the Army searchlight units, they soon began to score victories over the night bombers. The first occurred on the night of 5/6th August during a raid on Valletta when three of 43° *Stormo*'s Fiat BR.20Ms were claimed as destroyed: one by F/O Cassidy and two by P/O Barnwell. In fact just two BR.20Ms were actually lost that night, but the MNFU would go on to claim a steady stream of nocturnal victories throughout the rest of the month.

As the MNFU went about its business, the day fighters, having experienced a quiet period over Malta, went about theirs by making a nuisance of themselves in conducting offensive forays over Sicily searching for 'trade'. On 17th August, four Hurricane IIs from 126 Squadron attacked the seaplane base at Syracuse led by their CO, S/Ldr Rabagliati, (previously the CO of 46 Squadron) whose attack left two Cant Z.506Bs of 612^a *Squadriglia* in flames with four others damaged. The Italians, having decided that a daylight retaliation was in order, despatched a large formation of MC.200s from the newly arrived 10° *Gruppo* on the 19th but were spotted on radar approaching Malta. Scrambling to intercept, 12 Hurricanes from 126 Squadron engaged them over the Sicilian narrows where four of the enemy were shot down without loss. Flight Lieutenant HP Lardner-Burke DFC, who was beginning to make a name for himself over Malta, claimed three although his Hurricane was damaged in the process, and veteran 'Pip' Lefevre claimed the other.

A further strafing attack against Sicilian-based seaplanes was made by Rabagliati on 20th August, but this time the target was Augusta harbour where a Cant Z.506B was damaged as were petrol storage tanks and harbour installations. In retaliation the Italians sent 22 Macchi MC.200s to strafe Hal Far airfield at low level but little damage was done as by this time most of the airfield buildings had already been destroyed and replaced by freshly excavated underground tunnels containing orderly rooms, workshops, dormitories and other essential accommodation out of harm's way. The last real combat of the month occurred during the afternoon of 26th August when 18 Hurricane Is and IIs from 126 and

To counter the night raids each of Malta's Hurricane squadrons had taken it in turn to maintain a section on night duty until, in late July 1941, a dedicated Malta Night Fighter Unit (MNFU) was established at Takali with 12 Hurricane IIs drawn from all three fighter squadrons. The unit's pilots and ground crew were also drawn from within Malta's existing Hurricane force with the exception of its first CO, S/Ldr George Powell-Sheddon who was brought back to Malta having only recently left. 249 Squadron provided the MNFU with its first two flight commanders, one of whom had previous night fighter experience in the UK, plus three other pilots; 126 Squadron provided two pilots; and 185 Squadron sent three giving the MNFU a total of 11 pilots and 12 aircraft. The MNFU quickly began to score victories over the night bombers with the first being claimed on the night of 5th/6th August 1941 during a raid on Valletta when three newly-arrived Fiat BR.20Ms from 43° *Stormo* were claimed destroyed (though only two were actually lost). The unit's Hurricanes were initially painted overall black with red and blue B-type roundels, though in order to improve their camouflage properties later aircraft, such as this unidentified early Mk.IIa, had Dark Earth and Dark Green applied to their upper surfaces while retaining black undersides. This somewhat bent night-fighter was photographed at Takali following a landing accident and is coded 'Q'; it has a DH propeller and a fuselage roundel that has been toned down to become a B-type. Author's collection

185 Squadrons intercepted 15 MC.200s over the Sicilian narrows north of Gozo where they claimed four of the Italians destroyed. Rabagliati scored one of these kills in Hurricane I, V7103, P/O Lardner-Burke shot the tail off another and P/O Dickinson and Sgt McGregor claimed the last two while Sgt Greenhalgh claimed a probable after his cannon-fire left a Macchi smoking badly with an undercarriage leg dropped down. Unfortunately Sgt John Maltby failed to return and it would appear that he was shot down by one of two pilots from 86ª *Squadriglia* who both made claims for a Hurricane.

August 1941 proved to be a successful month for Malta's forces, a period in which the Hurricane's claimed 12 Italian aircraft destroyed, three probably destroyed and one damaged for the loss of one Hurricane, while the island's anti-shipping aircraft, warships and submarines busily engaged Axis convoys attempting to supply Rommel's *Afrika Korps*. The results were impressive: 63% of all stores sent by sea in August failed to arrive in North Africa. Success, however, was bought at a heavy cost as the casualties incurred during such attacks were often horrific especially amongst Malta's Blenheim crews. August also witnessed small changes for the *Regia Aeronautica* when, towards the end of the month, the Cant Z.1007*bis* bombers of 33° *Gruppo*, 9° *Stormo*, began to arrive at Chinisia in Sicily to commence operations against Malta while the SM.79s of 87° *Gruppo*, 30° *Stormo*, left Sicily for a rest from operations.

Also, the last day of the month saw W/C Hughie Edwards VC, the CO of 105 Squadron, relinquish his command to take a staff appointment and was replaced by W/C Don Scivier AFC who, on 21st September 1941, brought his Blenheim back to Luqa with one engine on fire following a daringly executed attack by two aircraft on a 24,000 ton troopship off Lampedusa. Unfortunately Scivier's luck did not last as he and his crew were killed next day following a mid-air collision near Homs when the tail of their Blenheim IV, Z7423 'H', was cut clean off. The other Blenheim involved, Z9606 'T' flown by Sgt Tommy Williams, was extensively damaged but he was able to nurse Z9606 the 218 miles back to Malta and land at Luqa. When he removed his flying helmet he found that the shock and strain of this sortie had turned his hair completely grey and within a month it was snow white, whilst his gunner was so traumatised by the incident that he never flew again. In fact, during July and August, the original 105 Squadron detachment had been all but wiped out with just two aircraft surviving from the dozen initially despatched from the UK (only 10 of which had reached Malta). As with most such detachments, losses were replaced by simply commandeering Blenheims as they staged through Malta en route to the Middle East to thus become the latest 'new' members of the

The smiling pilot of this Hurricane I appears to be Sgt Tom Hackston of 126 Squadron who was killed in action over Malta on 4th July 1941. He wears typical flying attire for RAF pilots based in Malta and has his seat-type parachute draped over his back ready for the straps to be fastened once he is in his cockpit; the 'cushion' inside the parachute pack is in fact his dinghy. Judging by the wrecked hangar in the background the surroundings appear to be Hal Far which was where 126 Squadron was based. The dark outer ring of the fuselage roundel is actually yellow yet appears dark as a result of orthochromatic film. *Frederick Galea*

detached unit. As for the surviving aircrew from 105 Squadron's original deployment to Malta, they departed for the UK on 28th August only to find themselves delayed upon arrival at Greenock due to a dock strike!

The next Blenheim detachment to arrive in Malta was the largest yet and came from 107 Squadron based at Great Massingham, Norfolk. They began to leave the UK on 22nd August with 26 aircraft and crews and were in place ready for operations by the first week of September. Once at Luqa, 107 Squadron joined forces with the remnants of 105 Squadron's detachment, which was now made up from replacement 'press-ganged' crews, until the latter left Malta on 11th October 1941.

With the advent of ASV-equipped Swordfish, almost all of the nocturnal sorties conducted by 830 NAS were now flown against convoys at sea and, on the night of 1st/2nd September 1941, nine Swordfish attacked five merchantmen and five destroyers using ASV to guide them into a perfect attacking position that resulted in four of the supply ships being torpedoed. One was a 6,338 ton freighter which, as it exploded, created a fireball so large that it was seen by the crew of a Hal Far-based Fulmar of 800X Flight flying a night intruder sortie 60 miles away over Sicily, and although this was the only ship sunk that night another was so badly

Having arrived at Takali this Hurricane IIb, Z3757, fitted with 44-gallon ferry tanks, has come to grief *circa* late July or August 1941. Assuming that this aircraft was not delivered to Malta via North Africa, then it is possible that it arrived during Operation *Railway II* on 30th July 1941. Z3757 was repaired and joined 185 Squadron where it received the code 'R'; later it went on to serve with both 249 and 605 Squadrons following which their aircraft were pooled. On 12th January 1942, P/O Wigley of 605 Squadron was at the controls when he helped shoot down a Ju 88, but on 6th April it was damaged beyond repair, probably by bombing. Beneath Z3757's wing sits another Hurricane which also appears to have come to grief. *Author's collection*

damaged that it never sailed again. This single action resulted in a loss to the Axis of 3,500 tons of bombs, –,000 tons of petrol, 5,000 tons of food, 25 Bf 109 engines, 25 cases of glycol coolant, and an entire tank repair workshop unit which would never reach Rommel's forces. Later that week another convoy was intercepted by Swordfish of the Tunisian coast where one ship was sunk and two others were damaged, while on the 12th, a 6,000 ton ammunition ship also exploded after it too had been torpedoed. It was, of course, often hard to judge the results of a night attack as a combination of smoke screens, heavy anti-aircraft fire and the darkness itself could make it difficult to determine the extent of any success or otherwise, therefore the Marylands of 69 Squadron were often called upon next morning to locate the convoy, assess any damage and count the ships.

Of course this offensive pressure was having a dramatic effect on events in North Africa as Rommel's Afrika Korps was being starved of supplies and fuel for its operations in the desert. Therefore, by September 1941, preparations were being put in hand for the *Luftwaffe* to return to Sicily in force once again in order to wipe Malta from the map, ready for a joint Italian and German airborne invasion. The epic battle for survival that followed, which would at last include Spitfires, will be covered in a later volume.

By summer 1941 most of the *Luftwaffe*'s Sicilian-based aircraft had departed for North Africa, the Balkans, or to participate in Operation *Barbarossa,* the invasion of the Soviet Union, leaving the *Regia Aeronautica* almost solely responsible for maintaining pressure on Malta. Almost, but not quite; some German units remained amongst which were the Bf 110Ds of ZG 26. Their main responsibility was to escort transport aircraft and merchant ships transiting between Sicily and North Africa, although they also escorted bombers to Malta and conducted sneak low-level fighter-bomber raids. This Bf 110D from III/ZG 26, coded 3U+DT, is seen escorting an Italian SM.79 from 30° *Stormo.* EN Archive Collection

Amongst the Italian bombers attacking Malta from late summer 1941 were the SM.79s of 32° *Gruppo*, 10° *Stormo ET* and this 57ª *Squadriglia* aircraft, which is having its engine covers removed, provides the backdrop for an impromptu game of volleyball in an idyllic setting amongst the olive groves on Chinisia airfield in Sicily. By this time the camouflage of Italian bombers was beginning to change as labour-intensive mottled schemes gave way to a two-coloured olive-green and blue grey 'Metropolitan' scheme consisting of *Verde Oliva Scoro* 2 upper surfaces with *Grigio Azzuro Chiaro* 1 undersurfaces. Author via www.military-aircraft.photos.com

Top: A formation of Z.1007bis bombers from 60ª *Squadriglia*, 33° *Gruppo*, 9° *Stormo* crossing the Sicilian countryside at low level in July 1941. This unit fought over Malta for a relatively long period after arriving in Sicily in June 1941 remaining there until November 1942, barring a short respite in Italy to re-equip with new aircraft and a detachment to Sardinia in June 1942 for anti-shipping operations against Malta-bound convoys. The camouflage appears to be *Giallo, Marrone* and *Verde Mimetico* with *Grigio Mimetico* undersides. EN Archive Collection

Above: A pair of 126 Squadron Hurricanes Is seen at Takali. The nearest Hurricane is coded 'XL', providing early evidence of the use of squadron codes in Malta, with 'X' being the unit designator and 'L' representing the aircraft's individual code within the unit. The presence of such a code dates this image to August 1941, as 126 Squadron only used this system for a month before it adopted the two-letter Squadron code 'HA'. Jack Paternoster via Colin Pomeroy

Hurricane IIa, DG626 '6', with pilot Len Davis at Kano, Nigeria, in September 1941 while en route to Egypt from Takoradi on the Gold Coast of West Africa, a route which offered an essential additional supply line to the Middle East. In order to complete their journey Hurricanes were equipped with a pair of 44-gallon long-range tanks while a temporary white finish was applied to the top of the cockpit to deflect heat. Additionally, white was applied to the top of the fuselage and tailplane to render the aircraft easier to locate if forced to crash, as visible on Hurricane Z4850 coded '7' in the background. DG626 appears to be painted in the usual Dark Earth and Dark Green scheme with light-coloured undersides, probably Sky Blue. Temporary white markings and numbers were also applied to all aircraft which flew this route. Originally built as Mk.I, V7061 was converted to a Mk.IIa and reserialled DG626. Following its arrival in Egypt, all that is known about DG626 is that it was struck of charge on 15th February 1942 as having been lost! Author via the late J Pickering

HAWKER HURRICANE I, N2622 'B', A-FLIGHT, 261 SQUADRON, TAKALI, LATE 1940 – EARLY 1941

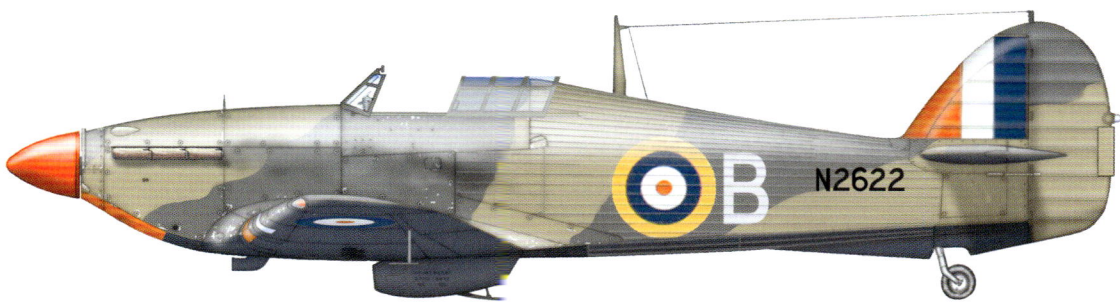

On 11th January 1941, Sgt Bill Timms took-off from Takali in this aircraft to intercept a high-altitude reconnaissance aircraft over Malta, but during the climb his engine over-revved and blew up at over 20,000 feet. Anoxia may have caused Timms to pass out and prevent him from altering his throttle and propeller pitch settings. It is assumed that he regained consciousness during the ensuing dive and tried to glide to Luqa, but, realising that he would not make it he bailed out at too low an altitude and was killed. N2622 crashed four miles north-west of Luqa airfield. By late-1940, the Hurricanes of 261 Squadron's A Flight featured red spinner-caps, a colour which on this aircraft (frequently flown by F/O 'Jock' Barber) extended for a distance beneath its nose too. A colour image exists showing Barber in a Hurricane which features the area of red described as well as the standard Dark Earth and Dark Green colour scheme with black-and-white halved undersides as depicted here. Sadly that Hurricane's serial number is not visible so the belief that the image depicts N2622 is speculative. Other factors however, suggest that this is the correct aircraft including 'Jock' Barber's logbook; it confirms that N2622 was the aircraft he most commonly flew at the time the photograph was taken. Additionally, as a senior member of A Flight, the code 'B' appears to be appropriate as 'A' was reserved for the CO. The area of red beneath the nose may have been used to indicate a flight commander's aircraft as it was by no means common.

FAIREY FULMAR I, N1881 'H', 806 NAS, HMS *ILLUSTRIOUS* AND HAL FAR, MALTA, JANUARY–MARCH 1941

N1881 was quite a successful aircraft being responsible for downing two Italian aircraft during 1940 while serving aboard *Illustrious*. Its camouflage is the usual S.1.E. Naval scheme found on early Fulmars consisting of Extra Dark Sea Grey and Dark Slate Grey uppers with Sky Grey sides and undersides. The propeller spinner is a dark colour, most likely black, though Sky Grey was also common within 806 NAS at this time; the serial and code 'H' are black. A1-Type roundels appear on the fuselage with large B-Type above the wings with a fin flash occupying the entire fin. The position of the colour demarcation running along the side of the fuselage could differ appreciably on early Fulmars though the same basic colour scheme remained. In the photograph used as a reference for N1881, the lower surfaces of the right-hand wing appears to be white, therefore the left wing would be black as depicted here; no roundels were applied beneath the wings.

JUNKERS Ju 87R-2 *STUKA*, S1+HK FROM 2/StG 3, TRAPANI, SICILY, JANUARY 1941

This aircraft is fully representative of those which launched the devastating dive-bombing attack against HMS *Illustrious* on 10th January 1941. It still wears the standard *Luftwaffe* European style RLM 70 *Schwarzgrun*, 71 *Dunkelgrun* and 65 *Hellblau* camouflage without any white theatre markings applied as yet and with a spinner which appears to have a blue tip, although this may have been red. The Ju 87R-2 was a long-range development of the Ju 87B and was ideally suited for anti-shipping sorties over the Mediterranean for which 300-litre long-range drop tanks were commonly carried, leaving the belly position free for a 500 kg (1,100 lb) bomb. A photograph of this aircraft appears on page 93.

FULMAR I, N1860 'M', 806 NAS, HMS *ILLUSTRIOUS* AND MALTA, JANUARY-MARCH 1941

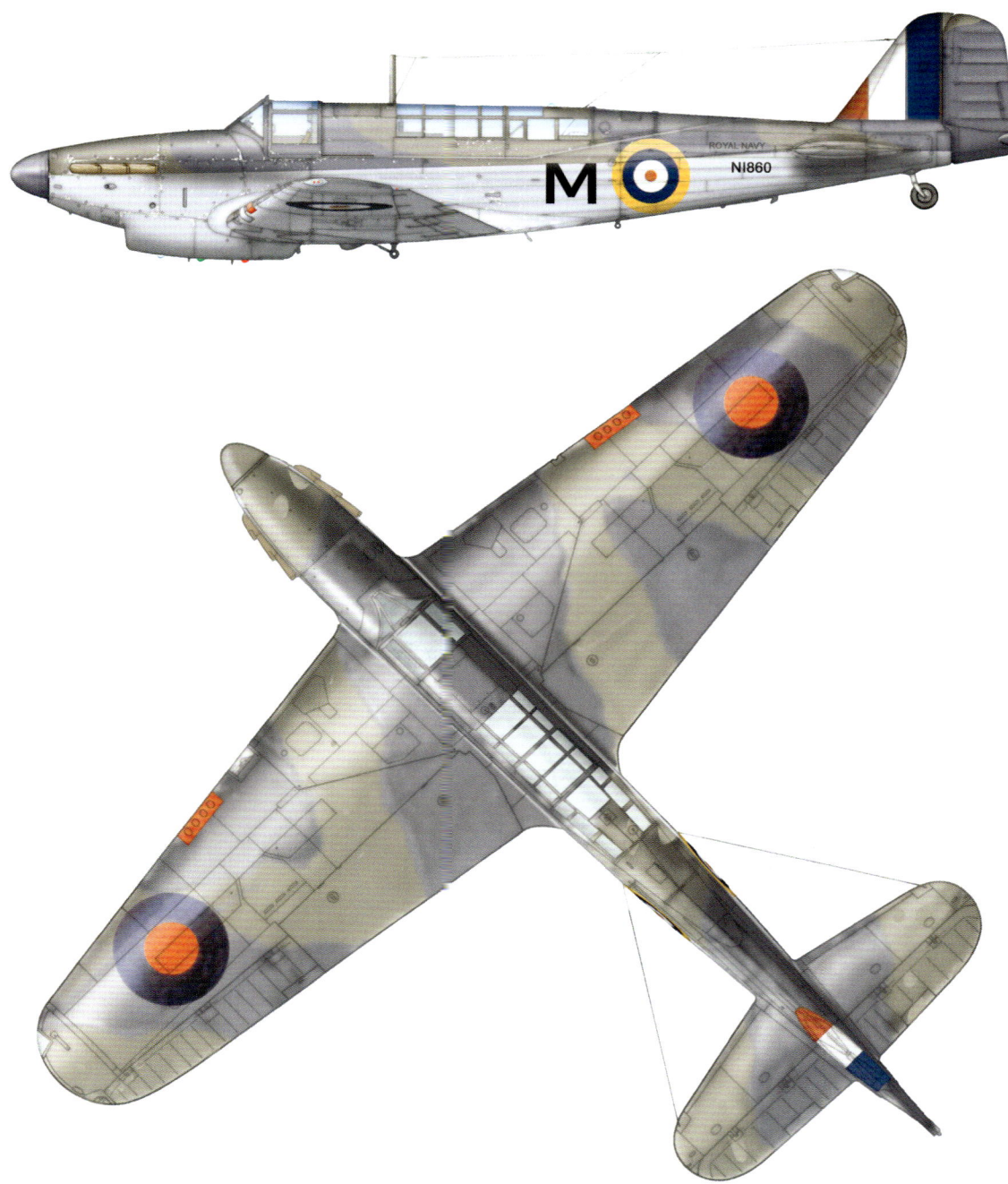

N1860 served with 806 NAS between 1st June 1940 and April 1941. This illustration is based on a photograph taken after it had returned to Egypt from Malta when it still retained the full naval S.1.E. camouflage scheme as described with Fulmar N1881 (qv), albeit without the black-and-white halved lower wings as seen on most of the unit's other aircraft. Other variations include: the retention of A-Type underwing roundels; 'Royal Navy' titles on the fuselage; a non-standard application of the code 'M' (codes, serials and titles are black); and either a faded Black or Extra Dark Sea Grey spinner. Additionally, N1860's rear fuselage colour demarcation line rises to finish level with the tailplane in this instance. A photograph of this aircraft appears on page 109.

FULMAR I, 'G', SERIAL UNKNOWN, 806 NAS, HMS *ILLUSTRIOUS* JANUARY 1941

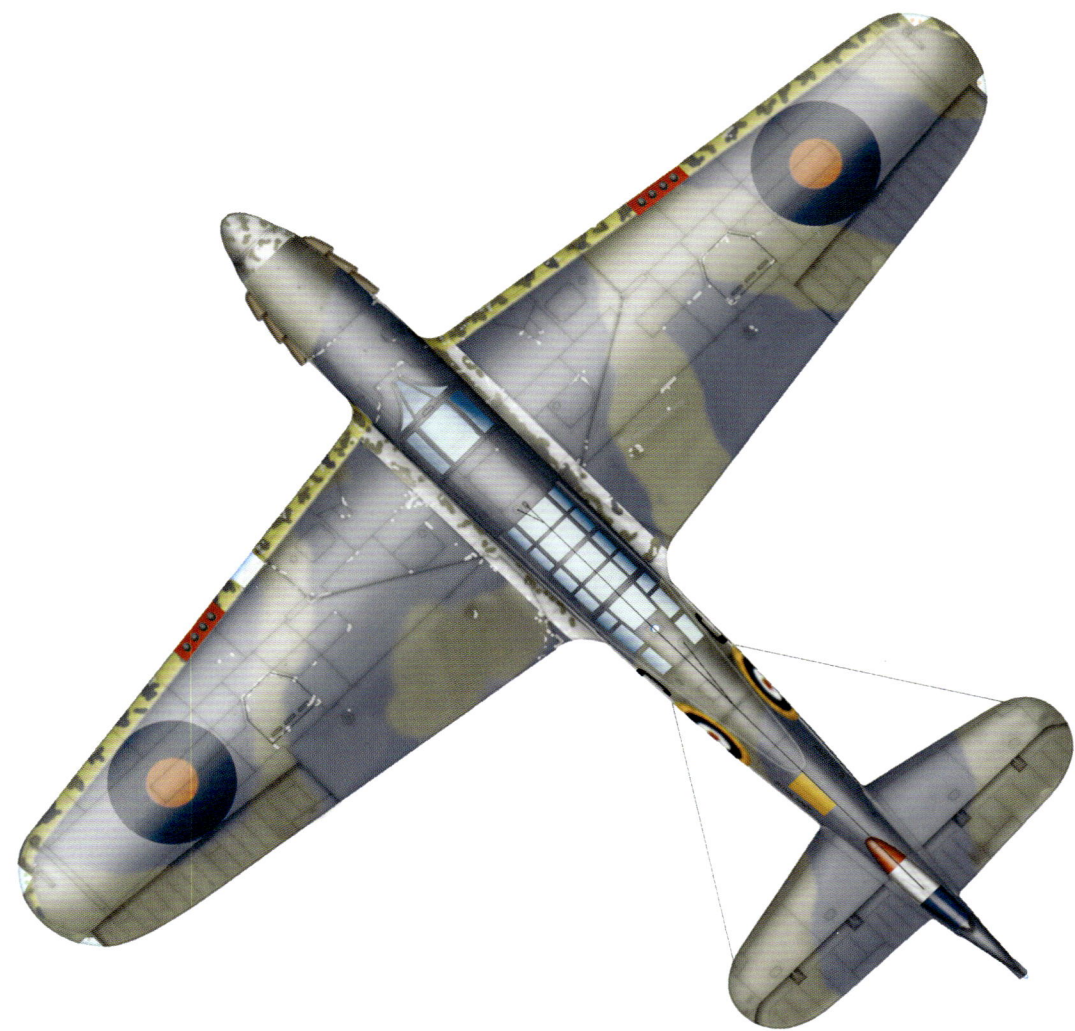

It is a fact that some RAF Hurricanes serving in the Western Desert, Greece and Crete in 1941/42 wore an Italian inspired camouflage finish on their nose and wing leading edges which was unofficially termed the 'Spaghetti' scheme and was intended to make the Hurricane appear more like an Italian fighter when viewed head-on. This, it was hoped, might allow their true identity to be concealed for a few vital seconds. What is less well known is that the originators of this scheme, in British service at least, appears to have been the naval fliers of 806 NAS who applied it to their Fulmars during 1940; the year before the RAF began using it. The most likely colour used for this unofficial scheme was a light brown base coat, possibly Middle Stone, with Dark Green and Dark Earth mottling applied on top, though there were no hard and fast rules. In fact this Fulmar appeared in a wartime newsreel which revealed that the mottling extended along the side of the fuselage and the wing roots, and that it appeared to have had a silver-painted spinner too (as did some other Fulmars and Hurricanes). The remainder of this Fulmar's camouflage complies with the standard naval S.1.E. scheme, although a variation in the fuselage demarcation line is once again evident, as too is a mustard-coloured gas-reactive patch on the upper left rear fuselage. When 806 NAS re-equipped with new Fulmars for service aboard HMS *Formidable* in 1941, they were finished in the later Temperate Sea Scheme in which the camouflage extended down the fuselage sides with Sky undersides and several had the Spaghetti scheme applied too.

THE HURRICANE TAKES THE STRAIN   149

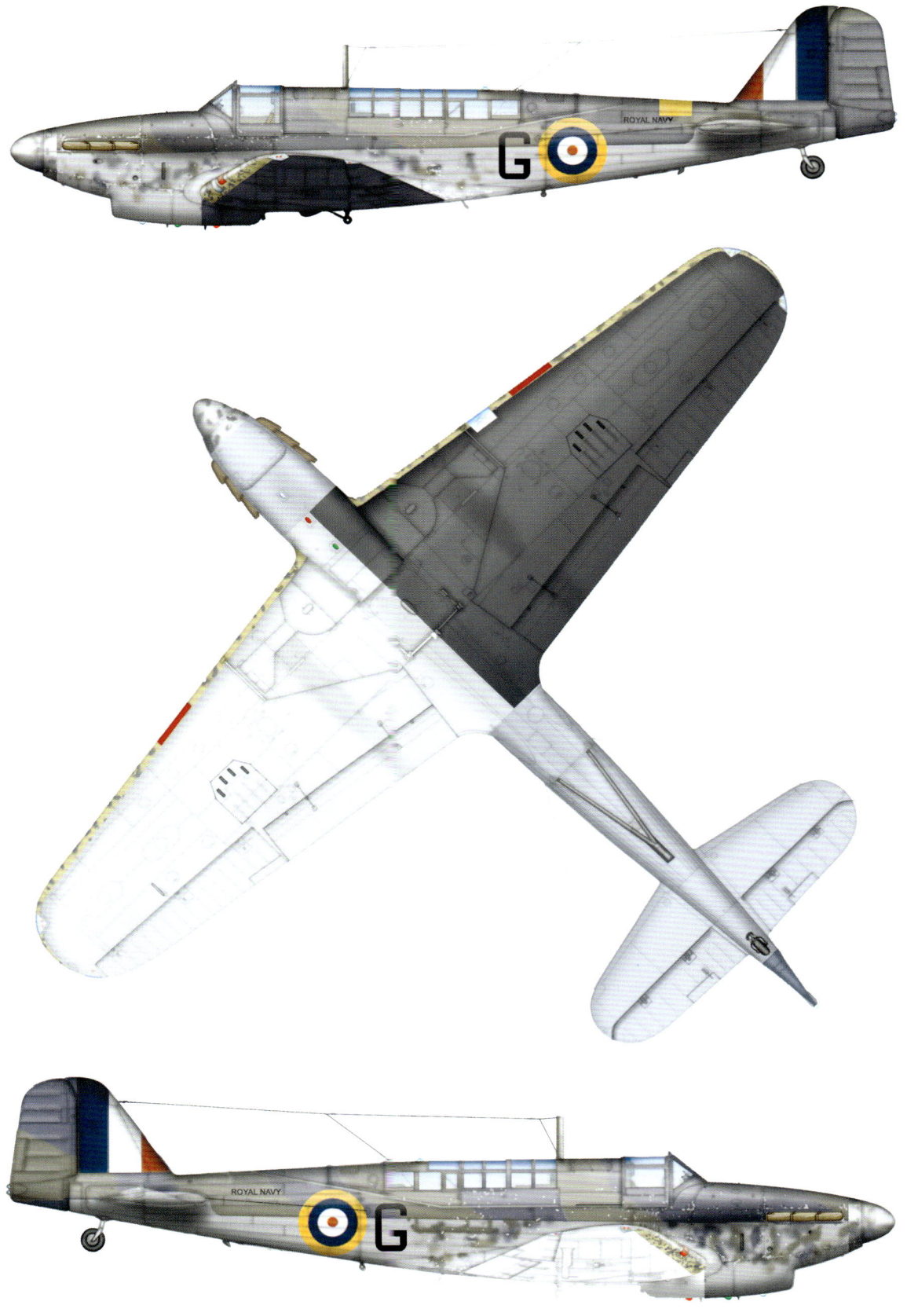

GLOSTER SEA GLADIATOR, N5520 'S', 261 SQUADRON RAF. N5520 'S', 806 NAS, HAL FAR. 1940-41

Photographs have appeared in recent years which show that Malta's surviving Sea Gladiators had been repainted by January 1941 in a scheme that extended their camouflage further down the sides of the fuselage. There is speculation that the colours used were Dark Earth and Dark Green as used by most of 261 Squadron's Hurricanes, although Middle Stone and Dark Earth remain an outside possibility. However, it is known that the Sea Gladiators were repainted at around the time they returned to naval charge (806 NAS at Hal Far) in January 1941, whereby the naval Temperate Sea Scheme of Dark Slate Grey and Extra Dark Sea Grey would seem to be a more likely choice of camouflage given, as one veteran has written, they 'looked smart in their new naval colours' for which the appropriate paints and dopes were still readily available at Kalafrana. By using a grey-scale in conjunction with the recently discovered images, the latter scheme does offer a very good match for the Sea Gladiators. Final definitive proof for either scheme is unfortunately lacking, therefore, two separate illustrations of N5520 are provided: one displays the RAF's Temperate Land Scheme of Dark Earth and Dark Green; the other shows the naval Temperate Sea Scheme. The undersides of 'both' aircraft remained black and white, while the underneath of the upper wing remained Sky Grey. Codes and serial were black.

The photograph shows a rare view of Sea Gladiator N5520 'S' seen in early 1941 following its transfer to 806 NAS. This particular aircraft arguably became the most famous of them all and ultimately became known as 'Faith' and was the last survivor. As previously explained the existing naval Dark Slate Grey and Extra Dark Sea Grey scheme was altered when the upper surface camouflage was extended down the fuselage sides, as appeared on Sea Gladiators elsewhere around this time, whilst the undersides themselves retained the black and white halved scheme applied previously with Sky Grey beneath the upper wing. The 'black' outer ring of the roundel was in fact yellow, the change in appearance having been caused by the use of orthochromatic film which shows both yellow and red as black, whereas both the code 'S' and serial actually were black. Lieutenant Jackie Sewell of 806 NAS, the first pilot to achieve five victories flying a Fulmar, was also a successful exponent of the Sea Gladiator in which he scored two kills over Malta, one of which was against a Ju 88 over Hal Far airfield on 24th January 1941, much to the joy of everybody watching from the ground and by the end of World War Two Sewell had scored 13 kills, seven of them shared. N5520's fuselage survives to this day and is currently preserved in Malta at the National War Museum in Fort St Elmo.
Frederick Galea

GLOSTER SEA GLADIATOR, N5524 'N', 261 SQUADRON RAF. N5524 'N', 806 NAS, HAL FAR, EARLY 1941

As with N5520, so to with N5524, albeit with subtle variations in their respective camouflage patterns, the most obvious visual difference applies to N5524's engine cowling which retained its original naval colours.

The photograph shows three of Malta's four surviving Sea Gladiators seen in early 1941 at Hal Far around the time of the Illustrious Blitz. They had been transferred from 261 Squadron (RAF) to naval charge with 806 NAS whose surviving Fulmars were also based at Hal Far following the attack on their ship. One of their Fulmars, 'F', which was flown by Lt Robert Henley and Midshipman Cullen during the Luftwaffe attack on Illustrious on January 10th 1941, is visible at the end of the line. The Sea Gladiators are: N5529 (nearest); N5524 (middle); and N5520. By this time all three had been repainted in what is likely to have been standard naval pattern S.1.E. camouflage amended to cover the entire fuselage. The camouflage, which is seen to extend down the sides of the fuselage, is confirmed by eyewitness accounts as having been the same naval colours as used previously i.e. Dark Slate Grey and Extra Dark Sea Grey. This would have been quite logical given their renewed naval ownership and the known fact that such colours were in fairly plentiful supply at Kalafrana. The middle aircraft incidentally has retained the original S.1.E. camouflage demarcation line on its engine cowling, while all three retain the half black, half white scheme beneath their lower wings, tail and fuselage. The undersides of their upper wings are Sky Grey which extends halfway down each wing strut. Fulmar 'F' wears the older S.1.E. scheme which was slowly being replaced with Sky Grey sides plus black-and-white undersides. Each Sea Gladiator has been fitted with an ex-Blenheim De Havilland three-bladed, variable-pitch metal propeller to improve their climb rate. *Courtesy of Frederick Galea and Wise Owl Publications*

JUNKERS Ju 88A-5 L1+FR FROM 7/LG 1, CATANIA, SICILY, JANUARY 1941

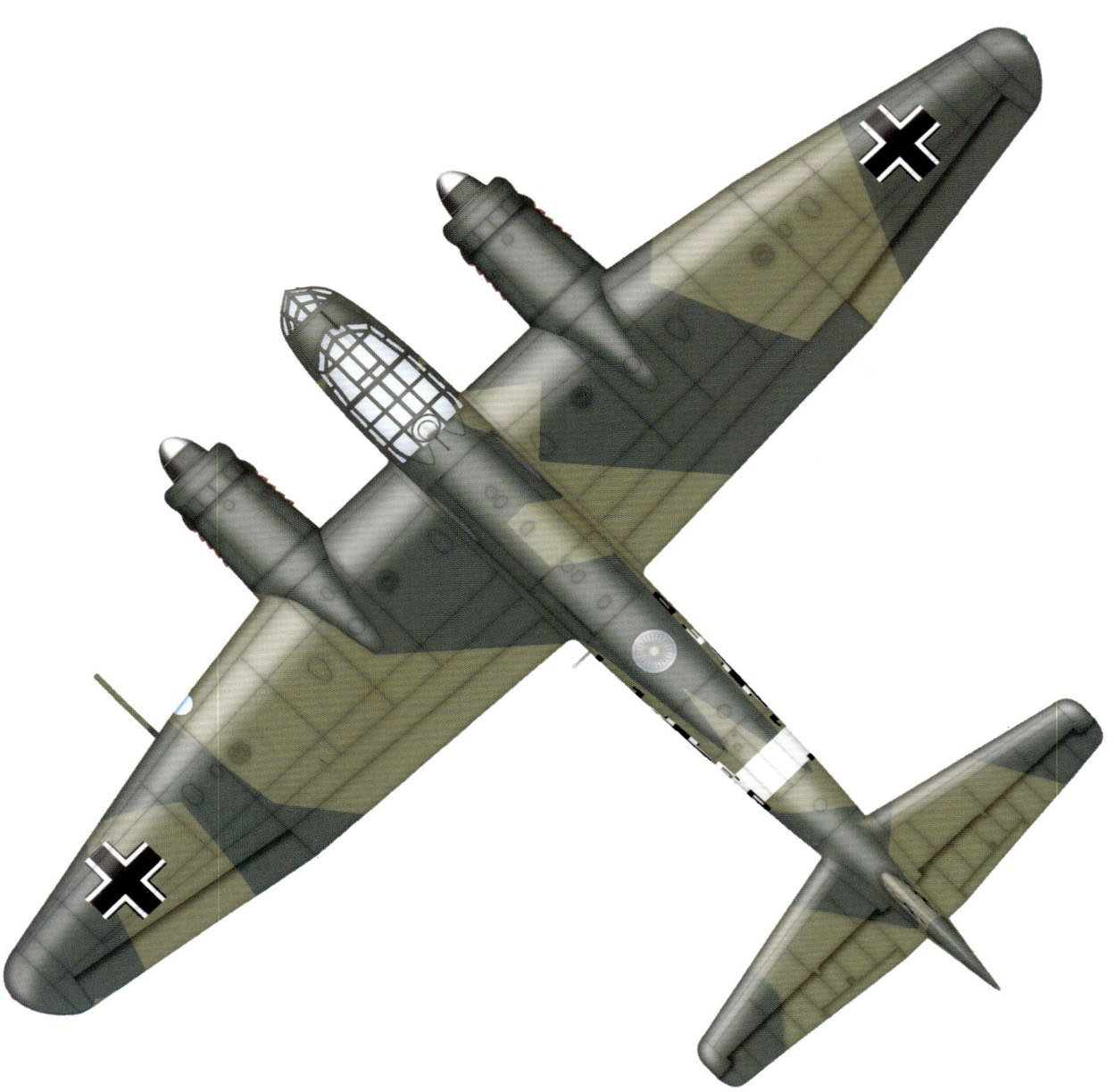

L1+FR features an early-style cockpit canopy with a single rear-facing 7.9mm MG 15 mg, a second facing forward with a third mounted in the ventral tub. It wears the *Luftwaffe*'s standard European bomber camouflage scheme of RLM 70 *Schwarzgrun*, 71 *Dunkelgrun* and 65 *Hellblau*. Its *Werk Nummer*, 2352, is in white at the tip of the fin. A white fuselage theatre band has been applied, the under-fuselage portion of which has been over-painted, possibly to render it more conspicuous against the predominantly blue-coloured undersides although its lower wingtips remain white. Spinners are black with white tips. The Ju 88A4 and A5 became Germany's primary bombers for operations against Malta and were considered tough opponents by British fighter pilots by virtue of being both fast and well armoured, making them hard to destroy even with the cannon-armed Hurricane IIc. A photograph of this aircraft appears on page 110.

THE HURRICANE TAKES THE STRAIN 153

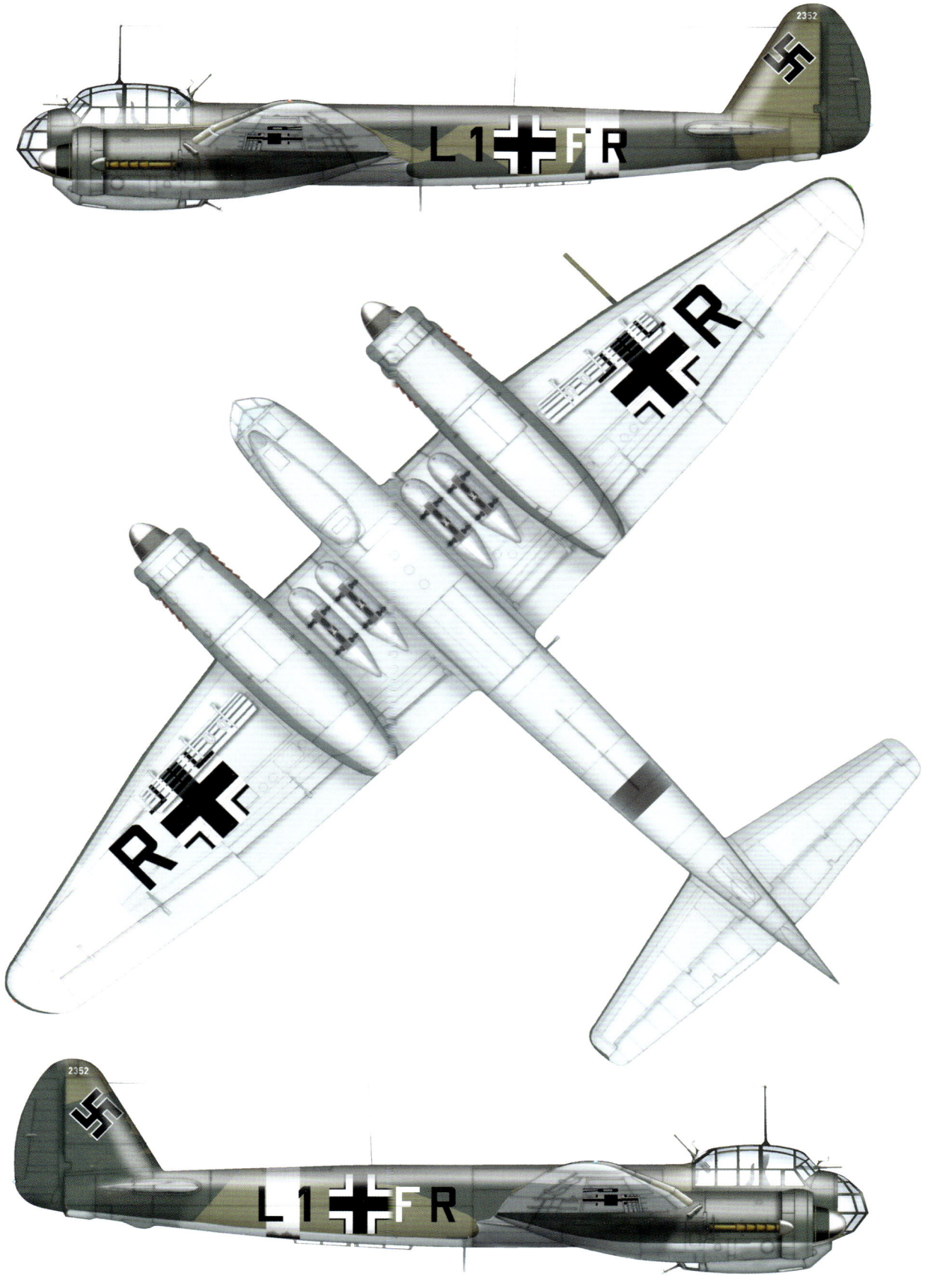

MESSERSCHMITT Bf 109E-7N 'WHITE 12', 7/JG 26. FLOWN BY JOACHIM MUNCHEBERG, SICILY, FEBRUARY 1941

This aircraft, a -7N sub-type with no filter over the air intake, was flown by the unit's CO, *Oberleutnant* Joachim Muncheberg, one of Germany's leading aces in 1941. On arrival in Sicily in February 1941 he had already amassed 23 kills over Poland, France and England and scored 19 more over Malta. Muncheberg continued to score (both in the West and for a time in the East) until killed on 23rd March 1943 over Tunisia when his 135th victim, a USAAF Spitfire, exploded directly in front of him bringing his own aircraft down too and although Muncheberg managed to bail out, he soon died of his injuries. His final tally was 135 kills: 102 against the Western allies and 33 against the Soviets. During operations over Malta, Muncheberg usually flew 'White 12', his personal aircraft, which, like the other aircraft in the *Staffeln* had a yellow nose containing his personal red love heart, while the *Jagdegeschwader* motif, a stylised 'S' inside a white shield, appeared under the windscreen. Deciding what constituted the precise colour scheme for Bf 109Es of this period can prove a contentious issue as they were then undergoing changes and the correct colour combination may never be known. Some reputable sources state that 7/JG 26's aircraft still wore a Battle of Britain era scheme of RLM 02 *Grau* and 71 *Dunkelgrun* on upper surfaces with RLM 65 *Hellblau* on the sides and undersides. Others, equally reputable, state they were finished in RLM 74 *Dunkelgrau*, 75 *Mittelgrau* and 76 *Lichtblau*, even though this scheme was only officially introduced later in 1941. Another theory is that field-mixed greys were applied to these aircraft on top of the first scheme in an approximation of the second, before the latter became official. Without positive proof to the contrary, any one of the three options may be considered viable. A division of opinion also exists as to whether 'White 12' wore a vertical white bar marking behind the fuselage cross or a white theatre band instead; perhaps both explanations are correct inasmuch that the theatre marking applied at a later date may have concealed the bar, who knows? This Bf 109E also had a triangular metal pennant attached to the radio mast.

THE HURRICANE TAKES THE STRAIN 155

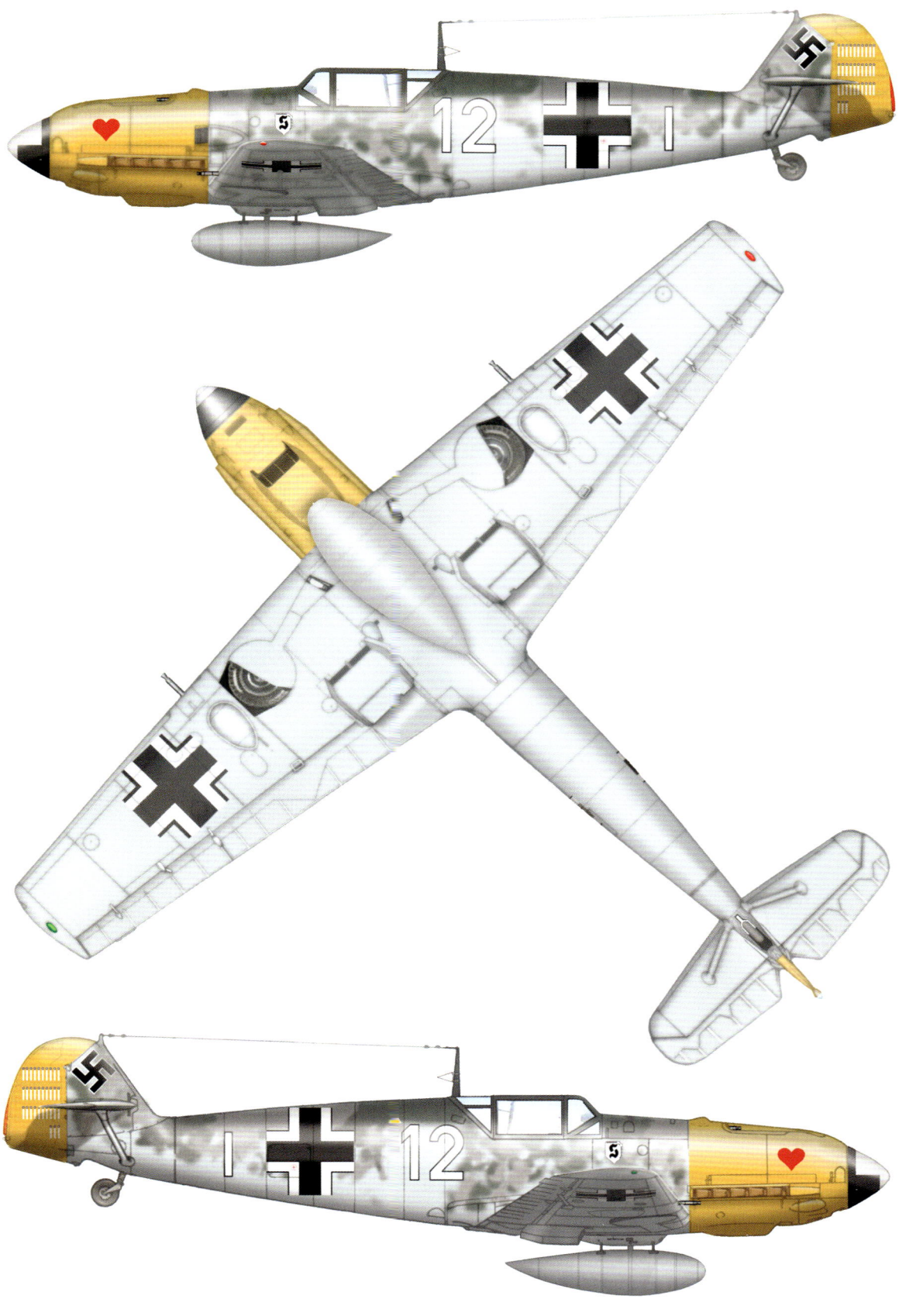

MESSERSCHMITT Bf 110D-3, 3U+LT, 9/ZG 26, SICILY, 1941-42

The primary function of ZG 26's Sicilian-based Bf 110Ds was to escort ships and transport aircraft crossing the Mediterranean between Italy and Libya. They were also employed against Malta directly as bomber escorts prior to the introduction of the Bf 109E to Sicily in 1941, after which they often mounted low-level fighter-bomber attacks against Malta's airfields. Initially these aircraft retained a European-style camouflage as shown here which consisted of RLM 74 *Dunkelgrau*, 75 *Mittelgrau* and 76 *Graublau* with a white theatre band and an RLM 27 *Gelb* nose. Eventually, most were repainted in desert colours, sometimes using Italian paints. The white cockerel denoting 9 *Staffeln* was placed on the nose in front of ZG 26's triangular Ladybird Motif, while 3U+LT's *Werk Nummer*, 3406, appears aft of the RLM 21 *Weisse* theatre band. The white band visible on the rudder may represent a repair or a rank or formation marking. The Bf 110D-3 was specifically designed for over-water operations with provision for 900-litre drop tanks (shown) and an extended tail which housed a dinghy. The letter 'N' on the engine cowling referred to the engine type fitted and the fuel required. A photograph of this aircraft appears on page 102.

JUNKERS Ju 88D-1, 7A+NH, 1.(F)/ 121, SICILY, 1941

Although often depicted as wearing a desert colour scheme (desert-yellow with blue undersides), 7A+NH was actually painted in overall RLM 65 *Hellblau* which was standard for other high-flying *Luftwaffe* reconnaissance aircraft like the Ju 86P and various Dornier types too. White theatre markings were applied to the rear fuselage, wingtips and spinner, while the *Gruppe's* white long-necked goose motif (illustrated) was placed below the cockpit. Although 7A+NH retains its original restrictive rear cockpit glazing, a pair of rear-facing 7.9mm MG 15 mgs were fitted – a somewhat cramped arrangement for the single gunner. As a means of extending its range the Ju 88D-1 was often fitted with 900-litre drop tanks inboard of the engines as seen here. A photograph of this aircraft appears on page 175.

HAWKER HURRICANE IIb, Z3580 'XJ', 126 SQUADRON, AUGUST 1941

This Hurricane wears a camouflage scheme consisting of Dark Earth and Dark Green with Sky Blue undersides which was standard for those RAF fighters of the period intended for overseas service. HQ Middle East Command had specifically requested that fighter aircraft despatched to them should not have Sky (i.e. light green) undersides upon receipt, and, as this colour was unsuitable for most other overseas theatres too, it was replaced by Sky Blue at the Maintenance or Packing Unit that prepared the aircraft for overseas service. The Dark Earth and Dark Green Temperate Land scheme applied to the upper surfaces was retained as it remained appropriate for the Far East, Greece and even Russia and was comparatively easy to modify if necessary; Egyptian MUs, for example, replaced Dark Green with Middle Stone, the result being better suited to operations in the desert. The roundels are standard 49in B-Type on top of the wing, 45in A-Type below and 35in A1-Type on the fuselage: the fin flash is 27in high, each segment being 8in wide. The code 'XJ' is Medium Sea Grey. Although 'XJ' had been allocated to 261 Squadron there is no evidence of them actually adopting this code and, in the event, it is believed that Z3580 was delivered to Malta during Operation *Railway 1* on 27th June 1941, the month after 261 Squadron had left the island! In this case 'X' represents the short-lived single code letter only used by 126 Squadron in Malta during August 1941, prior to their adoption of the two-letter code 'HA' with 'J' representing the aircraft's individual Squadron identifying letter. Z3580 was fitted with a long-spinner Rotol propeller and, though it remains unconfirmed, photographic comparisons indicate that the spinner was probably painted red. Additionally, despite being built as a Mk.IIb it is fitted with a Mk.I-style tail wheel, while the armament had been reduced from twelve to eight mgs to improve manoeuvrability.

HAWKER HURRICANE IIb, Z2961 'K', 185 SQUADRON, HAL FAR, SEPTEMBER 1941/1942

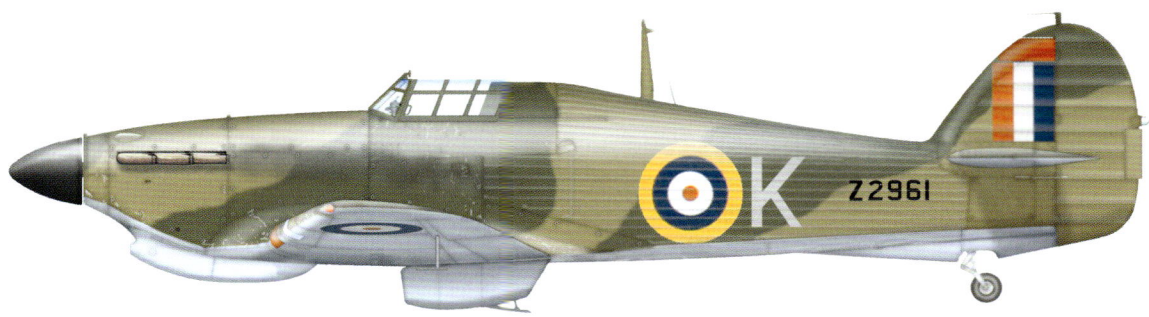

This Hurricane is shown as it appeared when serving at Hal Far in late 1941 wearing the standard overseas delivery scheme of Dark Earth and Dark Green with Sky Blue undersides. The red 'flash' at the top of the tail fin is apparent in a photograph of this aircraft and appears to represent a recent repair using fabric to which fresh red lead shrinking dope (as used over the wing gun ports) was applied. Although squadrons often shared aircraft without exchanging paperwork, the service history of this fighter seems to have been comparatively well recorded and, following tropicalisation in the UK, it served sequentially with the Malta Night Fighter Unit, 249, 185 and finally 605 Squadrons before being struck off charge on 13th March 1943. It was involved in shooting down a Ju 88 on 23rd March 1942 and was flown by a number of well known Malta pilots including P/O David Banwell, Sgt Tony Boyd & Sgt Garth Horrocks. The national insignia consists of 49in B-Type roundels on top of the wing, 45in A-Type roundels below and 35in A1-Type roundels on the fuselage: the fin flash is 27in high, each segment being 8in wide and the code 'K' is Medium Sea Grey. The serial is black as is the Rotol propeller spinner while the tailwheel is the later Mk.II type.

GLOSTER SEA GLADIATOR, N5520, 185 SQUADRON, LATE 1941/1942

Once they became obsolete as fighters, an event hastened by the arrival of the Bf 109E over Malta, surviving Sea Gladiators were retained for essential, yet often overlooked, meteorological reconnaissance duties that required at least one early morning sortie per day. For this the veteran biplanes were equipped with a psychrometer (a wet and dry bulb thermometer) fitted to the rear starboard interplane strut and an aneroid barometer mounted in front of the pilot to measure cloud base and wind speeds. N5520 was one of those used for 'Met' duties and apparently acquired the name 'Faith' too from 1941 onwards; a name that began to appear in pilots' logbooks in reference to this aircraft. Whether that name was physically applied to this aircraft in service is unknown, but when its refurbished remains were presented to Malta in 1943, the name 'Faith' had been painted below the cockpit. It might have been in early 1941, about the time that Malta's Sea Gladiator's returned to Naval control, that the names 'Faith' 'Hope' and 'Charity' actually became associated with the biplanes themselves. The trio of names, to the Maltese public at least, appear to have been the result of an article published by the *Times of Malta* in 1940, though it remains uncertain as to whether or not such names were ever actually applied to the aircraft, and if they were then it appears to have happened retrospectively. 'Hope' is thought to have been N5531, destroyed on 4th February 1941 during a raid on Hal Far. 'Charity' is thought to refer to N5519, shot down in 1940; while the name 'Faith' appears in pilots' logbooks in relation to N5520, by which time the old fighter was used solely for Meteorological Flights. It was during one such flight that N5520 was intercepted by at least three Bf 109Es from 7/JG 26 although the unknown pilot managed to survive unscathed by using the Sea Gladiator's famed manoeuvrability to turn inside each attack until they finally gave up and left.

In March 1941, 806 NAS left Malta for Egypt and the remaining Sea Gladiators were handed back to the RAF for use by Hal Far's Station Flight, although after 185 Squadron formed at Hal Far in May 1941, the Sea Gladiators and the meteorological duties passed to them. Unfortunately N5520 appears to have been severely damaged soon after it joined 185 Squadron, possibly in June 1941, when it ground-looped on landing. This type of accident was very common with Gladiators moving one old pilot to say 'There are only two types of Gladiator pilot, those who have ground looped upon landing and those that are going to ground loop'. Luckily the damage inflicted was repairable and N5520 was ready to fly again by August 1941 when Bill Metcalf recorded in his diary on 30th August 1941, that 'one of the trio of Gladiators is now back on the runway'. Only a select group of pilots were however allowed to fly the biplane, one of whom was Sgt Fred Sheppard, who mentioned that N5520 was regularly referred to as 'The Glad' and not 'Faith'. He also stated that N5520 was painted in a similar scheme to Hurricanes when it first appeared with 185 Squadron, albeit without a yellow outline to the fuselage roundel and that the words 'Royal Navy' remained, indicating perhaps that a further repaint had taken place into a Dark Green and Dark Earth scheme during the period of maintenance following the ground loop in June. Although details are sketchy it appears that N5520 may have suffered further damage during December 1941 which took a month or so to repair and at the time of its final flight, on 10th February 1942 (some references

state either January or 6th February 1942), the colour scheme had changed once again. By that date N5520 was painted in an overall silver scheme as this supposedly was the only dope for use on fabric as opposed to paint, still available on the besieged island. In the pilot's seat for what proved to be N5520's final flight was Sgt Arnold Jolly of 185 Squadron who had conducted an uneventful meteorological flight up to an altitude of 25,000ft. However, he failed to see a bomb crater when landing back at Hal Far which the Sea Gladiator fell into it and turned over and ended up on its back. An eyewitness: LAC Kenneth Cox remembered that; 'At the time I was waiting on the runway to refuel N5520 [which was] painted silver all over. Sergeant Jolly came out in one piece. We then righted the aircraft by lifting the tail up and pulling it over with a length of rope that had already been attached. The Gladiator was in a sorry state. Both wings sagged down to the ground, we had quite a job pushing it the two hundred yards or so to a place between two damaged hangars. The engine fitted to N5520 was a Blenheim Mercury [sic] with a three blade variable pitch propeller.' Before any repairs could be completed however, N5520's remains received a direct hit during a bombing raid and after the remnants of the wings and engine were removed the damaged fuselage was wheeled away into a nearby quarry and quietly forgotten about.

Having accrued five confirmed kills with five more probably shot down it appeared as if this was the end of the story for Malta's Sea Gladiators. However, N5520's mortal remains, bereft as they were of engine and wings, were rediscovered in 1943 by Corporal William Brown within the quarry in which it had been dumped and AVM Sir Keith Park decided to have the aircraft restored and presented to the people of Malta. The airframe was cosmetically restored and painted silver by a three-man team at Takali, one of whom was LAC Leslie Davies who also claims that traces of silver fabric were present but that this came as no surprise as it was the only colour of dope available there at the time. The airframe received a further application of silver dope and paint and had the name 'Faith' painted under the windscreen. As it was engineless a spare Mercury XI engine and a previously unused two-bladed Watts propeller were attached and N5520 was handed over to the people of Malta in a ceremony which took place at the Palace Square, Valletta on 3rd September 1943. The Sea Gladiator has remained in Malta ever since.

Today the RAF currently guards another island fortress during a period of renewed (May 2012) Argentine passion over the ownership of 'their' islands despite the opinions, beliefs and desires of the Falkland Islanders whose own wish, to remain British, does not appear to figure in Argentinean calculations. The Falkland's resident RAF fighter unit is in fact an old Malta unit No.1435 Flight (whose Badge is centred around a Maltese Cross) and which during the last 30 years has been equipped in turn with the Phantom FGR.2, the Tornado F.3 and currently the Typhoon FGR.4. While operating the Tornado F.3, and later the Typhoon, all were/are coded 'F', 'H', 'C' and 'D' (Desperation).

Photo credit, below: Charles Polidano – Touch the Skies

MACCHI MC.200 *SAETTA*, '86-5', 86ª *SQUADRIGLIA*, 7º *GRUPPO*, 54º *STORMO*, CATANIA-FONTANAROSA, SICILY, JUNE 1941

THE HURRICANE TAKES THE STRAIN   161

Equipped with the later style semi-enclosed cockpit beloved by Italian pilots, this aircraft was camouflaged in a three tone mottle scheme comprising *Bruno Mimetico* and *Giallo Mimetico* 4 mottling on a *Verde Mimetico* 2 background. The undersides were *Grigio Mimetico* with the unit's Tiger Motif below the cockpit: the aircraft's individual number '5' can be seen repeated on the undercarriage doors. Although it looked quite archaic with its open cockpit and radial engine the MC200 was actually a very good fighter and a good match for the Hurricane.

HAWKER HURRICANE PR.I, V7101, PHOTO RECONNAISSANCE CONVERSION, MAY-JUNE 1941

Hurricane PR.1, V7101, Luqa 1941. As it became increasingly dangerous for Marylands to venture too far inland over enemy territory in an attempt to obtain high-altitude reconnaissance photographs, it was decided that a Hurricane I should be adapted to conduct such sorties instead. V7101 had arrived aboard SS *Essex* in January 1941 and was subsequently placed under the supervision of S/Ldr Louks who stripped it of guns, armour and radio equipment and claimed that its range had been extended to 1,500 miles by fitting an additional 150-gallon fuel tank in the rear fuselage (salvaged from a crashed Wellington), while additional oxygen was provided for the pilot by utilising the now empty radio battery bay. Further additions included: a Rotol propeller (the shape of which can just be made out in the photograph); two F.24 cameras; an enlarged 25-gallon oil tank (fitted in the wing leading edge); a ventral Perspex panel which, if it was fitted, would only allow the pilot a very limited downward view; and a one-piece windscreen said to have been adapted from a Blenheim's cockpit side blister, although the latter had not been fitted when this image was taken as V7101 still retains a standard windscreen. Reputedly, V7101 could reach an altitude of 35,000ft, but its usual operating altitude was 30,000ft and though most sorties were flown over Sicily or Taranto it could apparently fly as far as Naples. One pilot who regularly flew this aircraft, F/Lt George Burges, stated that it was awful to fly. He recalled that its centre of gravity was too far aft making it liable to spin at any time, but he did not recall the additional fuel tank, suggesting that it may have been fitted originally but later removed. Another pilot to fly V7101 was Adrian Warburton who later flew a second PR Hurricane, (Mk.IIa, Z3053) which was similarly modified. The most obvious external change to V7101 in its new guise was probably its new colour scheme. Essentially overall blue, the paint was said to consist of: 'five gallons of De Lux [sic] Bosun Blue, seven pints of turpentine, 16 lbs of zinc powder and 3 lbs of De Lux Black.' The resulting colour would have been quite dark and very much like that applied to 2 PRU's reconnaissance aircraft based in Egypt. Taken with the full glare of a Maltese sun beating down upon V7101's airframe the photograph of this aircraft shows a 'washed-out' appearance, making it appear much lighter in colour than Bosun Blue would otherwise suggest. Close examination of the image reveals that a Dark Earth and Dark Green 'B' Pattern camouflage is still in existence, particularly along its port wing and fuselage, and has yet to be repainted. Additionally, as the fin and rudder are in shadow they reveal their true pattern and colours more readily. Therefore, though it has previously been stated that this image shows V7101 painted light blue with the fin and rudder in a separate camouflage finish, in fact it wasn't, although it is clearly undergoing role modification as signified by the removal of the radio mast. Having served with 261 and 69 Squadron, V7101 later served with 151 OTU until struck off charge on 1st March 1944.

This, the only known photograph of Hurricane I, V7101, depicts it midway through its conversion to a PR machine. A 'bubble' windscreen was intended for it but at the time this image was taken a standard windscreen remained in place and the airframe had yet to be painted 'Bosun Blue'. Consequently it is seen wearing its earlier Dark Green and Dark Earth camouflage scheme, as described in the accompanying text, and confirmed by examining other copies of this photo. Whether a Vokes filter was ever fitted to V7101 remains unconfirmed, however, one has been included in the colour profile. Author's Collection

HAWKER HURRICANE IIc, 'BD826', 185 SQUADRON, LATE 1941

Although its true identity has not been firmly established the Hurricane seen here, in both photographic and art form, is the same aircraft and is believed to be BD826 though some sources suggest BW826. The latter can be discounted as it was allocated to either a Grumman Goose amphibian or a Pitcairn PA-39 autogyro (depending on the source consulted), though in the event that serial was never actually applied to any aircraft. BD826 is much closer to the mark in as much that it was at least allocated to a Hurricane, albeit a Mk.IIb, and it is abundantly clear that this is a cannon-armed Mk.IIc: which might indicate an administrative error somewhere or that a set of Mk.IIc outer wings were fitted to replace the original Mk.IIb wings at some point, which was quite common. Preamble aside whatever its true identity this Hurricane did serve in Malta and it did enjoy an unusual colour scheme. The power of the 4 x 20mm cannons equipping this type was greatly appreciated by pilots in comparison to the rifle calibre mgs of the preceding variants, although their additional weight did impair manoeuvrability to a degree which occasionally led to the removal of two of the cannon. As can be seen, this example retains all four guns and is fitted with a pair of 44-gallon long-range tanks. Once it became apparent that Axis supply aircraft were flying between Sicily and North Africa, a series of long-range patrols were mounted by Hurricanes from Malta for which additional fuel was required. Therefore under wing tanks, previously used in delivering Hurricanes to Malta, were reused to supply the necessary range to interdict Axis aircraft crossing the Mediterranean. On close examination, this Hurricane wears a strange colour scheme that seems to have escaped previous comment, which, given its extensive exhaust staining appears to indicate that it had been operational in these colours for some time. It is the author's belief that the strange colours apparent on this aircraft was an attempt to camouflage it for long over-water flights and that the monotone dope which has been roughly applied to the rear fuselage and tail could well be a shade of blue-grey, or possibly an over-thinned or weathered Extra Dark Sea Grey, which oddly ends parallel with the windscreen. A matching blue-grey colour also appears in patches on top of the wings alongside a darker colour, most likely the original Dark Green. Forward of the windscreen the nose retains its original camouflage of Dark Green and Dark Earth but it is so damaged by the sun that the Dark Earth has bleached while the Dark Green has weathered darker. (The reason for leaving this area alone probably pertains to both the heat of the engine and oily panels which would cause roughly applied dope or paint to flake away). The Vokes filter looks darker than the rest of the undersides which appears to be Sky Blue, suggesting that it may have been taken from another aircraft with Azure Blue undersides. Speculatively speaking, the propeller spinner seems to be red rather than the more usual black or Sky which supports the probability that it was being used for long-range patrols near to the North African coastline as the local theatre marking for this area was a red spinner. The fuselage roundel is a non-standard variant of the A1-Type which was sometimes seen during 1941. *Photo credit: Frederick Galea*

APPENDICES

REGIA AERONAUTICA UNITS BASED IN SICILY – 10th JUNE 1940

Unit		Aircraft Type	No. per *Gruppo*	Base
1° *Stormo*	17° *Gruppo* CT 71ª, 72ª & 73ª *Squadriglia*	Macchi MC.200 But Fiat CR.32 & CR.42 were also used due to structural problems with the MC.200.	26	Boccadifalco
	157° *Gruppo* CT 384ª, 385ª, 386ª *Squadriglia*	Fiat CR.42	17	Trapani-Milo
11° *Stormo*	33° *Gruppo* BT 59ª & 60ª *Squadriglia*	Savoia Marchetti SM.79	17	Comiso
	34° *Gruppo* BT 67ª & 68ª *Squadriglia*	Savoia Marchetti SM.79	16	Comiso
30° *Stormo*	87° *Gruppo* BT 192ª & 193ª *Squadriglia*	Savoia Marchetti SM.79	14	Sciacca
	90° *Gruppo* BT 194ª & 195ª *Squadriglia*	Savoia Marchetti SM.79	13	Sciacca
34° *Stormo*	52° *Gruppo* BT 214ª & 215ª *Squadriglia*	Savoia Marchetti SM.79	14	Fontanarossa
	53° *Gruppo* BT 216ª & 217ª *Squadriglia*	Savoia Marchetti SM.79	13	Fontanarossa
36° *Stormo*	108° *Gruppo* BT 256ª & 257ª *Squadriglia*	Savoia Marchetti SM.79	16	Castelvetrano
	109° *Gruppo* BT 258ª & 259ª *Squadriglia*	Savoia Marchetti SM.79	16	Castelvetrano
41° *Stormo*	59° *Gruppo* BT 232ª & 233ª *Squadriglia*	Savoia Marchetti SM.79	9	Gela
	60° *Gruppo* BT 234ª & 235ª *Squadriglia*	Savoia Marchetti SM.79	9	Gela
Stormo *Autonomo*	108° *Gruppo* BaT 256ª & 257ª *Squadriglia*	Savoia Marchetti SM.85 and Junkers Ju 87B	16	Sciacca

Another unit, 76° *Gruppo* was equipped with Ro.37 Army Co-Operation aircraft at Boccadifalco but was not engaged in ops over Malta.

A 57ª *Squadriglia* SM.79 on Chinisia airfield with sheep grazing under the wing. Most Sicilian airfields were open to animals and shepherds who had traditionally used the land for grazing long before any airfields were built. The aircraft wears the two-coloured 'Metropolitan' scheme described on page 143 and illustrates how the upper surface colour wraps around the engine cowlings and over the leading edges of the wing. Author via www.military-aircraft.photos.com

REGIA AERONAUTICA ENGAGED ON OPERATIONS AGAINST MALTA IN LATE 1940

Unit		Aircraft Type	No. per *Gruppo*	Location in Sicily	Duration of Tour
1° *Stormo*	157° *Gruppo* CT 384ª, 385ª and 386ª *Squadriglia*	Fiat CR.42	24	Trapani-Milo	June-Dec 1940
	17° *Gruppo* CT 71ª, 72ª and 73ª *Squadriglia* Temporarily swapped aircraft for CR.32 biplane fighters due to ongoing structural problems	Macchi MC.200	24	Boccadifalco Trapani-Milo	June-Sept 1940 Sept 1940-June 1941
	6° *Gruppo* 79ª, 81ª and 88ª *Squadriglia*	Macchi MC.200	24	Fontanarossa	July 1940-Nov 1941
3° *Stormo*	23° *Gruppo Autonomo* 70ª, 74ª and 75ª *Squadriglia*	Fiat CR.42	24	Comiso	June-Aug 1940
4° *Stormo*	9° *Gruppo* CT 73ª, 96ª and 97ª Squadriglia	Fiat CR.42	24	Comiso	July 1940
11° *Stormo*	33° *Gruppo* 59ª and 60ª *Squadriglia*	Savoia Marchetti SM.79	17	Comiso	June-July 1940
	34° *Gruppo* 67ª and 68ª *Squadriglia*	Savoia Marchetti SM.79	16	Comiso	June 40-Aug 1941
30° *Stormo*	87° *Gruppo* 192ª and 193ª *Squadriglia*	Savoia Marchetti SM.79	14	Sciacca/ Castelvetrano	June 1940-Aug 1941
	90° *Gruppo* 194ª and 195ª *Squadriglia*	Savoia Marchetti SM.79	13	Sciacca/ Castelvetrano	June 1940-Aug 1941
34° *Stormo*	52° *Gruppo* 214ª and 215ª *Squadriglia*	Savoia Marchetti SM.79	14	Fontanarossa	June-Dec 1940
	53° *Gruppo* 216ª and 217ª *Squadriglia*	Savoia Marchetti SM.79	13	Fontanarossa	June-Dec 1940
36° *Stormo*	108° *Gruppo* 256ª and 257ª *Squadriglia*	Savoia Marchetti SM.79	16	Castelvatrano	June- Nov 1940
	109° *Gruppo* 258ª and 259ª Squadriglia	Savoia Marchetti SM.79	16	Castelvetrano	June 1940
41° *Stormo*	59° *Gruppo* 232ª and 233ª *Squadriglia*	Savoia Marchetti SM.79	9	Gela	June-Oct 1940
	60° *Gruppo* 234ª and 235ª *Squadriglia*	Savoia Marchetti SM.79	9	Gela	June-Oct 1940
46° *Stormo*	105° *Gruppo* CT 254ª and 255ª *Squadriglia*	Savoia Marchetti SM.79	9	Pisa San Giusto, Italian mainland	June- Oct 1940
	96° *Gruppo BaT* 236ª and 237ª *Squadriglia* (1 x SM.86W flown on trial)	Junkers Ju 87B/R *Picchiatelli*	14	Comiso/ Pantellaria	June-Oct 1940
	97° *Gruppo BaT* 238ª and 239ª Squadriglia	Junkers Ju 87B/R *Picchiatelli*	14	Comiso	Nov-Dec 1940
47° *Stormo*	106° *Gruppo* 260ª and 261ª *Squadriglia*	Cant Z.1007*bis*	16	Trapani-Milo/ Chinisia	August-Oct 1940
	107° *Gruppo* 262ª and 263ª *Squadriglia*	Cant Z.1007*bis*	16	Chinisia	Aug- Oct 1940
	83° *Gruppo* RM 184ª, 186ª and 189ª *Squadriglia* Maritime Patrol and Air Sea Rescue	Cant Z.506 Cant Z.501 Fiat RS.14B	26	Augusta Harbour	June 1940-Jul 1943

REGIA AERONAUTICA UNITS IN SICILY DURING EARLY 1941

Unit		Aircraft Type	No. of Aircraft	Base and Notes
Autonomo	6° *Gruppo Autonomo* CT 79ª, 81ª and 88ª *Squadriglia*	Macchi MC.200	12-27	Fontanarossa
1° *Stormo* CT	17° *Gruppo* CT 71ª, 72ª and 80ª *Squadriglia*	Macchi MC.200	18-27	Fontanarossa
	157° *Gruppo* CT 384ª, 385ª and 386ª *Squadriglia*	Macchi MC.200	18-27	Trapani-Milo Only until February 1941
Autonomo	156° *Gruppo Autonomo* CT 379ª and 380ª *Squadriglia*	Fiat CR.42	12-27	Comiso Took over 9 a/c from 23° *Gruppo* Jan 41 and built up to 31 a/c which passed back to 23° *Gruppo* in April 41. A single Re.2000 was also trialled.
Autonomo	96° *Gruppo* BaT 236° and 237° *Squadriglia*	Junkers Ju 87B/R *Picchiatelli*	12-18	Comiso
30° *Stormo* BT	87° *Gruppo* BT 192ª and 193ª *Squadriglia*	Savoia Marchetti SM.79	12-18	Sciacca
	90° *Gruppo* BT 194° and 195° *Squadriglia*	Savoia Marchetti SM.79	12-18	Sciacca
Autonomo	279ª *Squadriglia* Sil RM (*Aerosiluranti*)	Savoia Marchetti SM.79	6-9	Catania Torpedo Bombers
Autonomo	83° *Gruppo* RM 184°, 186° and 189° *Squadriglia*	Cant Z.506 & Z.501	12-18	Augusta Air Sea Rescue (ASR) and Maritime Recce (MR)
Autonomo	612ª *Squadriglia Autonomo*	Cant Z.506 & Z.501	6-9	Stagnone Air Sea Rescue (ASR) and Maritime Recce (MR)
Autonomo	144ª *Squadriglia Autonomo*	Cant Z.506 & Z.501	6-9	Stagnone Air Sea Rescue (ASR) and Maritime Recce (MR)

A rare colour image of Cant Z.1007s from 59ª *Squadriglia*, 33° *Gruppo*, 9° *Stormo* based at Trapani-Milo during June 1941. They wear white theatre stripes and yellow cowlings with a variety of different mottled camouflage patterns with the nearest aircraft displaying Cant's stylised company insignia below the cockpit in blue. Italian official image

REGIA AERONAUTICA UNITS OPERATING AGAINST MALTA FROM SICILY – MAY-JUNE 1941

Unit		Aircraft Type	No. of Aircraft	Base and Notes
Autonomo	6º *Gruppo* CT 79ª, 81ª and 88ª *Squadriglia*	Macchi MC.200 'Saetta'	18-27	Fontanarossa
Autonomo	17º *Gruppo* CT 71ª, 72ª and 80ª *Squadriglia*	Macchi MC.200 'Saetta'	18-27	Trapani-Milo
54º *Stormo* CT	7º *Gruppo* CT 76ª, 86ª and 98ª *Squadriglia*	Macchi MC.200 'Saetta'	18-27	Catania 76ª *Squadriglia* detached to Pantellaria
3º *Stormo* CT	23º *Gruppo* CT 74ª and 75ª *Squadriglia* 70ª *Squadriglia* Sezione Sperimentale	Fiat CR.42 'Falco' Fiat CR.42 'Falco' Reggiane Re.2000 Serie 1	15 9 9	Comiso Pantelleria Island Trapani-Milo (plus Pantellaria Island)
4º *Stormo*	10º *Gruppo* CT 84ª, 90ª and 91ª *Squadriglia*	Macchi MC.200 'Saetta'	8-27	Trapani Jul 41, Comiso Sep 41, Chinisia Nov 41 Palermo (91ª *Squadriglia* only)
Autonomo	23º *Gruppo* Autonomo CT 70ª, 74ª and 75ª *Squadriglia*	Fiat CR.42 'Falco' (some MC.200s from Sept 41)	12-27	70ª Sq- Trapani-Milo 75ª Sq & part of 74ª Sq-Pantellaria Island. Dets Boccadifalo (Convoy Escort Fighter)
Autonomo	101º *Gruppo* BaT 208ª and 238ª *Squadriglia*	Ju 87R *Picchiatelli*	12-18	Trapani, Gela, Comiso. Mostly employed in night operations
10º *Stormo* BT	30º *Gruppo* BT 55ª and 56ª *Squadriglia* 32º *Gruppo* BT 57ª and 58ª *Squadriglia*	Savoia Marchetti SM.79 Savoia Marchetti SM.79	12-18 12-18	Sciacca Chinisia
30º *Stormo* BT	87º *Gruppo* BT 192ª and 193ª *Squadriglia* 90º *Gruppo* BT 194ª and 195ª *Squadriglia*	Savoia Marchetti SM.79 Savoia Marchetti SM.79	12-18 12-18	Sciacca Sciacca
36º *Stormo* BT	108º *Gruppo* BT 256ª and 257ª *Squadriglia* 109º *Gruppo* BT 258ª and 259ª *Squadriglia*	Savoia Marchetti SM.79 Savoia Marchetti SM.79	12-18 12-18	Various Sicilian bases Various Sicilian bases
43º *Stormo* BT	31º *Gruppo* BT 65ª and 66ª *Squadriglia* 99º *Gruppo* BT 242ª and 243ª *Squadriglia*	Fiat BR.20M Fiat BR.20M	12-18 12-18	Catania Gerbini
Autonomo	83º *Gruppo* RM 170ª, 184ª and 186ª *Squadriglia*	Cant Z.501 & Z.506B	12-27	Augusta Seaplane Base (MR/ASR)
Autonomo	278ª *Squadriglia* AS Sil	Savoia Marchetti SM.79Sil	6-9	Various Sicilian bases Torpedo-Bomber-*Aerosiluranti* (Sil)
Autonomo	144ª *Squadriglia Autonomo* RM	Cant Z.501/Z.506B	6-9	Stagone/Syracuse Harbour (MR/ASR)
Autonomo	612ª *Squadriglia Autonomo* RM	Cant Z.506B	6-9	Stagone/Syracuse Harbour (MR/ASR)
Autonomo	173º *Squadriglia Autonomo* RST	Fiat CR.25	6-9	Catania/Boccadifalco (Long Range Heavy Fighter/Recce)

REGIA AERONAUTICA UNIT COMPOSITION

Unit	Abbreviation	Number of Aircraft		RAF Equivalent
Squadriglia	Sq	Fighters 9 (+3 reserve)	Bombers 6	Small Squadron
Gruppo	Gr	Fighters 18-27	Bombers 12-18	Small Wing
Stormo	St	Fighters 36-81	Bombers 24-54	Small Group
Squadriglia Autonomo	Sq Aut	6-9	–	Independent Small Squadron
Gruppo Autonomo	Gr Aut	12-27	–	Independent Small Wing

REGIA AERONAUTICA UNIT DESIGNATIONS

Abbreviation	Italian Designation	English Translation
AS or 'sil'	*Aerosiluranti*	Aerial torpedo-bomber
BM	*Bombardamento Marittima*	Maritime bomber
BaT	*Bombardamento a Tuffo*	Dive-bomber
BT	*Bombardamento Terrestre*	Land-based bomber
CT	*Caccia Terrestre*	Land-based fighter
CM	*Caccia Marittima*	Maritime fighter
OA	*Osservazione Area*	Tactical reconnaissance
RM	*Ricognizione Marittima*	Maritime reconnaissance
RST	*Ricognizione Strategica Terrestre*	Land-based strategic reconnaissance

REGIA AERONAUTICA RANKS: OFFICERS AND SENIOR NCOs

Rank	Abbreviation	English Translation	RAF Equivalent
Generale	Gen	General	Air Chief Marshal
Generale di Sqiaddra Aerea	-	Lieutenant General	Air Marshal
Generale di Divisione Aerea	-	Major General	Air Vice-Marshal
Generale di Bragata Aerea	Gen Brig	Brigadier General	Air Commodore
Colonnello	Col	Colonel	Group Captain
Tenente Colonnello	Ten Col	Lieutenant Colonel	Wing Commander
Maggiore	Magg	Major	Squadron Leader
Capitano	Cap	Captain	Flight Lieutenant
Tenente	Ten	1st Lieutenant	Flying Officer
Sottontenente	Sottoten	2nd Lieutenant	Pilot Officer
Sergente Maggiorre Capo	Serg Magg	Chief Sergeant Major	Warrant Officer 1
Sergente Maggiore	Serg Magg	Sergeant Major	Warrant Officer 2
Sergente	Serg	Sergeant	Sergeant

Cant Z.1007 *Alcione* (Kingfisher). An excellent image depicting the most obvious external identifying feature between the single- and twin-finned variants of the Cant Z.1007*bis*: both of which were employed against Malta. These aircraft, however, wear the codes of 190ª *Squadriglia*, 86° *Gruppo*, 35° *Stormo* which operated from Greece and North Africa (although the stylised 'M' denoting 95° *Gruppo*, also a component of 35° *Stormo*, appears on the tail fin of the nearest aircraft). As far as can be determined, 35° *Stormo* never deployed its Z.1007 units against Malta directly, although it did operate against Malta-bound convoys. Shown to advantage here is the usual C-10 Type, mottled camouflage usually seen on the Z.1007 comprising *Verde Memitico* 3, *Giallo Memitico* 3 and *Marrone Memitico* over *Grigio Memitico* undersides with white theatre band and yellow engine cowlings. Italian official image

FLIEGERKORPS X (10th AIR CORPS) – SICILY 1941

Unit	Aircraft Type	No. of A/C	Location	Role/notes
Stab LG 1	Junkers Ju 88A-4/5	4	Catania	Bomber (*Lehrgeswader* 1 = LG 1); Independent/Evaluation/
II/LG 1	Junkers Ju 88A-4/5	38	Catania	Demonstration/Training Wing 1; known as *Helbigfliers* after
III/LG 1	Junkers Ju 88A-4/5	38	Catania	their commodore *Hptm* Joachim Helbig
III/KG 30 Arrived 25th February 1941	Junkers Ju 88A-4/5	38	Gerbini	Bomber
1(F)/121	Junkers Ju 88D	17	Catania	Reconnaissance
2(F)/123*	Junkers Ju 88D	14	Catania	(*Arrived March 1941). Some Bf 110C/D later converted to Reconnaissance Role to work alongside Ju 88Ds
Stab StG 3	Junkers Ju 87R *Stuka*	9	Trapani-Milo	Dive-bomber. Joined from Northern France having been re-equipped following heavy losses during the Battle of Britain.
I/StG 1	Junkers Ju 87R *Stuka*	36	Trapani-Milo	The Ju 87B was replaced by the long range Ju 87R
II/StG 2	Junkers Ju 87R *Stuka*	35	Trapani-Milo	*Reichweitenausfuhrung* or Long Range version with extra oil and fuel tanks including a pair of under wing 300-ltr tanks to give a range of 1,255 km
II/KG 26	Heinkel He111H	37	Comiso	Bomber/Minelayer
4/KG 4	Heinkel He 111H	12	Comiso	Torpedo Bomber
III/ZG 26	Messerschmitt Bf 110D *Zerstorer*	34-40	Palermo	Long-range fighter
1/NJG 3	Messerschmitt Bf 110C *Zerstorer*	12	Gela	Night Fighter Formed from LG 1, February 1941
2/(F)123	Messerschmitt Bf 110C *Zerstorer*	n/k	Catania	Reconnaissance This Ju 88D equipped unit also operated a small number of Reconnaissance converted Bf 110Cs later in 1941
Kampfgruppe z.b.V.9	Junkers Ju 52/3m	29	Reggia Calabria	Transport (z.b.V = Special Duties Battle Group). Based on the Italian mainland and Sicily, under control of Luftflotte 2
III/KG z.b.V. 1	Junkers Ju 52/3m	48	Reggia Calabria	Transport Based on the Italian mainland and Sicily, under control of Luftflotte 2
Seenotberichskommando X	Dornier Do 24 and Heinkel He 59	n/k	Syracuse	Air Sea Rescue
7/JG 26	Messerschmitt Bf 109E-7	8-14	Gela	Fighter From 9th February 1941- CO- *Oblt* Joachim Muncheberg
I/JG 27	Bf 109E-4	30+	Gela	Fighter Flew some sorties over Malta during early March 1941 whilst staging through Sicily bound for North Africa
III/JG 27 *Jabo*	Bf 109E-4	30+	Gela	Fighter Bomber Detached to Sicily during May 1941 whilst en route back to Germany from the Balkan Campaign
JG 3	Bf 109E-4	n/k	Gela	Fighter One or two sorties may have been flown over Malta whilst staging through Sicily for North Africa

Units arrived in January 1941 unless indicated otherwise.

A GENERAL EXPLANATION OF *LUFTWAFFE* UNITS

Luftflotte — 'air flotilla'. A *Luftflotte* equated approximately to an RAF Command in size.

Fliegerkorps — or 'flying corps' approximated an RAF Group in size.

Geschwader — roughly equivalent to an RAF Wing, *Geschwaders* essentially consisted of three *Gruppe* (plural *Gruppen*) and a staff *Staffel* (plural *Staffeln*). A *Geschwader* would usually be equipped with approximately 100 or so aircraft and was abbreviated 'G'.

Added to the 'G' was a role indicator resulting in, for instance:

- **StG** *Sturzkampfgeschwader* — dive-bomber *Geschwader*
- **SG** *Schlachtgeschwader* — ground-attack *Geschwader*
- **JG** *Jagdgeschwader* — fighter *Geschwader*
- **KG** *Kampfgeschwader* — bomber *Geschwader*
- **LG** *Lehrgeschwader* — training and evaluation *Geschwader*
- **ZG** *Zerstorergeschwader* — 'destroyer' or heavy-fighter *Geschwader*

The abbreviated term was followed by a given unit's number; thus *Sturzkampfgeschwader* Two, became StG 2.

The component *Gruppen* of StG 2 would be numbered I/StG 2, II/StG 2 & III/StG 2. Most *Geschwaders* consisted of just three *Gruppen*, however, less orthodox units, e.g. LG 1, featured as many as five.

A *Gruppe* was broken down further into three *Staffeln* consisting of around 30 aircraft each. These were numbered as 1-3 *Staffeln* within I *Gruppe*, 4-6 *Staffeln* within II *Gruppe* & 8-10 *Staffeln* within III *Gruppe*, so the 5th *Staffeln* of StG 3 would be 5/StG 2 which was within II/StG 2.

Smallest of all was the *Stab*, a headquarters or staff flight which generally had a complement of three aircraft.

LUFTWAFFE RANKS

Rank	Abbreviation	English Translation	RAF Equivalent
Reichsmarschall	-	-	-
Generalfeldmarschall	GenFeldm	General Field Marshal	Marshal of the Royal Air Force (5 Star Rank)
General Oberst	GenOb	Colonel General	Air Chief Marshal (4 Star Rank)
General der Flieger	Gen dFl	General of Flyers, equivalent to Lt General	Air Marshal
General der Flak	GenFLAK	General of Flak, equivalent to Lt General	Air Marshal
General Leutnant	GenLt	Major General	Air Vice Marshal
General Major	GenMaj	Brigadier General	Air Commodore
Oberst	Oberst (Ob)	Colonel	Group Captain
Obersleutnant	Oberstlt (ObLt)	Lieutenant Colonel	Wing Commander
Major	Maj	Major	Squadron Leader
Hauptmann	Hptm	Captain	Flight Lieutenant
Ober Leutnant	Oblt	Lieutenant	Flying Officer
Leutnant	Lt	2nd Lieutenant	Pilot Officer
Stabsfeldwebel	Stabsfw	Senior Non Commissioned Officer	Warrant Officer 1st Class
Oberfähnrich	Obfhr	Senior Officer Cadet	(Cadet with Seniority of a Pilot Officer)
Oberfeldwebel	Obfw	Staff Sergeant	Flight Sergeant
Fähnrich (Fahnenjunker)	Fhr	Officer Candidate	Officer Cadet
Feldwebel	Fw	Sergeant	Sergeant
Unterfeldwebel	Ufw	Under Sergeant	Sergeant
Unteroffizier	Uffz	Corporal	Corporal
Hauptgefreiter	Hptgefr	Lance Corporal	Senior Aircraftman
Obergefreiter	Ogfr	Senior Airman	Leading Aircraftman
Gefreiter	Gefr	Airman	Aircraftman 1st Class

ROYAL AIR FORCE / FLEET AIR ARM RANKS AND ABBREVIATIONS USED IN THE TEXT

Royal Air Force

AVM	Air Vice-Marshal	F/O	Flying Officer	Sgt	Sergeant
W/C	Wing Commander	P/O	Pilot Officer	Cpl	Corporal
S/Ldr	Squadron Leader	W/O	Warrant Officer	LAC	Leading Aircraftman
F/Lt	Flight Lieutenant	F/Sgt	Flight Sergeant	AC1	Aircraftman 1st Class

Fleet Air Arm

Lt Cdr	Lt-Commander	PO	Petty Officer
Lt	Lieutenant	L/Air	Leading Airman
S/Lt	Sub-Lieutenant	Mid	Midshipman
N/Air	Naval Airman		

Abbreviations

AMES	Air Ministry Experimental Station	KOMR	King's Own Malta Regiment	RAMC	Royal Army Medical Corps
AA	Anti-Aircraft	MU	Maintenance Unit	RAOC	Royal Army Ordnance Corps
AFDU	Air Fighting Development Unit	MWF	Malta Wellington Flight	RASC	Royal Army Service Corps
AOC	Air Officer Commanding	NAS	Naval Air Squadron	RE	Royal Engineers
ASV	Air-to-Surface Vessel (radar)	NCO	Non-Commissioned Officer	REME	Royal Electrical & Mechanical Engineers
C-in-C	Commander-in-Chief	OADU	Overseas Air Delivery Unit	RM	Royal Marines
CMP	Corps of Military Police	OC	Officer Commanding	RMA	Royal Malta Artillery
CO	Commanding Officer	PR	Photo-Reconnaissance	RN	Royal Navy
CID	Committee of Imperial Defence	RA	Royal Artillery	RNAS	Royal Naval Air Station
FAA	Fleet Air Arm	RAF	Royal Air Force	RTR	Royal Tank Regiment
GR	General Recce (i.e. GR Flight)	RAFVR	Royal Air Force Volunteer Reserve	SD	Special Duties (i.e. SD Flight)

AIRCRAFT DELIVERIES TO MALTA BY AIRCRAFT CARRIER 1940-1941

Date	Operation	Carrier(s)	Types	Took off	Failed to arrive
02.09.40	*Hurry*	HMS *Argus*	Hurricane	12	0
			Skua	2	0
17.11.40	*White*	HMS *Argus*	Hurricane	12	8
			Skua	2	1
03.04.41	*Winch*	HMS *Ark Royal*	Hurricane	12	0
			Skua	2	0
27.04.41	*Dunlop*	HMS *Ark Royal*	Hurricane	24	1
			Fulmar	3	0
21.05.41	*Splice*	HMS *Ark Royal*	Hurricane	41	1
		HMS *Furious*	Fulmar	5	1
06.06.41	*Rocket*	HMS *Ark Royal*	Hurricane	44	1
		HMS *Furious*			
14.06.41	*Tracer*	HMS *Ark Royal*	Hurricane	48	2
		HMS *Victorious*			
27.06.41	*Railway I*	HMS *Ark Royal*	Hurricane	22	1
		HMS *Furious*			
30.06.41	*Railway II*	HMS *Ark Royal*	Hurricane	36	1
		HMS *Furious*			
24.07.41	*Substance*	HMS *Ark Royal*	Swordfish	7	0

AIRCRAFT SPECIFICATIONS – ROYAL AIR FORCE

Gloster Sea Gladiator

Top Speed	253mph (14,500ft)
Range	320 miles
Length	27ft 5in
Wingspan	32ft 3in
Engine	Bristol Mercury VIIIA/AS
Armament	4 x .303in Browning machine-guns (mgs)

Hawker Hurricane I

Speed	321mph at 20,000ft (non-tropicalised)
	286mph at 20,000ft (tropicalised)
Range	505 miles at optimum cruise speed (190mph) and height (15,000ft) with no fuel reserve. 460 miles for tropicalised variant. (935 miles with 2 x 44 gallon tanks).
Length	31ft 3in
Wingspan	40ft
Engine	RR Merlin III 12-cylinder inline (1,030hp)
Armament	8 x .303in mgs

Hawker Hurricane IIa

Speed	340mph at 20,000ft (non-tropicalised)
	333mph at 20,000ft (tropicalised)
Range	468 miles at optimum cruise speed (177mph) and height (15,000ft) with no fuel reserve. 440 miles for tropicalised variant at its higher optimised cruise speed of 185mph. (900 miles with 2 x 44 gallon tanks).
Length	32ft 2in
Wingspan	40ft
Engine	Merlin XX, 12-cylinder inline (1,280hp)
Armament	8 x .303in mgs

Hawker Hurricane IIb

Speed	328mph at 20,000ft (non-tropicalised)
	242mph at 20,000ft (tropicalised)
Range	465 miles at optimum cruise speed (177mph) and height (15,000ft) with no fuel reserve. 436 miles for tropicalised variant at its higher optimised cruise speed of 185mph. (950 miles with 2 x 44 gallon tanks)
Length	32ft 2in
Wingspan	40ft
Engine	Merlin XX
Armament	12 x .303in mgs

Hawker Hurricane IIc

Speed	328mph at 20,000ft (non-tropicalised)
	272mph at 20,000ft (tropicalised)
Range	460 miles at optimum cruise speed (178mph) and height (15,000ft) with no fuel reserve. 426 miles for tropicalised version at its higher optimised cruise speed of 188mph. (908 miles with 2 x 44 gallon tanks)
Length	32ft 2in
Wingspan	40ft
Engine	Merlin XX
Armament	4 x 20mm Hispano or Oerlikon cannon

Note: Of the Hurricane II variants the Mk.IIa enjoyed the better performance as it employed the same engine but weighed less than other Mk.II variants by virtue of their different weapons fit. The IIb had the worst performance due to the extra weight imposed by its four additional mgs and ammunition which also adversely influenced its manoeuvrability as that weight was distributed largely throughout the span of the wing and helps explain why many IIbs had their outer four guns removed in service. Unsurprisingly of course an individual cannon as fitted to a IIc was heavier than a single Browning mg; however, collectively, four cannon (plus ammunition) weighed less than the 12 mgs and ammunition of a IIb. Additionally, the cannon-armed Hurricanes had their weapons mounted well inboard by comparison, thereby restoring some of the manoeuvrability lacking in its immediate predecessor, despite which several IIcs still had their outboard cannon deleted in service in the interests of overall performance.

In respect of a Hurricane's 'maximum speed' those shown above represent the best achievable at an altitude of 20,000ft as most combats occurred between 20,000 and 25,000ft; the Mk.IIs supercharger having 'kicked-in' at 17,500ft.

Bristol Blenheim IV

Max speed	266mph
Range	1,125 miles
Length	39ft 9in
Wingspan	58ft 1in
Engines	2 x Bristol Mercury XV radials (920hp each)
Armament	Most Malta-based Mk.IV bombers were fitted with 4 x .303in mgs: one fixed (forward firing); one chin-mounted firing backwards; plus two others in the dorsal turret. However, early arrivals had only a single gun in the turret, while later arrivals featured two chin guns. Blenheim bombers could carry a 1,000 lb bomb load internally. The Blenheim IVf was a standard Mk.IV adapted to act as a fighter and as such received a ventral gun tray mounting four .303mgs to supplement the single fixed wing-mounted gun of the same calibre.

Bristol Beaufighter Ic

Max Speed	318mph
Range	1,470 miles
Length	41ft 8in
Wingspan	57ft 10in
Engines	2 x Bristol Hercules XVII 14-cylinder twin-row radials (1,770hp each)
Armament (fixed)	4 x 20mm cannon, 6 x .303in mgs: 2 x 250 lb bombs externally

Martin Maryland I

Speed	278mph
Range	1,210 miles
Length	46ft 8in
Wingspan	61ft 4in
Engines	2 x Pratt & Whitney R-1830-S3C4-G Twin Wasp radial (1,200hp each)
Armament	4 x .303in (fixed) mgs, 1 mg in dorsal position. 2,000 lb bombs internally (max) if required

Short Sunderland I

Max speed	212mph (cruise 150mph)
Range	3,000 miles
Length	85ft 4in
Wingspan	112ft 10in
Engines	4 x Bristol Pegasus XXII radials (1,010hp each)
Crew	7
Armament	1 x .303in mg in nose turret, 4 x .303in mgs in tail turret plus single .303in mgs in each of two beam position. 2,000 lb of bombs or depth charges mounted internally on lateral racks which were run out underneath the wings prior to an attack. ASV Mk.II radar was progressively fitted from October 1941 onwards.

Vickers Wellington Ic

Max Speed	235mph
Range	2,550 miles
Length	64ft 7in
Wingspan	86ft 2in
Engines	2 x Bristol Pegasus XVIII radials (1,000hp each) (Wellington II = 2 x Merlin III)
Armament	2 x .303in mgs in each of nose and tail turrets (plus beam mgs). 4,500 lb bombs internally (max)

Blenheim IV, V5872 'XD-V', 139 Squadron, taking off from Luqa during the unit's deployment to Malta from Horsham St Faith, Norfolk, between 16th May and 3rd June 1941. A colour illustration of this aircraft appears on page 36. Author's collection

AIRCRAFT SPECIFICATIONS – FLEET AIR ARM

Blackburn Skua

Max Speed	225mph
Range	435 miles
Length	35ft 7in
Wingspan	42ft 6in
Engine	Bristol Perseus XII 9-cylinder sleeve valve radial (905hp)
Armament	4 x .303in (fixed) mgs, 1 x flexible .303in mg, 1 x 500 lb bomb

Fairey Fulmar I

Speed	246mph
Range	650 miles (865 miles with extra tanks)
Length	40ft 2in
Wingspan	46ft 5in
Engine	Merlin VIII 12-cylinder inline (1,080hp)
Armament	8 x .303in mgs: plus a Thompson smg, pistol or toilet paper carried in rear cockpit! (See text Chapter 3)

Fairey Albacore I

Max Speed	161mph
Range	930 miles
Length	39ft 10in
Wingspan	50ft
Engine	Bristol Taurus XII radial engine (1,130hp)
Crew	3
Armament	1 x .303in (fixed) mg in starboard wing, 1 (later 2) x flexible .303in mgs: 1 x 18in torpedo, or 6 x 250 lb bombs, or 4 x 500 lb bombs beneath the wings.

Fairey Swordfish I

Speed	138mph
Range	1,030 miles
Length	35ft 8in
Wingspan	45ft 6in
Engine	Bristol Pegasus IIIM3 9 cylinder radial (690hp)
Armament	1 x fixed .303 mg – 1 x flexible .303in mg: 1 x 18in torpedo, or 1,500 lb bombs

AIRCRAFT SPECIFICATIONS – REGGIA AERONAUTICA

Fiat CR.42 *Falco*

Speed	267mph
Range	481 miles
Length	27ft 2in
Wingspan	31ft 10in
Engine	Fiat A.74 RC.38 twin-row 14-cylinder radial (846hp)
Armament	2 x 12.7mm (Breda SAFAT) mgs

Macchi C.200 *Saetta*

Speed	314mph
Range	540 miles
Length	27ft 1in
Wingspan	35ft 8in
Engine	Fiat A.74 RC.38 radial (846hp)
Armament	2 x 12.7mm mgs

Macchi C.202 *Folgore*

Speed	370mph
Range	475 miles
Length	29ft 6in
Wingspan	34ft 8in
Engine	Alfa Romeo RA.1000 RC.41-1 *Monsone* (1,200hp) licence-built Daimler-Benz DB 601A
Armament	2 (later 4) x 12.7mm mgs

Reggiane Re.2000 *Falco*

Speed	329mph
Range	522 miles
Length	27ft 8in
Wingspan	36ft 1in
Engine	Piaggio P.XI RC.40 14-cylinder twin-row radial (1,000hp)
Armament	2 x 12.7mm mgs

Savoia Marchetti SM.79-II *Sparviero*

Speed	267mph
Range	1,180 miles
Length	53ft 2in
Wingspan	69ft 6in
Engines	SM.79-I, 3 x Alfa Romeo 126 RC.34 radials (780hp each)
	SM.79-II, 3 x Piaggio P.XI RC.40 (1,000hp each)
Armament	3 x 12.7mm Breda Safat mgs, 1 x Lewis 7.7mm mg in beam position: 1,250kg of bombs carried vertically (facing upwards) inside the bomb bay which was offset to starboard, or 2 x 930kg Whitehead-Fiume torpedoes mounted externally (although only one was carried operationally due to handling difficulties and was mounted offset to port underneath the fuselage).

Cant Z.1007*bis Alcione*

Speed	280mph
Range	1,242 miles
Length	60ft 4in
Wingspan	81ft 4in
Engines	3 x Piaggio P.XI RC.40 14-cylinder radials (1,000hp each)
Armament	2 x 12.7mm mgs, 2 x 7.7mm mgs: 2,000kg of bombs

Fiat BR.20M *Cigogna*

Speed	267mph
Range	1,242 miles
Length	54ft 8in
Wingspan	70ft 8in
Engines	2 x Fiat A.80 RC.41 18-cylinder twin-row radials (1,030hp each)
Armament	1 x 12.7mm mg, 2 x 7.7mm mgs: 1,600kg of bombs

Left: Despite the arrival of the superior Macchi C.202, the older Macchi MC.200 still remained in widespread service. This MC.200 belonged to 92ª *Squadriglia*, 8° *Gruppo*, 2° *Stormo* which served in North Africa and was never involved in operations over Malta; however, this image is included as it clearly depicts the so-called 'Poached Egg' mottling as commonly applied to the type over a *Verde Mimetico* 2 background. The mottles are usually described as being *Bruno Memitico* with *Verde Mimetico* 4 edges, although in this instance the centre of the mottles appear more like mid-green. The white centres of the wing national markings have been over painted by hand to help tone them down, while the engine cowling is a rather pale yellow. Italian official image

Opposite: A reconnaissance Ju 88D based in Sicily during early 1941 with Mount Etna beyond. This aircraft, coded 7A+NH, is from *Auflarungsgruppe* 121 and although it has often been described in the past as wearing a desert colour scheme, it is in fact painted overall light blue most likely using standard RLM 65 *Hellblau* (Light Blue). Although its cockpit retains the early style (non-bulged) rear canopy, it has nonetheless been converted to mount twin rear-facing mgs and must have been very cramped, even if one gunner operated both guns. A colour illustration of this aircraft appears on page 156. EN Archive Collection

AIRCRAFT SPECIFICATIONS – LUFTWAFFE

Messerschmitt Bf 109E-7

Speed	348mph
Range	410 miles
Length	28ft 4in
Wingspan	32ft 4in
Engine	Daimler Benz DB-601N 12-cylinderinline (1,175hp)
Armament	2 x 20mm cannon, 2 x 7.9mm mgs; optional 500kg bomb or 300-litre drop tank

Messerschmitt Bf 110D

Speed	349mph at 22,965ft
Range	482 miles (without drop tanks)
Length	41ft 6in
Wingspan	53ft 3in
Engine	2 x Daimler Benz DB-601F (1,300hp each)
Armament	2 x 20mm cannon plus 4 x 7.9mm mgs (fixed), 1 x rear-facing 7.9mm mg; 2 x 500kg bombs and 2 x 900-litre drop tanks

Junkers Ju 87B *Stuka* (used by *Regia Aeronautica*)

Speed	211mph (sea level)
Range	528 miles
Length	37ft 8in
Wingspan	45ft 4in
Engine	Jumo 211D 12-cylinder inline (1,200hp)
Armament	2 x 7.9mm mgs, 1 rear-facing 7.9mm mg; 1,000kg bombs (max)

Junkers Ju 87R *Stuka*

Speed	255mph
Range	954 miles
Length	37ft 8in
Wingspan	45ft 4in
Engine	Jumo 211D 12-cylinder inline (1,200hp)
Armament (fixed)	2 x 7.9mm mgs, 1 rear-facing 7.9mm mg; 1,000kg bombs or 1 x SC500kg bomb and 2 x 300 litre drop tanks.

Junkers Ju 88A-4

Speed	269mph
Range	1,696 miles
Length	47ft 3in
Wingspan	65ft 7in
Engine	Jumo 211J-1 or J-2 12-cylinder inline (1,340hp each)
Armament	4 x 7.9mm mgs plus (on occasion) 1 x 20mm cannon; 3,600kg bombs

Heinkel He 111H

Speed	227mph
Range	1,212 miles
Length	53ft 10in
Wingspan	75ft 2in
Engine	2 x Jumo 211F-2 12-cylinder inline (1,350hp each)
Armament	1 nose-mounted 20mm cannon, 1 x dorsal 13mm mg, 4 x 7.9mm mgs in ventral gondola and beam positions; 2,500kg of bombs or torpedoes.

BIBLIOGRAPHY

249 At War: Brian Cull; *Grub Street,1997*.
Aeronautica Caccia & Assalto 1940/43 Pt I & II: P Waldis etc; *La Bancarella Aeronautica, 2002 & 2003*.
Aeronautica Italiana Caccia & Assalto 1940/45 Pt III: P Waldis etc; *La Bancarella Aeronautica, 2002 & 2008*.
Aircraft of the Aces, 18 Hurricane Aces 1939-40: Tony Holmes; *Osprey, 1998*.
Aircraft of the Aces, 34 Italian Aces of WW2: Giorgio Apostolo & Giovanni Massimello; *Osprey, 2000*.
Aircraft of the Aces, 44 Gloster Gladiator Aces: Andrew Thomas; *Osprey, 2002*.
Aircraft of the Aces, 57 Hurricane Aces 1941-45: Andrew Thomas; *Osprey, 2003*.
Aircraft of the Aces, 75 Royal Navy Aces of WW2: Andrew Thomas; *Osprey, 2007*.
Aircraft of the Aces, 90 Fiat CR.42 Aces of WW2: Hakan Gustavsson & Ludovico Slonga; *Osprey, 2009*.
Against All Odds; RAAF Pilots in the Battle For Malta 1942: Lex McAulay; *Hutchinson, Australia, 1989*.
Aircraft of World War II: Kenneth Munson; *Ian Allan Ltd, 1972*.
Anti-Aircraft, A History of Air Defence: Ian V Hogg; *Macdonald and Jane's (Publishers) Limited, 1978*.
Ardwick Boys Went To Malta, (The); A British Territorial Army Battalion During The Siege Of Malta 1940-1943: R Bonner; *Fleur de Lys Publishing, 1992*.
Armed Rovers; Beauforts & Beaufighters over the Mediterranean: Roy C Nesbit; *Airlife Publishing, 1995*.
Aviation Elite Units 25; Jadgeschwader 53 'Pik-As': John Weal; *Osprey, 2007*.
Battle Over Malta; Aircraft Losses and Crash Sites 1940-42: Anthony Rogers; *Sutton Publishing, 2000*.
Battle For The Mediterranean: Donald Macintyre; *BT Batsford Ltd, 1964*.
Battleships, Axis & Neutral in WWII: W Garzke JR & R Dulin JR; *Naval Institute Press, 1985*.
Big Gun Monitors: Ian Buxton; *Dent, 1978*.
Bomber Units of the Luftwaffe 1939/45 Vol 2: H dw Zeng, DG Stanley, Eddie Creek; *Classic/Ian Allan, 2008*.
Bristol Blenheim: Chaz Bowyer; *Ian Allan, 1984*.
British Carrier Aviation, Evolution of the Ships and their Aircraft: Norman Friedman; *Conway Maritime, 1988*.
British Cruisers, Two World Wars and After: Norman Friedman; *Seaforth Publishing, 2010*.
British & American Tanks of WWII: Chamberlain and Ellis; *Arms & Armour Press, 1977*.
British & Empire Warships of the Second World War: HT Lenton; *Greenhill Books, Lionel Leventhal Ltd 1998*.
Bomber Squadrons of the RAF and their Aircraft: P Moyes; *Macdonald & Jane's (Publishers) Limited, 1976*.
Chambers Dictionary of World History: *Chambers Harrap Publishers Ltd, 2004*.
Coastal Support and Special Squadrons of the RAF: JDR Rawlings; *Jane's Publishing Company Limited, 1982*.
Courage Alone; The Italian Air Force 1940-1943: Chris Dunning; *Hikoki Publications, 2009*.
Cross and the Ensign, The; A Naval History of Malta 1798-1979: Peter Elliott; *Harper Collins, 1994*.
Cunningham The greatest admiral since Nelson: John Winton; *John Murray (Publishers) Ltd, 1998*.
Engage the Enemy more Closely, The RN in WW Two: Corelli Barnett; *Hodder and Stoughton Ltd, 1991*.
Faith, Hope & Charity; The Defence of Malta: Kenneth Poolman; *New English Library Ltd, 1974*.
Fighter Squadrons of the RAF; John DR Rawlings; *Macdonald & Janes Ltd, 1978*.
Finest Years, Churchill As Warlord 1940-45: Max Hastings; *Harper Press, 2009*.
Fleet Air Arm Aircraft, Units and Ships 1920-39: R Sturtivant & D Cronin; *Air-Britain (Historians) Ltd, 1998*.
Fleet Air Arm Aircraft, 1939-1945: R Sturtivant with Mick Burrow; *Air-Britain (Historians) Ltd, 1995*.
Fleet Air Arm Camouflage and Markings, Atlantic and Mediterranean Theatres 1937-1941: Stuart Lloyd; *Dalrymple & Verdun Publishing, 2008*.
Flying Sailors at War 1939-June 1940, Vol 1: Brian Cull; *Dalrymple & Verdun Publishing, 2011*.
Flying Training and Support Units: R Sturtivant, J Hamlin; *Air-Britain (Historians) Ltd, 2007*.
Flying Units of the RAF: A Lake; *Airlife Publishing Ltd, 1999*.
Fortress Malta, An Island Under Siege 1940-1943: James Holland; *Orion Books Ltd, 2003*.
Gladiators Over Malta; Story of Faith, Hope and Charity: Brian Cull & Frederick Galea; *Wise Owl Pubs, 2008*.
Guns of the RAF 1939-1945: GF Wallace; *William Kimber and Co Ltd, 1972*.
Hawker Hurricane, An Illustrated History, The: Francis K Mason; *Crecy, 1990*.
Hitler's Mediterranean Gamble, North African Campaigns in WWII: D Porch; *Weidenfeld and Nicholson, 2004*.
Hurricane, The War Exploits of the Fighter Aircraft: Adrian Stewart; *William Kimber, 1984*.
Hurricanes Over Malta: Brian Cull & Frederick R Galea; *Grub Street, 2001*.
Illustrious & Implacable Classes of Aircraft Carrier 1940-1969, The: Neil McCart; *Fan Publications, 2000*.
Junkers Ju 87 Stuka: Manfred Griehl; *Airlife, 2001*.
Junkers Ju 88: Manfred Griehl; *Arms and Armour, 1990*.
Lest We Forget: RAF & Commonwealth Air Forces Servicemen Lost in the Defence of Malta: John A Agius MBE & Frederick Galea; *Malta Aviation Museum Foundation, 1999*.
Luftwaffe Colours, Kampflieger Vol.2 Bombers of the Luftwaffe: J Richard Smith & Eddie Creek; *Classic Colours/Ian Allan, 2004*.
Luftwaffe Colours, Sea Eagles Vol.2 Luftwaffe Anti-Shipping Units 1942-45: Chris Goss; *Classic Colours/Ian Allan, 2006*.
Malta, Blitzed But Not Beaten: Philip Vella; *Progress Press Co Ltd, 1985*.
Malta, An Aviation History: Alfred Coldman; *Publishers Enterprises Group Ltd, 2001*.
Malta Flypast, Volumes 1- 7: Malta Aviation Museum Foundation.
Malta, The Thorn In Rommels Side: Laddie Lucas; *Penguin Books, 1993*.
Malta, The Hurricane Years: Christopher Shores, Brian Cull & Nichola Malizzia; *Grub Street, 1999*.
Mediterranean Air War Volumes 1, 2 & 3: Christopher F Shores; *Ian Allan, 1972-73*.
Middle Sea, The. A History of the Mediterranean: JJ Norwich; *Chatto & Windus, 2006*.
Military Aviation in Malta GC. 1915-1993: John F Hamlin; *GMS Enterprises, 1994*.
Names With Wings: G Wansbrough-White; *Airlife Publishing Ltd, 1995*.
Naval Camouflage 1914-1945; A Complete Visual Reference; David Williams; *Chatham Publishing, 2001*.
Naval Weapons of World War Two: John Campbell; *Conway Maritime Press Ltd, 1985*.
Nelson to Vanguard, Warship Design and Development 1923-1945: DK Brown; *Chatham Publishing, 2000*.
Night Strike From Malta: Kenneth Poolman; *Janes Publishing Company, 1980*.
Onward to Malta: Wing Commander TF Neil DFC and bar, AFC; *Corgi Books, 1998*.
RAF Squadrons: CG Jefford; *Airlife Publishing Ltd, 1988 & 2001*.
Raiders Passed, Wartime Recollections of a Maltese Youngster: Charles B Grech; *Midsea Books, Malta, 1998*.
Regia Aeronautica, The Italian Air Force 1923-1945: Chris Dunning; *Chevron Publishing Ltd, 2009*.
Royal Air Force Aircraft serial monographs (various): *Air-Britain (Historians) Ltd*.
Royal Air Force Ground Crews, An 'Erk' on Malta: J Paternoster; *Malta Aviation Museum Foundation, 1998*.
Royal Navy and the Mediterranean Vol 1, The: Edited by C Page; *Frank Cass Publishers, 2002*.
Royal Navy and the Mediterranean Vol 2, The: Edited by C Page; *Frank Cass Publishers, 2002*.
Shiphunters, The: RE Gillman; *Purnell Book Services, 1976*.
Squadrons of the Fleet Air Arm, The: Ray Sturtivant and Theo Ballance; *Air-Britain (Historians) Ltd, 1994*.
Squadrons of the RAF and Commonwealth 1918-1988, The: JJ Halley; *Air-Britain (Historians) Ltd, 1988*.
Times Atlas of the Second World War, The: *Time Books Limited, 1989*.
Victory in the Air: Richard J Caruana; *Modelaid International Publications, 1996*.
War in a Stringbag: Commander Charles Lamb; *Book Club Associates, 1977*.
Warburton's War: Tony Spooner & Chris Goss; *Goodall/Crecy Publishing, 2003*.
Warplanes of the Third Reich: William Green; *Macdonald & Jane's (Publishers) Limited, 1979*.
With All Modesty: The Veterans Tales of the Battle of Malta; Colin Pomeroy; *Self Published, 2006*.
World Encyclopaedia of the Tank: Chris Chant; *PSL, 1994*.

Other Accounts
Diaries of the late Sub Lieutenant Graham Angus Hogg DSO, RNVR (806 NAS, Fleet Air Arm).
Letters & Correspondence from veterans, with especial thanks to Jack Paternoster, Walter Gillman, Harold Revill, Jack Waterfield, Colin White DSC, Malcolm Oxley, Ron Bramley, Douglas Newton, Harold Revill, Anthony Stephens & John Tipton.